The Bible, Qumran, and the Samaritans

Studia Judaica

Forschungen zur Wissenschaft des Judentums

Begründet von Ernst Ludwig Ehrlich

Herausgegeben von
Günter Stemberger, Charlotte Fonrobert,
Elisabeth Hollender, Alexander Samely, Irene Zwiep

Band 104

—

Studia Samaritana

Edited by
Magnar Kartveit, Gary N. Knoppers, Stefan Schorch

Volume 10

The Bible, Qumran, and the Samaritans

Edited by
Magnar Kartveit, Gary N. Knoppers

DE GRUYTER

ISBN 978-3-11-071052-6
e-ISBN (PDF) 978-3-11-058141-6
e-ISBN (EPUB) 978-3-11-058037-2
ISSN 0585-5306

Library of Congress Control Number: 2018945373

Bibliographic information published by the Deutsche Nationalbibliothek
The Deutsche Nationalbibliothek lists this publication in the Deutsche Nationalbibliografie;
detailed bibliographic data are available on the Internet at http://dnb.dnb.de.

© 2020 Walter de Gruyter GmbH, Berlin/Boston
This volume is text- and page-identical with the hardback published in 2018.
Printing and binding: CPI books GmbH, Leck

www.degruyter.com

———

In memoriam, Peter W. Flint
21 January 1951 – 3 November 2016

Table of Contents

Magnar Kartveit and Gary N. Knoppers
Qumran, Mount Gerizim, and the Books of Moses —— 1

Konrad Schmid
Overcoming the Sub-Deuteronomism and Sub-Chronicism of Historiography in Biblical Studies: The Case of the Samaritans —— 17

Emanuel Tov
Textual Harmonization in the Five Books of the Torah: A Summary —— 31

Reinhard Pummer
Samaritan Studies – Recent Research Results —— 57

Thomas Römer
Cult Centralization and the Publication of the Torah Between Jerusalem and Samaria —— 79

Christophe Nihan and Hervé Gonzalez
Competing Attitudes toward Samaria in Chronicles and Second Zechariah —— 93

Raik Heckl
The Composition of Ezra-Nehemiah as a Testimony for the Competition Between the Temples in Jerusalem and on Mt. Gerizim in the Early Years of the Seleucid Rule over Judah —— 115

Benedikt Hensel
Ethnic Fiction and Identity-Formation: A New Explanation for the Background of the Question of Intermarriage in Ezra-Nehemiah —— 133

Reinhard Pummer
An Update of Moses Gaster's "Chain of Samaritan High Priests" —— 149

Bibliography —— 173

List of Contributors —— 195

Index of Modern Authors —— 197
Index of Ancient Texts —— 201
Index of Subjects —— 209

Magnar Kartveit and Gary N. Knoppers
Qumran, Mount Gerizim, and the Books of Moses

The study of the Pentateuch and research on the Samaritans have changed fundamentally over the last decades in refreshingly different ways.[1] In this book, the focus is on the change created by new material emerging from two sets of disparate sources: the ancient manuscripts from the area of the Dead Sea, especially from Qumran, and the archaeological excavations and ancient inscriptions at Mount Gerizim. Material from these two sites has created a common field of research for two different groups: scholars working with the Pentateuch and experts on the Samaritans. Earlier, scholars who worked in Old Testament/Hebrew Bible studies could leave the Samaritan material mostly to experts in that area of research and scholars studying the Samaritan material needed only sporadically to engage in the academic study of the Hebrew Bible. Scholars in the field of early Judaism might wish to consult early Samaritan evidence and scholars in Samaritan studies might wish to work comparatively with early Judaic texts, but the study of the Hebrew Bible was considered, for the most part, to be anterior and distinct from Samaritan studies. This is no longer the case. The pre-Samaritan texts from Qumran and the results from the excavations on Mount Gerizim have created an area of study common to previously separate fields of research. Scholars coming from different directions meet in this new area and realize that they work on much the same questions and with much common material.

The first major change in Pentateuchal and Samaritan studies was the discovery of the pre-Samaritan texts from Qumran. This shift began in 1955 when Patrick W. Skehan presented what he called "Exodus in the Samaritan Recension from Qumran."[2] His article announced that among the Qumran texts there was a scroll of Exodus with features that were previously only known from the Samaritan Pentateuch. With the following words, Skehan introduced 4QpaleoExod^m:

---

[1] In editing the various contributions to this collection of essays, we wish to recognize two graduate students at the University of Notre Dame, who ably assisted in this effort: Raleigh C. Heth and Mark A. Lackowski. Raleigh Heth also carefully compiled the indices for this volume. The abbreviations in this book follow those employed in the second edition of *The SBL Handbook of Style for Biblical Studies and Related Disciplines*, ed. Billie Jean Collins, Bob Buller, and John F. Kutsko (Atlanta: Society of Biblical Literature, 2014) with one addition: StSam for Studia Samaritana.
[2] Patrick W. Skehan, "Exodus in the Samaritan Recension from Qumran," *JBL* 74 (1955): 182–87.

> The recension in question is the "Samaritan" recension, with all the essential characteristics of that fuller text, including its repetitious manner of recounting the plague episodes, its borrowings from Deuteronomy and its transpositions; this is true at almost every point where the extant fragments make verification possible.[3]

The significance of this discovery was enhanced by these observations: "The script cannot by any stretch of the imagination be called Samaritan. ... Neither is the orthography Samaritan."[4] Skehan's "surprise" was therefore that "the Samaritan recension ... is shown by this scroll to have been preserved with a measure of fidelity ... that compares not unfavorably with the fidelity of transmission of MT itself."[5]

Skehan's presentation opened new insights into the history of the text of the Torah. With all the Dead Sea manuscripts now published, we are able to work with this material on a broader basis. There is no doubt that the Samaritan Pentateuch has predecessors in Qumran, not only in 4QpaleoExod^m, but in several manuscripts of the so-called pre-Samaritan text type. They constitute some 11 percent of the total of Pentateuchal texts from the Dead Sea area.[6]

The second major development in this field is constituted by the results from the archaeological excavations on Mount Gerizim. The site, *Jebel eṭ-Ṭur*, had been excavated by A. M. Schneider from Göttingen in 1930, but new excavations were undertaken by Yitzhak Magen and his team, beginning in 1982. During the next 25 years, they discovered 395 inscriptions and fragments of inscriptions in Hebrew and Aramaic, as well as a number of inscriptions in Greek. No images were found, but some 300,000 fragmentary animal bones from sacrifices were discovered—all this in addition to the buildings, monumental walls, towers, and chambers that were uncovered.[7] Most importantly, a sacred precinct was discovered, the probable site for the Samaritan temple.

---

3 Skehan, "Exodus," 182.
4 Ibid., 182f.
5 Ibid., 183.
6 Emanuel Tov, *Textual Criticism of the Hebrew Bible*, 3rd rev. ed. (Minneapolis: Fortress, 2012), 108. Tov is revising this figure slightly down to 9 percent (personal communication), as his research continues. See recently his "The Development of the Text of the Torah in Two Major Text Blocks," *Text* 26 (2016): 1–27.
7 Yitzhak Magen, "The Dating of the First Phase of the Samaritan Temple on Mount Gerizim in Light of the Archaeological Evidence," in *Judah and the Judeans in the Fourth Century B.C.E.*, ed. Oded Lipschits, Gary N. Knoppers, and Rainer Albertz (Winona Lake, IN: Eisenbrauns, 2007), 157–211; idem, *Judea and Samaria Researches and Discoveries*, Judea and Samaria Publications 6 (Jerusalem: Israel Antiquities Authority, 2008); idem, *A Temple City*, vol. 2 of *Mount Gerizim Excavations*, Judea and Samaria Publications 8 (Jerusalem: Israel Antiquities Authority, 2008); idem, *The Samaritans and the Good Samaritan*, Judea and Samaria Publications 7 (Jerusalem:

The temple on Mt. Gerizim was thus built in the days of Sanballat the Horonite (Sanballat I), governor of Samaria in the days of Nehemiah, who arrived in the Land of Israel in 444 BCE (Neh. 2:1–10). The temple remained in use during the Ptolemaic and Seleucid periods, as well, and also withstood the destruction of the city of Samaria and the construction of a Macedonian city on its ruins.[8]

Josephus, however, wrongly ascribed its construction to the Sanballat who lived in the days of Alexander the Great; in fact, it was built by another Sanballat, who lived in the time of Nehemiah, some one hundred years earlier (Jos., *Ant.* 11: 302, 321–325).[9]

In the third century BCE, in the Hellenistic period, the temple and the sacred precinct were rebuilt, and a city began to rise around them. The city expanded until it reached its maximal size in the second century BCE, with an overall area of about 400 dunams (800 m. long and some 500 m. wide), becoming the capital of the Samaritan people and its religious and cultic center.[10]

If there was a Yahwistic temple on Mount Gerizim from the fifth to the second centuries BCE, the finalization of the contents and the text of the Pentateuch happened at a time when this temple existed. Old Testament/Hebrew Bible scholars have begun to realize over the last years the consequences of this momentous discovery and are increasingly relating their studies to this reality.

These two major developments in biblical and Samaritan studies formed the background for two sessions at the 22nd congress of The International Organization for the Study of the Old Testament (IOSOT). The congress took place at the University of Stellenbosch, South Africa, from September 4 to 9, 2016. For the first time in the history of this organization, a research group for Samaritan studies was set up. The good attendance at the sessions showed that the time had come for a reorientation in this area of research. The invitations to the presenters at the research group were met with positive responses and most of the invited scholars were able to attend the congress and contribute to the research group. Their presentations were followed by lively and interesting discussions. The presenters were free to choose topics for their own lectures, but the overall idea was to delve into the area where Samaritan studies and Old Testament/Hebrew Bible studies overlap. It is no longer desirable or even possible to conduct these studies in isolation from one another, but to engage in a dialogue for the common good. It is a pleasure to present in this volume the contributions delivered in

---

Israel Antiquities Authority, 2008); idem, *Flavia Neapolis: Shechem in the Roman Period*, Judea and Samaria Publications 11, 2 vols. (Jerusalem: Israel Antiquities Authority, 2009).
8 Yitzhak Magen, "Mount Gerizim," in *The Aramaic, Hebrew and Samaritan Inscriptions*, vol. 1 of *Mount Gerizim Excavations*, ed. Y. Magen, H. Misgav and L. Tsfania, Judea and Samaria Publications 2 (Jerusalem: Israel Antiquities Authority, 2004), 10.
9 Ibid., 6.
10 Ibid., 1.

Stellenbosch. All the lecturers readily agreed to have their presentations published in the series Studia Samaritana.

It was, therefore, with great sadness that we received the message that one of the presenters in Stellenbosch, Peter W. Flint, had died on November 3, 2016. He had been involved in research of the Dead Sea Scrolls for over 20 years. He was one of the 70 official editors of the Dead Sea Scrolls worldwide, and worked on the great Isaiah scroll and on the Psalms. In addition, he published books and articles on the Dead Sea Scrolls and related subjects.[11] It was an obvious choice to invite him to the research group inside the IOSOT-congress and he suggested a contribution on "Two Pre-Samaritan Scrolls found at Qumran: One Especially Close to the Samaritan Pentateuch, the Other a Transition Text between the S[amaritan] P[entateuch] and the Septuagint." The two scrolls were 4QpaleoExod^m (4Q22) and 4QNum^b (4Q27), but he also discussed a series of other texts of the pre-Samaritan and Reworked Pentateuch text types. Flint found 4QpaleoExod^m to be close to the Samaritan Pentateuch, whereas he found 4QNum^b to be a text in between the text type of the Samaritan Pentateuch and the text type of the Septuagint. In the presentation, he was able to exploit insights from relevant scholarly contributions, and to locate his own solutions to the problems in relation to these discussions. The paper in detail analyzed the material at hand and discussed many instances in which the Dead Sea Scrolls present particularly interesting readings. A lively discussion followed his presentation.

Peter W. Flint was born in South Africa in 1951, and in 1972 he completed his first B.A., from Witwatersrand, Johannesburg. From the University of South Africa in Pretoria he earned a B.A. in Classical Hebrew in 1979 and a M.A. in 1983. Seven years later he completed his second M.A., this time at the University of Notre Dame in Indiana, USA, followed by a Ph.D. in Old Testament and Second Temple Judaism at the same institution in 1993. It is a serious loss to this volume that Flint's paper cannot be included, but it is a small compensation to dedicate it to his memory. Full obituaries and overviews of his scholarly merits are offered elsewhere.[12] In this context, it is only possible to acknowledge his contributions

---

[11] To take a few examples, see Peter W. Flint, *The Dead Sea Psalms Scrolls and the Book of Psalms*, STDJ 17 (Leiden: Brill, 1997); idem (ed. with Tae Hun Kim), *The Bible at Qumran: Text, Shape, and Interpretation*, Studies in the Dead Sea scrolls and Related Literature (Grand Rapids, MI: Eerdmans, 2001); idem (ed. with Patrick D. Miller, Jr.), *The Book of Psalms: Composition and Reception*, VTSup 99 (Leiden: Brill, 2005); idem (with Eugene C. Ulrich), *Qumran Cave 1. II: The Isaiah Scrolls*, DJD 32, 2 vols. (Oxford: Clarendon, 2010); idem, *The Dead Sea Scrolls* (Nashville, TN: Abingdon, 2013).

[12] A *Festschrift* that was being prepared in his honor, edited by Andrew Perrin, Kyung S. Baek, and Daniel K. Falk, has now become a memorial volume: *Reading the Bible in Ancient Traditions*

to our field, his insights and suggestions for understanding the Dead Sea Scrolls and related matters, his courteous and generous presentations of material and the results of his research. Our disciplines have suffered a great loss from his death, but through his publications we are still able to benefit from his innovative and sound scholarship.

In addition to the five Stellenbosch lectures presented here, some other essays are included. A few scholars were invited to contribute to this volume. Reinhard Pummer is one of the most renowned scholars in Samaritan studies and he willingly agreed to write for the volume, even submitting two chapters. Benedikt Hensel also concurred to contribute. It is, therefore, possible to present a book covering a wide range of topics related to the central issues posed by the research group at the IOSOT congress.

A broad orientation in the field is provided in Konrad Schmid's contribution. He describes the general situation in Old Testament/Hebrew Bible historical studies subsumed under the catchwords Sub-Deuteronomism and Sub-Chronism, expressions that describe general scholarly tendencies to replicate, whether consciously or unconsciously, the assumptions, contours, and tropes of biblical presentations of Israelite history. Against such tendencies, it is incumbent to distinguish between the Israel as described in the Bible and the historical Israel as reconstructed by scholars. The two cannot be completely separated, but must be nevertheless held apart. The discoveries from the excavations on Mount Gerizim make this program more important than ever: the Samarians of the north and the Samaritans of Shechem and Mount Gerizim are made invisible or neglected or even vilified in some of the ancient literary sources. Scholars have to redress the imbalance and describe the groups, as well as their theologies and histories, in fairer and more defensible terms. In this process we may be led to read biblical texts anew, as Schmid does with Joshua 24, with a fresh perspective.

Readers will be intrigued by many of Schmid's ideas. What if, for example, the composition of a text, such as Joshua 24, reflects a socio-historical situation, when two major Yahwistic sanctuaries, one in Jerusalem and one on Mount Gerizim, coexisted in the land? Schmid discusses this scenario and offers a glimpse of what a theology of coexistence looked like at a time, when contemporaneous Yahwistic communities could be found in Samaria and in Judah. If this was the situation in the fifth century BCE, traditional scholarly portrayals of the Northerners and the Southerners in this period will have to be rewritten.

---

and Modern Editions: Studies in Textual and Reception History in Honour of Peter W. Flint, SBL Early Judaism and Its Literature Series 47 (Atlanta: Society of Biblical Literature, 2017).

Whereas Schmid explores the implications of the discoveries on Mt. Gerizim for gaining a better understanding of a critical biblical text, the essay by Emanuel Tov explores the implications of the other major area of discovery mentioned above: the Dead Sea Scrolls. His topic is the harmonizing tendencies in the Qumran biblical texts, in *tefillin*, and in liturgical texts. Summing up years of study on these texts, he offers a critical evaluation of his own and of other scholars' research. In particular, the feature of harmonization has been often cited as a major characteristic of the so-called pre-Samaritan texts, but Tov argues that the term requires clarification. As a rubric, the category of harmonization has been sometimes used broadly to include coordination and assimilation.[13] Tov opts for a narrow definition of harmonization, in differentiation from the classifications employed in many other scholarly publications. Yet, even accepting a narrow definition, harmonization on the textual level may be considered as widespread in biblical manuscripts. Considering the varied material found in the Bible, it is conspicuous that harmonization is a feature more prominent in the Pentateuchal manuscripts than in the manuscripts of the Former Prophets, Latter Prophets, and Writings. The historical texts of the Bible, especially those of Samuel-Kings and Chronicles, present many stories that could invite harmonization, but generally this is not found. Of all the parts of the Hebrew Bible, the Pentateuch was the arena where harmonizing work took place.

Although this phenomenon is typical of the pre-Samaritan manuscripts, it is not prominent in the Masoretic text. Where it is most prominent, came as a surprise to Tov, as it will be to his readers, both when the individual books of Moses are compared with each other and when the different textual witnesses are compared. One of the most salient findings, for example, is that the largest contingent of harmonizations appears within the books of the LXX, followed by the pre-Samaritan manuscripts and the Samaritan Pentateuch. Statistics are presented which show the situation, and readers will be intrigued by the picture they present.

Over against the background of detailed studies of the Dead Sea Scrolls from Qumran and other relevant textual evidence, scholars are beginning to develop new theories about the origins of the Samaritans.[14] If we compare our present

---

[13] David McLain Carr, *The Formation of the Hebrew Bible: A New Reconstruction* (Oxford: Oxford University Press, 2011), 90–98, who refers to other scholars with a similarly wide understanding of the expression.

[14] The proposals are wide-ranging; see e.g., József Zsengellér, *Gerizim as Israel: Northern Tradition of the Old Testament and the Early Traditions of the Samaritans*, Utrechtse Theologische Reeks 38 (Utrecht: University of Utrecht, 1998); Ingrid Hjelm, *The Samaritans and Early Judaism: A Literary Analysis*, JSOTSup 303 (Sheffield: Sheffield Academic Press, 2000); eadem, "Northern

knowledge with the standard presentation on the Samaritans written by James A. Montgomery in 1907,[15] it is conspicuous what a difference the empirical evidence from the area of the Dead Sea has made. Montgomery was on the right track in many of the assumptions he made, but he had no idea of the connection between the text of the Samaritan Pentateuch and the texts circulating in Jewish circles at the turn of the era. His comments on the Samaritan Pentateuch are telling of the state of knowledge in his time:

> Indeed it is not the disagreement that is remarkable so much as the great similarity of the two texts [the Masoretic and the Samaritan]. Apart from the few falsifications inserted by the Samaritans, there are no material differences, such for instance as would give the historian a different view of the age to which the composition belongs, or of the history which it relates ; the variations will never be more than of interest to the textual scholar, illustrative to him of the origin and processes of various text-traditions.[16]

Montgomery could not know that most of the "few falsifications" in the Samaritan text were harmonizations and instances of content editing, which are now amply attested in Judean Dead Sea Scrolls texts. Both the Samaritan Pentateuch and the so-called pre-Samaritan manuscripts at Qumran share such special features.[17] Moreover, the literary techniques Samaritans employed to produce a

---

Perspectives in Deuteronomy and Its Relation to the Samaritan Pentateuch," *HBAI* 4 (2015): 184– 204; Stefan Schorch, "La formation de la communauté samaritaine au 2e siècle avant J.–Chr. et la culture de lecture du Judaïsme," in *Un carrefour dans l'histoire de la Bible*, ed. Innocent Himbaza and Adrian Schenker, OBO 233 (Göttingen: Vandenhoeck & Ruprecht, 2007) 5–20; idem, "The Samaritan Version of Deuteronomy and the Origin of Deuteronomy," in *Samaria, Samarians, Samaritans: Studies on Bible, History, and Linguistics*, ed. József Zsengellér, SJ 66; StSam 6 (Berlin: de Gruyter, 2011), 23–37; Magnar Kartveit, *The Origin of the Samaritans*, VTSup 128 (Leiden: Brill, 2009); Gary N. Knoppers, *Jews and Samaritans: The Origins and History of Their Early Relations* (New York: Oxford University Press, 2013); Reinhard Pummer, *The Samaritans: A Profile* (Grand Rapids: Eerdmans, 2015); Dany R. Nocquet, *La Samarie, la Diaspora et l'achèvement de la Torah: territorialités et internationalités dans l'Hexateuque*, OBO 284 (Fribourg: Academic Press; Göttingen: Vandenhoeck & Ruprecht, 2017).
15 James A. Montgomery, *The Samaritans, the Earliest Jewish Sect: Their History, Theology, and Literature*, The Bohlen lectures 1906 (Philadelphia: J. C. Winston, 1907; repr. New York: Ktav, 1968).
16 Ibid., 289f.
17 The new multi-volume, diplomatic edition of the Samaritan Pentateuch being prepared by Stefan Schorch and József Zsengellér attempts to do justice to the textual variants among the Samaritan Pentateuch, the Masoretic Text, the Septuagint, and the Dead Sea Scrolls. See Stefan Schorch, "Der Pentateuch der Samaritaner: Seine Erforschung und seine Bedeutung für das Verständnis des alttestamentlichen Bibeltextes," in *Die Samaritaner und die Bibel: Historische und literarische Wechselwirkungen zwischen biblischen und samaritanischen Traditionen*, ed. Jörg

thin, but distinctive, theological layer in the Samaritan Pentateuch are consistent with the literary techniques attested elsewhere in the pre-Samaritan manuscripts of the Dead Sea Scrolls and in the Samaritan Pentateuch itself. In this sense, the Samaritans and the Judeans of Qumran share some vital features, as far as their Scriptures are concerned.

Peter W. Flint's observation in this respect is to the point: 4QpaleoExod^m (4Q22) is a version that comes very close to the Samaritan Pentateuch and may indeed have been one of the predecessors of that text. When the Samaritans produced their tenth commandment, appearing in the Samaritan Pentateuch of both Exodus 20 and Deuteronomy 5 (but not in other ancient witnesses), a text that draws almost exclusively upon the injunctions found in their *Vorlage* of Deut 11:29–30; 27:2–8, focusing on the commands to build an altar on Mount Gerizim and to inscribe the text of the Torah upon whole stones, they employed exactly the same literary method as was used for the content editing of the pre-Samaritan texts found at Qumran. By reusing, adapting, and expanding an existing Torah text type that was shared with Judeans and thus was non-sectarian, Samaritan scribes created an amplified Torah. Only the light additional stratum and not the base text the Samaritans shared with Judeans, may be viewed as distinctively Samaritan. By dealing intensively with harmonizations in the wider textual corpus from Qumran, Tov's essay thus illumines the broader intellectual milieu in which the pre-Samaritan texts were produced and out of which the Holy Text of the Samaritans emerged.

The Books of Moses are one of the pillars in the theological edifice of the Samaritans, from their early history until today. This is manifest in their creed:

> We say: My faith is in thee, Yhwh; and in Moses son of Amram, thy servant; and in the holy Law; and in Mount Gerizim Beth-El; and in the Day of Vengeance and Recompense.[18]

Even though the date of this version of the creed is the 17th century CE, the first four elements are found in *Memar Marqah/Tebat Marqe*, a collection of theological treatises in six books, the Aramaic parts dating from the late fourth century

---

Frey, Ursula Schattner-Rieser, and Konrad Schmid; SJ 70; StSam 7 (Berlin: de Gruyter, 2012), 5–29; idem, "A Critical *editio maior* of the Samaritan Pentateuch: State of Research, Principles, and Problems," *HBAI* 2 (2013): 100–20. For a review of this new work and other modern editions of the Samaritan Pentateuch, see Gary N. Knoppers, "Toward a Critical Edition of the Samaritan Pentateuch: Reflections on Issues and Methods," in *Reading the Bible in Ancient Traditions and Modern Editions: Studies in Textual and Reception History in Honour of Peter W. Flint*, ed. Andrew Perrin, Kyung S. Baek, and Daniel K. Falk, SBL Early Judaism and Its Literature 47 (Atlanta: Society of Biblical Literature, 2017), 163–88.

18 Montgomery, *Samaritans*, 207, with reference to *Ep. to the Brethren in England*, 1672.

CE.[19] Paralleled by Islam's article of faith in God's scriptures, but unparalleled in Judaism and Christianity, this article of faith in Scripture constitutes an old and central element of Samaritanism. Here, the Torah's status is in line with that of God, Moses, Mount Gerizim and the Judgment Day.

Scholars have therefore always known of these tenets of Samaritan theology, but not until recently realized the scope and content of the concentration on Mount Gerizim. The excavations conducted from 1982 onward have yielded a wealth of material that gives an impression of life in the city on the mountain, with its altar or temple. If a scholar needs texts to accompany the stones and structures, they are there: 395 inscriptions and fragments of inscriptions. Some are long, some contain a few letters, but together they present us with a congregation in existence around 200 BCE. From the same period come two inscriptions from the island of Delos in the Aegean Sea, also clearly Samaritan. A community with such a pronounced identity and self-awareness will have existed for some time before 200 BCE, and the enlargement of the city on Mount Gerizim around this time also testifies to such a situation.[20]

All this and much more is described in Reinhard Pummer's first article in this volume. He not only analyzes the implications of the excavations on the two summits of Mount Gerizim (*Tell er-Rās* and *Jebel eṭ-Ṭōr*), but also discusses the literary evidence (biblical, Josephus, Patristic) relevant for the reconstruction of the history of the area during the Persian, Hellenistic, and Roman periods. As part of his essay, Pummer reviews the archaeological excavations of possibly Samaritan cemeteries and tombs at a variety of sites in Palestine, enabling scholars to gain a better picture of Samarians and Samaritan material culture of the late Hellenistic, Roman, and Byzantine periods. Taken together, these material remains supply important evidence for the extent of the area occupied by the Samaritans in Palestine during different eras. Additionally, the Delos inscriptions show that a Yahwistic Samarian Diaspora existed far in the west and Josephus describes the Samari(t)ans as part of the population in Egypt.

Yet, Pummer's study of material artifacts also raises questions about the state of Samaritan-Jewish relations during the periods surveyed. Discussing tomb types, burial caves, storage jars, and grave goods, Pummer observes how closely they resemble their Jewish counterparts. If "the culture of the Samaritans was to a large extent indistinguishable from that of Jews," as he points out, how likely is it that deep hostility characterized Samaritan-Jewish relations during

---

19 A new edition of this important work is being prepared by Abraham Tal, *Tibåt Mårqe: The Ark of Marqe: Edition, Translation, Commentary*, StSam (Berlin: de Gruyter, forthcoming).
20 Magnar Kartveit, "Samaritan Self-Consciousness in the First Half of the Second Century B.C.E. in Light of the Inscriptions from Mount Gerizim and Delos," *JSJ* 45 (2014): 449–70.

this time? In short, the overview Pummer provides of recent studies of Samaritan material and literary culture furnishes readers with an up-to-date and insightful assessment of the field.

In light of the new situation created by the discovery of a cult on Mount Gerizim existing at a time when important parts of the Bible were produced, Thomas Römer in his article discusses anew the formation of the Pentateuch and of the Deuteronomistic History. Many recent scholarly discussions on the origins and development of the Pentateuch and of the Deuteronomistic History do not take the new discoveries into account and Römer recognizes the deficiencies of such approaches. This understanding leads him to take up questions hotly debated recently: how is the centralization command in Deuteronomy to be understood? Does Deuteronomy have a northern background? When was this book first created and how was it reworked and extended? Is the Pentateuch witness to common efforts in Yehud and Samaria to create a foundational document or common constitution? What is the significance of the appearance of Shechem both in Genesis 12, as Abram's first stop in the land, and in Joshua 24, as the site of an all-Israelite convocation? Similarly, what is the significance of the site Moriah in Genesis 22? Readers may be surprised by some of his proposals.

One of the curious features about the last section of Genesis (37–50), largely taken up by the Joseph Story, is that it features the progenitor of two of the most prominent northern tribes: Ephraim and Manasseh. Römer thus asks: where might the Joseph novella have originated? Römer's proposals concerning these and other issues he discusses may be met with consent by some scholars and with rejection by others. Whatever the case, all readers will benefit from dealing with the texts and problems taken up in this essay. Indeed, his intriguing study may open up new questions and stimulate new approaches to old questions, compelling scholars to reconsider traditional assumptions and positions.

While Thomas Römer covers much ground in his wide-ranging article, Christophe Nihan and Hervé Gonzalez in their chapter concentrate on only two particular verses in the Bible: 2 Chr 7:12 and Zech 11:14. Both essays will provoke, however, much discussion. Nihan and Gonzalez situate their studies of individual texts within the larger literary contexts of Chronicles and Zechariah, respectively. Yet, Nihan and Gonzalez, like Römer, attend to the issue of historical context, exploring the import of these passages in the (reconstructed) world in which they were written, a period in which a Yahwistic temple on Mount Gerizim coexisted with a Yahwistic temple on Mount Zion. Whatever precise nuances in the relationship between the Yahwists of Judah and the Yahwists of Samaria may have obtained at the times in which these two different texts were composed, it is safe to assume that relations between Jerusalem and Mount Gerizim were not yet completely severed.

In their essay, Nihan and Gonzalez discuss foreign policy developments in the southern Levant during the transition from Persian to Hellenistic overlords. In their view, the authors of Chronicles and Zechariah 9–14 confronted the situation in the North with different attitudes. While Römer finds cooperation between Yehud and Samaria in the production of the Pentateuch, Nihan and Gonzalez find nuanced attitudes in the particular historiographic and prophetic texts they discuss. On the one hand, Chronicles emphasizes the priority of the Jerusalem temple, while recognizing the Yahwists of the North to be Israelite in identity. Hence, the people of the North are approached with the view that they can and should support the sanctuary in Jerusalem. What this means, can be seen in the unparalleled divine proclamation presented in 2 Chr 7:12 in which YHWH employs the phraseology of Deuteronomy to speak of the Jerusalem temple as "chosen" by him to be for him a "place of sacrifice."

On the other hand, the second part of the book of Zechariah presents us with a complex and shifting set of attitudes toward the North. There are several new beginnings in Zechariah 9–14 each of which builds upon previous passages and develops themes from preceding literary units. The text of Zech 11:14 provides one window into this reality. What can be seen in the detailed contribution by Nihan and Gonzalez is the existence of a variety of theological stances within Jerusalem during this period—and Römer's proposals for growth in the development of the Pentateuch nicely adds to this picture. The essay by Römer and that of Nihan and Gonzalez thus illustrate two ways in which the excavations on Mount Gerizim have sparked a spate of new scholarship on the Pentateuch, in particular, and the Hebrew Bible/Old Testament, in general.

After all of the research that has been undertaken on Ezra-Nehemiah, is it possible to say something new? Evidently there is, as shown by two new monographs on the book by two German scholars, published in the same year, with the same publisher, in the same series. At first glance, it might seem to be a coincidence that the two monographs appeared simultaneously, but Raik Heckl's and Benedikt Hensel's extensive studies on Ezra-Nehemiah are both written against the background of the new insights gained from the Mount Gerizim excavations and so it is probably no coincidence. To some extent, the works follow the same line of thinking, yet the two are strikingly different.[21] The editors of this volume are pleased to present articles by both scholars, because such an inclusion of different perspectives allows readers to have the opportunity to read and

---

[21] Raik Heckl, *Neuanfang und Kontinuität in Jerusalem: Studien zu den hermeneutischen Strategien im Esra-Nehemia-Buch*, FAT 104 (Tübingen: Mohr Siebeck, 2016); Benedikt Hensel, *Juda und Samaria: Zum Verhältnis zweier nach-exilischer Jahwismen*, FAT 110 (Tübingen: Mohr Siebeck, 2016).

compare. Both contributions testify to the need to re-evaluate our understanding of well-known biblical texts on the basis of fresh material.

Raik Heckl presents a literary analysis of Ezra-Nehemiah so as to describe the discourses that resulted in the literary history of the book. He discusses the hermeneutical strategies that its last authors used to persuade their readers to accept the new text over against its *Vorlagen*. He emphasizes that the Cyrus edict, contextualized at the beginning of Ezra 1 represents the hermeneutical key to understanding Ezra 1–6. He provocatively contends that the version of the Cyrus edict in Ezra 1 anticipates not only the main elements of the Aramaic temple chronicle in Ezra 5–6, but also the versions of the Cyrus edict in Ezra 5:13–15 and 6:2–5. The opening of the Ezra story performs a similar function, connecting Jerusalem with the Torah through the person and activities of Ezra. As for the lists of persons in Neh 7 (//Ezra 2) and the communal covenant (אמנה) of Neh 10, the author argues that they are placed relatively close to the end of the exile.

One of the aims of the essay is to show how the literary growth of the book reveals a change in theological preferences over time. In this perspective, the literary material discussed in Ezra-Nehemiah does not reflect the historical circumstances of the Persian period. The writers wish to provide the Jerusalem temple with royal legitimacy and with a more ancient pedigree than the competing temple on Mount Gerizim. Additionally, they claim the Torah, understood as dating to an earlier time (the Persian period) and stemming from within a broad Yahwistic context, exclusively for the Jerusalem community and not for others.

Heckl readily acknowledges, of course, that the facts on the ground, pertaining to the two sanctuaries, could differ quite markedly from what one finds in the presentation of Ezra-Nehemiah. In this respect, the whole of Ezra-Nehemiah should be read as a text emerging from a later era than is often assumed by scholars. Readers will find in Heckl's essay suggestions that should trigger further reanalysis of the history of the relationship between Samaria and Jerusalem. In this reconstruction, Ezra-Nehemiah becomes a programmatic text in worsening relations between the two communities.

Taking as his starting point the separation from foreignness in Neh 13:30, Benedikt Hensel finds the focus on separation to be a leading motif in the Ezra-story in Ezra 1–10 and in Neh 8–10. Hensel addresses the particular notion of foreignness in the two books against the background of our present knowledge of the constitution of the population in the area. In so doing, he discovers an enigma, namely that there were not many foreigners to dissociate from. So what would have been the purpose of the injunction to separate from almost non-existent aliens? An answer to this question can be found by paying attention to the use of the term "Israel" in these books, a designation reserved for the returnees from exile. As "Israel" was a self-designation also of the emerging community around the Gerizim sanctuary, this usage in Ezra-Nehemiah attempts to redefine the relevant power relationships in the period, pro-Jerusalem and anti-Samaritan. Readers will be struck by a number of Hensel's proposals, including the suggestion that the designation of the "foreigner" functions in the text as a cipher for a particular conflict, by which the "Israelite" authors of Ezra demarcate themselves from other post-exilic Yahwisms, specifically the Samarian YHWH worshipers. Hensel's study thus revives suggestions of anti-Samaritan polemics in Ezra-Nehemiah, but with new material from Mount Gerizim and Delos as the impulse for a renewed attempt to understand the theological thrust of the book.

Any theory of the creation and redaction of the final stages of the Pentateuch will have to take into account the evidence furnished by the Pentateuchal scrolls discovered near the Dead Sea. Along with the inscriptions and material results from the excavations on Mount Gerizim, they constitute empirical evidence that needs to be weighed and sifted by scholars engaged in the study of the cultures of Samaria and Judah during the Persian, Hellenistic, Roman, and Byzantine periods. The essays here presented all testify to this situation, and they show how scholars are now wrestling with old questions in the light of new evidence.

"The head of the Samaritan community is the high priest," says Reinhard Pummer in his second contribution to this volume. Whatever the vagaries of human history during the many centuries of the Common Era, this fact has remained largely constant. The Samaritans assert a continuous chain of high priests from Aaron, the brother of Moses, to the present high priest, who they say is number 132 in an unbroken line of succession.[22] Indeed, the lineage of the first high priest (Aaron) is itself traced back to the first human (Adam). The Samaritan claim of a distinguished pedigree, extending from contemporary times back into hoary antiquity may be contrasted with the Judean assertions found in Neh 13:28f:

> And one of the sons of Jehoiada, son of the high priest Eliashib, was the son-in-law of Sanballat the Horonite; I chased him away from me. Remember them, O my God, because they have defiled the priesthood, the covenant of the priests and the Levites.

The text of Nehemiah acknowledges a marital connection between the Jerusalem priestly elite and the family of the contemporary governor of Samaria (Sanballat),

---

[22] Pummer's essay provides variants, including chronological notations and the names of additional high priests drawn from other relevant Samaritan sources, to complicate this picture.

but criticizes it by equating it with polluting the sacerdocy.[23] One of the grandsons of the high priest Jehoiada had violated the covenant of the priests and Levites by defiling his ancestral lineage. The first-century Jewish historian Josephus, whatever the precise version(s) of his source (a variant form of Ezra-Nehemiah or 1 Esdras with additional material), presents an account that recalls certain features of the Nehemiah narrative, but also makes additional claims:

> Now the elders of Jerusalem, resenting the fact that the brother of the high priest Jaddus was sharing the high priesthood while married to a foreigner, rose up against him, for they considered this marriage to be a stepping-stone for those who might wish to transgress the laws about taking wives and that this would be the beginning of intercourse with foreigners. They believed, moreover, that their former captivity and misfortunes had been caused by some who had erred in marrying and taking wives who were not of their own country. They therefore told Manassēs either to divorce his wife or not to approach the altar. And, as the high priest shared the indignation of the people and kept his brother from the altar, Manassēs went to his father-in-law Sanaballetēs and said that while he loved his daughter Nikasō, nevertheless the priestly office was the highest in the nation and had always belonged to his family, and that therefore he did not wish to be deprived of it on her account. But Sanaballetēs promised not only to preserve the priesthood for him but also to procure for him the power and office of high priest and to appoint him governor of all the places over which he ruled, if he were willing to live with his daughter; and he said that he would build a temple similar to that in Jerusalem on Mount Garizein—this is the highest of the mountains near Samaria—, and undertook to do these things with the consent of King Darius... But, as many priests and Israelites were involved in such marriages, great was the confusion which seized the people of Jerusalem. For all these deserted to Manassēs, and Sanaballetēs supplied them with money and with land for cultivation and assigned them places wherein to dwell, in every way seeking to win favour for his son-in-law. (*Ant*. 11.306–312)[24]

Josephus thus acknowledges that the Samaritans had a high priest with appropriate genealogical roots, but asserts that the circumstances of his appointment and the arrival of the high priestly institution in Samaria are driven by pure political

---

[23] Samaritan tradition also speaks of relationships within the Israelite priesthood as being severed by the establishment of a dissident faction, but blames this division within the Aaronic priesthood upon the machinations of Eli and his establishment of a renegade sanctuary at Shiloh. See Gary N. Knoppers, "Samaritan Conceptions of Jewish Origins and Jewish Conceptions of Samaritan Origins: Any Common Ground?" in *Die Samaritaner und die Bibel: historische und literarische Wechselwirkungen zwischen biblischen und samaritanischen Traditionen*, ed. Jörg Frey, Ursula Schattner-Rieser, and Konrad Schmid, SJ 70; StSam 7 (Berlin: de Gruyter, 2012), 81–118.
[24] Translated by R. Marcus, *Jewish Antiquities Books IX–XI*, LCL 326 (Cambridge, MA: Harvard University Press, 1937; repr. 1995), 461–67. See also the new edition of Paul Spilsbury and Chris Seeman, *Judean Antiquities 11*, Flavius Josephus: Translation and Commentary 6 A (Leiden: Brill, 2017), 109–13.

expediency, rather than by any longstanding sacerdotal tradition.²⁵ In this construction, the Samaritan high priesthood is late, suspect, and derivative of authentic Judean tradition. Moreover, the status of Manasseh, as a Judean priest, is sullied by his being "married to a foreigner." This would be a defilement (טמא) of the priesthood in Jerusalem, according to the terminology employed in Nehemiah.²⁶

Yet, as the list within Pummer's essay makes clear, Samaritan tradition does not know of such an incident, much less a high priest named Manasseh dating to this time. Research on the Samaritans, as well as on the historical relations between priests in Samaria and Judah, thus has to take strikingly different views into account: the Samaritan tradition, the claims made by Josephus, and all other relevant sources. Pummer's critically annotated and updated list of Samaritan high priests provides both basic data for further research and supplies us with the Samaritan view. Their voice should be heard in our volume.

So where will future scholarship lead us? The essays in this book represent a re-orientation in a period, when the full impact of new discoveries is being felt. Still, some scholars work as if the material presented and presupposed here is not very relevant.²⁷ But increasingly, the relevance and significance of the pre-Samaritan texts at Qumran and the discoveries on Mount Gerizim can be seen in publications.²⁸ The present volume is situated at the crossroads at which scholars are looking back and seeing forward. There is no better moment than when we have exciting times ahead.

---

25 On the challenges posed by the texts in question, see recently Reinhard Pummer, *The Samaritans in Flavius Josephus*, TSAJ 129 (Tübingen: Mohr Siebeck, 2009); Magnar Kartveit, "Josephus on the Samaritans – His *Tendenz* and Purpose," in *Samaria, Samarians, Samaritans: Studies on Bible, History, and Linguistics*, ed. József Zsengellér, SJ 66; StSam 6 (Berlin: de Gruyter, 2011), 109–20; Étienne Nodet, "Israelites, Samaritans, Temples, Jews," in *Samaria, Samarians, Samaritans*, 121–71; Gary N. Knoppers, "The Samaritan Schism or the Judaization of Samaria? Reassessing Josephus's Account of the Mt. Gerizim Temple," in *Making a Difference: Essays on the Bible and Judaism in Honour of Tamara Cohn Eskenazi*, ed. David J. A. Clines, Kent Richards, and Jacob L. Wright, Hebrew Bible Monographs 49 (Sheffield: Sheffield Phoenix, 2012), 163–78.
26 Compare Hensel's study of the separation from foreignness in Ezra-Nehemiah found elsewhere in this volume.
27 Thus, e.g., the new book of John J. Collins, *The Invention of Judaism: Torah and Jewish Identity from Deuteronomy to Paul* (Oakland, CA: University of California Press, 2017), exhibits many strengths, but it underestimates, in our view, the impact of the history of Samarian-Judean relations on the process of Judean identity formation.
28 E.g., Carr, *Formation*, 91–95, 170–71, 198–99, 473–76; Christian Frevel, *Geschichte Israels*, Kohlhammer Studienbücher Theologie 2 (Stuttgart: Kohlhammer, 2016), 317–28.

Konrad Schmid
Overcoming the Sub-Deuteronomism and Sub-Chronicism of Historiography in Biblical Studies: The Case of the Samaritans[1]

Biblical scholars discussing the Samaritans currently find themselves in a paradoxical situation. On the one hand, compared with other sources, evidence of the Samaritans is meager in the Hebrew Bible. On the other hand, recent scholarship has tended to assume that—historically speaking—the Samaritans must have been much more important than the biblical presentation alone suggests. Significant work along these lines includes the recent monographs on the Samaritans by Magnar Kartveit and on the Jews and the Samaritans by Gary Knoppers.[2] Stefan Schorch has offered a new overview of Samaritan scholarship in German.[3]

One of the most important insights of critical biblical studies that enabled these developments is the necessity of distinguishing between the biblical and the historical Israel, as Reinhard Kratz has put it in a recent book title.[4] The Israel of the Bible is different from the one inferred through historical reconstruction, though it needs to be stressed that the different aspects of what the term "Israel" can denote historically—basically the Northern Kingdom either without

---

[1] An earlier version of this paper in German was published as "Die Samaritaner und die Judäer: Die biblische Diskussion um ihr Verhältnis in Josua 24," in *Die Samaritaner und die Bibel: Historische und literarische Wechselwirkungen zwischen biblischen und samaritanischen Traditionen / The Samaritans and the Bible: Historical and Literary Interactions between Biblical and Samaritan Traditions*, ed. Jörg Frey, Ursula Schattner-Rieser, and Konrad Schmid, SJ 70; StSam 7 (Berlin: de Gruyter, 2012), 21–49.
[2] Magnar Kartveit, *The Origin of the Samaritans* (VTSup 128; Leiden: Brill, 2009); Gary N. Knoppers, *Jews and Samaritans: The Origins and History of Their Early Relations* (Oxford: Oxford University Press, 2013).
[3] Stefan Schorch, "Der Samaritanische Pentateuch in der Geschichte des hebräischen Bibeltextes," *VF* 60 (2015): 18–29.
[4] See, for example, Reinhard G. Kratz, *Historical and Biblical Israel*, trans. Paul Michael Kurtz (Oxford: Oxford University Press, 2015); idem, *The Composition of the Narrative Books of the Old Testament*, trans. John Bowden (London: T&T Clark, 2005); Christoph Levin, *The Old Testament: A Brief Introduction*, trans. Margaret Kohl (Princeton: Princeton University Press, 2005); Konrad Schmid, *The Old Testament: A Literary History*, trans. Linda M. Maloney (Minneapolis: Fortress, 2012).

or with the Judean southern kingdom[5]—are a witness to this development from the historical to the biblical Israel.

In practice, however, this distinction between the historical and the biblical is in many places ignored and *de facto* disregarded. The lack of this distinction proves to be the case quite often in the presentation of the history of Israel in the last century. In a 1993 review article, Manfred Weippert lamented what he fittingly called the widespread "Sub-Deuteronomism" with which particularly the pre-state history of Israel is reconstructed in textbooks.[6] What is meant by "Sub-Deuteronomism" is the subtle influence of the Bible's Deuteronomistic view of history as portrayed in the books from Genesis through Kings on how historians conceive the way that history might have played out. The danger of blurring the difference between biblical and historical Israel is quite natural because there are not many available extra-biblical sources, while the Bible offers at best tertiary sources that are difficult to evaluate.[7] For example, in several textbooks, one reads of a Patriarchal Era or the Era of the Judges, but these assumptions cannot be verified.[8] They rely on biblical images of Israel's pre-history that

---

[5] On the historical reasons and processes for the adoption of the term "Israel" for the South, see Nadav Na'aman, "The Israelite-Judahite Struggle for the Patrimony of Ancient Israel," *Bib* 91 (2010): 1–23; idem, "Saul, Benjamin and the Emergence of Biblical Israel," *ZAW* 121 (2009): 216–224, 335–349; Daniel Fleming, *The Legacy of Israel in Judah's Bible: History, Politics, and the Reinscribing of Tradition* (Cambridge: Cambridge University Press, 2012). See also, with a strong emphasis on the mediating function of the sanctuary of Bethel, Ernst Axel Knauf, "Bethel: The Israelite Impact on Judean Language and Literature," in *Judah and the Judeans in the Persian Period*, ed. Oded Lipschits and Manfred Oeming (Winona Lake, IN: Eisenbrauns, 2006), 291–349. A different approach is taken by Kristin Weingart, *Stämmevolk—Staatsvolk—Gottesvolk? Studien zur Verwendung des Israel-Namens im Alten Testament*, FAT II/68 (Tübingen: Mohr Siebeck, 2014).

[6] Manfred Weippert, "Geschichte Israels am Scheideweg," *ThR* 58 (1993): 71–103, 73.

[7] On the methodological discussion, see, e.g., Christof Hardmeier, "Zur Quellenevidenz biblischer Texte und archäologischer Befunde: Falsche Fronten und ein neues Gespräch zwischen alttestamentlicher Literaturwissenschaft und Archäologie," in *Steine—Bilder—Texte: Historische Evidenz außerbiblischer und biblischer Quellen*, ed. idem, Arbeiten zur Bibel und ihrer Geschichte 5 (Leipzig: Evangelische Verlagsanstalt, 2001), 11–24; Christoph Uehlinger, "Bildquellen und 'Geschichte Israels': Grundsätzliche Überlegungen und Fallbeispiele," in *Steine*, ed. Hardmeier, 25–77; Joachim Schaper, "Auf der Suche nach dem alten Israel? Text, Artefakt und 'Geschichte Israels' in der alttestamentlichen Wissenschaft vor dem Hintergrund der Methodendiskussion in den Historischen Kulturwissenschaften," *ZAW* 118 (2006): 1–21, 181–196. See also the contributions in Hugh G.M. Williamson, ed., *Understanding the History of Ancient Israel* (Oxford: Oxford University Press, 2007).

[8] See the reflections in Konrad Schmid, *Genesis and the Moses Story: Israel's Dual Origins in the Hebrew Bible*, trans. James D. Nogalski, Siphrut 3 (Winona Lake, IN: Eisenbrauns, 2010); Philippe Guillaume, *Waiting for Josiah: The Judges*, JSOTSup 385 (London: T&T Clark, 2004).

are unlikely to be wholly fiction, but they at the same time transcend the sphere of history into a mythic past.

Such problems with biblically inspired reconstructions of the history of Israel likewise apply to questions about the Samaritans. The "Sub-Deuteronomism" that depicts Judah as the real Israel such that the territory of the former Northern Kingdom plays no role after 722 and 587 BCE is concretized in numerous modern publications on the history of Israel.[9] As a result, one can even identify a "Sub-Chronicism" that often extends the usual "Sub-Deuteronomism." The basic assumptions of the Deuteronomic view of history for the exilic and postexilic periods is thereby modified through the basic assumptions of the Chronistic view of history. The history of Israel essentially takes place in Judah. The territory of the former Northern Kingdom ideally remains a part of Israel, but it remains caught in its antagonism toward Judah and thereby rejects the offer to participate in the Judean restoration efforts.

When one considers customary presentations of the history of Israel, the topic of the Samaritans—apart from a few exceptions (Sacchi, Miller-Hayes, Widengren)[10]—is usually treated in about 2–3 pages, as is the case in of the discussions of Manfred Metzger,[11] Siegfried Hermann,[12] Herbert Donner,[13] J. Alberto Soggin,[14] Gösta Ahlström,[15] and Michael D. Coogan.[16] However, Christian Frevel's

---

[9] See Gary N. Knoppers, "In Search of Post-Exilic Israel: Samaria after the Fall of the Northern Kingdom," in *In Search of Pre-Exilic Israel: Proceedings of the Oxford Old Testament Seminar*, ed. John Day, JSOTSup 406 (London: T&T Clark, 2004), 150–180, 151: "The Deuteronomistic Interpretation of Israel's fall has also influenced modern scholarship."

[10] See Paolo Sacchi, *The History of the Second Temple Period*, JSOTSup 285 (Sheffield: Sheffield Academic Press, 2000), 152–59. J. Maxwell Miller and John H. Hayes, *A History of Ancient Israel and Judah* (Philadelphia: Westminster, 1986), 337–339 present their own solution that merely addresses the fall of Samaria as it is presented in 2 Kgs 17:21–40. Comparatively extensive is the treatment of the Samaritans in Geo Widengren, "The Persian Period," in *Israelite and Judean History*, ed. John H. Hayes and J. Maxwell Miller (London: SCM, 1977), 489–538.

[11] Manfred Metzger, *Grundriss der Geschichte Israels* (Neukirchen-Vluyn: Neukirchener Verlag, 1963), 172–74.

[12] Siegfried Hermann, *Geschichte Israels* (Stuttgart: Kohlhammer, 1973), 399–400.

[13] Herbert Donner, *Geschichte des Volkes Israel und seiner Nachbarn in Grundzügen*, 2nd ed., GAT 4/2 (Göttingen: Vandenhoeck & Ruprecht, 1995), 469–470.

[14] J. Alberto Soggin, *Einführung in die Geschichte Israels und Judas: Von den Ursprüngen bis zum Aufstand Bar Kochbas* (Darmstadt: Wissenschaftliche Buchgesellschaft, 1991), 219–222. Treatment of the Samaritans is completely missing in, e.g., Shmuel Safrai, *Das jüdische Volk im Zeitalter des Zweiten Tempels* (Neukirchen-Vluyn: Neukirchener Verlag, 1978).

[15] Gösta Ahlström, *The History of Ancient Palestine* (Sheffield: Sheffield Academic Press, 1993), 901–904.

new book on the "Geschichte Israels" is quite detailed about the Samaritans in the Persian period, elaborating his case in 7 pages.[17] Apparently, the policy is starting to change.

The widespread neglect of the Samaritans, at least in older literature, is, to put it bluntly, a biblicism. The Bible is an important source for Israel's history, but it is focused on Judah and Jerusalem.[18] The presentation is weighted entirely toward the South, and where the North comes up, it is generally mentioned in a defensive and even discriminatory manner. Primarily, the explicit passages in 2 Kgs 17:24–40; Ezra 4:1–5; Neh 13:28–30; and 2 Chr 30:1–18 are of interest with regard to the Samaritans. They are open for a historical investigation, but they are colored in different ways by bias—in particular their pro-Judean stance. The Samaritans appear as a syncretistic community with dubious political ambitions.

Older scholarship on the Samaritans remained markedly under the banner of the biblical accentuations. The study by J. W. Rothstein *Juden und Samaritaner* from the year 1908 bears the subtitle, *Die grundlegende Scheidung von Judentum und Heidentum: Eine kritische Studie zum Buch Haggai und zur jüdischen Geschichte im ersten nachexilischen Jahrhundert* ("The Fundamental Separation between Judaism and Paganism: A Critical Study on the Book of Haggai and the Jewish History in the First Postexilic Century").[19] The parallelism of the title and subtitle show clearly that the Samaritans are pagans according to Rothstein, as is the case in much Jewish polemic of antiquity.[20]

A similarly difficult viewpoint appears in James A. Montgomery's book *Samaritans: The Earliest Jewish Sect: Their History, Theology, and Literature*,[21] even when taking into account that the English term "sect" is more neutral

---

16 Leonard J. Greenspoon, "Between Alexandria and Antioch: Jews and Judaism in the Hellenistic Period," in *The Oxford History of the Biblical World*, ed. Michael D. Coogan (Oxford: Oxford University Press, 1998), 346–349.
17 Christian Frevel, *Geschichte Israels* (Stuttgart: Kohlhammer, 2016).
18 On the historical processes, see n. 4 above.
19 J. W. Rothstein, *Juden und Samaritaner: Die grundlegende Scheidung von Judentum und Heidentum: Eine kritische Studie zum Buch Haggai und zur jüdischen Geschichte im ersten nachexilischen Jahrhundert*, BZAW 3 (Leipzig: Hinrichs, 1908).
20 See Lester Grabbe, *Judaism from Cyrus to Hadrian, 2: The Roman Period* (Minneapolis: Fortress, 1992), 503.
21 James A. Montgomery, *Samaritans: The Earliest Jewish Sect: Their History, Theology, and Literature* (Philadelphia: John C. Winston, 1907; repr. 1968). Cf. Ingrid Hjelm, *The Samaritans and Early Judaism: A Literary Analysis*, JSOTSup 303 (Sheffield: Sheffield Academic Press, 2000), 13–22.

and more widely used than the German word "Sekte."²² Lester Grabbe also treats the Samaritans in his presentation *Judaism from Cyrus to Hadrian* under the section "Individual Sects and Movements."²³ This very categorization of Samaritans as a Jewish group or sect is problematic, as they regard themselves not as a part of Judaism, but as "Israelites."

However, the situation just sketched above as characterizing 20th century textbooks should also be relativized, as already noted with Frevel's new "Geschichte Israels." The "Sub-Deuteronomism" and "Sub-Chronicism" in the field of the history of Israel has undergone considerable criticism over the past 20 years, and its faulty perspectives and methods have clearly been recognized in biblical studies.²⁴ Of course, there were earlier contrarian voices, such as the well-known essay by Albrecht Alt on the Samaritans' role in the formation of Judaism, which had to be updated, however, by newer findings on Yehud's provincial status already in the early Persian period.²⁵

Most responsible for this development is the considerable rise of archaeology in Israel, which has substantially altered the biblical picture of the history of Israel in various places. In terms of reception within biblical studies, notable works were those of David Jamieson-Drake, Hermann Michael Niemann, and Nadav Na'aman, all from the early 1990s,²⁶ which on the basis of various indirect indicators established that the Northern Kingdom was more developed in terms

---

22 On the example of the Qumran community, see the remarks in John J. Collins, *Beyond the Qumran Community: The Sectarian Movement of the Dead Sea Scrolls* (Grand Rapids: Eerdmans, 2009), 7–9, as well as the elaborations of David J. Chalcraft, ed., *Sectarianism in Early Judaism: Sociological Advances* (London: Equinox, 2007).
23 Grabbe, *Judaism from Cyrus to Hadrian*, 2, 502–7.
24 See especially the contributions by Hans G. Kippenberg, *Garizim und Synagoge: Traditionsgeschichtliche Untersuchungen zur samaritanischen Religion der aramäischen Periode*, RVV 30 (Berlin: de Gruyter, 1971).
25 Albrecht Alt, "Die Rolle Samarias bei der Entstehung des Judentums (1934)," in *Kleine Schriften zur Geschichte des Volkes Israels II*, ed. idem, 2nd ed. (Munich: Kaiser, 1959), 316–337; idem, "Judas Nachbarn zur Zeit Nehemias," in ibid., 338–45; cf. Sebastian Grätz, "Zu einem Essay von Albrecht Alt: Die Rolle Samarias bei der Entstehung des Judentums," in *Kontexte: Biografische und forschungsgeschichtliche Schnittpunkte der alttestamentlichen Wissenschaft*, FS Hans Jochen Boecker, ed. Thomas Wagner et al.; (Neukirchen-Vluyn: Neukirchener Verlag, 2008), 171–184.
26 David Jamieson-Drake, *Scribes and Schools in Monarchic Judah: A Socio-archaeological Approach*, JSOTSup 109 (Sheffield: Sheffield Academic Press, 1991; repr. Winona Lake, IN: Eisenbrauns, 2010); Hermann Michael Niemann, *Herrschaft, Königtum und Staat: Skizzen zur soziokulturellen Entwicklung im monarchischen Israel*, FAT 6 (Tübingen: Mohr Siebeck, 1993); Nadav Na'aman, "The 'Conquest of Canaan' in the Book of Joshua and in History," in *From Nomadism to Monarchy: Archaeological and Historical Aspects of Early Israel*, ed. Nadav Na'aman and Israel Finkelstein (Jerusalem: Israel Exploration Society, 1994), 218–81.

of culture and was more politically important than the Southern Kingdom. Israel Finkelstein's 2014 book on the *Forgotten Kingdom* is a neat synthesis of the recent findings that corroborate this view, but his title still reflects the traditional negligence of the North: Its basic quality is having been forgotten. The prevalence of the North is a natural conclusion, based on consideration of its geographic realities. Some have recently argued for the simultaneity of the cultural development of Judah and Israel, but at present there is little to uphold this contrary position.

In terms of the history of scholarship on the relationship between the North and South, one can reach a conclusion similar to what is the case for Israel and its neighboring cultures: The biblical account and focus have turned out to be one-sided and call for historical adjustments, which have since taken place. Israel – in the greater sense – was not the center of the ancient Near East, let alone its historically and culturally most powerful element. Only through the massive history of reception, particularly of the Bible, did Israel become more important than Egypt or Mesopotamia in Western academia. Judah was neither the only nor the central factor of the history of Israel after 722 BCE. Again, Judah's *de facto* prevalence is a product of the Bible, not of ancient Judean history.

Probably the most important turning point in appraising the significance of the Samaritans for the history of Israel took place around 20 years ago. New archaeological findings played a decisive role, bringing about a broadening of the sources and a calibration of the biblical picture. In particular, the findings hinting at a comparatively early existence of a Samaritan temple on Gerizim[27] show that, as early as the Persian and also in the Hellenistic period, there were two possibilities in the land of Israel for worshipping the biblical God—on Gerizim and in Jerusalem. Consequently, especially since the 1990s, many new publications on the Samaritans saw the light of day and significantly increased scholars' understanding in this area, leading to different and new perspectives.[28]

---

27 Cf. Ephraim Stern and Yitzhak Magen, "Archaeological Evidence for the First Stage of the Samaritan Temple on Mount Gerizim," *IEJ* 52 (2002): 49–57; Yitzhak Magen, "The Dating of the First Phase of the Samaritan Temple on Mount Gerizim in Light of the Archaeological Evidence," in *Judah and the Judeans in the Fourth Century B.C.E.*, ed. Oded Lipschits, Gary N. Knoppers, and Rainer Albertz (Winona Lake, IN: Eisenbrauns, 2007), 157–211; Yitzhak Magen et al., eds., *The Aramaic, Hebrew and Samaritan Inscriptions*, vol. 1 of *Mount Gerizim Excavations*, Judea and Samaria Publications 2 (Jerusalem: Israel Antiquities Authority, 2004); Yitzhak Magen, *A Temple City*, vol. 2 of *Mount Gerizim Excavations*, Judea and Samaria Publications 8 (Jerusalem: Israel Antiquities Authority, 2008), 167–205.
28 Cf. the works by Jürgen Zangenberg, *ΣAMAPEIA: Antike Quellen zur Geschichte und Kultur der Samaritaner in deutscher Übersetzung*, Texte und Arbeiten zum neutestamentlichen Zeitalter 15 (Tübingen: Francke, 1994); Gary N. Knoppers, "Mt. Gerizim and Mt. Zion: A Study in the Early

As a result of the new sensibilities regarding the Samaritans in biblical studies, one may ask whether certain biblical texts need to be interpreted differently when read with eyes that are not staring at Judah alone. I shall illustrate this by looking at the concluding chapter of the book of Joshua (Joshua 24). I will not address the post-biblical Samaritan traditions about Joshua 24, since Ingrid Hjelm has already dealt with this topic.[29] After the portrayal of the conquest of the land of Canaan by the tribes of Israel, this chapter contains Joshua's farewell address in which he commits the tribes to YHWH, their God. Of course, Joshua 24 plays out during a time when separation between Samaritans and Jews was not an issue, since there were no Jews or Samaritans at the time of the narrative setting. But given the general consensus that Joshua 24 was written in a period later than the time of its literary scenery, this relationship could have been and, I will argue, was in fact a reality.

Joshua 24 is a high profile text in biblical studies that has been treated by multiple monographs[30] and addressed even more frequently in articles and essays. Although nearly every possible dating has been proposed for it, in recent scholarship, the assumption that this chapter is a postexilic text has increased significantly—and rightly so, to my mind.[31] Of primary importance is the literary

---

History of the Samaritans and Jews," *SR* 34 (2005): 309–338; idem, "Revisiting the Samarian Question in the Persian Period," in *Judah and the Judeans in the Persian Period*, ed. Oded Lipschits (Winona Lake, IN: Eisenbrauns, 2006), 265–289; Hjelm, *Samaritans*; eadem, *Jerusalem's Rise to Sovereignty: Zion and Gerizim in Competition*, JSOTSup 404 (London: T&T Clark, 2004); eadem, "What do Samaritans and Jews Have in Common? Recent Trends in Samaritan Studies," *Currents in Biblical Research* 3 (2004): 9–59; Bob Becking, *The Fall of Samaria: An Historical and Archaeological Study*, SHANE 2 (Leiden: Brill, 1992); idem, "Do the Earliest Samaritan Inscriptions Already Indicate a Parting of the Ways?," in *Judah and the Judeans in the Fourth Century B.C.E.*, 213–222; Yitzhak Magen, *The Samaritans and the Good Samaritan* (Jerusalem: Israel Antiquities Authority, 2008), 3–40; Magnar Kartveit, *The Origin of the Samaritans*, VTSup 128 (Leiden: Brill, 2009).

29 Hjelm, *Jerusalem's Rise*, 195–210.

30 See, e.g., Götz Schmitt, *Der Landtag von Sichem*, AzTh I/15 (Stuttgart: Calwer, 1964); Herbert Mölle, *Der sogenannte Landtag zu Sichem*, Forschung zur Bibel 42 (Würzburg: Echter, 1980); William T. Koopmans, *Joshua 24 as Poetic Narrative*, JSOTSup 93 (Sheffield: Sheffield Academic Press, 1990); Moshe Anbar, *Josué et l'Alliance de Sichem (Josué 24:1–28)*, BET 25 (Frankfurt am Main: Peter Lang, 1992). See also Thomas Römer, "Das doppelte Ende des Josuabuches: einige Anmerkungen zur aktuellen Diskussion um 'deuteronomistisches Geschichtswerk' und 'Hexateuch,'" *ZAW* (2006): 523–48, 535 n. 39.

31 Jean L'Hour, "L'alliance de Sichem," *RB* 69 (1962): 5–36, 161–184, 350–368; Andrew D. H. Mayes, *The Story of Israel between Settlement and Exile: A Redactional Study of the Deuteronomistic History* (London: SCM Press, 1983), 51; Anbar, *Josué*; Thomas Römer, *Israels Väter: Untersuchungen zur Väterthematik im Deuteronomium und in der deuteronomistischen Tradition*, OBO 99 (Fribourg: Universitätsverlag and Göttingen: Vandenhoeck & Ruprecht, 1990), 325–326.

horizon that Joshua 24 reflects. Verses 2–4 name the three patriarchs, and therefore look back to Genesis. Particularly striking is the note in Josh 24:32 on the burial of Joseph's bones, which concludes a narrative thread beginning in Gen 50:25 and is found again in Exod 13:19.³² The parallelism between Joseph and Joshua in the 110 years of their lives should also be mentioned here. As for the setting of Joshua 24 in Shechem, one can also detect a reference back to Gen 12:6, 8—namely, Abraham's construction of an altar in Shechem.³³ Israel's history in Genesis through Joshua ends where it began.

If one follows the mainstream at least of European pentateuchal or, as the case may be, hexateuchal scholarship, which assumes that the hexateuchal theme from the patriarchs to the conquest originated at a late point in the narrative books' literary history,³⁴ then this literary horizon of Joshua 24 already speaks decidedly against an early date. This position can be substantiated further by some specific tradition-historical and redaction-historical observations. The main concern of the chapter, namely the call to serve Yhwh and renounce other gods, can hardly be older in terms of theological history than the first commandment of the Decalogue, which itself presupposes the Shema Israel, traditionally placed in the Josianic period, as well as the literary and functional core of Deuteronomy.³⁵

Among the inner-biblical affiliations in Joshua 24, the reception of the Priestly document is of preeminent importance for the date of this chapter. Joshua 24 is clearly familiar with Priestly language: הר שעיר as Esau's place of residence (Josh 24:4) appears only in Gen 36:8–9, a text normally accorded to "P."³⁶ The designation ארץ כנען (Josh 24:3) is also a term that is used especially in the Priestly

---

32 On this, see Markus Witte, "Die Gebeine Josefs," in *Auf dem Weg zur Endgestalt von Genesis bis II Regum*, FS Hans-Christoph Schmitt zum 65. Geburtstag, ed. Martin Beck and Ulrike Schorn, BZAW 370 (Berlin: de Gruyter, 2006), 139–56.
33 Finally, the casting aside of the "foreign gods" from "beyond the river" in Josh 24:13–28 refers back to the renunciation scene in Gen 35:1–5, esp. 35:2b, 4. However, Gen 24:2b, 4 is likely a post-Josh 24 corrective to this pro-Samaritan perspective, see below n. 40.
34 See the overview in Kratz, *Composition*; Jan C. Gertz, Konrad Schmid and Markus Witte, eds., *Abschied vom Jahwisten: Die Komposition des Hexateuch in der jüngsten Diskussion*, BZAW 215 (Berlin: de Gruyter, 2002); Tom Dozeman and Konrad Schmid, eds., *A Farewell to the Yahwist? The Composition of the Pentateuch in Recent European Interpretation*, SBLSS 34 (Atlanta: SBL, 2006); Jan C. Gertz et al., eds., *T&T Clark Handbook of the Old Testament: An Introduction to the Literature, Religion and History of the Old Testament* (London: T&T Clark, 2012), 237–272.
35 Cf. Reinhard G. Kratz, "Der vor- und der nachpriesterschriftliche Hexateuch," in *Abschied*, ed. Jan C. Gertz et al., 295–323.
36 See Mölle, *Landtag*, 208.

document in Genesis.³⁷ Particularly the expression כל ארץ כנען is specifically Priestly, designating the further settlement areas of all Abrahamic descendants in the Levant, namely the Edomites and the Arabians, according to Gen 17:8.

The prominent mention of Aaron in Josh 24:5 (cf. v. 33) would be difficult to explain without the Priestly version of the exodus.³⁸ The beginning of v. 5 could possibly be a literary addition, since it is omitted from the LXX. Finally, the depiction of the miracle of the Sea in Josh 24:6–7 in particular indicates that an edition of Exodus 14 that is interlaced with "P" is received here³⁹ (cf. רדף Exod 14:4, 8–9, 23 "P"; פרש/רכב Exod 14:9, 17–18, 23, 26 "P"; כסה Exod 14:28 "P"⁴⁰). Therefore, the Priestly Document should be taken as the *terminus ante quem non* for Joshua 24—if not in its entirety, then at least for a considerable portion of it.⁴¹

A relative literary *terminus ante quem* for the formation of Joshua 24 can be found in Neh 13:28–30, since this text presents a clear and critical response to the position of Joshua 24. While Joshua 24 still promotes the inclusion of the Samaritans and calls for the dismissal of "foreign" gods with an all-Israel perspective and a setting in Shechem, Nehemiah 13 views the Samaritans themselves as "foreign." Nehemiah prides himself on having expelled one of the sons of Jerusalem's High Priest because he intermarried with the Samaritans: "And one of the sons of Jehoiada, son of the high priest Eliashib, was the son-in-law of Sanballat the Horonite; I chased him away from me....Thus I cleansed (טהר)⁴² them from everything foreign (נכר)." (Neh 13:28–30)

---

37 See Anbar, *Josué*, 87.
38 See Heinrich Valentin, *Aaron: Eine Studie zur vor-priesterschriftlichen Aaron-Überlieferung*, OBO 18 (Fribourg: Universitätsverlag and Göttingen: Vandenhoeck & Ruprecht, 1978), 36–45; Peter Mommer, *Samuel: Geschichte und Überlieferung*, WMANT 65 (Neukirchen-Vluyn: Neukirchener Verlag, 1991), 126.
39 See also Blum, "Knoten," 197 and n. 68.
40 Volkmar Fritz, *Das Buch Josua*, HAT I/7 (Tübingen: Mohr Siebeck, 1994), 249 (he naturally sees the relevant text portions in Josh 24:6–7 as "additions" because his basic text originates from "DtrH"); Anbar, *Josué*, 98–99. Klaus Bieberstein, *Josua—Jordan—Jericho: Archäologie, Geschichte und Theologie der Landnahmeerzählungen Jos 1–6*, OBO 143 (Fribourg: Universitätsverlag and Göttingen: Vandenhoeck & Ruprecht, 1995), 399, sees in Josh 24:7,11, however without any detailed explanation, "nur eine allgemeine Abhängigkeit von der so genannten 'jahwistischen Fassung' von Ex 14" ("only a general dependence on the so-called 'Yahwistic version' of Exod 14").
41 Albert de Pury views "P^g as the absolute beginning," in *Les dernières rédactions du Pentateuque, de l'Hexateuque et de l'Ennéateuque*, ed. Konrad Schmid and Thomas Römer, BEThL 203 (Leuven: Peeters, 2007), 99–128.
42 On the terminology of "purity" of the communication see Saul Olyan, "Purity Ideology in Ezra-Nehemiah as a Tool to Reconstitute the Community," *JSJ* 35 (2004): 4–10; Rainer Albertz,

A similar case appears in Gen 35:2b, 4, which according to the hypothesis of Yair Zakovitch, Nadav Na'aman, and Hans Rapp presents a critical reception of Joshua 24:[43] The sanctuary near Shechem that is in use in the background scenery of Joshua 24 is in reality nothing other than and nothing less than a *favissa* in which Jacob disposed of his family's idols. These portions of the verses are, however, quite difficult to date. Joshua 24 is, therefore, later than the Priestly Document, which belongs in the early Persian period, but earlier than Nehemiah 13 and Genesis 35. Therefore, it likely emerged between the end of the 6th and the 4th centuries BCE, at a time when Jews and Samaritans co-existed side by side.

Whether one can narrow the date further based on the archaeology of ancient Shechem—which plays a prominent role in Josh 24:1 as the gathering place for all the tribes—depends on how one interprets the content of Joshua 24. Ancient Shechem, *Tel Balāta*, appears to have been unsettled between 480 – 330 BCE. Depending on how pro-Samaritan one finds Joshua 24, then 480 BCE could present a further *terminus ante quem*. If Joshua 24 were an offer to the North to join cultically and politically with the South, then the setting in Shechem would fit better with a settlement that was still in existence. If Joshua 24 instead drafts a theological ideal of all Israel that was conceived in the South but did not really push for a realization by equals, then a date after 480 BCE would be more plausible. From this perspective, Joshua 24 could take place in Shechem in the sense of a theological gesture, but one would not need to fear any competition with Jerusalem.

At any rate, the opening of Josh 24:1 is of particular importance for our topic: "Then Joshua gathered all the tribes of Israel to Shechem, and summoned the elders, the heads, the judges, and the officers of Israel; and they presented themselves before God." Why does Joshua 24 play out in Shechem?[44] Joshua's speech

---

"Purity Strategies and Political Interest in the Policy of Nehemiah," in *Confronting the Past*, ed. S. Gitin, J.E. Wright, and J.P. Dessel (Winona Lake: Eisenbrauns, 2006), 199–206.

43 Cf. Yair Zakovitch, "The Object of the Narrative of the Burial of Foreign Gods at Shechem," BetM 25 (1980): 30–37; Nadav Na'aman, "The Law of the Altar in Deuteronomy and the Cultic Site Near Shechem," in *Rethinking the Foundations: Historiography in the Ancient World and in the Bible*, FS J. Van Seters, ed. Steven L. McKenzie and Thomas Römer, BZAW 294 (Berlin: de Gruyter, 2000), 141–161, 160–61 n. 54; Hans A. Rapp, *Jakob in Bet-El: Gen 35,1–15 und die jüdische Literatur des 3. und 2. Jahrhunderts*, Herders Biblische Studien 29 (Freiburg i.Br.: Herder, 2001), 62–63. Critical are Römer, "Ende": 542 n. 103 and note also the considerations in Uwe Becker, "Jakob in Bet-El und Sichem," in *Die Erzväter in der biblischen Tradition*, FS Matthias Köckert, ed. Anselm C. Hagedorn and Henrik Pfeiffer, BZAW 400 (Berlin: de Gruyter, 2009), 159–185, 181–182.

44 The LXX, however, has: καὶ συνήγασεν Ἰησοῦς πάσας φυλὰς Ισραηλ εἰς Σηλω, therefore reading "Shiloh" instead of "Shechem" (also in v. 25). These readings might have arisen from the

is addressed to "all the tribes of Israel," meaning all Israel, the North and South. Especially the invitation to the North precipitates the choice of an appropriate location. Shechem arises easily from the scenery of Deuteronomy and the book of Joshua.[45] There are, however, other reasons for specifically choosing Shechem. According to 1 Kgs 12:1, Shechem is the location where Rehoboam must go in order to be made king. Shechem, therefore, seems to have been the place where kings in Israel were enthroned. Because Joshua 24 basically reports nothing less than the choice of Yhwh as king, the founding legend of the theocracy, Shechem is the logical choice. Joshua 24 does not seem to portray Shechem as only the Northern Kingdom's primary reference point. Even though it emphasizes the North, the chapter addresses all the tribes of Israel. Additionally, the beginning of the ancestral story is a factor: According to Gen 12:6, Shechem is the first place in the land where Abraham built an altar.[46] Joshua 24 therefore constructs a narrative arc back to Genesis 12. The promulgation of the law in Shechem takes place at the same location where the first cultic place for Yhwh was set up in the land.

Joshua 24 then continues in v. 2: "And Joshua said to all the people, 'Thus says the Lord, the God of Israel: Long ago your ancestors—Terah and his sons Abraham and Nahor—lived beyond the Euphrates and served other gods.'" The beginning of Joshua's speech assumes the idolatry of Israel's ancestors in Mesopotamia. This motif of Abraham's liberation from Mesopotamian idol worship became common in the history of reception, but it is noteworthy that it is not mentioned in Genesis 11–12. If one considers the postexilic audience of Joshua 24, then it appears that Josh 24:2 clearly views its addressees as a syncretistic religious community that worships Mesopotamian deities, though not exclusively.

Remarkably, this position is quite similar to what 2 Kgs 17:24–31 states to characterize the syncretistic religious history of the North after 722 BCE: "So these nations worshipped the Lord, but also served their carved images; to this day their children and their children's children continue to do as their ancestors did" (2 Kgs 17:41). Of course, 2 Kgs 17:24–41 can hardly provide an adequate view into the historical religious situation in the North. However, it is still conspicuous that the authors of 2 Kings 17 could, in their time, describe

---

anti-Samaritan slant in the Hebrew *Vorlage* of the LXX. See the discussions in Hjelm, *Jerusalem's Rise*, 197 and n. 197; Christophe Nihan, "The Torah between Samaria and Judah: Shechem and Gerizim in Deuteronomy and Joshua," in *The Pentateuch as Torah: New Models for Understanding its Promulgation and its Acceptance*, ed. Gary N. Knoppers and Bernard M. Levinson (Winona Lake, IN: Eisenbrauns, 2007), 187–223, 197 n. 31.
45 Cf. Blum, "Knoten."
46 Römer, "Ende," 544 n. 118.

the religious practices in the North in this way (cf. 2 Kgs 17:34, 41: "until this day").

A longer exposition reprising the ancestral and exodus story then follows. Joshua's speech culminates in vv. 14–15 in the call that connects with the problem presented.

> "Now therefore revere Yhwh, and serve him in sincerity and in faithfulness; put away the gods that your ancestors served beyond the River and in Egypt, and serve Yhwh. Now if you are unwilling to serve Yhwh, choose this day whom you will serve, whether the gods your ancestors served in the region beyond the River or the gods of the Amorites in whose land you are living; but as for me and my household, we will serve Yhwh."

Joshua presents the tribes of Israel with a clear choice: either Yhwh or the other deities. Eventually, the people agree in Shechem to do so. What does this entail for the meaning of Joshua 24 at the time of its authors and their contemporary readers? In light of the literary connections between Joshua 24 and other biblical texts, I propose a dating of this text after "P" and before Nehemiah, so likely around the 5th century BCE.

For the readers of Joshua 24, Samaria and Yehud were independent provinces. Joshua 24 opts for a theocratic constitution for all Israel within the framework of a religious orientation that—in biblical terms—renounces both the deities of the ancestors from beyond the River as well as the deities of the Amorites, focusing instead on God alone. In prohibiting the tribes of Israel from serving other deities, it is hard to say exactly what Joshua 24 has in mind for readers in the 5th century BCE. There is no evidence that the Samaritans were sacrificing to multiple deities. Maybe the background of this claim is the polemic of 2 Kgs 17:29–34 that is factored in here, especially 2 Kgs 17:33a: "So they worshiped YHWH but also served their own gods." The choice of Shechem[47] as the location of the scene allows little doubt that in both the narrative world and the world of the narrator, the North is the specific addressee.

---

[47] Shechem was a relatively unimportant location during the Persian period. It was unsettled from ca. 480 to ca. 330 BCE (Karl Jaroš, *Sichem: Eine archäologische und religionsgeschichtliche Studie mit besonderer Berücksichtigung von Jos 24*, OBO 11 (Fribourg: Universitätsverlag, 1976), 47–48; cf. Römer, "Ende," 545 n. 121). The city was fortified again only in the Hellenistic period, Edward F. Campbell, "Shechem," *NEAEHL* 4:1345–54; Ahlström, *History*, 901. See however Ephraim Stern, *The Assyrian, Babylonian, and Persian periods 732–332 B.C.*, vol. 2 of *Archaeology of the Land of the Bible*, ABRL (New York: Doubleday, 2001), 427–28, who is arguing for an ongoing settlement into the 4th century. On the discussion of the tree sanctuary, see Ludwig Wächter, "Zur Lokalisierung des sichemitischen Baumheiligtums," *ZDPV* 103 (1987): 1–12.

This reading of Joshua 24 suggests a text quite close to the basic convictions of the Chronistic History. Israel is all Israel; unlike Chronicles, however, Joshua 24 is not centered on Jerusalem. This could also be linked to the literary fiction of the scenery of Joshua 24: Jerusalem had not yet been conquered by the Israelites. During the time in which Joshua 24 is set, Shechem remained a legitimate sanctuary.

What does this mean for the history of Samaria and Yehud in the 5th century BCE? It appears that the categories for describing relations between Samaritans and Judeans in terms of competition and then separation are inadequate. For the period prior to the competition surrounding the building of the wall under Nehemiah, one should likely reckon with a phase of concordance, as Benedikt Hensel has also proposed in a recent study.[48] Joshua 24 implies a relationship between Judeans and Samaritans in which living side by side in the two provinces appears to have been understood not in terms of competition but of concordance. Joshua 24 is thus in agreement with various postexilic texts, in particular from the prophetic tradition, that nourished hopes of the restitution of all Israel following the exile: Jer 30:3, 8–9; 31:27–28, 31–34; Ezek 34:23–21; 37:15–28; Obad 18–21; Isa 11:11–16; Jer 3:18; Zech 9:9–13; 10:6–12.[49] The competitive claims of Samaria and Judah in the time of Nehemiah and finally in the combative actions of John Hyrcanus against the Samaritans completely turned this vision of restitution into an idea of the past.

---

48 Benedikt Hensel, *Juda und Samaria: Zum Verhältnis zweier nach-exilischer Jahwismen*, FAT 110 (Tübingen: Mohr Siebeck, 2016).
49 Erhard Blum, *Die Komposition der Vätergeschichte*, WMANT 57 (Neukirchen-Vluyn: Neukirchener Verlag, 1984), 59.

Emanuel Tov
Textual Harmonization in the Five Books of the Torah: A Summary

The five books of the Torah share a special phenomenon that is unusual within the Hebrew Bible: all five of them feature exactly the same textual characteristics despite containing different content genres. As strange as it may sound, harmonization is the most central textual feature in a large group of textual witnesses of the Torah, appearing in the LXX, the SP (Samaritan Pentateuch), and several Hebrew manuscripts, but not in the Masoretic Text (MT). This situation implies that several witnesses of these five books underwent the same type of textual development, which is understandable as they form one unit. It should be pointed out that textual harmonization is not a natural or expected phenomenon, but it developed nevertheless in certain texts. What is unusual is that this phenomenon is prominent in the Torah and not in the other Scripture books that probably provide more occasion for harmonization. See section 10.

1 What is Harmonization?

There are many contradictory details in Scripture that a harmonizing approach would have removed or altered. When such contradictions appear in all textual sources and not merely in some of them, they relate to literary criticism rather than to textual criticism. Content differences become a text-critical issue only when individual manuscripts differ from one another and one of them is harmonized to agree with another one.[1]

Harmonization is recognized when a detail in source A is changed to another detail in source A or in source B because they differ. Scribes adapted many elements in a verse to other details in the same verse, the immediate or a similar context, the same book, or in parallel sections elsewhere in Scripture. Some of the examples of harmonization pertain to strikingly different texts, but most of

---

1 It is not always easy to distinguish between the two realms in matters of harmonization or coordination (as in the terminology of David Carr). David McLain Carr, *The Formation of the Hebrew Bible: A New Reconstruction* (Oxford: Oxford University Press, 2011), 90–98 provides a wealth of important information, definitions, and examples, but he constantly moves between phenomena that in my view are different: coordination and harmonization at the compositional level of books and harmonization at the scribal level. In this study, I deal only with the latter.

https://doi.org/10.1515/9783110581416-003

the examples in the Torah are of a different type. They pertain to very similar texts in which harmonization seems to be unnatural. Found frequently in direct speech, they often pertain to small literary differences in formulation that were harmonized because of a formal approach to Scripture, according to which a God-inspired text should only include formulations that are perfectly in harmony with one another. Some harmonizing changes must have been inserted unconsciously, but most were inserted because of a theological concern for perfection, especially in harmonizing pluses. Harmonization is by definition a secondary feature, and in the SP and LXX it is coupled with similar secondary features such as various forms of adaptation of details to the context.

In this study, I summarize the situation regarding harmonizations in the Torah as analyzed in my earlier studies of the five individual books.[2] The study of harmonization[3] has become an increasingly more central issue in textual analysis, as I have come to realize that in the Torah all the textual witnesses can be divided between a block of texts in which harmonization is a central textual feature and a block in which there is little harmonization.[4] See section 11.

Let us turn first to some examples. The Torah offers several schematic descriptions that differ slightly in detail, such as the description of the days in the creation account and many narratives in the patriarchal stories.[5] For exam-

---

[2] "Textual Harmonizations in the Ancient Texts of Deuteronomy," in Emanuel Tov, *Hebrew Bible, Greek Bible, and Qumran: Collected Essays*, TSAJ 121 (Tübingen: Mohr Siebeck, 2008), 271–82; "Textual Harmonization in the Stories of the Patriarchs," in Emanuel Tov, *Textual Criticism of the Hebrew Bible, Qumran, Septuagint: Collected Writings, Volume 3*, VTSup 167 (Leiden: Brill, 2015), 166–88; "The Harmonizing Character of the Septuagint of Genesis 1–11," in Tov, *Collected Writings, Volume 3*, 470–89; "Textual Harmonization in Leviticus," forthcoming; "The Septuagint of Numbers as a Harmonizing Text," forthcoming; "Textual Harmonization in Exodus 1–24," *TC: A Journal of Biblical Textual Criticism* 22 (2017). http://rosetta.reltech.org/TC/v22/TC-2017-Tov.pdf

[3] For theoretical studies on harmonization, see my own study "The Nature and Background of Harmonizations in Biblical Manuscripts," *JSOT* 31 (1985): 3–29; Ronald S. Hendel, *The Text of Genesis 1–11: Textual Studies and Critical Edition* (New York: Oxford University Press, 1998), 82–92; Bénédicte Lemmelijn, *A Plague of Texts? A Text-Critical Study of the So-Called 'Plagues Narratives' in Exodus 7:14–11:10*, OTS 56 (Leiden: Brill, 2009), 212–15; Corrado Martone, "From Chaos to Coherence and Back: Some Thoughts on the Phenomenon of Harmonization in the Bible and the Dead Sea Scrolls," in *"Let the Wise Listen and Add to Their Learning" (Prov 1:5). Festschrift for Günter Stemberger on the Occasion of his 75th Birthday*, ed. Constanza Cordoni and Gerhard Langer; SJ 90 (Berlin: De Gruyter, 2016), 29–38.

[4] See Emanuel Tov, "The Development of the Text of the Torah in Two Major Text Blocks," *Text* 26 (2016): 1–27. http://www.hum.huji.ac.il/units.php?cat=5020&incat=4972

[5] Likewise, in the Homeric epos, recurring events such as the beginning of the day, battle scenes, and descriptions of meals are described with exactly the same words.

ple, the reader hears the story of Joseph's encounter with Potiphar's wife three times, as told by the narrator (Gen 39:7–13), by Potiphar's wife to the members of her household (39:14–15), and in her account to Potiphar (39:17–19). The dreams of Pharoah's cupbearer (40:9–12) and chief baker (40:16–17) are repeated in Joseph's interpretation (40:12–15; 18–19). The details of Pharaoh's dream (41:1–7) are repeated in the interpretation (41:25–36) and in the words of the narrator (41:47–57). Likewise, there is much repetition in the words of Abraham's senior servant at the well (24:10–14), the account of the senior servant and Rebekah at the well (24:15–27), and the former's account to Laban (24:33–49). In all these repeated episodes, the biblical stories introduce many small variations, and they must have been thorns in the sides of formalistic scribes. These small variations provide an opportunity for harmonization, as indeed occurred often in the textual sources. In some stories, harmonizing changes were made on almost every possible occasion.

By the same token, any combination of two or three from among the words מצוה, משפט, חק, and משמרת, which are often juxtaposed in Deuteronomistic phraseology, may attract the addition of a third or fourth word in the manuscript tradition.[6]

Some of the changes and pluses in the textual witnesses of Leviticus had halakhic implications and they have been analyzed in important studies on the LXX by Zacharias Frankel, Leo Prijs and David Andrew Teeter for all the textual witnesses.[7] Some harmonizing changes and pluses were indeed based on legalistic interpretations (see section 6) but, as a rule, it was merely the formal similarity between verses that led a scribe to adapt one verse to another in legal passages. For example, some verses in Leviticus describe a cleaning ritual consisting of two elements (11:25, 28, 40 *bis*), יכבס בגדיו וטמא עד־הערב ("he shall wash his clothes and remain unclean until evening"). Other verses contain a slightly expanded ritual consisting of three elements (15:5, 6, 7, 8, 10, 21, 22, 27; 17:15): יכבס בגדיו ורחץ במים וטמא עד־הערב ("he shall wash his clothes, bathe in water, and remain unclean until evening"). It was to be expected that some manuscripts with verses containing two elements would add the third one harmonis-

---

6 See Deut 11:1 MT SP; 28:15 MT SP; 30:10 LXX in Tov, "Textual Harmonizations in the Ancient Texts of Deuteronomy," 275, 278.
7 Zacharias Frankel, *Vorstudien zu der Septuaginta* (Leipzig: Fr. Chr. Wilh. Vogel, 1941); idem, *Über den Einfluss der palästinischen Exegese auf die alexandrinische Hermeneutik* (Leipzig: J. A. Barth, 1851); Leo Prijs, *Jüdische Tradition in der Septuaginta* (Leiden: Brill, 1948); David Andrew Teeter, *Scribal Laws: Exegetical Variation in the Textual Transmission of Biblical Law in the Late Second Temple Period*, FAT 92 (Tübingen: Mohr Siebeck, 2014).

tically, "and shall wash himself in water."[8] This happened in the LXX of 11:40b, but not in vv. 25, 28, 40a and in the SP of v. 25, but not in vv. 28, 40a, 40b. The harmonizing pluses were thus added *inconsistently*.

2 Investigation Procedure

In the studies mentioned in n. 2, the data have been recorded for the LXX, SP, and MT. The largest group (1) includes harmonizations exclusive to the LXX, while group (2) contains similar data from both the LXX and the SP. Far fewer harmonizations are exclusive to the SP (3) and even fewer to the MT (groups 4 and 5).

I distinguish between harmonizations influenced by: (a) the immediate context, (b) the remote context, and (c) an addition or expansion of a subject or object on the basis of the context. Usually such instances are not considered harmonizations, but as long as the contextual base of these pluses can be indicated, I consider them harmonizing. In the case of additions based on remote contexts, one usually recognizes the idea or phrase that triggered the harmonizing change (§ 1a). I suggest that most harmonizations of groups (a) and (b) were conscious, while those of group (c) could have been unconscious. The harmonizations of groups (a) and (b) reflect a certain conception, almost ideology, according to which intertextual links should be added in order to perfect the biblical stories. Harmonizations to remote contexts show how well the editor or scribe knew the biblical text (see section 5).

The following groups are excluded from the examination:

a. Instances of apparent harmonizing additions in the LXX that cannot be evaluated adequately because of our limitations in evaluating the translation technique of the LXX. Thus, when analyzing the harmonizing addition of תוך in MT Deut 23:12 אל תוך (SP אל; cf. v. 11 אל תוך), the evidence of the LXX (εἰς) cannot be brought to bear on this issue since this preposition renders both אל (passim) and אל תוך (Num 17:12; Deut 13:17; contrast 21:12; 22:2).

b. Differences between texts that are not due to harmonization: non-harmonizing pluses or changes in the LXX (e. g., Lev 5:5, 21; 26:41; Num 4:14 for which cf. vv. 9, 13b, 10, 12; and 36:1) and textual complications (e. g., in Lev 15:3; 17:4;

---

[8] The longer formula is based on the remote 15:5: ואיש אשר יגע במשכבו יכבס בגדיו ורחץ במים וטמא עד־הערב ("Anyone who touches his bedding shall wash his clothes, bathe in water, and remain unclean until evening" [JPS]).

23:41[9] or Num 1:18 + ἔτους [cf. 1:1]; 14:31 MT SP וידעו; LXX וירשו [καὶ κληρονομήσουσιν], based on v. 24).

c. A few frequently occurring formulaic additions for which no exact source text can be indicated: אלהיך, אלהים, etc. added to יהוה; כל, נא, כן, גם, גם, כה, pronominal prepositions such as בך, לך, et sim. These instances are not harmonizing additions in the strict sense of the word,[10] and rather should be considered adaptations to formulaic expressions.

d. Possible cases of harmonization for which no source text could be found.[11]

e. Misleading agreements between the SP and the LXX. For example, in Lev 12:4, the unusual plural form of the MT for "blood" in בדמי טהרה is represented by the singular form in the SP בדם טהרה and the LXX ἐν αἵματι ἀκαθάρτῳ αὐτῆς. At first sight, this could appear to be a case of an extra-Masoretic agreement between the SP and the LXX, but this agreement is misleading because elsewhere in the Pentateuch the LXX also renders the rare occurrences of the plural דמים with the singular αἷμα.[12]

3 Harmonization in Liturgical Hebrew Witnesses

All textual sources contain harmonizations of the type described in the previous sections, and in the Torah this feature plays a major role in the LXX and SP (not in the MT) as well as in three liturgical Torah texts and fifteen *tefillin*. The latter sources are not treated here, because of their small size and sometimes fragmentary state. The three Qumran texts that contain the same pericopes as the *tefillin* are 4QDeut[j,k1,n] [13] and they do not contain complete copies of Deuteronomy and Exodus.[14]

---

9 The texts in Lev 15:3 and 17:4 at first sight appear to represent pluses in the shared text of the LXX SP, but actually they reflect textual omissions (*homoioteleuta*) in the MT.
10 Except for such cases in which a clear source can be indicated.
11 E.g., Deut 13:16 ואת בהמתה לפי חרב.
12 Gen 4:10, 11; Exod 4:25, 26; Lev 12:5, 7; 20:18.
13 The liturgical character of 4QDeut[j] is supported by its small size. See Tov, *Hebrew Bible, Greek Bible, and Qumran*, 37. Note further that both 4QDeut[j] and 4QDeut[n] start with Deut 5:1 and continue until the beginning of ch. 6. Both texts also contain a fragment that covers 8:5–10. See Esther Eshel, "4QDeut[n]: A Text That Has Undergone Harmonistic Editing," *HUCA* 62 (1991): 151.
14 4QDeut[j] contains sections from Deuteronomy 5, 8, 10, 11, 32 and Exodus 12, 13; 4QDeut[kl] contains sections from Deuteronomy 5, 11, 32.

While the proto-MT and MT-like *tefillin* do not contain harmonizations, in the LXX-SP *tefillin* they constitute the major textual feature, as in the case of the LXX of the running texts (see section 7).[15] For example, most of the differences between 4QPhyl A and the other texts may be ascribed to various types of harmonization.[16] This also pertains to the many (17) harmonizing changes of 4QDeut^n towards the text of Exodus, especially in the Decalogue in Deuteronomy 5 towards Exodus 20.[17] A striking example is the long addition in the Deuteronomy scroll of the argument for the Sabbath from Exod 20:8–11 (the creation of the world in six days), added after the argument of Deut 5:15 (remembrance of the slavery in Egypt). This harmonizing addition in 4QDeut^n links us directly to the *tefillin*, since two *tefillin*, one *mezuzah* and the Nash Papyrus[18] replace the argument for the Shabbat in the text of Deuteronomy with that in Exodus, viz., 4QPhyl G, 8QPhyl III, 4QMez A.[19]

---

15 Two types of *tefillin* were found in the Judean Desert. For the texts from cave 4, see Józef Tadeusz Milik, "Tefillin, Mezuzot et Targums (4Q128–4Q157)," in *Qumrân grotte 4.II: I. Archéologie, II. Tefillin, Mezuzot et Targums (4Q128–4Q157)*, ed. Roland de Vaux and Józef Tadeusz Milik, DJD 6 (Oxford: Clarendon, 1977), 33–79; for 8QPhyl, see Maurice Baillet, "Phylactère," in *Les 'petites grottes' de Qumrân: exploration de la falaise, les grottes 2Q, 3Q, 5Q, 7Q à 10Q, le rouleau de cuivre*, ed. Maurice Baillet, Józef Tadeusz Milik, and Roland de Vaux, DJD 3 (Oxford: Clarendon, 1962), 154. Group (i) contains four proto-MT and MT-like *tefillin* (MT orthography) that are close to codex L and cover only the scriptural pericopes required by the rabbis (MurPhyl, 34SePhyl, 8QPhyl I, XHevSePhyl). A larger group of fifteen *tefillin* (ii), reflecting the LXX-SP text (conservative as well as Qumran Scribal Practice orthography), covers not only the pericopes required by the rabbis, but also additional passages. Two *tefillin*, 4QPhyl C and D-E-F, reflect a special group since they reflect the SP-LXX text together with MT orthography, but they consist only of the required passages of the rabbis. These *tefillin* show that in the last centuries BCE and the first two centuries CE the rabbinic circles were apparently less strict than the later rabbinic circles since in earlier times the rabbinic rules were also applied to *tefillin* of a different textual character. For an analysis, see my study "The *Tefillin* from the Judean Desert and the Textual Criticism of the Hebrew Bible," in *Is There a Text in This Cave? Studies in the Textuality of the Dead Sea Scrolls in Honour of George J. Brooke*, STDJ 119 (Leiden: Brill, 2017), 277–92.
16 I classify twelve of the variants (frequently shared with the LXX and/or SP) as harmonistic: Deut 10:13, 21; 11:2, 4, 6, 7, 8, 10, 11, 13; Exod 12:50; 13:3, 5 and 9 as representing various textual categories: Deut 5:3, 32; 10:13, 18, 18, 22; 11:10, 12, 16.
17 See the analysis of Eshel, "4QDeut^n," 117–54 (esp. 142–47).
18 See William Foxwell Albright, "A Biblical Fragment from the Maccabaean Age: The Nash Papyrus," *JBL* 56 (1937): 145–76; Stanley Arthur Cook, "A Pre-Massoretic Biblical Papyrus," *Proceedings of the Society of Biblical Archaeology* 25 (1903): 34–56.
19 In all these texts, harmonization, including the addition of small pericopes, is the main textual-editorial feature. See section 11.

4 Harmonizations in the LXX: Hebrew or Greek Background?

Harmonizations occur mainly in the LXX and SP (but not the MT) together with those found in the liturgical texts and *tefillin*. These harmonizations are analyzed in the following sections, while in this section we turn to the question of whether the harmonizations in the LXX should be conceived of as an inner-Greek phenomenon or as relating to the *Vorlage* of the LXX.

It has been suggested that the Greek translator inserted these harmonizations, but I wish to suggest that most of them were already found in his *Vorlage*, although this cannot be proven conclusively. The first scholar to claim that the translators inserted these harmonizations was Theophilus Toepler (1830), who provided a long list of examples.[20] He was followed by Zacharias Frankel who based himself on Toepler and added several examples, but he usually ascribed the phenomenon to anonymous editors of the manuscripts (*diaskeuastes*),[21] although occasionally he ascribed them to the translator.[22] In recent times, several scholars have returned to the earlier view of ascribing the harmonizations to the translators of the book of Numbers.[23]

In 1985, I suggested that these harmonizations were inserted into the Hebrew *Vorlage* of the LXX, rather than being the work of the translators.[24] This approach is supported by the following arguments: (1) the translators' fidelity to their sources; (2) the level at which the harmonization took place; (3) the frequent agreement of the SP with the LXX; and (4) the occasional agreement of the LXX with Qumran scrolls. These arguments have been exemplified in the various studies

---

20 Theophilus Eduardus Toepler, *De Pentateuchi interpretationis alexandrinae indole critica et hermeneutica* (Halle: C. Schwetschke, 1830), 8–16.
21 Frankel, *Einfluss*, 58–63; 103–04; 163–64, 187–88; 221–23. The basis for Frankel's approach was laid in his earlier *Vorstudien*, 78–79.
22 See, e.g., Frankel's remarks in *Einfluss*, 187–88.
23 Gilles Dorival, *La Bible d'Alexandrie, 4: Les Nombres* (Paris: Cerf, 1994), 42–43. See also his summarizing methodological remark on p. 40; John William Wevers, *Notes on the Greek Text of Numbers*, SCS 46 (Atlanta: Scholars Press, 1998), xvii–xviii; Martin Rösel, "Die Septuaginta und der Kult: Interpretationen und Aktualisierungen im Buch Numeri," in *La double transmission du texte biblique: Études d'histoire du texte offertes en hommage à A. Schenker*, ed. Yohanan Goldman and Christoph Uehlinger, OBO 179 (Fribourg/Göttingen: Éditions Universitaires/Vandenhoeck & Ruprecht, 2001), 25–40 (29–30).
24 "The Nature and Background of Harmonizations." This argument was accepted by Hendel, *The Text of Genesis 1–11*, 82–92 ("Harmonizing Tendencies in S and G").

on the books of the Torah in the studies quoted in n. 2 with examples from these books, and will be accompanied here by select examples.

1. *The translator's fidelity.* If a translation was literal, by implication the harmonizations reflected in that translation took place in his *Vorlage* because harmonization is a sign of great freedom. The overall impression of the LXX translation technique in the books of the Torah is one of fidelity to the Hebrew parent text, but the translation technique of each of the books needs to be investigated further.

2. *The level at which the harmonization took place.* If all or most instances of harmonization were created by the same hand, the changes must have taken place at the Hebrew level and were not created by the translator. This suggestion is based on the fact that in some cases the content of the two Greek texts—the text that was changed by way of harmonization and the text from which it was adapted—differs, rendering it impossible that the translator himself was influenced by the Greek context. Examples are provided below of differences in Hebrew *Vorlage*, vocabulary, and construction:

Vorlage (the plus is based on a slightly different *Vorlage*):

Lev 10:15 MT SP LXX ולבניך; SP LXX + ולבנתיך + (καὶ ταῖς θυγατράσιν σου). Based on v. 14 MT SP, and not on the LXX because the LXX reflects a different *Vorlage*, אתה ובניך וביתך (σὺ καὶ οἱ υἱοί σου καὶ ὁ οἶκός σου).

Lev 22:18 MT SP בני; LXX (ישראל) קהל (συναγωγῇ Ἰσραήλ). Based on 16:17 MT SP קהל ישראל. The LXX in 16:17 combines the two readings (συναγωγῆς υἱῶν Ἰσραήλ). Therefore, the harmonization could not have taken place at the translational level.

Num 29:11 MT SP LXX ונסכיה(ם); LXX + כמשפטם לריח ניחח אשה ליהוה + (κατὰ τὴν σύγκρισιν, εἰς ὀσμὴν εὐωδίας, κάρπωμα κυρίῳ). Based on v. 6 (κατὰ τὴν σύγκρισιν αὐτῶν, εἰς ὀσμὴν εὐωδίας κυρίῳ) with a different *Vorlage* (כמשפטם לריח ניחח ליהוה).

Num 31:6 MT SP LXX אלעזר; LXX + בן אהרן + (υἱοῦ Ἀαρών). Based on 26:1, the only verse in Numbers in which Moses appears together with Eleazar and the latter's father. The LXX of 31:6 could not have been based on the LXX of 26:1 since the phrase "son of Aaron" is missing in the LXX *ad loc.*

Vocabulary (the wording of the plus differs from that of the source of the harmonization):

Lev 6:8 MT SP LXX המזבח(ה); SP LXX + אשה + (κάρπωμα). Based on 2:2 (θυσία).

Lev 13:39b MT SP LXX בעור; LXX + בשרו + (τῆς σαρκὸς αὐτοῦ). Based on v. 11 (τοῦ χρωτός). Similar argument in Lev 13:43 based on v. 2.

Lev 25:50 MT SP LXX שכיר; LXX + שנה בשנה + (ἔτος ἐξ ἔτους). Based on v. 53 (ἐνιαυτὸν ἐξ ἐνιαυτοῦ).

Lev 26:20 MT ועץ הארץ; SP LXX ועץ השדה (καὶ τὸ ξύλον τοῦ ἀγροῦ). Based on v. 4 (καὶ τὰ ξύλα τῶν πεδίων).

Num 27:12 MT SP LXX הר העברים הזה; LXX + הר נבו + (ὄρος Ναβαύ). Based on Deut 32:49, where Moses is told "Ascend these heights of Abarim to Mount Nebo." The two Greek renderings of הר העברים הזה differ (27:12 τὸ ἐν τῷ πέραν τοῦτο; Deut 32:49 τὸ ὄρος τὸ Αβαριν τοῦτο) and therefore the borrowing must have taken place at the Hebrew level.

Num 33:9 MT SP LXX ויחנו שם; LXX + על המים + (παρὰ τὸ ὕδωρ). Based on Exod 15:27 (παρὰ τὰ ὕδατα).

Different construction (the construction of the plus differs from that of the source of the harmonization)

Lev 25:25 MT SP LXX אחיך; LXX + עמך + (ὁ μετὰ σοῦ). Based on v. 39 (παρὰ σοί).
Lev 25:46 MT SP LXX לרשת; LXX + והיו לכם + (καὶ ἔσονται ὑμῖν). Based on v. 45 (ἔστωσαν ὑμῖν).
Lev 26:21 MT SP LXX ואם; LXX + באלה + (μετὰ ταῦτα). Based on v. 23 (ἐπὶ τούτοις).
Num 23:7 MT SP LXX init; LXX + ותהי רוח אלהים עליו + (καὶ ἐγενήθη πνεῦμα θεοῦ ἐπ' αὐτῷ). Based on 24:2 (καὶ ἐγένετο πνεῦμα θεοῦ ἐν αὐτῷ).
Num 27:12 MT SP LXX ישראל; LXX + לאחזה + (ἐν κατασχέσει). Based on Deut 32:49 (εἰς κατάσχεσιν).

While usually no judgment can be made on the vocabulary of any two Greek texts because the Greek renderings use common LXX vocabulary, in the aforementioned cases a strong argument against inner-LXX harmonization may be made.

3. *Frequent agreement of the SP with the LXX.* The fact that the LXX agrees with the SP in so many harmonizations in all five books of the Torah strengthens the assumption of a Hebrew background also for the other harmonizations in which they do not agree. See section 8 below.

4. *Occasional agreement of the LXX with a Qumran scroll.* In several instances, the LXX agrees with a Qumran scroll and these agreements support the idea that the LXX reflects a Hebrew text:

Exod 2:11 MT SP LXX בימים; 4QExod[b] LXX + הרבים + (ταῖς πολλαῖς). Based on v. 23.
Exod 7:15 MT SP LXX הנה; 4QpaleoExod[m] SP LXX + הוא (יצא) + (αὐτὸς ἐκπορεύεται). Based on 4:14. Similarly 8:16.
Lev 26:24 MT SP בקרי; 11QpaleoLev[a] LXX בחמת קרי (θυμῷ πλαγίῳ). Based on v. 28.
Num 22:11 MT SP LXX הארץ; 4QNum[b] LXX + והוא יושב ממולי + (καὶ οὗτος ἐγκάθηται ἐχόμενός μου). Based on v. 5.
Num 22:11 MT SP LXX וגרשתיו; 4QNum[b] LXX + מן הארץ + (ἀπὸ τῆς γῆς). Based on v. 6 (ἐκ τῆς γῆς). Difference in Greek.
Num 22:18 MT SP LXX או גד(ו)לה; 4QNum[b] LXX + בלבי + (ἐν τῇ διανοίᾳ μου). Based on v. 13. Also 25:16; 26:33; 35:21.

Beyond the examples provided above, I believe that it is unlikely that Greek translators, certainly relatively literal ones, harmonized scriptural verses, especially when dealing with remote contexts. This is not the same as the influence of the translation of the Greek Torah on that of the later translators,[25] which is felt especially in the vocabulary of the later books. The frequent agreement between the LXX and such Hebrew sources as the SP and pre-Samaritan scrolls makes it difficult to maintain a view that harmonization is an inner-Septuagintal phenomenon.[26] In addition to all these, it should be pointed out that harmonization in small details is the major textual phenomenon in a series of Hebrew liturgical biblical texts and *tefillin*, all of which support the likelihood of harmonization taking place also in the *Vorlage* of the LXX. See section 3.

5 Harmonization Types and Techniques

Most of the examples of harmonization are rather straightforward in that a change is inserted in text A in accord with text B, such as described in section 1. Some special techniques are noticed:

Rewriting
All five books of the Torah resemble one another with regard to the procedures followed in the course of inserting harmonizations, but in one aspect Exodus is somewhat different. Sometimes, the act of harmonizing was combined with some rewriting of the content, and in Exodus there are more such instances than in the other books of the Torah.

---

25 Especially the vocabulary of certain key passages such as the influence of Deuteronomy 32 on the Greek Isaiah. See my study "The Septuagint Translation of the Torah as a Source and Resource for the Post-Pentateuchal Translators," in *Die Sprache der Septuaginta, The Language of the Septuagint*, vol. 3 of *Handbuch zur Septuaginta, Handbook of the Septuagint, LXX.H*, ed. Eberhard Bons and Jan Joosten (Gütersloh: Gütersloher Verlag, 2016), 316–28.
26 Inner-LXX influence is not impossible, but such instances would be very rare. I submit one such possible instance in which the translation equivalents common to Exodus and Numbers show the possibility of such influence. The description of the features of God in LXX Num 14:18 יהוה ארך אפים ורב־חסד ואמת נשא עון ופשע וחטאה is expanded twice in Numbers in accord with Exod 34:6–7: "The Lord is slow to anger, and abounding in steadfast love <u>and faithfulness</u>, forgiving iniquity and transgression <u>and sin</u>." The underlined words have been added in the LXX of Num 14:18 (Κύριος μακρόθυμος καὶ πολυέλεος <u>καὶ ἀληθινός</u>, ἀφαιρῶν ἀνομίας καὶ ἀδικίας <u>καὶ ἁμαρτίας</u>). Cf. the wording of Exod 34:6–7: Κύριος ὁ θεὸς οἰκτίρμων καὶ ἐλεήμων, μακρόθυμος καὶ πολυέλεος καὶ ἀληθινός, ⁷καὶ δικαιοσύνην διατηρῶν καὶ ποιῶν ἔλεος εἰς χιλιάδας, ἀφαιρῶν ἀνομίας καὶ ἀδικίας.

Exod 4:18 MT SP LXX לשלום; LXX + ויהי אחרי הימים הרבים האלה וימת מלך מצרים (μετὰ δὲ τὰς ἡμέρας τὰς πολλὰς ἐκείνας ἐτελεύτησεν ὁ βασιλεὺς Αἰγύπτου). Based on 2:23 with free rewriting of the context.

Exod 6:20 MT SP LXX ואת משה; SP LXX + ואת מרים אחותם (καὶ Μαριὰμ τὴν ἀδελφὴν αὐτῶν). Based on Num 26:59.

Exod 17:9 MT SP אנשים; LXX אנשי חיל (ἄνδρας δυνατούς). Based on 18:25. The original text was rewritten to fit a different situation since the mighty men in chapter 18 describe the judges, while those in chapter 17 describe the Israelite soldiers who are to fight with Amalek.

Exod 19:10 MT SP לך אל העם; LXX רד העד בעם (Καταβὰς διαμάρτυραι τῷ λαῷ). Based on v. 21. The two divine commands have been combined.

Exod 19:13 MT SP במשך הקלת והיבל והענן מן ההר; LXX במשך הי(ו)בל (המה [הם] יעלו בהר) (ὅταν αἱ φωναὶ καὶ αἱ σάλπιγγες καὶ ἡ νεφέλη ἀπέλθῃ ἀπὸ τοῦ ὄρους). Based on v. 16.[27] By way of harmonization, all three phenomena that accompanied the theophany have been combined in an unusual manner (addition of קלת and ענן) together with the words "from the mountain."[28]

Num 3:10 MT SP LXX את כהנתם; LXX + ואת כל דבר למזבח ולמבית לפרכת (or sim.) + (καὶ πάντα τὰ κατὰ τὸν βωμὸν καὶ τὰ ἔσω τοῦ καταπετάσματος). This harmonization was added by way of the creative rewriting of 18:7 (κατὰ πάντα τρόπον τοῦ θυσιαστηρίου καὶ τὸ ἔνδοθεν τοῦ καταπετάσματος). Both the Greek and Hebrew formulations differed.

Num 27:12: ויאמר יהוה אל־משה עלה אל־הר העברים הזה הר נבו וראה את־(ה)ארץ כנען אשר אני נתתי לבני ישראל לאחזה. "The Lord said to Moses, 'Go up this mountain of the Abarim, Mount Nebo, and see the land of Canaan that I have given to the Israelites for a possession.'" Several elements in this verse are harmonized with Deut 32:49: 27:12 MT SP LXX הר העברים הזה; LXX + הר נבו + (ὄρος Ναβαύ). Based on Deut 32:49 where Moses is told "Ascend these heights of Abarim to Mount Nebo." The two Greek renderings of הר העברים הזה differ (27:12 τὸ ἐν τῷ πέραν τοῦτο; Deut 32:49 τὸ ὄρος τὸ Αβαριν τοῦτο) and therefore the borrowing must have taken place at the Hebrew level.

Num 32:11 MT SP LXX ומעלה; LXX + אשר ידעו רע וטוב (οἱ ἐπιστάμενοι τὸ κακὸν καὶ τὸ ἀγαθόν). Based on Deut 1:39 (οὐκ οἶδεν σήμερον ἀγαθὸν ἢ κακόν), with an unusual twist of meaning and in the reverse sequence. In the original verse, Deut 1:39, these words refer to

---

27 The exegesis is unusual as the verb משך originally referred only to the horn, cf. Josh 6:5, but it now includes also the other two subjects.

28 The MT and the LXX of this verse represent different scenarios, whereby the LXX foreshadows the picture of v. 16 since the addition of the cloud in the translation of v. 13 is based on v. 16 where the trumpet and the cloud are mentioned together ("a thick cloud on the mountain, and a blast of a trumpet"). The interpretation of the sound of the trumpet differs in both texts. In the MT, the people are told that they may go up the mountain "when the trumpet sounds a long blast," but in the LXX these actions are to take place when the sounds "end" (ἀπέλθῃ) and are thus based on a different interpretation of the Hebrew verb. Here and in 21:12, משכו וקחו – ἀπελθόντες λάβετε, the Greek translator may have had the root מוש in mind. Furthermore, the LXX adds two elements that are based on v. 16, the "sounds" and the "cloud." Harmonization with v. 16 is thus at the base of the LXX rendering of v. 13, while this verse also reflects midrashic elements. See David Willoughby Gooding, "On the Use of the LXX for Dating Midrashic Elements in the Targums," JTS 25 (1974): 1–11 (4–6).

the generation of those born in the desert that will reach the promised land, while in the plus in the LXX they refer to the generation of those who left Egypt.[29] A similar plus from Deut 1:39 is included in the LXX of 14:23, which is closer to the text of Deuteronomy.

Harmonizations to remote verses show the scribe's expertise in the content of the Bible:

Gen 17:14 MT SP LXX לא ימול את בשר ערלתו; SP LXX + ביום השמיני + (τῇ ἡμέρᾳ τῇ ὀγδόῃ). Based on Lev 12:3 MT SP LXX.

Gen 50:25 MT SP LXX והעלתם את עצמתי מזה; SP LXX + אתכם + (μεθ' ὑμῶν). Based on Exod 13:19 MT SP LXX והעליתם את עצמתי מזה אתכם. Joseph's words in Gen 50:25 are quoted with a small expansion in Exod 13:19, and this expansion was in turn inserted in the SP LXX in Genesis.

Lev 10:9 MT יין ושכר אל־תשת אתה ובניך אתך בבאכם אל־אהל מועד (ולא תמתו חקת עולם לדרתיכם); LXX Οἶνον καὶ σικερα οὐ πίεσθε, σὺ καὶ οἱ υἱοί σου μετὰ σοῦ, ἡνίκα ἂν εἰσπορεύησθε εἰς τὴν σκηνὴν τοῦ μαρτυρίου, ἢ προσπορευομένων ὑμῶν πρὸς τὸ θυσιαστήριον. The scribe/editor of this verse remembered the parallel verse in Exodus in which the approaching of the Tent of Meeting was mentioned together with the nearing of the altar with similar implications of danger:[30] Exod 30:20 בבאם אל־אהל מועד ירחצו־מים ולא ימתו או בגשתם אל־המזבח (לשרת להקטיר אשה ליהוה).

Num 9:14, 15:14 MT SP LXX גר; LXX + בארצכם + (ἐν τῇ γῇ ὑμῶν). Based on Lev 19:33, this harmonization displays an intricate knowledge of the regulations regarding proselytes.

Num 14:10 MT SP LXX נראה; LXX + בענן + (ἐν νεφέλῃ). Based on Exod 16:10. In these verses, the "presence of the Lord" appears in two different localities (in the Tent of Meeting in Numbers and in the desert in Exodus), but the *Vorlage* of the LXX nevertheless transferred the image of the cloud from Exodus to Numbers.

In several verses, the LXX supplied a description of the execution of a command to that of the command itself, similar to the practice of the SP in Exodus 7–11 and elsewhere. This practice, which hitherto was considered typical of the SP group, was foreshadowed by the Hebrew text underlying the LXX of the Torah. This feature is also found elsewhere on rare occasions (LXX of Gen 1:9; 1 Sam 9:3b based on v. 3a; 1 Kgs 18:36 based on v. 37).

Exod 17:10 MT SP LXX אמר לו משה; LXX + ויצא + (καὶ ἐξελθών).[31] Based on v. 9.

Num 23:3b MT SP LXX והגדתי לך; LXX + הלך לקראת אלהים + (καὶ παρέστη Βαλὰκ ἐπὶ τῆς θυσίας αὐτοῦ, καὶ Βαλαὰμ ἐπορεύθη ἐπερωτῆσαι τὸν θεόν). Based on v. 3a.

---

29 According to Wevers, *Notes on the Greek Text of Numbers*, xviii, the change was made by the translator.
30 The words in the two Greek versions are identical but this does not necessarily point to borrowing at the Greek level since they serve as general LXX equivalents.
31 Thus Rahlfs with the main manuscripts. Wevers records this variant in the apparatus.

By definition, all harmonizing additions represent secondary developments. They were made in order to adapt one context to another one. However, the fullness of the wording is often artificial and even tautological. This was noticed occasionally by Frankel, who claimed that some of these harmonizations create impossible contexts.[32]

Gen 11:31 MT LXX ואת שרי + ואת מלכה + כלותו אשת אברם בנו; SP ואת שרי כלותו אשת אברם + ונחור + כלותו אשת אברם + בניו = v. 29. The plus of the SP is based on v. 29, where the two daughters-in-law of Terah are mentioned together. The SP could not imagine that Abraham would have left Ur Kasdim with his wife, while Nahor left without his wife, Milkah, and therefore Milkah was added. However, the position of the plus in the SP betrays its secondary nature: MT LXX "Sarai, his daughter-in-law, the wife of his son Abraham" was changed in the SP to "Sarai and Milkah, his daughters-in-law [note the hybrid form כלותו], the wife of his son Abram and Nahor his sons." The addition of Nahor in the SP is equally as secondary as the change of "his son" to "his sons."

Gen 20:14 MT SP LXX אלף כסף + SP LXX ויקח אבימלך (צאן ובקר ועבדים ושפחת); + χίλια δίδραχμα). Based on v. 16 MT SP LXX. The harmonization in this verse reveals its secondary nature. According to v. 14 MT, Abimelech gave Abraham "sheep and oxen, and male and female slaves," but according to v. 16 MT SP LXX he told Sarah that he had given him "a thousand pieces of silver." That monetary unit probably represented the monetary value of the items he had given Abraham according to v. 14. However, the SP LXX version of v. 14 added this detail from v. 16, and thus according to that version Abraham received twice as much in reparation.

Gen 32:20 (19) MT SP LXX (τῷ השלישי את השני גם את (ויצו; LXX + הראשון את + πρώτῳ). Based on v. 18(17) MT SP LXX הראשון את ויצו. This verse quotes Jacob's words to the second and third servants, but the Hebrew parent text of the LXX found it necessary to complete the picture by adding the "first." However, the "first one" was already mentioned in v. 18 (17), making this addition superfluous.

Num 2:2b MT SP LXX יחנו; LXX + ישראל בני; איש על־דגלו באתת לבית אבתם יחנו בני ישראל מנגד סביב לאהל־מועד יחנו, "Each one in his respective regiment, under ensigns by his ancestral house, they shall camp, the Israelites; facing the Tent of Meeting on every side they shall camp." The Vorlage of the LXX created a parallel structure by repeating the subject at the end of the sentence: παρεμβαλέτωσαν οἱ υἱοὶ Ισραηλ ἐναντίοι κύκλῳ τῆς σκηνῆς τοῦ μαρτυρίου παρεμβαλοῦσιν οἱ υἱοὶ Ισραηλ as if reading: facing the Tent of Meeting on every side they shall camp, *the Israelites.*

Num 15:36 MT SP LXX באבנים; LXX + מחוץ למחנה + (ἔξω τῆς παρεμβολῆς): "So the whole community took him outside the camp and stoned him to death *outside the camp.*"

---

32 Frankel, *Einfluss*, 187 described the addition in Num 7:88 according to Exod 28:41 as "unsinnig" ("nonsensical"). The LXX there αὕτη ἡ ἐγκαίνωσις τοῦ θυσιαστηρίου ("this was the dedication of the altar") has been supplemented with μετὰ τὸ πληρῶσαι τὰς χεῖρας αὐτοῦ ("after he filled his hands"). On the same p. 187, Frankel describes a harmonization as a "misunderstanding," and on p. 188 he describes another harmonization as "unsinnig." Similar evaluations are presented on pp. 163–64.

+ מות יומת הרוצח LXX + ‎4QNumᵇ ;ויומת מות יומת המכה רצח הוא Num 35:21 MT SP LXX (θανάτῳ θανατούσθω ὁ φονευτής): "The assailant shall be put to death; he is a murderer; *the assailant shall be put to death.*" Based on v. 18 מות יומת הרצח (θανάτῳ θανατούσθω ὁ φονευτής). Even though the verdict has already been pronounced in v. 21, the plus, repeating the formulation of v. 18, is tautological.

6 In Which Types of Literature were Harmonizations Inserted?

Textual harmonization in small details is visible throughout the Torah, especially in the LXX and SP as well as in the *tefillin* and liturgical texts. When reviewing the instances of harmonization, we note that they have been inserted mainly in narratives, lists, and the phraseology of the laws. Seemingly, the legal material is changed as frequently as the narratives, but this pertains mainly to details in the formulation of the laws and not to their content.

From the outset, we do not expect a great amount of harmonization in legal material because such harmonization would create an unusual situation. After all, the Torah is replete with laws on similar or identical matters that contradict one another. For example, the laws regarding the Hebrew servant in Exod 21:11 differ from those in Deut 15:12–18. The laws pertaining to Pesach and the feast of the *matzot* differ from one another in the different law codes (Exodus 12; 13:3–10; 23:15, 18; 34:18, 25; Lev 23:5–14; Num 9:1–14; 28:16–25; Deut 16:1–8), and so do the laws regarding the tithe (Lev 27:30–33; Num 18:21–32; Deut 14:22–29). Had someone harmonized these laws at the content level, we would have been left with a law code with no internal differences among the books of the Torah. The Mishnah is a good example of such a harmonious law code, and the Temple Scroll, which uses a different system than that in the Mishnah, presents another such example.

In view of this, it is understandable that the substance of the laws is rarely harmonized within a specific pericope or between parallel law codes in the textual witnesses. The aforementioned LXX of Deut 16:7, which is harmonized with Exod 12:9, forms an exception.[33]

The following examples are likewise rare. Most harmonizations in the textual witnesses that deal with legal details are of a secondary nature as they are concerned with small and insignificant details of formulation. For example:

---

[33] For an extensive discussion, see Teeter, *Scribal Laws*, 127, 195–96.

Exod 21:2 MT יעבד; SP LXX יעבדך (δουλεύσει σοι). Based on Deut 15:22.

Exod 23:15 MT SP LXX תשמר; LXX + לעשות + (ποιεῖν). Based on 31:16. The formulation of the laws regarding the *matzot* festival is harmonized to that of the *Shabbat*, but this addition does not change the essence of the law.

Lev 2:12; 23:13 MT SP LXX לריח ניחח; LXX + ליהוה +. Based on 2:9.

Lev 2:13 MT SP LXX קרבנך תקריב; LXX + ליהוה אלהיכם + (κυρίῳ τῷ θεῷ ὑμῶν). Based on v. 9.

7:25 MT SP האכלת (הנפש); LXX ההיא. Based on v. 21 (ונכרתה הנפש ההוא).

Sometimes, however, the difference is slightly more substantial:

Lev 1:10 MT SP LXX יקריבנו; LXX + וסמך את ידו על ראשו + (καὶ ἐπιθήσει τὴν χεῖρα ἐπὶ τὴν κεφαλὴν αὐτοῦ). Based on vv. 3–4. The description of the cattle offering in vv. 3–4 is very similar to that of the sheep in v. 10, but v. 3 adds a detail that is not provided in v. 10. According to v. 3, the person who brings the cattle offering "shall lay his hand upon the head of the animal," and this detail has been added in v. 10 in the LXX.

The number of harmonizations that introduce a new legal interpretation in the textual witnesses of Hebrew and translated Scripture is not large. In a penetrating study,[34] Teeter adduces many examples of such interpretations, but it should be remembered that these examples are gathered from the totality of the available textual witnesses in Hebrew and translation. Therefore, their number may be misleading, and most of them are insignificant. The examples adduced by Teeter show that scribes inserted their exegesis into Hebrew manuscripts at a relatively late stage in the transmission of the text, and probably much less frequently than in the non-legal material.[35] It is remarkable that certain groups of variants/changes reflect rabbinic exegetical tendencies such as "minor expansions in accordance with whether they serve to extend or to restrict the legal requirement" (pp. 119–28). For example:

Exod 21:28 MT SP LXX שור; SP + וכל בהמה +. Based on 22:9 או שור או שה או כל בהמה. The inclusive legal interpretation of SP by way of harmonization changes the subject matter of the law.[36]

Exod 21:33 MT SP LXX שור או חמור; SP + או כל בהמה +. Based on 22:9.

Exod 21:35 MT SP LXX שור רעהו; SP + עד כל בהמה +. Based on 22:9.

Exod 22:3 MT משור עד חמור עד שה; LXX מחמור עד שה (ἀπό τε ὄνου ἕως προβάτου); SP + או כל בהמה +. Based on 22:9.

---

34 Teeter, *Scribal Laws*.
35 Many of the examples given by Teeter have no bearing on the phenomenon of harmonization, while many others do.
36 Teeter, *Scribal Laws*, 119: "A minor expansion functions to specify the wider application of the law." The same pertains to the next examples from 21:33, 35; 22:3, 4.

Exod 23:4 MT SP LXX או חמור ;SP + או כל בהמתו +. Based on 22:9.
Exod 22:13 MT SP LXX או מת ;LXX + או נשבה + (ἢ αἰχμάλωτον γένηται). Based on v. 9. "When a man borrows [an animal] from another and it dies or is injured, its owner not being with it, he must make restitution." Since this verse continues the legal situation described in v. 9, the addition of the LXX in accord with that verse is logical.[37]

Harmonizations in laws refer mainly to the phraseology, especially in Leviticus.

As a rule, harmonizing changes are inserted more often in prose than in poetry because the lack of incongruence is felt more readily in prose segments than in poetry and it is much easier to rewrite prose than poetry. This is clearly visible in Numbers as only a few harmonizing changes were made in the poems in chapters 21–24.

7 Different Frequencies of Harmonization within the Torah

The instances of harmonization have been analyzed in the monographic studies mentioned in n. 2. These studies attempted to present exhaustive material, and the combined data can now be compared for the five books of the Torah.[38] Since the books differ in length and content, statistics are relevant. The study of Exodus is limited to chapters 1–24 due to the special complications of the tabernacle chapters, which do not relate to their internal harmonizations but to the editorial changes, large and small, in these chapters.

The two major foci in studying the frequency of the harmonizations are:
a. Differences between the textual sources;
b. Differences between the books of the Torah.

The investigation pertains only to the LXX, SP, and MT, with partial data regarding the pre-Samaritan scrolls in section 9.

---

[37] This instance was mentioned already by Abraham Geiger, המקרא ותרגומיו (Jerusalem: Mosad Bialik, 1972), 302–03.
[38] In all these studies, the large editorial pluses of the SP have been disregarded. These large additions, sometimes involving as much as nine verses, are part of a special editorial reworking of the Torah not known from other books. This reworking is visible especially in Exodus 7–11 and in the chapters in Exodus and Numbers that run parallel to Moses's speech in Deuteronomy 1–3. These changes involve duplications of other Torah verses and a few rearrangements based on the inclination of the SP group to improve the consistency of the divine message. Editorial changes are distinct from the small harmonizing alterations in SP. The principle and substance of the small harmonizing changes is shared with the LXX, while the editorial changes described above are characteristic of the SP group only.

Table 1 records the frequencies of the harmonizations according to the categories that have been recorded. The witnesses that are mentioned first (LXX in group 1) are the ones that are supposed to evidence the harmonizations.
1. LXX ≠ MT SP
2. SP LXX ≠ MT
3. SP ≠ MT LXX
4. MT SP ≠ LXX
5. MT ≠ SP LXX
6. MT LXX ≠ SP (extant only in Deuteronomy)

Table 1: Groups of Harmonizations in the Torah[39]

	Total	LXX	%	SP	%	MT	%	SP-LXX	%	MT-SP	%	MT-LXX	%
Gen	346	196	56	40	12	0	0	63	18	47	14	0	0
Exod	208	137	66	18	9	2	1	31	15	18	9	0	0
Lev	314	201	64	8	2.5	5	1.5	80	25.5	20	6.5	0	0
Num	284	179	63	16	6	1	0	45	16	43	15	0	0
Deut	202	99	49	22	11	2	1	27	13	44	22	8	4

The data need to be read horizontally. In this way, the total number of harmonizations in Genesis are as follows when recorded both for the individual sources LXX: 196 (56%), SP: 40 (12%), MT (0%), and for combined sources SP-LXX 63 (18%), MT-SP: 47 (14%), and MT-LXX (0%), together 100%.

Different types of conclusions may be drawn from the data:

1. *Preponderance of harmonizations in the LXX.* The unique harmonizations of the LXX, SP, and MT may be compared by examining columns 3, 5, and 7. In Genesis, by far the most numerous examples of harmonization are found in the unique readings of the LXX (196), followed remotely by the SP (40) and MT (0). In whatever way we count the shared readings, the LXX of Genesis has far more harmonizations than the SP does, while the number of harmonizations in the MT is negligible.

When reviewing all five books in this way according to Table 1, the same picture is repeated with a range of 49–66% for the unique readings of the LXX, 2.5–12% for those of the SP, and 0–1.5% for those of the MT.

---

[39] Cases of shared harmonization are counted once, in separate categories.

This picture reveals the LXX as the harmonizing source *par excellence* among the textual witnesses, with the SP as a remote second.[40] To these investigations, we have to add partial information about two groups of texts that are probably equally as harmonizing as the LXX: the pre-Samaritan Hebrew scrolls (see section 9) and the liturgical texts (see section 3).

Table 2 provides the total number of instances of harmonization for each book with inclusive counting that records the common instances of harmonization twice, once for each source in order to obtain better results for each source (e.g., in Numbers, the 45 harmonizing pluses in the SP LXX to the shorter text of the MT are counted twice, once for the SP and once for the LXX).[41]

Table 2: Combined Numbers of Harmonizations in the Torah

	Total	LXX	%	SP	%	MT	%
Gen	457	259	57	151	33	47	10
Exod	257	169	66	66	26	18	8
Lev	414	281	**68**	108	26	25	6
Num	371	224	60	105	28	44	12
Deut	281	134	48	93	33	54	**19**

While there is some imprecision in this method of counting in which the common instances are counted twice, this table presents a picture similar to that in Table 1. As in Table 1, the LXX presents the largest source of harmonization in the Torah, 57–68%, followed by the SP with 26–33%, and the MT with 6–19%.

2. *Different frequencies in books of the Torah.* When the books of the Torah are compared, the largest percentage of harmonization in the LXX is found in Leviticus (Table 2 and Table 1 [with the inclusion of the common SP-LXX cases of harmonization]) and Exodus (Table 1). In whatever way we count the shared readings, the LXX of Genesis has far more harmonizations than the SP, while the number of harmonizations in the MT is negligible.

---

40 A similar conclusion was reached by Hendel, *The Text of Genesis 1–11*, 81–92 relating to chs. 1–11, in which the largest number of harmonizations was found in the LXX, followed by the SP (with half of such instances), with the MT reflecting only a few such features.

41 In this way, the combined number of harmonizations of the LXX in Numbers is calculated as 224 (179 unique instances and 45 shared with the SP). The number of instances in the SP is calculated as 105 (16 unique cases, 44 shared with the LXX, and 43 shared with the MT).

Table 3: Unique Harmonizations in the Torah Compared with the Length of the Books[42]

	Pages acc. to Adi Ed.	LXX Harm	Aver. per page	SP Harm	Aver. per page	MT Harm	Aver. per page
Gen	63	194	3.24	40	0.63	–	–
Exod	29	137	4.72	18	0.62	2	0.06
Lev	37	201	5.43	8	0.21	5	0.67
Num	53	179	3.37	16	0.30	1	0.13
Deut	46	99	2.15	22	0.47	2	0.09

Table 3 presents a meaningful analysis of the frequencies of the harmonizations in the five books of the Torah based on a comparison of the number of the *unique* harmonizations in each book with the length of the book.

Compared with the length of the books, the LXX of Leviticus remains the most frequently harmonizing book. The reason is clear: The stereotyped formulation of the laws renders their framework, not their content, an ideal candidate for harmonization.

Within the SP, most cases of harmonization are found in the stories of Genesis.

8 Harmonizations Shared by the LXX and SP

The shared harmonizations of the LXX and SP form an important part of the statistics adduced in section 7. These two texts also share many additional readings. The recognition that the LXX and the SP share a significant number of readings against the MT goes back to the research of the seventeenth century, and remarkably the two texts agree especially often in secondary readings such as in harmonizations.[43] The statistics in Table 1 speak for themselves. Furthermore, in addition to harmonizations, the LXX and SP share further details against the MT. They very often share remarkable secondary readings, sometimes in common with additional sources, and rarely also a primary variant, but we are focusing here on the harmonizations that they share exclusively, sometimes shared with a pre-Samaritan scroll belonging to the same group. For example:

---

42 Cases of shared harmonization are counted once, in a separate category.
43 See my study "The Shared Tradition of the Septuagint and the Samaritan Pentateuch," in *Die Septuaginta: Orte und Intentionen*, ed. Siegfried Kreuzer et al., WUNT 361 (Tübingen: Mohr Siebeck, 2016), 277–93. The numbers of harmonizations quoted in that study are larger than those in this study as they also include grammatical and linguistic simplifications.

Exod 7:10 MT פרעה אל; 4QpaleoExod^m SP LXX לפני פרעה (ἐναντίον Φαραώ). Based on v. 9.
Exod 10:24 MT SP LXX משה אל; 4QpaleoExod^m SP LXX + ולאהרן +. Based on 9:29 and passim.
Num 14:18 MT SP LXX ורב חסד; SP LXX + ואמת + (καὶ ἀληθινός). Based on Exod 34:6.
Num 21:21 MT SP LXX האמרי; SP LXX + דברי שלום + (λόγοις εἰρηνικοῖς). Based on Deut 2:26.
Num 30:6 MT הניא; SP LXX הנא יניא (ἀνανεύων ἀνανεύσῃ) = 11QT^a XIII:20. Based on the structure of v. 7 היו תהיה.

In the course of my research, I became increasingly aware of the closeness of the SP and the LXX. For example, in most of the differences between the SP and MT in Jacob's blessing in Genesis 49, the SP agrees with the LXX.[44] This closeness is visible especially in their shared harmonizing pluses, but also in non-harmonizing readings.

These details led to the suggestion that the LXX and SP derived from a common base. The assumption of a common ancestor of the LXX and SP group was first surmised in the 1815 monograph by Wilhelm Gesenius, who guided the discussion of the SP and LXX in a sound direction.[45] In Gesenius's view, the two texts derived from a common source that he named the "Alexandrino-Samaritan edition."[46] Central to this analysis are both the large number of agreements between the SP and the LXX and their special nature.[47] In all books of the Torah, these two sources agree frequently in secondary readings, especially in harmonizing pluses. This agreement is extended to the so-called pre-Samaritan Qumran scrolls (section 9).

---

44 This pertains to fourteen of the twenty different content differences between the MT and the SP in vv. 3, 5, 6, 7, 8, 10, 11, 12, 13, 14, 22, 23, and 26.
45 Wilhelm Gesenius, *De Pentateuchi Samaritani origine, indole et auctoritate commentatio philologico-critica* (Halle: Bibliotheca Rengeriana, 1815).
46 Gesenius, *Pentateuchi Samaritani origine*, 14. Gesenius explained the background of the similarity between the SP and the LXX by saying that "the Alexandrian translation and the Samaritan text derived from Judean codices which were similar to each other." This text, adopted by both the Jews of Alexandria and the Samaritans in Palestine, removed many problems from the original text and should therefore be characterized as secondary. Gesenius's approach was followed by Samuel Kohn, *De Pentateucho Samaritano ejusque cum versionibus antiquis nexu* (Leipzig: Kreysing, 1865) and John W. Nutt, *Fragments of a Samaritan Targum: Edited from a Bodleian Manuscript, with an Introduction, Containing a Sketch of Samaritan History, Dogma and Literature* (London: Trübner, 1874), 98.
47 For a detailed analysis of the close relation between the LXX and the SP group, see my study "The Shared Tradition."

While the LXX and SP share a common background in secondary readings, they also disagree as often as they agree.[48] The assumption that the LXX and SP derived from a common base text is supported[49] by the fact that several rewritten Bible compositions are closer to the common text of the LXX and the SP than to the MT:[50]

1. 11QT^a
2. 4Q252 (4QComm Gen A)
3. *Jubilees* in its Ethiopic versions (the Hebrew texts are too fragmentary for analysis)
4. Pseudo-Philo
5. Genesis Apocryphon
6. 4QTestimonia

In fact, there are no rewritten Bible compositions that are based clearly on the MT as opposed to the LXX and SP.

An additional group of texts based on the common LXX-SP base are the liturgical texts (mentioned in section 3), further supporting the argument of the existence of a large text block.

Determining relationships between manuscripts is precarious when so many ancient texts have been lost, but in the case of the Torah we can attempt to do so because the evidence seems to be reliable. It seems to me that the SP group distanced itself further from the common LXX-SP tradition than did the *Vorlage* of the LXX. This is suggested by the large editorial changes in Exodus 7–11 in the SP group, the addition of parallels to Deuteronomy 1–3 in Exodus and Numbers,

---

48 The use of secondary readings as a guiding principle in composing the stemma follows Paul Maas's principle of *Leitfehler* (indicative errors): Paul Maas, *Textual Criticism*, trans. Barbara Flower (Oxford: Clarendon, 1958), 42–49 = "Textkritik," in *Einleitung in die Altertumswissenschaft*, I, VII, ed. Alfred Gercke and Eduard Norden, 3rd ed. (Leipzig: Teubner, 1957). These common secondary readings are so significant that the occurrence of a good number of them suffices to characterize textual witnesses. By the same token, the occurrence of a good number of common harmonizations in the SP and the LXX suffices to characterize these two sources as being textually close to each other. When this is recognized, the large deviations of the SP can be ascribed easily to a secondary factor (subsequent content editing of the SP) even though these editorial manipulations are of a greater magnitude than the harmonizations themselves.

49 Scholars who noticed the close connection of texts to both the LXX and the SP were not necessarily aware of Gesenius's theory, and therefore their witness may be considered independent support of the theory described here.

50 For an analysis and bibliographical references to the studies dealing with these compositions, see my study "The Textual Base of the Biblical Quotations in Second Temple Compositions," in *Hā-'îsh Mōshe: Studies in Scriptural Interpretation in the Dead Sea Scrolls and Related Literature in Honor of Moshe J. Bernstein*, ed. Binyamin Y. Goldstein, Michael Segal, and George J. Brooke, STDJ 122 (Leiden: Brill, 2017), 280–302..

and the addition of the tenth Samaritan commandment.⁵¹ At the same time, there are no unmistakable instances of major secondary elements in the *Vorlage* of the LXX,⁵² with the possible exception of Exodus 35–40.⁵³ I therefore think that the LXX remained in closer proximity to the common LXX-SP base than did the pre-Samaritan texts and the SP.

9 Harmonizations in Pre-Samaritan Sources

The harmonizing readings of LXX-SP are also shared by the pre-Samaritan scrolls, that is, early Qumran scrolls that share central features with the SP and undoubtedly belong to the same group as SP.⁵⁴

In the present study, the investigation of the occurrence of harmonization has been limited to the main texts in which it occurred (the LXX and SP) together with the MT. These examinations are now expanded to include the pre-Samaritan scrolls since they contain a similar number of harmonizations to those in the SP and the LXX, and probably more.⁵⁵ These texts are closer to the SP than to the LXX, while 4QNumᵇ, a transition text, is close to both the SP and the LXX.⁵⁶ These texts were not included in our earlier examinations since these scrolls are fragmentary.

The closeness between the LXX and the SP and the earlier pre-Samaritan texts in harmonizations shows that this feature goes back to an early period

---

51 See my study *Hebrew Bible, Greek Bible, and Qumran*, 57–70.
52 At the same time, I note that the LXX—in my view reflecting an earlier stage in the development than the SP—contains many small harmonizing pluses in Numbers that adapt the text to Exodus, Leviticus, and Deuteronomy. See 9:14, 15 (cf. Lev 19:33); 14:10 (cf. Exod 16:10); 21:2 (Exod 34:15); 27:12 (Deut 32:49). See also the examples analyzed by Teeter, *Scribal Laws*, 118–74.
53 See Anneli Aejmelaeus, "Septuagintal Translation Techniques: A Solution to the Problem of the Tabernacle Account," in eadem, *On the Trail of the Septuagint Translators: Collected Essays* (Kampen: Kok Pharos, 1993), 116–30 (118). See further my own analysis in "The Source of Source Criticism: The Relevance of Non-Masoretic Textual Witnesses," in *Text – Textgeschichte – Textwirkung, Festschrift zum 65. Geburtstag von Siegfried Kreuzer*, ed. Thomas Wagner et al., AOAT 419 (Münster: Ugarit-Verlag, 2015), 283–301.
54 See my study "The Samaritan Pentateuch and the Dead Sea Scrolls."
55 See "The Samaritan Pentateuch and the Dead Sea Scrolls."
56 Due to the fragmentary preservation of the pre-Samaritan texts, only some of this evidence is available. Examples are provided in "The Samaritan Pentateuch and the Dead Sea Scrolls," especially for 4QNumᵇ.

as Table 4 shows that there are more harmonizations in the pre-Samaritan scrolls than in the other sources.[57]

Table 4: Harmonizations in the Pre-Samaritan Scrolls Compared with Other Texts

	No. in Scroll	SP	LXX	MT
4QpaleoExod[m]	8	12	9	5
4QExod-Lev[f]	8	6	3	4
4QNum[b]	15	1	6	1
4QRP[a] (4Q158)	0	0	0	0
4QRP[b] (4Q364)	10	5	7	5

These figures show that the greatest numbers of harmonizations are found in 4QExod-Lev[f], 4QNum[b], and 4QRP[b], while the SP contains the largest number for the data covered by 4QpaleoExod[m].[58] Some examples of these harmonizations have also been mentioned in other sections.

10 Harmonization in the Torah Compared with the Other Biblical Books

In my research of the last few years, it came as a great surprise to find so many secondary features in the LXX of the Torah.[59] The LXX reflects many primary readings, but the textual feature that characterizes the *Vorlage* of that translation most is its many harmonizing pluses. These harmonizations (mainly pluses) appear more frequently in the LXX than any other textual phenomenon such as interchanges of letters, scribal mistakes, or literary variants. Further, these harmonizing pluses appear more frequently in the LXX than in any other textual witness in the Torah or any other Scripture book with the possible exception

---

[57] Examined for the stretches of texts covered by the pre-Samaritan texts. Harmonizations cannot be examined in Genesis as no pre-Samaritan texts have been preserved for that book. The main stumbling block in this analysis is the fragmentary nature of the Qumran scrolls, which complicates statistical analysis.

[58] Coincidence plays a part in the analysis of the fragmentary scrolls since harmonizations do not appear with the same frequency in all chapters. For example, no cases of harmonization are spotted in the fragments of 4QRP[a].

[59] The first scholar to reach this conclusion was Hendel with regard to Genesis 1–11; see n. 40 above.

of the fragmentary pre-Samaritan scrolls. The common base of the harmonizations of the SP and LXX makes it likely that the Greek pluses were rendered from Hebrew (section 8), and were not created by the Greek translator. In addition, internal differences between these Greek renderings also indicate that the harmonizations were not carried out at the Greek level (section 4).

In no other Scripture book does the reconstructed *Vorlage* of the LXX present a similar level of harmonization to that in LXX-Pentateuch.[60] Opportunities for harmonization present themselves first and foremost in Samuel–Kings//Chronicles, but also in Joshua//Judges, within Jeremiah, between Jeremiah 52 and 2 Kgs 24:18–25:30, in Isa 36:1–38:8//2 Kgs 18:13–20:11, among the oracles against the foreign nations in the prophetic books, etc. Massive harmonization in Chronicles towards Samuel–Kings would have been counterproductive, as in such a case the two books would have been close to identical. While there is always some harmonization in the mentioned parallel segments, basically they remain dissimilar.

It remains to be determined why the textual witnesses of the Torah were harmonized more than the other books of Hebrew Scripture. See section 11.

11 Harmonizing Texts and the Development of the Text of the Torah

The harmonizations described in this study characterize the LXX and SP as well as the pre-Samaritan scrolls, liturgical scrolls, and *tefillin*. These texts belong to a large text block to which additional texts also belonged. In my earlier studies,[61] I named this group block II, which is characterized by secondary features, while block I, in which these secondary features are minimal, contains only the MT and its congeners.

Harmonization is not absent from the MT; it is minimal. After all, in Tables 1–3 we found several instances of unique harmonization in the MT together with several significant examples of harmonization common with other sources, such

---

[60] This pertains also to the harmonizations detected in the other translations, but in those cases the harmonizing process, pertaining to small details only, is inner-translational. For some data, see Chaim Heller, *Untersuchungen über die Peschitta zur gesamten hebräischen Bibel, I* (Berlin: Poppelauer, 1911), 21–25; Alexander Sperber, *The Bible in Aramaic*, vol. 4a (Leiden: Brill, 1968), 44–45.

[61] See "The Development of the Text of the Torah" (n. 4).

as the plus of Deut 1:39 אשר אמרתם לבז יהיה in MT SP, which was added to the text of the LXX and 4QDeut[h] (apparently) based on the parallel verse, Num 14:31.[62]

The novel idea of subdividing the textual witnesses of the Torah into two text blocks is closely connected to the perception of two different scribal approaches, conservative and popularizing. The approaches themselves have been mentioned in the scholarly literature, but without connection to specific texts or text groups beyond the occasional mentioning of the SP, 1QIsa[a], and the Qumran Scribal Practice as examples of a popularizing approach, and MT as an example of a conservative text. The description of these approaches had not yet been developed when Kahle described the SP as a popularizing vulgar recension[63] and the MT as an official and reliable recension.[64] It was developed further in the subsequent research, such as in my own writing in which I contrasted the conservative and popularizing approaches of copying and translating.[65] A number of other scholars have written about different scribal approaches, and a good summarizing analysis was presented by D. Andrew Teeter.[66] Teeter distinguished between two main approaches to the biblical witnesses, which have been given various names (conservative/official/standard,

---

[62] See the analysis of Alexander Rofé, "Historico-Literary Aspects of the Qumran Biblical Scrolls," in *The Dead Sea Scrolls: Fifty Years After Their Discovery: Proceedings of the Jerusalem Congress, July 20–25, 1997*, ed. Lawrence H. Schiffman, Emanuel Tov, and James C. VanderKam (Jerusalem: Israel Exploration Society and the Shrine of the Book, Israel Museum, 2000), 30–39 (33).

[63] Paul Kahle, "Untersuchungen zur Geschichte des Pentateuchtextes," *TSK* 88 (1915): 399–439; repr. in id., *Opera Minora* (Leiden: Brill, 1956), 3–37, especially 5–12. Various scholars accepted from Kahle's writings the concept of "vulgar" texts, albeit with certain changes. Henrik Samuel Nyberg, "Das textkritische Problem des Alten Testaments am Hoseabuche demonstriert," *ZAW* 52 (1934): 241–54; Gillis Gerleman, *Synoptic Studies in the Old Testament* (Lund: Gleerup, 1948); Moshe Greenberg, "The Stabilization of the Text of the Hebrew Bible Reviewed in the Light of the Biblical Materials from the Judean Desert," *JAOS* 76 (1956): 157–67; Saul Lieberman, *Hellenism in Jewish Palestine*, 2nd ed. (New York: Jewish Theological Seminary, 1962), 20–27; and Edward Yechezkel Kutscher, *The Language and Linguistic Background of the Isaiah Scroll (1 Q Is[a])*, STDJ 6 (Leiden: Brill, 1974), 77–89 ("vernacular and model texts") posited in their descriptions the "careful" tradition of the MT alongside "vulgar" texts. The scribes of these "vulgar" texts (e.g., 1QIsa[a] and the SP) approached the biblical text in a free manner and inserted changes of various kinds, including orthography.

[64] Kahle, "Untersuchungen," 26–37 (35).

[65] Emanuel Tov, *Textual Criticism of the Hebrew Bible*, 3rd ed., revised and expanded (Minneapolis: Fortress Press, 2012), 184–85, and idem, "Approaches towards Scripture Embraced by the Ancient Greek Translators," in *Der Mensch vor Gott: Forschungen zum Menschenbild in Bibel, antikem Judentum und Koran. Festschrift für Herrmann Lichtenberger zum 60. Geburtstag*, ed. Ulrike Mittmann-Richert et al. (Neukirchen-Vluyn: Neukirchener Verlag, 2003), 213–28.

[66] Teeter, *Scribal Laws*, 240 and passim.

etc., versus vulgar/popular/harmonizing/interpretive, etc.). However, all these analyses were theoretical. I now associate the conservative approach with block I and the popularizing approach with block II in the Torah.

The primary nature of the texts cannot be proven in this binary division. Therefore, the discussion moves to the presence of secondary readings, among which harmonizations play a central role. The texts of block I are characterized by the absence of secondary features, and those of block II are characterized by their presence.

When stressing the secondary features of block II, I focus not only on elements that enable the characterization of these texts, but also try to grasp their central features. It so happens that harmonizing additions represent the most characteristic *textual* feature of the LXX in the Torah. In a similar fashion, Esther Eshel has argued that the pre-Samaritan scrolls should be named "harmonistic" and not "pre-Samaritan," and she expanded that group to include texts such as 4Q158, *tefillin,* and *mezuzot.*[67] I expand that group even further.

The Torah constituted the most popular text of all and, as such, it was read, used, and revised more than the other biblical books. A large block of sources improved the text of the Torah, so to speak, with many harmonizations. Only the MT remained relatively free of that tendency.

---

67 Eshel, "4QDeut^n."

Reinhard Pummer
Samaritan Studies – Recent Research Results

The aim of this contribution is to highlight a number of recent developments in Samaritan studies whose importance reaches beyond this specific area of research, particularly into the study of Israelite history and the Bible. As is well known and amply illustrated in this volume, Qumran studies have opened new vistas on the Hebrew Pentateuch in its two main forms – the Masoretic text and the Samaritan Pentateuch – and raised new questions regarding its origins and development. The excavations of the remains of a sanctuary and the surrounding city on Mount Gerizim, together with the epigraphic finds that came to light in the process, have shed new light not only on crucial questions concerning the sanctuary on Mt. Gerizim, famously described by Josephus, but also on the relationship between the Yahwistic Samarians and the Yahwistic Judeans in the period of the Second Temple.[1] The present paper will focus on these particular aspects. It is not intended to be a comprehensive account of the current state of Samaritan studies; such an account can be found in my recent book *The Samaritans: A Profile*.[2]

In any attempt to clarify the question of the origin of the Samaritans and the time when Samaritans and Jews began to go their separate ways, and what the status of the sanctuary on Mt. Gerizim was, the results of the excavations on the mountain carried out in the years from the early eighties of the twentieth century to the early twenty-first century are of particular importance. The excavations uncovered not only the relics of sacred precincts that enclosed a sanctuary and numerous fragments of inscriptions, but also remains of a large city surrounding the sanctuary in the Hellenistic period. However, one of the unsolved enigmas is the absence of burials of the inhabitants of that city. Elsewhere, Samaritan cemeteries and tombs did come to light, both inside and outside of Samaria. But compared to the Mt. Gerizim discoveries and the antique Samaritan synagogues uncovered over the last several decades, these burial sites are a generally

---

[1] Concerning the terminology, "Samaritans" are the Yahwistic community that developed in the second century BCE. Before this time, the Yhwh worshipers in Samaria should properly be called Yahwistic Samarians (see now the detailed and extensive discussions in Benedikt Hensel, *Juda and Samaria: Zum Verhältnis zweier nach-exilischer Jahwismen*, FAT 110 [Tübingen: Mohr Siebeck, 2016]).
[2] Reinhard Pummer, *The Samaritans: A Profile* (Grand Rapids, MI: Eerdmans, 2016).

less well known subject that has recently been described and analyzed in a number of specialized publications. Their importance lies in the fact that they allow us another glimpse of the material culture and the settlements of the Samaritans in the Roman-Byzantine era, a time for which for the most part very little information about the Samaritans is available. The following is an overview of what has so far been unearthed on and off the Samaritans' sacred mountain in this area, and what conclusions we can draw from it.

Sanctuaries on Mt. Gerizim

For a long time, it was thought that the Samaritan temple stood on Tell er-Ras, the lower peak of the mountain (831 m above sea level). The excavators of the site believed that the large cube of stones underneath the visible remains of the Roman temple was the Samaritan altar of sacrifice or the Samaritan temple.[3] The renewed excavations by Yitzhak Magen have shown that the large podium was constructed as a platform for the Roman temple built by Antoninus Pius (138–161 CE) in the second century CE. Most scholars now have abandoned the theory of a Samaritan altar or temple in this spot.[4] It is now clear that the Samaritan sanctuary stood on the highest peak of Mt. Gerizim (881 m above sea level) either underneath or in the vicinity of the Byzantine church whose ruins are still visible. So far, however, the sanctuary itself has not been unearthed. It is therefore still a matter of debate whether it was an open-air altar on which sacrifices were offered or a temple building. What has been excavated are remains of the precinct that encompassed the sanctuary, or rather, remains of two precincts – an earlier and a later one – as well as remains of a city surrounding the sanctuary. While most scholars believe that there was a temple with walls and a roof on Mt. Gerizim, some think that at least the earlier sanctuary was an altar. The contemporary Samaritans categorically deny that a legitimate temple ever existed on the mountain. This is, however, a consequence of their theology rather than a historically based statement.[5] In the last analysis, the

---

[3] For references see Reinhard Pummer, "Was There an Altar or a Temple in the Sacred Precinct on Mt. Gerizim?" *JSJ* 47 (2016): 1–3.

[4] However, in 1997 Joe D. Seger, in the same encyclopedia in which Robert J. Bull put forward once more his thesis of Tell er-Ras as the place where the Samaritan temple stood, reiterates the same view as Bull (Joe D. Seger, "Shechem," in *OEANE*, ed. Eric M. Meyers [New York; Oxford: Oxford University Press, 1997], 23).

[5] See the discussion in Pummer, "Was There an Altar or a Temple in the Sacred Precinct on Mt. Gerizim?" 10–13.

question "altar" or "temple" can only be definitively answered after further excavations of the site.

Flavius Josephus on the Samaritan Temple

As is well known, Flavius Josephus describes the building of a temple on Mt. Gerizim in his *Jewish Antiquities* in connection with his second account of the origin of the Samaritans in *Ant.* 11.297–347.[6] According to this account, the temple was built in the time of Alexander the Great.[7] At the death of the high priest Joannes (Johanan in the Bible), the latter was succeeded by his son Jaddus (Jadua), who had a brother by the name Manasses (Manasseh) to whom the satrap of Samaria, Sanaballetes (Sanballat), had promised his daughter, Nikaso, in marriage in order to secure the goodwill of the Jewish nation (*Ant.* 11.303). Sanballat is said to be a member of the Cuthean race, the same race to which the Samaritans belonged. The fact that Manasses was married to a foreigner while he was "sharing" the high priesthood[8] was considered to set a dangerous precedent for others who wanted to ignore the prohibition to marry women from a different country (γυναῖκας οὐκ ἐπιχωρίας), something which had brought misfortune over the Jews in the past. The elders of Jerusalem and Jaddus told Manasses therefore to divorce his wife or not to officiate at the altar. Manasses, who did not want to do either, informed his father-in-law of this state of affairs. The latter did not want Manasses to divorce his daughter and promised to build a temple for him where he could be high priest; moreover, he will make him governor in his stead. Manasses accepted the offer and many others who had married foreign wives joined him. With the permission of Alexander, the temple was built and Manasses was made high priest. One of the arguments for building a second temple presented by Sanballat to Alexander was that in case of a revolution the people would be divided and not stand together and "so give trouble to the kings" (*Ant.* 11.323).[9] In the conclusion to this section, Josephus explicitly states that the temple continued to exist even after Alexander's death (*Ant.* 11.346). It was de-

---

6 The first account is Josephus' version of 2 Kgs 17: 24–41 in *Ant.* 9.288–291.
7 For a discussion, see Reinhard Pummer, *The Samaritans in Flavius Josephus*, TSAJ 129 (Tübingen: Mohr Siebeck, 2009), 103–52.
8 On this expression see Pummer, *The Samaritans in Flavius Josephus*, 109, and Paul Spilsbury and Chris Seeman, *Judean Antiquities 11*, vol. 6 A of *Flavius Josephus: Translation and Commentary* (Leiden; Boston: Brill, 2017), 110 (n. 1035).
9 For a possible reference ("to the kings" in plural) see Spilsbury and Seeman, *Judean Antiquities 11*, 118 (n. 1112).

stroyed, according to Josephus, by John Hyrcanus I in 130 or 129 BCE (*War* 1.62–63 // *Ant.* 13.254–256) when he captured "Shechem and Garizein and the Cuthaean nation, which lives near the temple built after the model of the sanctuary at Jerusalem" (*Ant.* 13.256 // *War* 1.63). Thus, according to the dates given by Josephus, the temple had existed for approximately 200 years (see Josephus' statement to this effect in *Ant.* 13.256). The historian gives no reason for the destruction, leaving the field wide open to scholarly theories about Hyrcanus' possible motives – from an intense hatred for the Samaritans[10] to the intention to integrate them by force into the Hasmonean state.[11]

Before the new excavations on the main peak of Mt. Gerizim by Yitzhak Magen, Josephus' accounts were the only descriptions of the erection and destruction of the Samaritan temple. We now know that a number of his assertions need to be corrected, above all his dating of the building and the destruction of the sanctuary. In Josephus' account of the building of the temple on Mt. Gerizim, one can discern two stages. The first is Sanballat's promise to give his daughter Nikaso in marriage to Manasseh, to build a temple for him and to make him high priest (*Ant.* 11.306–311). This episode is dated by Josephus in the time of Darius when Sanballat was an old man (*Ant.* 11:310–311). The second is the actual building of the temple in the time of Alexander the Great (*Ant.* 11.322–324). Between the two parts of his account Josephus narrates Alexander's victory at Issus, his conquest of Damascus and Sidon, and his siege of Tyre (*Ant.* 11.316–320). It seems that Josephus confused Darius II (424–405) and Darius III (336–332 BCE) and the account as it stands now appears to date the building of the temple in the late fourth century BCE. Archaeology and a renewed analysis of the sources has shown, however, that the temple was built in the fifth century BCE and the city around it as well as the enlargement of the precinct took place in the Ptolemaic and Seleucid periods (third century, or maybe already fourth century, to early second century BCE).[12] Other aspects of Josephus' stories –

---

[10] Yitzhak Magen, Haggai Misgav, and Levana Tsfania, eds., *The Aramaic, Hebrew and Samaritan Inscriptions*, vol. 1 of *Mount Gerizim Excavations*, Judea and Samaria Publications 2 (Jerusalem: Israel Antiquities Authority, 2004), 12, and Yitzhak Magen, *A Temple City*, vol. 2 of *Mount Gerizim Excavations*, Judea and Samaria Publications 8 (Jerusalem: Israel Antiquities Authority, 2008), 178.

[11] Jonathan Bourgel, "The Destruction of the Samaritan Temple by John Hyrcanus: A Reconsideration," *JBL* 135 (2016): 505–23. For various other explanations, see Pummer, *The Samaritans in Flavius Josephus*, 209. See now also the discussion in Hensel, *Juda and Samaria*, 239–40.

[12] Jan Dušek, *Les manuscrits araméens du Wadi Daliyeh et la Samarie vers 450–332 av. J.-C.*, CHANE 30 (Leiden; Boston: Brill, 2007), 538–48; see also pp. 603–4. Dušek believes the building of the second precinct began only in the early second century BCE, whereas Magen believes

such as the supposed reasons for the construction of the temple – are also subject to doubt but can, of course, not be verified or falsified by archaeology. Furthermore, Josephus' assumption that Judeans and Samarians were one people during the Persian period (*Ant.* 22.323) is incorrect.[13] On the whole, in his passages on the Samaritans, Josephus sees the past through the lens of his own time. As to the time of the destruction of the sanctuary, the find of numerous coins has shown that it was destroyed in 111/110 BCE,[14] not in 130 BCE (*War* 1.62) or 129 BCE (*Ant.* 13.254), as Josephus claims.[15] The excavations have unearthed evidence of the conflagration all over the mountain. The make-shift fortifications put up by the Samaritans immediately before the attack were no match for Hyrcanus' forces.[16] Only a relatively small number of pottery, glass and stone vessels, weapons, tools, domestic utensils and jewelry have been excavated.[17] It may well be that the residents of the city left when the Hasmoneans began the siege and took many personal items with them.[18] Although the absence of any substantial traces of possessions or any remains of bodies can also be a sign that the booty was removed and the dead were buried before the city was burnt.[19]

The Sacred Precincts on Mt. Gerizim

As noted, the remains of two sacred precincts surrounding a sanctuary were unearthed on the main peak of Mt. Gerizim, one from the Persian period and the other from the Hellenistic period. The older precinct was smaller than the later one. It measured approximately 96 x 98 m, was constructed of large field stones and was perhaps accessed through three gates, each with six or eight chambers. Only the gate in the northern wall is preserved; the other two gates were partially (southern gate) or completely (eastern gate) destroyed by later constructions.[20]

---

the building of the city is to be dated after 331 BCE when the Samaritans were expelled from Samaria.
13 As pointed out by Gary N. Knoppers, *Jews and Samaritans: The Origins and History of Their Early Relations* (New York: Oxford University Press, 2013), 122–23.
14 Magen, Misgav, and Tsfania, *Aramaic, Hebrew and Samaritan Inscriptions*, 13.
15 See Pummer, *The Samaritans: A Profile*, 61–62, 86.
16 Magen, Misgav, and Tsfania, *Aramaic, Hebrew and Samaritan Inscriptions*, 12.
17 They are described and illustrated in Magen, *Temple City*, 209–23.
18 Magen, *Temple City*, 209.
19 Regarding the absence of burials on the mountain see below.
20 Gudme concludes: "Magen's assertion that the Persian period sanctuary contained three gates is a hypothesis only and a hypothesis at that, which seems more than a little influenced by a reading of the Book of Ezekiel" (Anne Katrine de Hemmer Gudme, *Before the God in This*

There was no gate in the western wall, possibly because it was the wall where the Holy of Holies of the sanctuary was located. The site designated by the present-day Samaritans as "The Twelve Stones"[21] may have been the area of the Holy of Holies.[22] The discovery of a considerable quantity of burned bones and ashes in a large building (11 x 12 m) to the east of the northern gate points to the performance of sacrifices on an altar.[23] On the basis of the coins found in the area, the ceramic finds, and Carbon-14 examinations of wood and bones,[24] the earlier sanctuary is dated by the excavator to the mid-fifth century BCE.[25] In 2007 Magen published an article that was to end once and for all the dispute about the date when the Gerizim temple was built.[26] However, the debate continued. New arguments were advanced in favor of a date for the founding of the temple in the time of Darius II, i.e. between 424 and 407 BCE.[27] This dating is based mainly on a re-interpretation of Josephus' account about Sanballat along the lines indicated above, the dates of the coins, and the Elephantine letter of 407 BCE.

The evidence of the coins for a mid-fifth century date is not as strong as it appears. Of the 68 or 69 identifiable coins from the Persian period, one coin from Cyprus dates from 480 BCE; one from Tyre dates from between 450 and 400 BCE; another coin from Tyre is dated between 400 and 332 BCE, and a

---

Place for Good Remembrance: A Comparative Analysis of the Aramaic Votive Inscriptions from Mount Gerizim, BZAW 441 [Berlin: Walter de Gruyter, 2013], 67).

21 See Deut 27:4 (SP) and Josh 4:20. For a view as they appeared before the recent excavations see Reinhard Pummer, *The Samaritans*, Iconography of Religions 23.5 (Leiden: Brill, 1987), Pl. XVb.

22 So Yitzhak Magen, "The Dating of the First Phase of the Samaritan Temple on Mount Gerizim in Light of the Archaeological Evidence," in *Judah and the Judeans in the Fourth Century B.C.E.*, ed. Oded Lipschits, Gary N. Knoppers, and Rainer Albertz (Winona Lake, IN: Eisenbrauns, 2007), 160.

23 Magen, "The Dating of the First Phase of the Samaritan Temple," 161; Magen thinks this was "possibly the 'House of Ashes' adjoining the altar in which the burning of the sacrifices was completed."

24 For tables, drawings and photographs of these finds see Magen, *Temple City*, 192–205, and Magen, "The Dating of the First Phase of the Samaritan Temple," 180–81 and 194–211.

25 Magen, *Temple City*, 162–64, and Magen, "The Dating of the First Phase of the Samaritan Temple," 162–64.

26 Magen, "The Dating of the First Phase of the Samaritan Temple," 176.

27 Dušek, *Les manuscrits araméens du Wadi Daliyeh*, 546–47 and 603–604. Dušek held firm to his dating from 2007 in his 2013 book Jan Dušek, *Aramaic and Hebrew Inscriptions from Mt. Gerizim and Samaria between Antiochus III and Antiochus IV Epiphanes*, CHANE 54 (Leiden: Brill, 2012), 3.

coin from Sidon dates from the late fifth century BCE.[28] Thus, only one coin dates from the first half of the fifth century BCE; all the other coins are from the second half of the fifth century. However, the evidence may well be skewed because Persian coins are very small and initially metal detectors were not allowed in the excavations – during the manual sifting of the soil many may well have gone unnoticed.[29] Furthermore, both extant drafts of the Elephantine letter dated 407 BCE mention that the Jews of the Egyptian fortress had sent a petition to "Jehohanan the High Priest and his colleagues the priests who are in Jerusalem" and to "Delaiah and Shelemiah sons of Sanballat governor of Samaria" (TAD A4.7 // A4.8). Neither a high priest nor other priests are mentioned for Samaria, unless the two sons of the governor Sanballat, Delaiah and Shelemiah, functioned as priests in the Gerizim temple,[30] and, thus, implicitly the religious authorities in Samaria would also have been addressed. However, the memorandum in reply to this letter was sent from Bagohi and Delaiah. Although their titles are not mentioned, this Bagohi is probably the governor of Judah to whom the petition was addressed;[31] Delaiah may then be the son of Sanballat who had become governor of Samaria after his father.[32] If so, and if no appeal to priests in Samaria was made, it would mean that the sanctuary on Mt. Gerizim had not yet been in existence. It could be argued, though, that, if the temple *was* built around 450 BCE, the authors of the letter chose to ignore it in their appeal; or they were not aware of its existence, even though the Jews in Elephantine were otherwise well informed about certain religious developments in Palestine, notwithstanding the fact that circumcision and certain feasts are not mentioned in their correspondence.[33]

When the Samarians burnt Andromachus, Alexander's representative in Samaria,[34] the city of Samaria was destroyed and the population fled; Samaria was

---

28 See Magen, *Temple City*, 168, 194–95; Magen, "The Dating of the First Phase of the Samaritan Temple," 197, 207–208; Dušek, *Les manuscrits araméens du Wadi Daliyeh*, 544.
29 See Magen, *Temple City*, 168.
30 So Magen, "The Dating of the First Phase of the Samaritan Temple," 182.
31 On the difficult question of identifying the historical Bagohi see Spilsbury and Seeman, *Judean Antiquities 11*, 98–101.
32 See Dušek, *Les manuscrits araméens du Wadi Daliyeh*, 528.
33 Paul-Eugène Dion, "La religion des papyrus d'Éléphantine: un reflet du Juda d'avant l'exil," in *Kein Land für sich allein: Studien zum Kulturkontakt in Kanaan, Israel/Palästina und Ebirnâri für Manfred Weippert zum 65. Geburtstag*, ed. Ulrich Hübner and Ernst Axel Knauf, OBO 186 (Freiburg, Schweiz: Universitätsverlag; Göttingen: Vandenhoeck & Ruprecht, 2002), 246–49.
34 Josephus omits this event; it is mentioned by Curtius Rufus (Menahem Stern, *Greek and Latin Authors on Jews and Judaism, I* [Jerusalem: The Israel Academy of Sciences and Humanities, 1974], 448).

settled by Macedonians. Before its destruction, Samaria was probably the seat of the Samarian Yahwistic priests, including the high priest. Josephus' claim that Shechem was the chief city of the Samaritans (*Ant.* 11.30) cannot be accurate for this period[35] since the city was abandoned between 475 and 325 BCE,[36] although it may not have been *completely* abandoned, as evidenced by ceramic finds from the Persian period in Tell Balatah and an Achaemenid tomb probably containing Persian soldiers. It may be that the city contained a Persian garrison. In any case, it is unlikely that the Samarians made Tell Balatah their capital. Rather, the Persian fortress was probably replaced at the time of Alexander or shortly thereafter by a Macedonian military center.[37] The Yahwist Samarians fled therefore to Mt. Gerizim which "became the religious, national, economic, and political center of the Samaritans during the Ptolemaic period," their capital.[38] As mentioned, in the late fourth or early third century BCE a city was founded on the mountain.[39] The date is determined by the coins from the Ptolemaic period that were found not only in the sacred precinct but also outside of it, particularly in the southern quarter (Area B). The latter seems to represent the earliest part of the city which eventually extended approximately 800 m in length and approximately 500 m in width, covering thus an area of 40 ha.[40] Magen believes it was initially a priestly city, most of the inhabitants serving the temple. The very location of it on a high mountain without a source of running water and without any arable land for the growing of crops indicates that it must have been built for religious reasons.[41] Eventually, however, its population grew to several thousand, living in five residential quarters, and in one residential quarter even outside the city itself (Area N).[42] Except for the sacred precinct, there is an absence of urban planning, ascribed by the excavator to the priestly nature of the city.[43]

---

[35] Underlined by Magen (see, e.g., Magen, *Temple City*, 175). See now also the discussion in Hensel, *Juda and Samaria*, 68–75.
[36] Nancy L. Lapp, "The Stratum V Pottery from Balaṭah (Shechem)," *BASOR* 257 (1985): 25; eadem, *Shechem IV: The Persian-Hellenistic Pottery of Shechem/Tell Balâṭah*, ASOR Archaeological Reports 11 (Boston: American Schools of Oriental Research, 2008), 1, 3, 15 n. 4.
[37] See Yitzhak Magen, *The Samaritans and the Good Samaritan*, Judea and Samaria Publications, 7 (Jerusalem: Israel Antiquities Authority, 2008), 17.
[38] Magen, "The Dating of the First Phase of the Samaritan Temple," 182; Magen, Misgav, and Tsfania, *Aramaic, Hebrew and Samaritan Inscriptions*, 12.
[39] For a detailed and copiously illustrated description see Magen, *Temple City*, 3–93.
[40] The sacred precinct in the Hellenistic period measured 3 ha (Magen, *Temple City*, 9).
[41] Pointed out by Magen, *Temple City*, 4.
[42] Magen, Misgav, and Tsfania, *Aramaic, Hebrew and Samaritan Inscriptions*, 3.
[43] Magen, *Temple City*, 89.

The Mount Gerizim Inscriptions

In the course of the excavations on Mt. Gerizim, numerous inscription fragments were discovered that shed light on various aspects of the sanctuary and its visitors.[44] Unfortunately, except for one (no. 223), they were not in their original position so that the dating of them on the basis of the stratigraphy is impossible. Scholars must, therefore, rely on palaeography / epigraphy. The *editio princeps* is Yitzhak Magen, Haggai Misgav, and Levana Tsfania, *Mount Gerizim Excavations I: The Aramaic, Hebrew and Samaritan Inscriptions*. The Aramaic and Hebrew inscriptions were thoroughly analyzed by Jan Dušek in his book *Aramaic and Hebrew Inscriptions from Mt. Gerizim between Antiochus III and Antiochus IV Epiphanes*. A comparative analysis of the Aramaic votive inscriptions from Mount Gerizim was published by Anne Katrine de Hemmer Gudme in her book *Before the God in This Place*. The final edition of the inscriptions is yet to be published. In the introduction to volume II of *Mount Gerizim Excavations*, Magen points out that the book is a preliminary account of the results of the excavations, and three additional volumes "are in various stages of preparation."[45]

Before discussing the inscriptions, a short clarification of the terminology used for the scripts is in order, since the editors' terminology differs from the way these terms are usually understood. For one type of script the *editio princeps* uses the term "lapidary" script. As was rightly pointed out, this is misleading, because all the inscriptions found on Mt. Gerizim are lapidary in the sense that they are incised on stones. It is, therefore, preferable to call this script "monumental." Furthermore, the term proto-Jewish script is inappropriate because the inscriptions are Samarian, not Jewish or Judean. And since this script is derived from the official Aramaic cursive script of the Persian time, it should be called "cursive."[46] With neo-Hebrew the editors mean the script that usually is called "paleo-Hebrew," a term that is preferable because it is the customary term.[47]

Almost four hundred inscriptions were found; according to the excavators, this is a small portion of what must have been several thousand. The largest

---

[44] On these inscriptions see also Magnar Kartveit, *The Origin of the Samaritans*, VTSup 128 (Leiden; Boston: Brill, 2009), 209–16. For a study of them within the wider cultural environment see Gudme, *Before the God in This Place*.

[45] Magen, *Temple City*, IX.

[46] Dušek, *Aramaic and Hebrew Inscriptions*, 5.

[47] Hensel points out that what Frank Moore Cross and other scholars in his wake call "paleo-Hebrew" – used in some texts in post-exilic times – is more recent than "Hebrew", the script that was used in pre-exilic times; he uses, therefore, a new term, *neo-paläohebräisch*, instead of "paleo-Hebrew" (Hensel, *Juda and Samaria*, 53 n. 84).

number of inscriptions are in Aramaic script, 381 in all (nos. 1–381);[48] seven are in paleo-Hebrew script (nos. 382–388); and several are written in a mixture of cursive Aramaic and paleo-Hebrew (nos. 152–154, 191, 197, 198, 201, 389). A number of Greek inscriptions were also discovered, a few dating from the Hellenistic period, but most from the Roman and Byzantine periods. A selection has been published in Yitzhak Magen, *Mount Gerizim Excavations* II.[49] Four inscriptions in Samaritan script (nos. 392–395) date probably to the Middle Ages.[50]

As mentioned above, the dating of the inscriptions can only be done with the help of palaeography. On this basis, the authors of the *editio princeps* in one place are of the opinion that some inscriptions "may belong to the earliest period of the sacred precinct (fifth-fourth centuries BCE)," while the majority "should be dated to the Hellenistic period (third-second centuries BCE)."[51] In their summary statement, however, they affirm: "All the inscriptions date from the Hellenistic period (third-second centuries BCE);"[52] the Persian period is no longer mentioned. Dušek has meticulously re-analyzed all the Aramaic and Hebrew inscriptions to answer the two questions: "a. Are the Aramaic inscriptions in monumental style older than or contemporary with those in cursive script? b. Are all the Aramaic inscriptions from the Hellenistic period or can some of them be dated to the Persian period?"[53] Through comparison with dateable inscriptions from other parts of the Near East he comes to the following conclusions: The cursive Aramaic inscriptions were all carved in roughly the same time span and can be dated to the first half of the second century BCE.[54] The Aramaic inscriptions in monumental style do not date to the Persian period, but were most likely carved in the Hellenistic period, and comparison with the cursive Aramaic script makes it possible to narrow the time more precisely to the early second century BCE.[55] The same applies to the inscriptions in mixed script – they were probably written in the first half of the second century BCE.[56] The dating of the paleo-Hebrew inscriptions is difficult because of the scanty remains – only small fragments are extant and very few letters. As a hypothesis, Dušek proposes for them too the

---

48 The numbering of the inscriptions is that of the Catalogue in Magen, Misgav, and Tsfania, *Aramaic, Hebrew and Samaritan Inscriptions*, 45–264.
49 Magen, *Temple City*, 246–49.
50 Magen, Misgav, and Tsfania, *Aramaic, Hebrew and Samaritan Inscriptions*, 261–64.
51 Magen, Misgav, and Tsfania, *Aramaic, Hebrew and Samaritan Inscriptions*, 14.
52 Magen, Misgav, and Tsfania, *Aramaic, Hebrew and Samaritan Inscriptions*, 41.
53 Dušek, *Aramaic and Hebrew Inscriptions*, 6.
54 Dušek, *Aramaic and Hebrew Inscriptions*, 26.
55 Dušek, *Aramaic and Hebrew Inscriptions*, 36–37.
56 Dušek, *Aramaic and Hebrew Inscriptions*, 39.

first half of the second century BCE.⁵⁷ The probable context in which all the inscriptions were written, is the second stage of the construction of the sacred precinct in the first half of the second century BCE under the rule of Antiochus III (223–187 BCE).⁵⁸ Among the thousands of coins discovered from the Seleucid period on Mt. Gerizim,⁵⁹ the majority, 1,773, comes from the rule of this monarch, which corroborates the dating of the second phase of the sanctuary in this period.

The seven fragments inscribed with paleo-Hebrew letters and the one in a mixed script (cursive Aramaic and paleo-Hebrew) seem to come from the priestly milieu. They contain fragments of the words כהן and כהנים (nos. 382, 388, 389) and יהוה (no. 383). No. 384 seems to read "Pinḥas" and possibly כהן הגדל, "high priest". Pinḥas is a typically priestly name among the Samaritans; it occurs also on nos. 24–25 and 61. No. 388 speaks of a priest and his wife and his sons. Five of the fragments (nos. 382–385 and 387) show ruling lines and may come from the same inscription, although this cannot be proven.⁶⁰ These paleo-Hebrew inscriptions are the only inscriptions containing ruling lines. Dušek categorizes them as public inscriptions because they were more meticulously incised and the surface of the stones was treated with more care than private inscriptions.⁶¹ The other paleo-Hebrew inscriptions, i.e., nos. 386, 388 and 389, do not have ruling lines and were discovered in a different location.⁶² According to Dušek, nos. 386 and 388 are to be classified with the dedicatory inscriptions.

Dedicatory inscriptions form the majority of the inscriptions. They are written in Aramaic and in mixed script. Unfortunately, with one exception (no. 223), they were not found *in situ* but were engraved on paving stones and building blocks. Apart from three extremely fragmentary inscriptions which were found on construction rollers in private houses (nos. 347–8 and 373),⁶³ most were found in or near the sacred precinct on top of the mountain. All dedicatory inscriptions are private inscriptions, i.e., they were requisitioned by private individuals, not by a public body. They took on a public character by being placed

---

57 Dušek, *Aramaic and Hebrew Inscriptions*, 54 and 59.
58 Dušek, *Aramaic and Hebrew Inscriptions*, 59.
59 At the time of the publication of Magen, *Temple City*, 14,000 coins were identified (Magen, *Temple City*, 170).
60 Dušek, *Aramaic and Hebrew Inscriptions*, 54–58.
61 Dušek, *Aramaic and Hebrew Inscriptions*, 62.
62 Magen, Misgav, and Tsfania, *Aramaic, Hebrew and Samaritan Inscriptions*, 256–59.
63 For construction rollers see Magen, *Temple City*, 91.

in the sacred precinct,[64] possibly on the inner wall separating the sanctuary from the rest of the courtyard. Essentially, the inscriptions contain two formulae – a shorter and a longer version of the dedicatory text. The shorter version mentions the name of the donor and his son and, in some instances, the name of the donor's residence, and the family members for whom the donation was made: "That which *Personal Name* son of *Personal Name* (from *Geographical Name*) offered for himself, his wife and his sons" (זי הקרב פלוני בר פלוני [מן מקום פלוני] על נפשה על אנתתה ועל בנוהי). The longer version adds the request for good remembrance: "That which *Personal Name* son of *Personal Name* (from *Geographical Name*) offered for himself, his wife and his sons for good remembrance before the god in this place" (זי הקרב פלוני בר פלוני [מן מקום פלוני] עלוהי ועל אנתתה ובנוהי לדכרן טב קדם אלהא באתרא דנה). The object of the dedication is not explicitly mentioned, except in two instances, nos. 147 and 148, where it is "this stone" (אבנה דה). It can be posited that the stones on which the inscription appears, is the object.[65] However, in the case of these two inscriptions the stone may have been explicitly mentioned because it was exceptionally large, and no conclusion should be drawn as to the object of the donation in other cases.[66] The editors of the inscriptions assume that those inscriptions "in which the root קרב appears, relate to contributions of money."[67] Thus, the gift may not have been the stone as such, but a donation which equalled the value of the stone or which was considered a contribution to the upkeep of the sanctuary; "this would make it a gift to the deity to whom it was dedicated, and the donor and her or his beneficiaries could obtain the 'right of dedication' to a certain stone and the right to have an inscription made on this stone, commemorating the gift and the donor."[68] Two inscriptions (nos. 156 and 212) may refer to the reason for the donation – possibly a vow (אסר – no. 156; נדר – no. 212).[69] In all other cases we are not told what the reason was. The formula that asks for good remembrance before the god in this place requests from the deity a reward for the donation.

---

64 Dušek, *Aramaic and Hebrew Inscriptions*, 60.
65 Joseph Naveh believed that the stone or the wall was the object (Joseph Naveh and Yitzhak Magen, "Aramaic and Hebrew Inscriptions of the Second-Century BCE at Mount Gerizim," ʿAtiqot 32 [1997]: 13*, 16*).
66 Magen, Misgav, and Tsfania, *Aramaic, Hebrew and Samaritan Inscriptions*, 138.
67 Magen, Misgav, and Tsfania, *Aramaic, Hebrew and Samaritan Inscriptions*, 17.
68 Gudme, *Before the God in This Place*, 88.
69 In the context of inscription no. 212, Magen points out that "Vows are not present in the Mt. Gerizim inscriptions, except for a single additional doubtful case, in no. 156" (Magen, Misgav, and Tsfania, *Aramaic, Hebrew and Samaritan Inscriptions*, 181).

Short and fragmentary as these inscriptions may be, they allow us glimpses into the onomasticon of the visitors to the sanctuary, the places where they lived and came from, the gender of the donors, and the type of worship practiced on Mt. Gerizim in the Hellenistic period. On the whole, about 89 names can be identified among the 144 people mentioned, some of the names appearing more than once.[70] Many personal names are composed with a Yahwistic element, from Delaiah (דליה) to Shemaiah (שמעיה). Biblical names range from Elnatan (אלנתן) to Simeon (שמעון). In inscription no. 49 Yehudah (י]הודה[) appears and in no. 43 the three preserved letters may be the ending of Yehud (הוד...). This shows that some Samarians bore the name Judah.[71] Other names are foreign – Arabic, Palmyrene, Greek, and two are of undetermined origin.[72] Most of the names are Hebrew and well known from Jewish sources; a quarter of the names are Greek. The latter appear not only in Greek inscriptions, but also in Aramaic inscriptions. In some cases, a title is added to the personal name of the donor, such as "priest" (in nos. 24, 25, 382, 388, and 389), or "governor" (שר) / "satrap" (שדרפנא[אה]) of Daphna (דפנא) (in no. 26). The occurrence of such famous names from the history of Israel as Amram, Eleazar, Ephraim, Judah, Jacob, Joseph, Jehoseph, Ephraim, Levi, and Phinehas may indicate that "some residents of Samaria identified with earlier figures in Israelite history."[73]

As to the gender of the donors and their families, by far the greater number are men. The formulae name the donor and his father; the donations are made in the donor's own name and that of his wife and his sons. The name of the wife is not mentioned. There are instances where husband and wife together are said to have made a contribution, such as inscription no. 6 ("That which offer]ed Yish[ma'el...]tb and [his] wi[fe...]"), and no. 103, if the editors' restoration is correct. In inscription no. 1, the names of both the husband and the wife are mentioned: "That which El'azar [son of PN] offered [for himself and] for his wife Imma and [his] so[ns...]." In a few inscriptions, women alone are mentioned as donors. An example is no. 17: "That which Miriam offered for herself and for her sons."[74] The editors conjecture that "These apparently were independent

---

70 Magen, Misgav, and Tsfania, *Aramaic, Hebrew and Samaritan Inscriptions*, 25–27.
71 See also below.
72 What was read as a Persian name, Bagohi, in inscription no. 27 has to be reconstructed differently, according to Dušek: "the three letters והי[...] more probably correspond to the pronominal suffix of 3rd pers.sg.m. of the substantive in plural and the more probable reconstruction is בנ[והי] 'his sons'" (Dušek, *Aramaic and Hebrew Inscriptions*, 83 n. 181).
73 Knoppers, *Jews and Samaritans*, 127–28.
74 See also the fragmentary inscription no. 45.

women, perhaps divorced or widowed, or possessing property of their own."[75] Some inscriptions specify the name of a woman donor and that of her husband. An example is no. 19: "[That whi]ch offe[red PN ...] wife of 'l[...]." These donations were made "possibly by women whose husbands died shortly before the donations, and who were still known as 'PN's wife'; women whose husbands were religious or public figures; or married women who nevertheless decided to make a donation on their own."[76]

The places, from where the donors came, include Samaria (שמרין, Shamrayin; nos. 14 and 15; cf. Ez. 4:10, 17), a sign that despite the Hellenization of the city under the Ptolemies, Yahwistic Samarians still resided in it in the second century BCE. Three inscriptions (nos. 12, 36, 39) mention Shechem (שכם), modern Tell Balatah,[77] which had been resettled in the time of Alexander and probably was a Hellenistic center in Ptolemaic times. Smaller towns or villages named in the inscriptions were Kfar Ḥaggai (כפר חגי) (no. 3), today probably the Arab village Ḥajja west of Tell Balatah. ʿAvarta or ʿAwarta (כפר עב֯ר[תא] or עוורתא), mentioned in inscription no. 8, contains the tombs – venerated to this day by the Samaritans – of Eleazar son of Aaron, his son Pinḥas, and the Seventy Elders. Other place names are Yoqmeʿam (יקמעם) (no. 7), identified with different modern sites by various authors, and Ṭura Ṭaba (טורא ט[ב]א) (no. 11), mentioned by Josephus in *Ant.* 18.86. Only part of what may have been the name Mabartha (מעברתא) – mentioned in *War* 4.449 – is preserved in inscription no. 76. It was the site on which in 72 CE Neapolis was built. Thus, the donors for whom the name of the place of residence is preserved came from the vicinity of Mt. Gerizim, unless one agrees with Knoppers' conjecture that the names Yehud and Yehudah mentioned above, may indicate that "the dedicator was from Judah or Benjamin." Either way – whether the person's name was Yehud / Yehudah or he came from Judah – this controverts the assumption by some that there was a long standing and profound hostility between the two communities of Samarian and Judean Yahwists.[78]

The offering "before the god in this place" implies that there was a sacred place on the mountain. Furthermore, the inscription no. 199 speaks of young bulls (פרין) that were sacrificed in the house of sacrifice:

---

[75] Magen, Misgav, and Tsfania, *Aramaic, Hebrew and Samaritan Inscriptions*, 20.
[76] Magen, Misgav, and Tsfania, *Aramaic, Hebrew and Samaritan Inscriptions*, 21.
[77] Magen notes that "it is unclear if the intent is to Tell Balatah or to Maʿabarta on the northern slopes of Mt. Gerizim, the future site of the city of Neapolis" (Magen, *The Samaritans and the Good Samaritan*, 81).
[78] Knoppers, *Jews and Samaritans*, 127.

..]° and bulls in all [...
... sacrific]ed in the house of sacrifice [...
...] '/znh mhw/rd' [...

It has been repeatedly pointed out that בית דבחא is the Aramaic equivalent of the Hebrew בית זבח in 2 Chron. 7:12. Similarly, in the Elephantine papyri (TAD, A.4.9:3) the Jews, requesting that their temple be rebuilt, call the latter בית מדבחא, "house of the altar." Other expressions, apart from "this place" (אתרא דנה), are מקדש, "sanctuary" and אגרה, possibly "shrine."[79] For the inscription no. 211 the editors propose the reading ה[כ]לה ... in the meaning of "temple."[80] Additional evidence for the existence of a sanctuary are the "hundreds of thousands of burnt animal bones inside thick layers of ash," belonging to goats, sheep, cattle and pigeons, most under three years old, and some under one year old. These finds are in keeping with the sacrifices named in Lev 1–6.[81] Together with the mention of priests[82] – and possibly of a high priest – these data clearly point to the existence of a sanctuary on the mountain in the Hellenistic period. Although, up to the present, remains of a temple building have not been identified by archaeology, it stands to reason that this sanctuary was a temple rather than an altar.[83] Something of which not even traces have been discovered, are burials of the inhabitants of the city surrounding the sanctuary.

Samaritan Cemeteries and Tombs

As pointed out, in the Hellenistic period the city on Mt. Gerizim was home to several thousand individuals, but no cemetery or tombs have been found on the mountain. Because Mt. Gerizim was sacred to the Samaritans, the latter probably

---

79 See Bob Becking, "Is There a Samaritan Identity in the Earliest Documents?" in *Die Samaritaner und die Bibel: Historische und literarische Wechselwirkungen zwischen biblischen und samaritanischen Traditionen = The Samaritans and the Bible: Historical and Literary Interactions between Biblical and Samaritan Traditions*, ed. Jörg Frey, Ursula Schattner-Rieser, and Konrad Schmid, SJ 70; StSam 7 (Berlin: De Gruyter, 2012), 61–62.
80 Magen, Misgav, and Tsfania, *Aramaic, Hebrew and Samaritan Inscriptions*, 181; in parallel to the inscription on the Giv'at Hamivtar ossuary, the editors conjecture that היכל, normally referring to the Holy in the temple, in the Gerizim inscription means the temple in general.
81 Magen, Misgav, and Tsfania, *Aramaic, Hebrew and Samaritan Inscriptions*, 9.
82 Knoppers points out that the evidence is too slim to allow the inference that these priests served the sanctuary on Mt. Gerizim (Knoppers, *Jews and Samaritans*, 129).
83 On the question "altar" or "temple" see Pummer, "Was There an Altar or a Temple in the Sacred Precinct on Mt. Gerizim?"

refrained from burying their dead on it.[84] Where they buried them, is still unknown. A particular problem concerns the Samaritans that were killed in the battle with the forces of John Hyrcanus I. As noted, the excavations failed to uncover remains of bodies or a substantial number of personal items, and it can therefore be presumed that the dead were buried and their possessions were plundered before the city was set on fire. Magen conjectures that the many Samaritan fighters that fell in the battle with the Hasmoneans were "almost certainly removed from the houses in the city and buried by the Hasmonean soldiers."[85] For them, the mountain was not sacred, and nothing would therefore have prevented them from interring the dead Samaritans on it. However, if this were so, we would expect to find graves of the city's defenders, but, as noted, so far, no tombs from this period have been discovered on the mountain. Only in other localities – inside and outside Samaria – Samaritan cemeteries and burials have been found, albeit most dating from the Roman-Byzantine time.

One Samaritan cemetery was found in the vicinity of Qedumim, approximately 10 km south of Tell Balata.[86] Five tombs have been excavated – one *arcosolia* type tomb, three *kokhim* (*loculi*) type tombs, and one that combines three different types of burial: burial on ledges, in *kokhim* and in sarcophagi.[87] The tombs were in use by the Samaritans from the late second century BCE to the Byzantine period. The many bodies in Tomb A, including those of children, are believed to come from casualties of the Samaritan revolt in 529 CE under Justinian I.[88]

Another cemetery was located at Khirbet Samara (south of the Nablus – Tulkarm road). As in Qedumim, tombs were closed with a rolling stone, one of which is preserved; for the others, tracks are visible. The tombs, all of the *arcosolia* type, have ledges with headrests.[89] They probably date from the Roman and Byzantine periods.

None of these burials have anything that could be seen as characteristically Samaritan. It is the geographical context alone that allows us to associate them

---

[84] Magen, *The Samaritans and the Good Samaritan*, 197–98. See also Yitzhak Magen, *Flavia Neapolis: Shechem in the Roman Period*, Volume 1, Judea and Samaria Publications 11 (Jerusalem: Israel Antiquities Authority, 2009), 330.
[85] Magen, *The Samaritans and the Good Samaritan*, 198.
[86] See Yitzhak Magen, "Qedumim," in *NEAEHL 4*, ed. Ephraim Stern (Jerusalem: The Israel Exploration Society, 1993), 1225–27.
[87] Magen, *The Samaritans and the Good Samaritan*, 205–8.
[88] Magen, *The Samaritans and the Good Samaritan*, 199.
[89] Magen, *The Samaritans and the Good Samaritan*, 208–9.

with the Samaritans, i.e., they were found in areas known from archaeological and literary sources to have been settled by Samaritans.

Samaritan cemeteries outside Samaria were described and analyzed in the recent book *Samaritan Cemeteries and Tombs in the Central Coastal Plain* by Oren Tal and Itamar Taxel.[90] The sites discussed are Khirbet al-'Aura / Tel Barukh, Khirbet al-Ḥadra and Tell Qasile. Today, they are all situated within the northern limits of Tel Aviv, an area that is known from archaeological and literary evidence to have included a substantial number of Samaritans in Roman-Byzantine times. Moreover, amulets and finger rings inscribed with Samaritan script were discovered in Tel Barukh and Khirbet al-Ḥadra; and in Tell Qasile the remains of a Samaritan synagogue with an inscription in Samaritan script (and two Greek inscriptions) have been found. The types of tombs represented in these three sites are *arcosolia* tombs, the most common type in Palestine in the late Roman and Byzantine periods; *loculi* tombs; and a combination of both, a comparatively rare type. In all three cases, the tombs were located close to the settlements. Storage jars with a disconnected upper body part[91] in some caves indicate "that primary infant burials and/or secondary burials of adults were also carried out" in the Tel Barukh cemetery.[92] These storage jars were placed in subsidiary chambers within some of the tombs.[93] The grave goods in Samaritan burials – jewelry, cosmetics, daggers, chisels, lamps, pottery and glass vessels, amulets, coins – show that they were mainly of local provenance and the Samaritan communities represent "'middle class' villagers who maintained some contacts with more remote locations."[94] Neither the types of burial nor any other feature of the tombs are specifically Samaritan. The presence of subsidiary chambers (maybe for jar burials) in the three sites analyzed by Tal and Taxel cannot count as a typically Samaritan characteristic, but at the most as distinctive of the Samaritan community of this region. On the

---

90 See also Oren Tal and Itamar Taxel, "Samaritan Burial Customs Outside Samaria: Evidence from Late Roman and Byzantine Cemeteries in the Southern Sharon Plain," *ZDPV* 130 (2014): 155–80.
91 The upper body parts of these jars were detached (after being cut away) below the handles and they are therefore missing their neck and rim. See Oren Tal and Itamar Taxel, *Samaritan Cemeteries and Tombs in the Central Coastal Plain: Archaeology and History of the Samaritan Settlement outside Samaria (ca. 300–700 CE)*, ÄAT 82 (Münster: Ugarit-Verlag, 2015) 51.
92 Tal and Taxel, *Samaritan Cemeteries and Tombs*, 197.
93 Tal and Taxel, *Samaritan Cemeteries and Tombs*, 198.
94 Tal and Taxel, *Samaritan Cemeteries and Tombs*, 200.

whole, the material culture, including the burial practices, of the Samaritans hardly differed from that of the Jews.[95]

So far, no intact ossuaries have been found in Samaritan tombs. If there were secondary burials in bag-shaped storage jars, as the evidence suggests, bone gathering must have taken place, although some scholars think that the Samaritans neither practiced bone gathering nor used ossuaries.[96] The alleged absence of ossuaries is ascribed to the Samaritans' disbelief in individual, physical resurrection, as *mKutim* 2:8 states.[97] However, it has now been shown that ossuaries have nothing to do with the belief in resurrection, but they were used by Jews in imitation of customs common in the Greco-Roman world.[98] It is, therefore, entirely conceivable that the Samaritans used ossuaries. And in fact, one hundred years ago, L. H. Vincent identified numerous ossuary fragments in a tomb complex located on the western outskirts of modern Nablus, i.e. on the south-eastern slope of Mount Ebal.[99] Judging by the remains left after the complex had been looted, it once contained at least fifteen sarcophagi and an even greater number of ossuaries.[100] Although Vincent hypothesizes that Jews may have lived in Shechem after the destruction of the city by John Hyrcanus, he believes that their presence there was short-lived.[101] Therefore, the large necropolis of which the burial caves must have been part, possibly belonged to Samaritans.[102] Comparable to Judea, the tomb complex may have held the remains of a clan or an association, and when it became too small to introduce additional large sarcophagi,

---

[95] Reinhard Pummer, "Samaritan Material Remains and Archaeology," in *The Samaritans*, ed. Alan D. Crown (Tübingen: J.C.B. Mohr [Paul Siebeck], 1989), 156.

[96] Magen, *The Samaritans and the Good Samaritan*, 198 and 209.

[97] Magen, *Flavia Neapolis: Shechem in the Roman Period*, 1, 339; idem, *The Samaritans and the Good Samaritan*, 198 and 209.

[98] See the thorough two-volume Ph.D. thesis Dina Teitelbaum, "The Jewish Ossuary Phenomenon: Cultural Receptivity in Roman Palestine," Ph.D. thesis (Ottawa: University of Ottawa, 2005), and Jodi Magness, "Ossuaries and the Burials of Jesus and James," *JBL* 124 (2005): 121–54, especially pp. 135–140.

[99] L.H. Vincent, "Un hypogée antique à Naplouse," *RB* 29 (1920): 128 (tombs 11 and 12 in Magen, *Flavia Neapolis: Shechem in the Roman Period*, 1, 322; for the location, see the map on p. 290). Vincent notes that a number of ossuaries were spread over the city, probably because they were decorated or displayed inscriptions and thus were of commercial interest to the "excavators".

[100] Vincent, "Un hypogée antique à Naplouse," 128.

[101] Although a number of Jews may have settled in the vicinity, particularly in Sychar (so Jürgen Zangenberg, "Between Jerusalem and the Galilee: Samaria in the Time of Jesus," in *Jesus and Archaeology*, ed. James H. Charlesworth [Grand Rapids, MI: Eerdmans, 2006], 416–17).

[102] Vincent, "Un hypogée antique à Naplouse," 135. The complex was re-examined by Félix-Marie Abel; see especially Félix-Marie Abel, "Notre exploration à Naplouse," *RB* 31 (1922): 94, 96 and 98.

the desiccated bones of the ancestors were collected into small ossuaries. Vincent dates the tomb complex between the first century BCE and the first century CE. But because of the necropolis's location facing Mt. Gerizim, he inclines towards a Samaritans affiliation, lowering the date to the middle of the first century.[103] We may, thus, have here an instance of the use of ossuaries by Samaritans.

A number of other burial caves attributed to the Samaritans were excavated in Shechem, Neapolis, Khirbet ʿAmurieh, Raqit, ʿArʿara, Kafr Samir/Castra, Ṭira HaCarmel, Caesarea, and Mughar el-Sharaf.[104] The mausoleum of ʿAskar, northeast of Tell Balatah,[105] is said by Magen to have "belonged to a family from Neapolis or from a Samaritan village at the city's outskirts," because on the basis of Greek inscriptions he concludes that the "wife of the mausoleum's builder, and perhaps the other named person, Sabbathai, were of Samaritan extraction," although the founder's origins are unknown.[106] The mausoleum was built in the second century CE and served as a burial site until the Muslim period. The decorations of the tomb and the sarcophagi show, according to Magen, "the profound assimilation of the Samaritans in Neapolis during the Roman period."[107] To all of the tombs known so far, applies Oren Tal's and Itamar Taxel's conclusion about the burials investigated by them: "the great majority of archaeologically traceable burial methods and customs known from Palestine – at least in its central regions – between the 4th and 7th centuries were common among the contemporaneous religious and ethnic groups"[108] and not specific to the Samaritans. Location in an area known to have been inhabited by Samaritans and finds with inscriptions in Samaritan script are therefore the only ways to identify burial caves as Samaritan.

A special case are the so-called Samaritan sarcophagi, found not only in Shechem and in Samaria but also in the Shephelah and the coastal plain.[109] They are different from the Roman sarcophagi as well as from the sarcophagi

---

103 Vincent, "Un hypogée antique à Naplouse," 134–35. Magen prefers the second century CE (Magen, *Flavia Neapolis: Shechem in the Roman Period*, 1, 322).
104 For references to the respective publications, see Tal and Taxel, *Samaritan Cemeteries and Tombs*, 201–2.
105 Magen, *Flavia Neapolis: Shechem in the Roman Period*, Volume 1, 293–305.
106 Magen, *Flavia Neapolis: Shechem in the Roman Period*, Volume 1, 305.
107 Magen, *Flavia Neapolis: Shechem in the Roman Period*, Volume 1, 305.
108 Tal and Taxel, *Samaritan Cemeteries and Tombs*, 202.
109 A map of the distribution of these sarcophagi can be found in Rachel Barkai, "Samaritan Sarcophagi," in *The Samaritans*, ed. Ephraim Stern and Hanan Eshel (Jerusalem: Yad Ben-Zvi Press; Israel Antiquities Authority; Staff Officer for Archaeology, Civil Administration for Judea and Samaria, 2002 [Hebrew]), 311.

of the Beth Sheʿarim cemetery. What sets them apart are their dimensions – they are never more than 2 m long and are narrow and low; they are made of soft limestone and their sides are thin. Apart from Rachel Barkai's research,[110] they have been studied especially by Yitzhak Magen.[111] He comes to the conclusion that "the initial use of the 'Samaritan' types of sarcophagi is not necessarily related to the Samaritans, nor did they originate in Samaria," although Samaritans too did use them, as did the pagans. They were not a product of the Samaritans nor did the whole Samaritan population use them.[112]

In addition to the information about Samaritan cemeteries, the new research on Samaritan burial places has made an important contribution to our knowledge of the expansion of the Samaritans to the central Coastal Plain, the Carmel region, the Beth She'an valley and the southern coast in late Roman and early Byzantine periods.[113] In the wake of Rabbinic sources it is usually thought that the Samaritan expansion started either after the destruction of the Jerusalem temple or after the Bar-Kokhba revolt and continued in the third and fourth centuries CE.[114] Some, however, believe that it was rather the bleak economic and security circumstances that lead to the migration to different areas, such as the Roman cities.[115] In any event, in the third and fourth centuries the movement by Samaritans to places that earlier were vacated by the Jews increased. Tell Qasile is one of the sites where an earlier Jewish population was replaced by Samaritans, most likely after some time in which the site was unoccupied. But new Samaritan settlements also were founded, as the study of Khirbet al-ʿAura / Tel Barukh and Khirbet al-Ḥadra and other sites has shown. In this way, certain re-

---

[110] She has described the sarcophagi in several publications, from her M.A. thesis Rachel Barkai, "Samaritan Sarcophagi of the Roman Period from the Land of Israel," M.A thesis (Jerusalem: Hebrew University, 1984), (Hebrew) to her article of 2002 Barkai, "Samaritan Sarcophagi".
[111] Yitzhak Magen, "The 'Samaritan' Sarcophagi," in *Early Christianity in Context: Monuments and Documents*, Studium Biblicum Franciscanum, Collection Maior 38, ed. Frédéric Manns and Eugenio Alliata (Jerusalem: Franciscan Printing Press, 1993), 149–66; Magen, *The Samaritans and the Good Samaritan*, 209–16; idem, Magen, *Flavia Neapolis: Shechem in the Roman Period*, Volume 1, 339–48, all with ample illustrations.
[112] Magen, *The Samaritans and the Good Samaritan*, 216.
[113] See Tal and Taxel, *Samaritan Cemeteries and Tombs*, 202–5.
[114] Cf. Gedaliah Alon, *The Jews in Their Land in the Talmudic Age (70–640 C.E.)*. Vol. 2, ed. and trans. Gershon Levi (Jerusalem: Magness Press, Hebrew University, 1984), 563. See also Magen, *The Samaritans and the Good Samaritan*, 83–85.
[115] Magen believes that already before the destruction of the Jerusalem temple individual families migrated to Roman cities, and that the crushing of the Jewish revolt was not the foremost reason for the Samaritan expansion; instead, it is economic reasons why the Samaritans migrated (Magen, *The Samaritans and the Good Samaritan*, 84–85).

gions were dominated by Samaritans, such as both sides of the river Yarkon, the Sharon plain, and the Carmel range.

Conclusion

The archaeological finds discussed above have shown that in the Hellenistic period a sanctuary existed on Mt. Gerizim to which people contributed through donations that demonstrate their veneration of Yhwh in this location. Nothing indicates, however, that the worship of Yhwh on Mt. Gerizim at that time differed from the one in Jerusalem. Thus, strictly speaking, the sanctuary was Samarian rather than Samaritan in the sense in which this term is applied to the later community that developed its own narrative of the Israelite tradition. The burials, albeit from a later period than the inscriptions on Mt. Gerizim, show once more that the culture of the Samaritans was to a large extent indistinguishable from that of the Jews.

One other consideration flows from the above evidence. Just as there was no difference between the worship of Yhwh in Judea and Samaria at the time of the two temples on Mt. Zion and on Mt. Gerizim, there was no difference in other areas in later times. The burial practices and the institution of the synagogue are two examples; they were the same in both religions. The only difference is discernible in synagogue art; as far as we know at the present time, it did not include the depiction of animate beings.[116] This sameness, in turn, should caution us against reading into ancient sources a strong antagonism between the two communities. Jewish criticism of the Samaritans is believed to be expressed or implied in certain Jewish Second Temple period sources. It is true that there is evidence of Jewish hostility against the Samaritans – and *vice versa* – in this era in some narratives in Josephus and, to a lesser extent, in a small number of New Testament passages. But the serious conflicts that erupted in the fifth and sixth centuries were between Samaritans and Christians, not between Samaritans and Jews. Of course, gradually the rabbis changed their attitude towards the Samaritans, and in the Talmudic period they were eventually seen as standing outside the fold of Israelite religion or on its fringes. But even then, the separation between the two communities was not absolute, as the adoption of a number of Jewish ideas and texts by the Samaritans in later centuries shows.

---

[116] See my forthcoming article "Synagogues – Samaritan and Jewish: A New Look at their Differentiating Characteristics."

Thomas Römer
Cult Centralization and the Publication of the Torah Between Jerusalem and Samaria

Some decades ago Peter Frei postulated the existence of a Persian policy of 'imperial authorization' of local law codes. He suggested that occasionally, the central administration would have bestowed local legal documents with imperial authority. Together with K. Koch, he proposed that the publication of the Pentateuch and its acceptance as 'Torah' in Yehud should be viewed as an example of such imperial authorization.[1] The imperial administration would have encouraged Judeans to codify their traditional customs into an authoritative document, which it would subsequently have ratified.

Several scholars accepted the theory that such an 'imperial authorization' instigated the publication of the Pentateuch.[2] However, more recently, this explanation has been criticized.[3] There are indeed quite few inscriptions dealing with specific legal matters, which often are written in two or three languages. The only partial parallel to an 'imperial authorization' would be the so-called 'codification' of Egyptian law under Darius I, but this latter case is quite different and the text it is based on makes no mention of the codification of law.

---

[1] Peter Frei, "Zentralgewalt und Lokalautonomie im Achämenidenreich," in *Reichsidee und Reichsorganisation im Perserreich*, ed. Peter Frei and Klaus Koch, OBO 55 (Göttingen: Vandenhoeck & Ruprecht, 1996).
[2] Frank Crüsemann, *Die Tora: Theologie und Sozialgeschichte des alttestamentlichen Gesetzes* (München: Chr. Kaiser, 1992); Rainer Albertz, *From the Exile to the Maccabees*, vol. 2 of *A History of Israelite Religion in the Old Testament Period* (London: SCM Press, 1992); Ernst A. Knauf, "Audiatur et altera pars. Zur Logik der Pentateuchredaktion," *BK* 53 (1998): 118–26; Joseph Blenkinsopp, "Was the Pentateuch the Civic and Religious Constitution of the Jewish Ethnos in the Persian Period?" in *Persia and Torah. The Theory of the Imperial Authorization of the Pentateuch*, ed. James W. Watts, SBL Symposium Series 17 (Atlanta, GA: Society of Biblical Literature, 2001): 41–62; Kyong-Jin Lee, *The Authority and Authorization of the Torah in the Persian Period*, CBET 64 (Leuven: Peeters, 2011).
[3] Udo Rütersworden, "Die persische Reichsautorisation der Thora: fact or fiction," *ZABR* 1 (1995): 47–61; Gary N. Knoppers, "An Achaemenid Imperial Authorization of Torah in Yehud?" in *Persia and Torah: The Theory of the Imperial Authorization of the Pentateuch*, ed. James W. Watts, SBL Symposium Series 17 (Atlanta, GA: Society of Biblical Literature, 2001): 115–34; Jean-Louis Ska, "'Persian Imperial Authorization': Some Question Marks," in *Persia and Torah: The Theory of the Imperial Authorization of the Pentateuch*, ed. James W. Watts, SBL Symposium Series 17 (Atlanta, GA: Society of Biblical Literature, 2001): 161–82.

Therefore, one should probably search for more 'internal' explanations for compilation of the Pentateuch. In this context, the Pentateuch is often viewed as a document of compromise between different scribal schools in Jerusalem during the fourth century BCE or maybe even later.[4] Different groups agreed to bring the different traditions they regarded as authoritative – for example, the Priestly writing – and to combine them to create a normative account or a foundation myth of the origins of 'Israel.' That normative account, while it preserved conflicting views, was nevertheless unified by a comprehensive narrative framework stretching from the origins of the world (Genesis 1) to the death of the divine mediator, Moses (Deuteronomy 34), with this Moses being its main figure.[5]

It is often claimed that the Torah was composed in Jerusalem. Recent archaeological investigation about the population of Yehud and Jerusalem in the Persian period reveal however that Jerusalem was only very sparsely inhabited during this time.[6] Of course, one cannot exclude that some priests and scribes around the Temple were enough to compose the Pentateuch. But one should also take into account the political and economic strength of the Babylonian and the Egyptian Diaspora. Even if the story of Ezra bringing a 'law' from Mesopotamia to Jerusalem in Ezra 7 is totally invented,[7] it reflects in one way or another the implication of the Babylonian Diaspora in the compilation of the Torah.

It seems clear now that there was a (Yahwistic) sanctuary on mount Gerizim built probably after the resettlement of Shechem circa 480 – 475 BCE,[8] if not ear-

---

[4] See the different contributions in Gary N. Knoppers and Bernard M. Levinson, eds., *The Pentateuch as Torah: New Models for Understanding Its Promulgation and Acceptance* (Winona Lake, IN: Eisenbrauns, 2007). See also the summary of the recent discussion in Thomas Römer, "Der Pentateuch," in Walter Dietrich et al, *Die Entstehung des Alten Testaments*, Theologische Wissenschaft 1 (Stuttgart: Kohlhammer, 2014), 69–89.

[5] Rolf P. Knierim, "The Composition of the Pentateuch," in *SBL Seminar Papers 24* (Atlanta: Scholars Press, 1985): 393–415.

[6] See the discussion between Israel Finkelstein, "The Territorial Extent and Demography of Yehud/Judea in the Persian and Early Hellenistic Periods," *RB* 117 (2010): 39–54, and Oded Lipschits, "Demographic Changes in Judah between the Seventh and the Fifth Centuries B.C.E.," in *Judah and the Judeans in the Neo-Babylonian Period*, ed. Oded Lipschits and Joseph Blenkinsopp (Winona Lake, IN: Eisenbrauns, 2003): 323–76.

[7] According to Sebastian Grätz, *Das Edikt des Artaxerxes: Eine Untersuchung zum religionspolitischen und historischen Umfeld von Esra 7,12–26*, BZAW 337 (Berlin: de Gruyter, 2004), this text was composed only during the Hellenistic period.

[8] Yitzhak Magen, "Mount Gerizim – Temple City," *Qadmoniot* 120 (2000): 74–118; Ephraim Stern and Yitzhak Magen, "Archaeological Evidence for the First Stage of the Samaritan Temple on Mount Gerizim," *IEJ* 52 (2002): 49–57.

lier, so that it is even possible that the Temple of Jerusalem and the sanctuary on Gerizim where built more or less at the same time, both apparently tolerated by the Persian administration. If the Pentateuch had originated only in Judah and the Golah it is hardly understandable why the Samaritans would have adopted this document. The very negative picture about Samaria and its governor Sanballat in the book of Nehemiah does probably not reflect a situation of the beginning of the 5th century BCE, but points to a much later date. The documentation from Elephantine shows that the Judeans living there wrote simultaneously to the governors of Jerusalem and of Samaria concerning the question of the rebuilding of the Yahu-Temple. They received as an answer a common statement of Bagavahyah, governor of Judah and of Delaiah the son of the governor of Samaria, Sanballat.

This suggests a friendly relationship between Samaria and Jerusalem at the end of the 5th century BCE,[9] at a time where the sanctuary on Gerizim probably already existed. One could suspect, as suggested by Granerød that the Judean and Samaritan leaders had some extraterritorial authority in religious questions over the Judeans (and Israelites?) in Elephantine.[10] Apparently, the Yhwh-worshippers in Elephantine considered that the leaders of Judah and Samaria had some common influence over the rebuilding of the Yhwh-sanctuary and other cultic concerns. These observations indicate a close collaboration between Jerusalem and Samaria. If there was such a contact, it seems quite plausible that it should have applied also to the promulgation of the Pentateuch. How should we then imagine this collaboration? And how does the idea of cult centralization fit to the fact that at the time of the promulgation of the Pentateuch there were at least two sanctuaries of Yhwh?

A Northern Origin of the Book of Deuteronomy?

Recent scholarship about the question of Samaritan implication in the compilation of the Pentateuch has paid much attention to the book of Deuteronomy. In this context, some scholars take up again a quite old idea of the Northern origin of Deuteronomy, making it a "Proto-Samaritan" manifesto. There is no need to summarize the whole discussion. This has been done in a recent volume of "Hebrew Bible and Ancient Israel," especially in the review of scholarship by Cyn-

---

9 Gard Granerød, *Dimensions of Yahwism in the Persian Period: Studies in the Religion and Society of the Judaean Community at Elephantine*, BZAW 488 (Berlin: de Gruyter, 2016), 41–44.
10 Granerød, *Dimensions of Yahwism*, 43.

thia Edenburg and Reinhard Müller.[11] A major question is how to understand Deuteronomy's claim about the place that Yhwh will choose for himself. Stefan Schorch has argued for a Northern origin of the first edition of Deuteronomy arguing that the centralization law in Deuteronomy 12 referred to the altar in Gerizim mentioned in Deuteronomy 27.[12]

This theory however is problematic in two regards. First, the Northern origin of Deuteronomy can be ruled out with a high degree of probability. The strong parallels between the earliest texts of the book of Deuteronomy and the Loyalty oath of Esarhaddon (VTE) suggest that the authors of the "Ur-Deuteronomium" knew this text.[13] That means that we can establish a *terminus a quo* in 672 BCE. And as Levinson and Stackert have pointed out the recently discovered copy of this Succession treaty at Tell Tayinat "confirms the Assyrian employment of this text with its western vassals."[14] It is therefore very plausible that there was a copy of this treaty in the Temple of Jerusalem.[15] The second problem is the assumption that Deuteronomy 12 refers to Deuteronomy 27. Or, as shown by Na'aman, Nihan, and others, Deuteronomy 27 is quite probably an insert between chapters 26 and 28, because it interrupts the continuity between chapters 26 and 28.[16] Moses speaks here in the 3rd person, together with the elders (v. 1) and the Levites (v. 9). This scenario is not at all prepared in the foregoing chapter. If Deuteronomy 27 is an addition, probably added in several stages, the same holds true for Deut 11:29–32.[17] If this diachronic analysis has some plausibility,

---

11 Cynthia Edenburg and Reinhard Müller, "A Northern Provenance for Deuteronomy? A Critical Review," *HeBAI* 4 (2015): 148–61.
12 Stefan Schorch, "The Samaritan Version of Deuteronomy and the Origin of Deuteronomy," in *Samaria, Samarians, Samaritans. Studies on Bible, History and Linguistics*, ed. József Zsengellér, SJ 66; StSam 6 (Berlin: de Gruyter, 2011): 23–37.
13 Hans Ulrich Steymans, *Deuteronomium 28 und die adê zur Thronfolgeregelung Asarhaddons: Segen und Fluch im Alten Orient und in Israel*, OBO 145 (Göttingen: Vandenhoeck & Ruprecht, 1995).
14 Bernard M. Levinson and Jeffrey Stackert, "Between Covenant Code and Esarhaddon's Succession Treaty: Deuteronomy 13 and the Composition of Deuteronomy," *Journal of Ancient Judaism* 3 (2012): 132.
15 See also Hans Ulrich Steymans, "Deuteronomy 28 and Tell Tayinat," *Verbum et Ecclesia* 34 (2013): 13.
16 Nadav Na'aman, "The Law of the Altar in Deuteronomy and the Cultic Site Near Shechem," in *Rethinking the Foundations. Historiography in the Ancient World and in the Bible: Essays in Honour of John Van Seters*, ed. Steven L. McKenzie and Thomas Römer, BZAW 294 (Berlin: de Gruyter, 2000): 141–61; Christophe Nihan, "Garizim et Ébal dans le Pentateuque: Quelques remarques en marge de la publication d'un nouveau fragment du Deutéronome," *Sem* 54 (2011): 185–210.
17 Edenburg and Müller, "Northern Provenance," 158.

the question of the identity of the chosen place in Deuteronomy 12 must be answered differently. Deuteronomy 12 insists several times on the fact that Yhwh will choose or has chosen for himself one place; the topic of the chosen place then appears as a refrain throughout the whole Deuteronomic Law (altogether 20 occurrences).

The Centralization Law in Deut 12:13–18

I will not discuss in detail the literary stratigraphy of this chapter. There are still good arguments that the oldest version of the topic of the chosen place which occurs 20 times inside the Deuteronomic Law is contained in verses 13–18.[18] Contrary to the MT that has the *yiqtol*-form *yibḥar*, the Samaritan text constantly displays the *qatal*-form of *baḥar*. As Schenker has shown the Samaritan text is supported by textual witnesses from the LXX, the Old Latin, and the Coptic, so that we clearly do not have a late sectarian revision, but a tradition that competes with the Masoretic one.[19] The Samaritan reading is also supported by Neh 1:9, which presents itself as a quote from Moses' speech, and uses the *qatal*-form: "I will gather them from there and bring them to the place at which I have chosen to establish my name אקבצם והבואתים אל־המקום אשר בחרתי לשכן את־שמי שם)." If the *qatal*-form is older, as Schenker argues, what would be the consequence? Would a *qatal*-form exclude the identification of the *maqom* with Jerusalem in Deuteronomy 12? This is clearly not the case. In many instances in Deuteronomy the *qatal*-form expresses the idea of a future action, which is prior to another action in the future.[20] Deut 16:17, for instance, alludes to future divine blessing when the people will be in the land: "all shall give as they are able, according to the blessing Yhwh your God will have given to you (איש כמתנת ידו כברכת יהוה אלהיך אשר נתן־לך). A similar use of the *qatal* occurs in Deut 28:20, where Moses announces that Israel's abandonment of Yhwh will only take place after the conquest of the land: "because of the evil of your deeds, through which you will have abandoned me (מפני רע מעלליך אשר עזבתני)."

---

18 Thomas Römer, *The So-Called Deuteronomistic History: A Sociological, Historical and Literary Introduction* (London: T & T Clark, 2005), 56–65.
19 Adrian Schenker, "Le Seigneur choisira-t-il le lieu de son nom ou l'a-t-il choisi? L'apport de la Bible grecque ancienne à l'histoire du texte samaritain et massorétique," in *Scripture in Transition: Essays on Septuagint, Hebrew Bible, and Dead Sea Scrolls in Honour of Raija Sollamo*, ed. Jutta Jokiranta and Anssi Voitila (Leiden: Brill, 2008): 339–51.
20 Innocent Himbaza, "'Le lieu que Yhwh aura choisi': Une perspective narrative, historique et philologique," *Sem* 58 (2016): 115–34.

Accordingly, in Deuteronomy 12, the *qatal*-form can indicate a choice that has taken place in Yhwh's mind but will be revealed later. We need to ask, however, how the differences between the MT and the SP are to be explained? In my view this is related to the broader context in which Deuteronomy 12 was thought to be read and understood. Before addressing this point, I would like to reassert that the chosen place in Deuteronomy 12, and especially in 12:13–18 was originally meant to be Jerusalem. The passage first opposes the totality or multitude of sacred places (*kol-maqom*) to the sanctuary that Yhwh will choose in only one tribe. This statement is a quite clear allusion to the Josianic reform. The "one tribe" out of which Yhwh will elect the place for his sanctuary can only be Judah. The same ideology can be found in Psalm 78, where Yhwh refuses to choose Ephraim (the North), but chooses "the tribe of Judah, the mountain of Zion which he loves (ויבחר את־שבט יהודה את־הר ציון אשר אהב)" (v. 68). The author of Deut 12:13–18 takes up the tradition of the election of Zion and transforms it into an exclusive election, which does not allow any other sanctuary. Finally, the above-mentioned text in Neh 1:9 which alludes in the *qatal*-form to Yhwh's chosen place clearly witnesses the identification of the place of Jerusalem.[21] Why is Jerusalem then not mentioned?

It is somewhat astonishing that Deut 12:13–18 is mainly concerned with the practical consequences of the centralization law (the so-called 'profane slaughter') and that there is not much insistence on the theological explanation of this centralization. In an article, that has not received much scholarly attention, Lohfink had assumed that the version of Deut 12:13–18 has replaced a somewhat older form of the centralization law, which we are unable to reconstruct.[22] This sounds quite speculative but it is possible that if Deut 12:13–18 was originally not conceived as a Moses speech, but a kind of a royal or divine decree, Jerusalem or Zion could have been mentioned. The name of the chosen place would have been removed when Deuteronomy was constructed as Moses' last will and became the opening of the so-called Deuteronomistic History.

---

[21] Magnar Kartveit, "The Place that the Lord Your God Will Choose," *HeBAI* 4 (2015): 205–18.
[22] Norbert Lohfink, "Fortschreibung? Zur Technik von Rechtsrevisionen im deuteronomischen Bereich, erörtert an Deuteronomium 12, Ex 21,2–11 und Dtn 15,12–18," in *Das Deuteronomium und seine Deutungen*, ed. Timo Veijola, Schriften der Finnischen Exegetischen Gesellschaft 62 (Göttingen: Vandenhoeck & Ruprecht, 1996): 127–71.

The Centralization Law in the Context of the Deuteronomistic History

The redactors of the Deuteronomistic History were of course convinced that the Jerusalemite temple was indeed the only legitimate place of Yhwh worship. For that reason, all the Northern kings are heavily condemned and the 'original sin' of Jeroboam is the foundation of competing Yhwh sanctuaries in Bethel and Dan (1 Kings 12). However, they had also to cope with the fact that in the older traditions that they integrated in their history other cultic places for Yhwh worship occurred that had no negative connotations. This was especially the case for Shiloh related to the Samuel and Ark traditions. Apparently the Deuteronomists found a compromise for their idea of centralization. They admitted that in the pre-monarchic times, before the construction of the Jerusalemite Temple, there was another chosen place, Shiloh. When Deuteronomy became the opening of the Deuteronomistic History the *qatal*-form of בחר in Deuteronomy 12 was then changed into a *yiqtol* in order to suggest the idea that Yhwh may choose different sanctuaries in the future.

In an exilic or postexilic perspective this idea was even easier to accept since Shiloh had been destroyed centuries before the destruction of the First Temple.[23] The theory that Yhwh did choose Shiloh before Jerusalem is clearly set out in Jeremiah 7, which in my view is a text that had been revised if not written by a "Deuteronomist." In Jeremiah's temple speech, the prophet in announcing the destruction of the Temple and in comparing it to Jerusalem uses a formula, which is reminiscent of Deuteronomy 12:

> [12]Go now to my place (מקומי) that was in Shiloh, where I made my name dwell at first (אשר שכנתי שמי שם בראשונה), and see what I did to it for the wickedness of my people Israel. [13]And now, because you have done all these things, says Yhwh, and when I spoke to you persistently, you did not listen, and when I called you, you did not answer, [14]therefore I will do to the house that is called by my name (אשר נקרא־שמי), in which you trust, and to the place that I gave to you and to your ancestors, just what I did to Shiloh. (Jer 7:12–14)

In regard to the narrative construction of the Deuteronomistic History, the Deuteronomists could accept the idea that there were "legitimate" Yhwh-sanctuaries before the construction of the Jerusalemite Temple, even Northern ones. This idea of a prior divine choice, which was then revoked, can be compared to the election of Saul, who was then rejected because of David. Once the Temple of Jer-

---

23 See Israel Finkelstein, "Seilun, Khirbet," *ABD* 5: 1069–72.

usalem was built, all other sanctuaries, especially the Northern ones were of course criticized.

Summing up, in the context of the Deuteronomistic History, the centralization law in Deut 12:13–18 still means the Jerusalemite Temple and this was made clear by the addition of verses 8–12, which introduce the idea of the 'rest,' alluding to the construction of the Temple. When the book of Deuteronomy was cut off from the books of Joshua-Kings and became the end of the Torah, things changed.

The Centralization Law in the Context of the Pentateuch

If we accept the idea that the Torah is not only a Judean and Babylonian production we need to look for 'Samaritan voices' and probably not only Judean concessions to the Samaritans, although those certainly also exist. One of those concessions can be the subtle reformulation of Deut 12:14 in 12:5. Most scholars would agree that Deut 12:2–7 belong to the latest revision of Deuteronomy 12, and it is possible that this revision took place when Deuteronomy had already become the last scroll of the Pentateuch. Contrary to Deut 12:14, which announces that Yhwh will choose his place from only one tribe, Deut 12:5 speaks about a choice out of all tribes:

12:14   כי אם־במקום אשר־יבחר יהוה באחד שבטיך
12:5   כי אם־אל־המקום אשר־יבחר יהוה אלהיכם מכל־שבטיכם

The idea that Yhwh can choose his place out of all the tribes allows for the possibility to understand the chosen place as referring to a different place than Jerusalem. Deuteronomy 12:2–7 adopt a very intolerant position towards the sanctuaries of the people that need to be destroyed, but apparently allows for a more open interpretation as for the place or places of legitimate Yhwh-worship.

One Place or Many Places: Deuteronomy 12, Exodus 20, and Exodus 25–31, 35–40

When Deuteronomy was added to the Pentateuch, the Deuteronomic law went into competition with the "Covenant Code" in Exodus 21–22. Although it may be possible that the earliest form of Deuteronomy 12–26 had been created to replace the Covenant Code,[24] the editors of the Pentateuch made the choice to integrate both codes into the Torah.[25]

The Covenant Code, whose original opening was probably "These are the ordinances you shall set before them" (Exod 21:1), has been expanded by the addition of Exod 20:22–26 immediately before it, to become the new opening of the work. It begins "Thus Yhwh said to Moses: Thus you shall say to the Israelites" (v. 22).[26] The section deals, after the prohibition of images (v. 23), with the building of sacrificial altars, and Yahweh promises to come and bless the people at *every place* he causes his 'name' to be remembered. In this way, the opening of the Covenant Code is made parallel to the Deuteronomistic Code,[27] which begins with the stipulation by Yhwh that he will select a single place for sacrificial offerings to be made to him.

At the same time, however, Exod 20:24–26 might be seen to correct the 'single altar' claim of Deuteronomy by allowing the legitimate construction of other sacrificial altars in places of worship wherever Yhwh worshippers live, assuming the unit post-dates Deuteronomy 12.

Exod 20:24	בכל־המקום אשר אזכיר את־שמי אבוא אליך וברכתיך
Deut 12:14	במקום אשר־יבחר יהוה באחד שבטיך
Deut 12:4	אל־המקום אשר־יבחר יהוה אלהיכם מכל־שבטיכם לשום את־שמו שם

It is indeed possible that Exod 20:22–26 was added in a late stage of the process of the promulgation of the Pentateuch, maybe by a group that wanted to offer an

---

[24] Bernard M. Levinson, *Deuteronomy and the Hermeneutics of Legal Innovation* (Oxford: Oxford University Press, 1997); Eckart Otto, *Das Deuteronomium. Politische Theologie und Rechtsreform in Juda und Assyrien*, BZAW 284 (Berlin: de Gruyter, 1999).

[25] According to Johannes Unsok Ro, "The Portrayal of Judean Communities in Persian Era Palestine Through the Lens of the Covenant Code," *Sem* 56 (2014): 249–89, the Covenant Code and the Deuteronomic Code both emerged in the Persian period, in different socio-geographical contexts.

[26] Some authors see in v. 22* the original opening, and in 20:24–26 additions to the original *mishpatim*, as for instance Wolfgang Oswald, *Israel am Gottesberg: Eine Untersuchung zur Literaturgeschichte der vorderen Sinaiperikope Ex 19–24 und deren historischem Hintergrund*, OBO 159 (Göttingen: Vandenhoeck & Ruprecht, 1998), 111–12. For another solution see John Van Seters, "The Altar Law of Ex 20,24–26 in Critical Debate," in *Auf dem Weg zur Endgestalt von Genesis bis II Regum. Festschrift für Hans-Christoph Schmitt zu seinem 65. Geburtstag*, ed. Martin Beck and Ulrike Schorn, BZAW 370 (Berlin: de Gruyter. 2006): 157–74.

[27] See Eckart Otto, "Die Rechtshermeneutik des Pentateuch und die achämenidische Rechtsideologie in ihren altorientalischen Kontexten," in *Kodifizierung und Legitimierung des Rechts in der Antike und im Alten Orient*, ed. Markus Witte and Marie Theres Fögen, BZABR 5 (Wiesbaden: Harrassowitz, 2006): 71–116.

alternative to the Deuteronomic centralization law and to allow for several Yhwh sanctuaries. The redactors of Exod 20:24–26 tried in this way to legitimate the existence of altars in diaspora communities outside 'the Land' while endorsing two single sites within that territory—at Mount Gerizim for the residents of Samaria and at Jerusalem for the residents of Yehud.

A similar strategy can be detected in the Priestly account of the construction of the mobile sanctuary in Exodus 25–31 and 35–40. This mobile sanctuary can easily be identified with different sanctuaries: For the Judeans, it can be read as alluding to the Jerusalemite Temple, whereas for the Samarians, it is possible to see the sanctuary as foreshadowing their Temple on Gerizim. If this is the case, one could imagine that the 'Priestly document' (P) did perhaps not only originate in Yehud. Maybe P should be seen as a 'mixed' group of priests from Samaria and from Jerusalem.[28] Flavius Josephus reports that dissident priests from Jerusalem, who disagreed with the measures of Ezra and Nehemiah, founded the temple of Gerizim.[29] Although his presentation is more ideological than historical, it acknowledges a relation between the priesthood from Gerizim and from Jerusalem. According to Neh 13:28 the son of Eliashib, the high priest of Jerusalem, was married with the daughter of the Samaritan governor Sanballat.[30] We should therefore change our view about the origin of the Pentateuch.

It is not a Judean and Babylonian production that was then adopted by the Samaritans. Our present knowledge of the archeological and historical facts requires, as Ingrid Hjelm puts it "new scenarios that present the Samaritans on Gerizim as (co-)authors, rather than as receivers of a fully formed tradition."[31] That means we should not only speak of 'concessions' made to the Samaritans but imagine a more intensive redaction of the Pentateuch from the Samaritan side, or at least from a mixed group of Judeans and Samaritans. In the following I just would like to offer two examples of a possible Samaritan revision of the nascent Torah. I will not deal with Deuteronomy 27 because this text has largely been analyzed and commented in recent publications.[32] I will rather offer some

---

[28] For a similar idea, see Walter Houston, "Between Salem and Mount Gerizim: The Context of the Formation of the Torah Reconsidered," *Journal of Ancient Judaism* 5 (2014): 311–34.
[29] Josephus, *Ant.* 11.309–312; 11.346.
[30] See also Josephus, *Ant.* 11:302–312.
[31] Ingrid Hjelm, "Northern Perspectives in Deuteronomy and Its Relation to the Samaritan Pentateuch," *HeBAI* 4 (2015): 193.
[32] See Na'aman, "Law of the Altar;" Nihan, "Garizim;" Detlef Jericke, "Der Berg Garizim im Deuteronomium," *ZAW* 124 (2012): 213–28; Gary N. Knoppers, *Jews and Samaritans: The Origins and History of their Early Relations* (Oxford: Oxford University Press, 2013), 206–8.

comments on a 'Shechem frame' and a possible 'Samaritan-connection' in the Joseph-novella.

The Shechem-frame of the Hexa- and Pentateuch

The first stop that Abraham makes in the land of Canaan where he receives his first divine revelation, is at Shechem at the oak of More, and here he builds his first altar (Gen 12:6–7). Scholars traditionally explain Abraham's link with Shechem with the assumption that the passage about Abraham's travel into the land of Canaan in Gen 12:1–9 takes up important places from the Jacob tradition and relates those also to Abraham. But interestingly Abraham's second stop is between 'Bethel and Ai,' and not in Bethel; and Ai does not play any role in the Jacob narrative. Therefore, one may consider an alternative explanation and postulate that the beginning of the Abraham narrative was reworked in a pro-Samaritan perspective. Read in the light of Exod 20:24–26 Abraham's altar in Shechem is the first place that Yhwh has chosen for his cult. There is a hint to the reference to Shechem at the very end of the Pentateuch when Moses is allowed to see the Promised Land, which he cannot enter. The repetition of the land promise in Deut 34:4 is indeed a quotation of Yhwh's promise to Abraham in Shechem:

Gen 12:7   לזרעך אתן את־הארץ הזאת
Deut 34:4   הארץ אשר נשבעתי לאברהם ליצחק וליעקב לאמר לזרעך אתננה

Interestingly the Samaritan Pentateuch has a very different description of the land that Moses is allowed to contemplate: "from the river of Egypt to the great river, the river of Euphrates, unto the utmost Sea." This large description, absent from the MT of Deut 34:2–3, has a more inclusive view of the Promised Land including Diaspora locations in Mesopotamia and also in Egypt. It is possible that the description centered on the land and tribes of Israel in Deut 34:2–3 MT is a later correction of the 'unrealistic view' of Moses according to the SP.

The Shechem location is even more obvious at the end of the book of Joshua. In Joshua 24, Joshua enacts the divine laws and the 'book of the law of God' at Shechem. The link with Gen 12:7 is made evident by the mention of the 'oak' in 24:26.[33] As I have argued elsewhere Joshua 24 was created in order to produce a

---

[33] The MT plural reading is a tendentious attempt to play down the holy character of the oak. The original reading, attested by the Greek, is the singular.

Hexateuch, and to integrate the book of Joshua into the Torah.³⁴ The Northern, 'Samaritan' location of Joshua 24 can hardly be a Judean invention. This is also shown by the LXX, which reads Shiloh instead of Shechem and reflects a Hebrew text from the second or first century presupposing the so-called "schism" between both groups after the destruction of the sanctuary of Gerizim.³⁵ We should see Josh 24 therefore probably as a co-production of Samaritans and Judeans, if not a pure Samaritan version. Although the idea of a Hexateuch could not be materialized in a Torah containing six scrolls, the figure of Joshua remained popular among the Samaritans, as shown by the Samaritan Chronicle of Joshua.³⁶

A Samaritan 'Shechem revision' is maybe also perceptible in Genesis 22. In this text God asks Abraham to go to the land "Moriah" and to sacrifice Isaac on of the mountain that God will indicate to him. Scholars generally argue that Moriah in Genesis 22 is an allusion to Jerusalem since in 2 Chr 3:1 the temple mount is called 'Mount Moriah.' But it is not clear at all that this text was in the mind of the author or redactor who added this geographical indication in Gen 22:2. As Nihan has argued in a forthcoming article, 'Moriah' in Genesis 22 may have a link with Shechem, and the Samaritan המורה allude to the oak of Shechem in Gen 12:6 (SP: אלון מורא). The Masoretic spelling (הַמֹּרִיָּה) could have been introduced at the same time that 2 Chr 3:1 was written. But it is quite possible that a Samaritan editor of the Pentateuch added the location Moriah in Gen 22; by doing so he wanted to suggest that the place of Abraham's sacrifice was identical with the place where he built already an altar when he arrived in the Land.

The Joseph Novella and Its Possible Northern, Samaritan Connections

Let us return for a moment to Joshua 24. At the end of that chapter the author reports the burying of Joseph's bones in Shechem (24:32). This action brings to an end a motif that occurs at the end of the Joseph story in Gen 50:26, and appears again in Exod 13:19, when the Israelites leave Egypt. In recent scholarship

---

34 Thomas Römer, "Das doppelte Ende des Josuabuches: einige Anmerkungen zur aktuellen Diskussion um 'deuteronomistisches Geschichtswerk' und 'Hexateuch,'" *ZAW* 118 (2006): 523–48. See also Thomas Römer and Marc Z. Brettler, "Deuteronomy 34 and the Case for a Persian Hexateuch," *JBL* 119 (2000): 401–19.
35 *Pace* Ernst A. Knauf, *Josua*, ZBK.AT 6. (Zürich: Theologischer Verlag, 2008), 195.
36 Ingrid Hjelm, *The Samaritans and Early Judaism: A Literary Analysis*, JSOTSup 303 (Sheffield: Sheffield Academic Press, 2000), 241–44.

there is a trend to understand the Joseph story as a Diaspora novella that would have been written down in order to legitimate the existence of an Egyptian diaspora.[37] The question remains, however, why Joseph is a "Northern" figure. In the prophetic books 'Joseph' or the 'house of Joseph' is indeed used to designate the North. And in Gen 41:51–52, Joseph becomes indeed the father of Ephraim and Manasseh. This Northern setting has sometimes been explained with the idea that the Joseph story could have originated in Elephantine, a colony that according to some scholars could have had Northern origins.[38] But the location of the Joseph story in Elephantine is not clear at all, nor is the presupposed Northern origin of the colony.

Another option would be to relate the Joseph narrative to a 'Samaritan' diaspora. According to Flavius Josephus there were also Samaritans living in Egypt during the Hellenistic time and perhaps earlier from the end of the Persian era onward.[39] He also reports that under Ptolemy VI (180–145 BCE) there was a conflict between Jews and Samaritans living together in Alexandria about the question of whether the Temple of Jerusalem or the sanctuary on Gerizim had been built according to the prescriptions the Torah.[40] Andronicus, speaking for Jerusalem "persuaded the king to decide that the temple in Jerusalem had been built in accordance with the laws of Moses."[41] If those tensions between Judeans and Samaritans arose only in the second century BCE, we might assume that there was a quite pacific cohabitation of both groups in Egypt in late Persian and early Hellenistic times. If this were the case the Joseph story could have been originated in a Samaritan context. When it was inserted into the Torah, the role of Judah was strengthened in order to create a balance between the North and the South. Admittedly these are speculations, but we need to investigate more seriously texts in the Torah that possibly have a Northern, Samaritan background.

---

37 Thomas Römer, "Joseph approché. Source du cycle, corpus, unite," in *Le livre de traverse: De l'exégèse biblique à l'anthropologie*, ed. Oliver Abel and Françoise Smyth, Patrimoines (Paris: Cerf., 1992): 73–85; Alessandro Catastini, *Storia di Guiseppe (Genesi 37–50)* (Venezia: Marsilio, 1994); Jean-Marie Husser, "L'histoire de Joseph," in *La Bible et sa culture: Ancien Testament*, ed. Michel Quesnel and Philippe Gruson (Paris: Desclée de Brouwer, 2000): 112–22; Christoph Uehlinger, "Fratrie, filiations et paternités dans l'histoire de Joseph (Genèse 37–50*)," in *Jacob: Commentaire à plusieurs voix de Gen. 25–36. Mélanges offerts à Albert de Pury*, ed. Jean-Daniel Macchi and Thomas Römer, MdB 44 (Genève: Labor et Fides, 2001): 303–28.
38 Karel van der Toorn, "Anat-Yahu, Some Other Deities, and the Jews of Elephantine," *Numen* 39 (1992): 80–101.
39 Josephus, *Ant*. 11.321–322; 12.7–10.
40 Josephus, *Ant*. 13.74–79.
41 Josephus, *Ant*. 13.79.

Conclusion

The centralization formula arose in a seventh-century "Urdeuteronomium," which was not a Northern but a Judean scroll, in order to demonstrate that the only legitimate sanctuary for sacrificing to Yhwh was the Temple of Jerusalem. When Deuteronomy became the opening of the so-called DtrH, the Deuteronomistic redactors had to explain the fact that before the construction of the Temple, Yhwh had been worshipped in other places. The Deuteronomistic temple speech in Jeremiah 7 claims that Yhwh did choose another sanctuary before Jerusalem, Shiloh. But just as Shiloh had been destroyed, the Temple in Jerusalem could also be put to ashes. In the context of the Pentateuch, the centralization law in Deuteronomy 12 is in tension with the introduction to the Covenant Code in Exod 20:24–26 which allows for a diversity of chosen places. A similar strategy can be found in the Priestly idea of a mobile sanctuary, which could be understood as a prototype for the Jerusalem Temple, but also for the Temple of Gerizim. This possibility of 'double entendre' can perhaps be explained by the idea that the Priestly authors were not only Judean but also Samaritan priests. Samaritan interventions can also be detected in the importance given to Shechem in the beginning of the Abraham narrative and in Joshua 24. And finally we may ask whether the Joseph novella did arise in the context of a Samaritan diaspora in Egypt. Much further investigation is necessary. But we need to imagine for the Samaritans a more active role in the production of the Torah.

Christophe Nihan and Hervé Gonzalez
Competing Attitudes toward Samaria in Chronicles and Second Zechariah

Our aim in this essay is to reexamine two passages preserved in broadly contemporaneous works from the late Persian and early Hellenistic period, namely, Chronicles and Zech 9–14 (so-called Second Zechariah).[1] The first passage, 2 Chr 7:12, is a key passage in Chronicles' account, which arguably reflects the rivalry between the Judean temple on Mt. Zion and the Samarian temple on Mt. Gerizim—a feature of this text which has not been sufficiently recognized in the scholarly discussion. The second passage, Zech 11:14, preserves one of the earliest pieces of evidence for the idea of a definitive separation between Judah and Samaria. Yet the meaning of this passage remains obscure and controverted. The following essay will argue that when these two passages are repositioned in their proper literary and historical context, they exemplify basic differences of attitude toward the Samarians and their temple within Judean scribal circles of the postexilic period; and that these differences are primarily related to the conceptualization of the Davidic dynasty in relation to the Jerusalem temple. As such, the comparison between 2 Chr 7:12 and Zech 11:14 casts some further light on the variety, or plurality, of Judean attitudes toward Samaria in the pre-Hasmonean period.[2]

---

[1] The first draft of this paper was presented by Christophe Nihan during the 22nd Congress of the International Organization for the Study of the Old Testament in September 2016. The present essay represents a revised and augmented version of this paper, which benefitted from the collaboration of Hervé Gonzalez for the second part devoted to Zech 9–14. The authors express their sincere thanks to Julia Rhyder (Lausanne), who undertook the revision of the English.
[2] A brief note regarding the dating of these two works is in order here. The dating of Chronicles in the late Persian/early Hellenistic period (fourth or third century BCE) is commonly accepted now. For a good survey of the main arguments to that effect, see Gary N. Knoppers, *I Chronicles 1–9*, AB 12 (New York: Doubleday, 2004), 101–17. In our opinion, a dating in the third century is more likely, as already argued, for example, by Rainer Albertz, *Religionsgeschichte Israels in alttestamentlicher Zeit – Teil 2: Vom Exil bis zu den Makkabäern*, GAT 8.2 (Göttingen: Vandenhoeck & Ruprecht, 1992), 607–22. However, this issue can remain open here. In the case of Zech 9–14, this corpus has long been recognized as one of the latest prophetic collections preserved in the Hebrew Bible, which was often dated to the period of Ptolemaic domination in the southern Levant (third century BCE). Despite recent arguments to the contrary, this dating remains in our view the most likely one. For a recent and comprehensive discussion of this issue, see Hervé Gonzalez, "Zechariah 9–14 and the Continuation of Zechariah during the Ptolemaic Period," *JHebS* 13 (2013): 1–43, especially 15–21. In any event, the analysis of Zech 11 below corroborates

We begin with 2 Chr 7:12. This passage introduces the second manifestation of YHWH to Solomon in 2 Chr 7:11–22. It follows the dedication of the temple (2 Chr 5:2–7:10), and provides the Chronicler with an opportunity to comment on the significance of the temple's building in Jerusalem under Solomon. Chronicles' version of YHWH's speech to Solomon consists of two parts, vv. 12–16 and vv. 17–22. The second part, vv. 17–22, takes up the content of the parallel passage in 1 Kgs 9 (1 Kgs 9:4–9), but the first part, vv. 12–16, considerably develops the opening statement found in 1 Kgs 9:3.³

12 וירא יהוה אל־שלמה בלילה ויאמר לו שמעתי את־תפלתך ובחרתי במקום הזה לי לבית זבח: 13 הן אעצר השמים ולא־יהיה מטר והן־אצוה על־חגב לאכול הארץ ואם־אשלח דבר בעמי: 14 ויכנעו עמי אשר נקרא־שמי עליהם ויתפללו ויבקשו פני וישבו מדרכיהם הרעים ואני אשמע מן־השמים ואסלח לחטאתם וארפא את־ארצם: 15 עתה עיני יהיו פתחות ואזני קשבות לתפלת המקום הזה: 16 ועתה בחרתי והקדשתי את־הבית הזה להיות־שמי שם עד־עולם והיו עיני ולבי שם כל־הימים:

12 YHWH appeared to Solomon in the night and told him: "I have listened to your prayer [cf. 1 Kgs 9:3], and so I have chosen this place to be my house of sacrifice. 13 When I shut up the heavens so that there is no rain [cf. 2 Chr 6:26], or command the locust to devour the land [cf. 2 Chr 6:28],⁴ or send pestilence among my people [cf. 2 Chr 6:28], 14 if my people, upon whom my Name is called, humble themselves, and if they pray, and seek my face, and turn from their evil ways, then I will hear from the heavens [cf. 2 Chr 6:21], and I will forgive their sin [cf. 2 Chr 6:25, 27] and heal their land. 15 Now⁵ my eyes will be open and my ears will be attentive to the prayer of this place. 16 For now, I have chosen and consecrated this house [2 Chr 7:12 + 1 Kgs 9:3] so that my Name will be there forever; my eyes and my heart will be there for all time.

---

the general view that Zech 9–14 cannot be from the same hand as Zech 1–8 (see Heiko Wenzel, *Reading Zechariah with Zechariah 1:1–6 as the Introduction to the Entire Book*, CBET 59 [Leuven: Peeters, 2011]) and Zech 11 must postdate the building of the Samarian sanctuary on Mt. Gerizim. In terms of relative chronology, this conclusion implies that the composition of Zech 11 (and presumably Zech 12–14 as well) cannot be dated before the second half of the Persian period, at the earliest.

3 The LXX and other ancient versions preserve few significant variants for this passage. Those variations which are preserved will be discussed in the text below. Unless otherwise specified, all translations in this essay are our own.

4 The LXX reads τὸ ξύλον = העץ instead of הארץ in the MT. Presumably, this represents an error on the part of a Greek translator. Whether this error arose when the text was read aloud to a scribe (Leslie C. Allen, *The Greek Chronicles: The Relationship of the Septuagint of I and II Chronicles to the Masoretic Text – Part II Textual Criticism*, VTSup 27 [Leiden: Brill, 1974], 2.123, 156, who thinks of a phonetic error), or during a process of copying is an intriguing question, but remains difficult to decide on the basis of this example alone. The reading of the MT broadly corresponds to the contents of 2 Chr 6:28a, although the wording differs.

5 Against BHS, there is no cogent reason to correct ועתה into מעתה, "from now on."

Specifically, 2 Chr 7:12 begins in the same way as 1 Kgs 9:3, where YHWH declares to Solomon, "I have listened to your prayer," but continues with an entirely new statement: "I have chosen this place to be a house of sacrifice for me" (ובחרתי במקום הזה לי לבית זבח). In the context of 2 Chr 5–7, "this place" can evidently only refer to the royal temple built in Jerusalem by Solomon. The notion that YHWH has "chosen" the temple of Jerusalem is then repeated once more in 2 Chr 7:16, where it is combined with the promise of 1 Kgs 9:3 that YHWH will "consecrate" the temple so that his name may reside there forever. In this way, the entire unit formed by 2 Chr 7:12–16 is framed by two parallel verses, vv. 12 and 16, which take up and develop the earlier statement in 1 Kgs 9:3a.⁶ The section in between vv. 13–15 takes up for its part the language of Solomon's prayer in 2 Chr 6,⁷ to conclude in v. 15 that YHWH's ears will be "attentive to the prayer of this place" (אזני קשבות לתפלת המקום הזה).⁸ Despite its brevity, YHWH's statement in v. 12b, ובחרתי במקום הזה לי לבית זבח, is remarkable in several ways.

First, the assertion that YHWH has "chosen" (בחר) the "place" (מקום) built by Solomon is unmistakably reminiscent of the language of cult centralization in Deuteronomy, and thereby identifies Solomon's temple with Deuteronomy's central place.⁹ This identification is further corroborated by the parallel statement in

---

6 Compare ויאמר לו שמעתי את־תפלתך (2 Chr 7:12bα) with ויאמר יהוה אליו שמעתי את־תפלתך (1 Kgs 9:3a). In 2 Chr 7:16, the first phrase ועתה בחרתי corresponds to 2 Chr 7:12, as noted above; but the rest of the verse, והקדשתי את־הבית הזה להיות־שמי שם עד־עולם והיו עיני ולבי שם כל־הימי הימים, reproduces almost verbatim the contents of 1 Kgs 9:3.

7 See especially the various threats enumerated in 2 Chr 7:13, all of which have parallels in 2 Chr 6:22–29, although the language used is somewhat unusual: lack of rain (6:26), locusts (6:28), pestilence (6:28). Verse 14 likewise contains motifs already present in 2 Chr 6, such as the idea that YHWH will "hear from heaven" and "forgive their [Israel's] sins;" both expressions effectively correspond to central concerns previously voiced by Solomon in his prayer. For further parallels between the language of vv. 13–14 and 2 Chr 6, see the detailed analysis by William Johnstone, *1 and 2 Chronicles. Volume 1: 1 Chronicles 1–2 Chronicles 9. Israel's Place among the Nations*, JSOTSup 253 (Sheffield: Sheffield Academic Press, 1997), 357–58.

8 The construction לתפלת המקום הזה is somewhat ambiguous. From a grammatical perspective, the most obvious meaning is that YHWH will be attentive to prayers which are offered to him *on the site* of the temple; but it is possible that the expression also includes the possibility that YHWH will hear the Israelite prayer that is simply directed "toward" (אל) the temple, as is stated in 2 Chr 6:34, 38.

9 As noted by various authors already: see, for example, Sara Japhet, *The Ideology of the Book of Chronicles and Its Place in Biblical Thought*, BEATAJ 9 (Frankfurt: Peter Lang, 1997), 89–90; eadem, *I & II Chronicles: A Commentary*, OTL (Louisville: Westminster John Knox, 1993), 614–15. As is well known, the combined usage of בחר and מקום to refer to the central place of cult is distinctive of Deuteronomy, see Deut 12:5, 11, 14, 18, 21, 26; 14:23, 24, 25; 15:20; 16:2, 6, 7, 11, 15, 16; 17:8, 10; 18:6; 23:17; 26:2; 31:11. Otherwise, a similar phraseology is only found in Josh 9:27; Neh 1:9 and 2 Chr 7:12.

v. 16 that YHWH has "chosen" (בחר) the temple of Jerusalem so that his Name (שם) may reside there, which is likewise reminiscent of the conception found in Deut 12 and related passages of Deuteronomy.[10] It is important to note that, while the identification of the Jerusalem temple with Deuteronomy's central place is already implied in some passages of Kings, such identification always remains implicit in this book.[11] In effect, 2 Chr 7:12 is the *only* passage, in the Hebrew Bible, where the temple of Jerusalem is expressly said to be "chosen" by YHWH.

Second, the identification of the Jerusalem temple with Deuteronomy's central place is followed in 2 Chr 7:12 with a description of that temple as a "house of sacrifice" (בית זבח). Although this designation of the temple is unparalleled in the Hebrew Bible, it is documented in two Aramaic sources that are broadly contemporaneous with Chronicles, as some scholars have already pointed out.[12] One of these sources is the "memorandum" of the reply sent in 407 BCE by Bagohi and Delaiah to the community of Elephantine, which refers to the temple of that community as a "house of sacrifice" (בית מדבחא).[13] The second is an inscription in lapidary Aramaic from the site of Mt. Gerizim, probably dating from the third or second century BCE, which mentions "bulls in all… [sacrific]ed in the

---

[10] For the idea that YHWH's name will reside in the central place, see Deut 12:5, 11, 21; 14:23, 24; 16:2, 6, 11; 26:2. Note, however, that Deuteronomy uses either the formula לשכן שמו שם, or the formula לשום את שמו שם, but never the expression להיות שמי שם. This expression is already used in 1 Kgs 8:16 and its parallel in 2 Chr 6:5–6; the choice of להיות שמי שם in 2 Chr 7:16 may well be intended, therefore, to connect the latter passage with this central statement.

[11] On this the discussion, see Christophe Nihan, "Cult Centralization and the Torah Traditions in Chronicles," in *The Fall of Jerusalem and the Rise of the Torah*, ed. Peter Dubovsky, Dominik Markl, and Jean-Pierre Sonnet, FAT 107 (Tübingen: Mohr Siebeck, 2016), 253–88, especially 256–57.

[12] Reinhard Pummer, *The Samaritans in Flavius Josephus*, TSAJ 129 (Tübingen: Mohr Siebeck 2009), 42; Bob Becking, "Do the Earliest Samaritan Inscriptions Already Indicate a Parting of the Ways?" in *Judah and the Judeans in the Fourth Century BCE*, ed. Oded Lipschits, Gary N. Knoppers, Rainer Albertz (Winona Lake, IN: Eisenbrauns, 2007), 217; Gary N. Knoppers, *Jews and Samaritans. The Origins and History of Their Early Relations* (Oxford: Oxford University Press, 2013), 128.

[13] See *TAD* A4.9.1.3. For more on this, see Avi Hurvitz, "Terms and Epithets Relating to the Jerusalem Temple Compound in the Book of Chronicles: The Linguistic Aspect," in *Pomegranates and Golden Bells: Studies in Biblical, Jewish, and Near Eastern Ritual, Law, and Literature in Honor of Jacob Milgrom*, ed. David P. Wright, David N. Freedman, and Avi Hurvitz (Winona Lake, IN: Eisenbrauns, 1995), 178–79, especially 178 n. 49, who also mentions further Syriac and Mandaic parallels for this expression.

house of sacrifice [בית דבחה]" (no. 199).¹⁴ These two sources provide clear evidence, therefore, that around the time of the composition of Chronicles the expression "house of sacrifice" could be applied to various Israelite sanctuaries, such as the temple of Elephantine or the temple on Mt. Gerizim.

While scholars have long noted the significance of 2 Chr 7:12–16, they have usually interpreted it against the background of Kings' revision in Chronicles. In particular, Sara Japhet and other commentators have remarked that the designation of Solomon's temple as a "house of sacrifice" involves a significant correction of the conception stated in 1 Kgs 8 (Solomon's prayer), where the temple of Jerusalem is never mentioned as the place where sacrifices are made but exclusively as the place toward which the Israelites must pray.¹⁵ In 2 Chr 7, this association of the temple with prayer is maintained, as v. 15 makes clear; but it is now prefaced in v. 12 with the reaffirmation that the temple, as the place "chosen" by YHWH, is primarily the site where the Israelites may legitimately bring their sacrifices.¹⁶ The resulting description in 2 Chr 7 thus combines the conceptions of Deut 12 and 1 Kgs 8, by defining simultaneously the temple as a "house of sacrifice" and as the place where the deity will hear the prayers of the Israelites.¹⁷

The idea that 2 Chr 7:12 involves a revision of the conception of the temple in Kings, especially in 1 Kgs 8, to align it more closely with the conception stated in Deuteronomy is certainly convincing. But there is more to this phenomenon than a mere literary development, and Kings is not the only relevant context for interpreting the unique formulation preserved in 2 Chr 7:12. Although this point has

---

14 See Yitzhak Magen, Haggai Misgav, Levana Tsfania, *The Aramaic, Hebrew and Samaritan Inscriptions*, vol. 1 of *Mount Gerizim Excavations*, Judea and Samaria Publications 2 (Jerusalem: Israel Antiquities Authorities, 2004). Compare also the comments by Becking, "Do the Earliest," 217; Knoppers, *Jews and Samaritans*, 128. For the argument that most of the inscriptions date to the third and second centuries BCE, see the comprehensive paleographic analysis by Jan Dušek, *Aramaic and Hebrew Inscriptions from Mt. Gerizim and Samaria between Antiochus III and Antiochus IV Epiphanes*, CHANE 54 (Leiden: Brill, 2012), 3–63; note, however, that Dušek himself does not preclude an earlier date in the fifth or fourth centuries for some of these inscriptions (Dušek, *Aramaic*, 59–60).
15 See 1 Kgs 8:30, 33, 35, 42, 44, 48; compare 2 Chr 6:21, 24, 26, 32, 34, 38.
16 See in this regard the comment by Japhet: "In his prayer, Solomon never mentions sacrifices or asks that God accept the offerings of His people; in fact, he ignores the Temple's ritual function. Yet, in 2 Chr 7:2ff., God answers Solomon *as if the latter had sought divine approval of the Temple as a site of sacrificial worship* [emphasis ours]" (Japhet, *Ideology*, 79); compare eadem, *I & II Chronicles*, 614.
17 Japhet (*Ideology*, 80) aptly observes that the Chronicler "views prayer and sacrifices as two sides of the same coin," and that the same "organic" connection between prayer and sacrifice is also reflected in other postexilic texts, such as Isa 56:7.

been little noted so far, an even more significant context for the statement in 2 Chr 7:12 is provided by the textual evidence showing that the identification of Deuteronomy's central place of sacrifice was a disputed issue between Judeans and Samarians from the Persian period onward. It is now widely agreed that the reading בהרגריזים ("on Mt. Gerizim") in Deut SP 27:4, which is also attested by one Old Latin manuscript (Codex 100 of Lyon) and by Pap. Giessen 19, is earlier than the alternative reading בהר עיבל ("on Mt. Ebal") in the MT, which arguably represents a later, polemical revision.[18] This observation demonstrates that the identification of Deuteronomy's central place with Mt. Gerizim is not a late "sectarian" development – as it was initially believed – but was already well-established around the time when the Pentateuch was finalized (i.e., the fourth century BCE), if not somewhat earlier.[19] This finding, in turn, provides an important background for understanding the statement about the Jerusalem temple in 2 Chr 7:12. The dating of Chronicles in the fourth or third century BCE (and certainly not earlier) is fairly consensual,[20] and the idea that other passages of this book – such as Abijah's speech in 2 Chr 13:8–12 – reflect a context of rivalry between the Judean and Samarian communities of the late Persian and early Hellenistic periods has already been convincingly demonstrated by Gary Knoppers.[21] Similarly, the unique emphasis on the Jerusalem temple as the place "chosen" by YHWH in 2 Chr 7:12 takes on new significance when it is read against a background of Judean-Samarian rivalry. In a context where the location of Deuteronomy's central place was disputed between both communities,

---

[18] For a recent reassessment of the evidence, see Gary N. Knoppers, "The Northern Context of the Law-Code in Deuteronomy," *HBAI* 4 (2015): 162–83; idem, *Jews and Samaritans*, 202–203; Ingrid Hjelm, "Northern Perspectives in Deuteronomy and its Relation to the Samaritan Pentateuch," *HBAI* 4 (2015): 184–204; Magnar Kartveit, "The Place That the Lord Your God Will Choose," *HBAI* 4 (2015): 205–18; Christophe Nihan, "The Torah between Samaria and Judah: Shechem and Gerizim in Deuteronomy and Joshua," in *The Pentateuch as Torah: New Models for Understanding Its Promulgation and Acceptance*, ed. Gary N. Knoppers and Bernard M. Levinson (Winona Lake, IN: Eisenbrauns, 2007), 187–223. Compare also the recent discussion by Eugene Ulrich, *Dead Sea Scrolls and the Developmental Composition of the Bible*, VTSup 169 (Leiden: Brill, 2015), 47–65, who offers a somewhat different solution. While he agrees that the reading "Mount Gerizim" is older than "Mount Ebal" he argues that both names are later additions; initially, Deut 27:4 did not mention a specific place for the altar, but implicitly located it in Gilgal. This solution is possible, but it is also more hypothetical, especially since no ancient witness attests to a text where the location of the altar would remain unspecified in Deut 27:4.
[19] See on this the comments in Nihan, "The Torah."
[20] See note 2 above.
[21] See Gary N. Knoppers, "Mt. Gerizim and Mt. Zion: A Study in the Early History of the Samaritans and Jews," *SR* 34 (2005): 309–38; in the case of Abijah's speech, see the comments in Nihan, "Cult Centralization," 275–82.

this passage clearly asserts that the legitimate sanctuary is the temple built in Jerusalem by Solomon, and none other. Furthermore, while the epigraphic evidence we have recalled above shows that the expression "house of sacrifice" was effectively associated with various sanctuaries in Persian and Hellenistic times the use of this expression in 2 Chr 7:12, in conjunction with the key term מקום, highlights the point that – in keeping with Deuteronomy's program of centralization – there can in fact only be *one* legitimate place of sacrifices, namely, the temple of Jerusalem.

It is important to observe, at this point, that the identification in 2 Chr 7:12 of the Jerusalem temple with the central place of Deuteronomy represents the climax of a broader trend that permeates Chronicles' account of the building of the temple, one which consistently highlights Solomon's role as the divinely chosen agent to enforce Deuteronomy's program of centralization. This notion is already present in Kings (esp. 1 Kgs 5:17–18), but it has been considerably developed in Chronicles. In particular, 1 Chr 22:9–10 (a passage with no parallel in Kings) describes Solomon as "the man of rest" (איש מנוחה) to whom "YHWH will give rest [נוח Hiphil] from all his surrounding enemies."[22] Later, in 1 Chr 28:2, the temple built by Solomon is itself described as the "house of rest" (בית מנוחה), a unique designation in the Hebrew Bible which obviously complements the previous designation of Solomon as "the man of rest."[23] The association of Solomon and the temple with the theme of Israel's "rest" (מנוחה) provides a clear reference to Deut 12:8–12 (esp. vv. 9–11),[24] and serves therefore in Chronicles to identify Solomon's reign as the time when the obligation for the Israelites to bring their sacrifices to the central place was eventually fulfilled. Other, additional associations between Solomon's temple building account in Chronicles and Deut 12 could be noted. But in the context of this essay the point to be stressed is that the

---

22 The latter statement was already applied to David in 2 Sam 7:1 (but contrast 1 Kgs 5:17–18), whereas it has been omitted in Chronicles' retelling of the Dynastic Oracle (cf. 1 Chr 17:1), presumably in order to emphasize the exclusive association between Solomon's reign and the "rest" of Israel.

23 The connection between the designation of Solomon as the "man of rest" and the designation of the temple as the "house of rest" is all the more significant since the term מנוחה does not occur in Chronicles outside of this passage. The phrase בית מנוחה is a *hapax legomenon* in the Hebrew Bible, although the use of the term מנוחה to denote the place where YHWH resides (or is represented) has parallels in some texts from the Second Temple period, like Isa 66:1 or Ps 132:13–14. For more, see Hurvitz, "Terms," 174–77.

24 According to Deut 12:8–12, the obligation for the Israelites to bring their sacrifices to the central place chosen by YHWH applies only *after* they have arrived in the "place of rest" (מנוחה), which apparently denotes here the promised land, and after YHWH has given them "rest" (נוח Hiphil) from their enemies (see Deut 12:9–11).

key statement in 2 Chr 7:12 forms the climax of a larger historiographical trend, the purpose of which is to make perfectly clear that the temple built by Solomon represents the fulfillment of Deuteronomy's program of centralization.[25]

Furthermore, the conception stated in 2 Chr 7:12, which identifies the temple of Jerusalem with the central place of Deuteronomy, also has a programmatic function regarding the subsequent story told in Chronicles. For the Chronicler, and contrary to Kings, the temple of Jerusalem remains the central sanctuary of Israel even *after* the separation of the northern tribes under Rehoboam. According to this conception, the northern tribes are automatically disloyal to YHWH when they worship him at any site other than Jerusalem – as Abijah's speech in 2 Chr 13:8–12 makes clear – but these tribes also have the possibility to return to the legitimate place of cult in Jerusalem, as the account of Hezekiah's Passover emphasizes (2 Chr 30–31). For the Chronicler, therefore, the separation between the south and the north is not definitive and can be overcome, if the northern tribes are willing to return to the temple in Jerusalem. In this regard, the temple of Jerusalem operates, in Chronicles, as the main symbol of a glorious past associated with the united monarchy under David and Solomon, when all Israel was ruled by a single king in Jerusalem. Presumably, this was still true for the Chronicler in his own time. In this conception, the temple and the united monarchy are really two sides of the same coin, supporting together what could be called an agenda of "cultic annexation" of the north to Jerusalem.[26]

We turn now to our second passage, Zech 11:14. The passage represents the climax of a complex dystopian account in Zech 11:4–14, in which the prophet is commanded to shepherd the "flock of the slaughter" (את־צאן ההרגה; v. 4b); the command itself is interpreted in v. 6 as the sign that YHWH has forsaken the "inhabitants of the land." The prophet's attempt to shepherd the flock ends in fail-

---

[25] On this issue, see the discussion in Nihan, "Cult Centralization," 263–67.
[26] For this reason, the question of whether Chronicles privileges the Davidic monarchy or the temple strikes us as a false alternative. It is clear that, from Chronicles' perspective, the prime obligation of the Davidic kings is toward the cult: 2 Chr 13:8, for instance, mentions "the kingship of YHWH which is in the hands of the sons of David" (ממלכת יהוה ביד בני דויד), thereby positioning the Davidides as vice-regents of the divine king, YHWH. On the relationship between YHWH's and David's kingship, see Japhet, *Ideology*, 395–411; for a different view, which is, however, somewhat misbalanced in our opinion, see Steven J. Schweitzer, *Reading Utopia in Chronicles*, LHBOTS 442 (London: T&T Clark International, 2007), 76–131. On the other hand, the centrality of the Jerusalem temple cannot be dissociated, in Chronicles' perspective, from the memory of the Davidic dynasty. In fact, one could even argue that one of the main functions of Chronicles' account (albeit certainly not the only one) was to remind the Chronicler's audience that the temple of Jerusalem derived its authority and legitimacy from the Judean monarchs.

ure (vv. 7–9), following which the prophet smashes the two staffs that he used as a shepherd (vv. 10–14).

10 ואקח את־מקלי את־נעם ואגדע אתו להפיר את־בריתי אשר כרתי את־כל־העמים: 11 ותפר ביום ההוא וידעו כן עניי הצאן השמרים אתי כי דבר־יהוה הוא: 12 ואמר אליהם אם־טוב בעיניכם הבו שכרי ואם־לא חדלו וישקלו את־שכרי שלשים כסף: 13 ויאמר יהוה אלי השליכהו אל־היוצר אדר היקר אשר יקרתי מעליהם ואקחה שלשים הכסף ואשליך אתו בית יהוה אל־היוצר: 14 ואגדע את־מקלי השני את החבלים להפר את־האחוה בין יהודה ובין ישראל:

10 I took my staff "Pleasant" and smashed it,[27] thereby breaking my covenant which I made with all the peoples.[28] 11 It was broken on that day, and the merchants[29] of the flock who were watching me knew that it was a word of YHWH. 12 Thus I told them: "If it is good in your eyes, give me my wages, and if not, let it be." They weighed my wages: thirty [shekels] of silver. 13 YHWH told me: "Deposit it with the caster [MT: היוצר],[30] this lordly price at

---

[27] In the LXX, vv. 10, 11, and 12a are included in the speech that began in v. 9, with the effect that the main verbs in these verses are translated with future indicatives, as in the case of v. 9 already. For a justification of the translation of the verb גדע with "to smash" here and in v. 14, see Al Wolters, *Zechariah*, HCOT (Leuven: Peeters, 2014), 376.

[28] While it has sometimes been proposed that עמים would refer to Israel here (e.g., Carol L. Meyers and Eric M. Meyers, *Zechariah 9–14: A New Translation with Introduction and Commentary*, AB 25C [New York: Doubleday, 1993], 270–71; Paul L. Redditt, *Zechariah 9–14*, IECOT [Stuttgart: Kohlhammer, 2012], 9–14, 85; Wolters, *Zechariah*, 377–78), this reading seems rather unlikely. The use of the plural form עמים to refer to Israel, while possible, is rare (as admitted, for example, by Meyers and Meyers, *Zechariah*, 271); furthermore, elsewhere in Zech 9–14 the form עמים always refers to other nations, and never to Israel: compare Zech 10:9; 12:2, 3, 4, 6; 14:12. Additionally, as noted by various authors, the reference to other nations makes good sense in the context of Zech 11:4–17, especially following the allusion to the exile in v. 9. For example, see Robert L. Foster, "Shepherds, Sticks, and Social Destabilization: A Fresh Look at Zechariah 11:4–17," *JBL* 126 (2007): 747.

[29] Reading כנעניי (instead of MT כן עניי), "Canaanites" = "merchants," as in v. 7 already. This reading is supported by the LXX in both verses. For a recent and thorough discussion of this issue, see Hervé Gonzalez and Jan Rückl, "*Lectio difficilior potior?* Zacharie 11,7a.11b dans le texte massorétique et la Septante," *Sem* 56 (2014): 333–57; compare also Mark J. Boda, *The Book of Zechariah*, NICOT (Grand Rapids, MI: Eerdmans, 2016), 657.

[30] The MT makes perfect sense if we assume that the text is referring here to the foundry of the temple in Jerusalem (see also Zech 13:7–9; further Mal 3:3–4), and does not need to be corrected to האוצר following the Peshitta. Greek, which reads χωνευτήριον, "(smelting) furnace," also supports the MT's reading. For further discussion of this issue, see, for example, Wolters, *Zechariah*, 383–85; Boda, *Zechariah*, 670. For the presence of a foundry in the temple of Jerusalem during the Persian period, see, for example, Mathias Delcor, "Le trésor de la maison de Yahweh des origins à l'exil," *VT* 12 (1962): 372–77; and more recently Joachim Schaper, "The Jerusalem Temple as an Instrument of the Achaemenid Fiscal Administration," *VT* 45 (1995): 528–39; Hervé Gonzalez, "Zacharie 9–14 et le temple de Jérusalem: Observations sur le milieu de production d'un texte prophétique tardif," *Judaïsme Ancien – Ancient Judaism* 5 (2017): 40–46, 57–61.

which I was valued by them [?]."³¹ I took the thirty [shekels] of silver and deposited them to the House of YHWH, with the caster. 14 Then I smashed my second staff "Bonds," thereby breaking the kinship between Judah and Israel.

As is well known, the interpretation of this section, and especially of vv. 11–13, raises considerable difficulties. In the context of this essay, however, our discussion will focus on the motif of the two staffs in vv. 10 and 14. The smashing of the first staff is identified with the breaking of the covenant made by YHWH with "all the peoples" (v. 10). The interpretation of this motif is disputed, but it presumably refers to the notion that YHWH will no longer protect his people from other nations, as the parallel with Hos 2:20 suggests.³² The breaking of the second

---

31 This remains in our opinion the most likely reading of the Hebrew at this place. Wolters (*Zechariah*, 386–87) proposes that the MT אֶדֶר be repointed אֶדֹּר, and thus be interpreted as a yiqtol first person singular from נדר, "to vow." But the resulting translation ("I will vow the weight I am worth") makes little sense in context and is too far removed from the Hebrew. The meaning of this divine statement remains a complex issue, which has not been fully clarified yet. We agree with Wolters and a few others that the case for reading the divine comment as a derogatory statement has been overstated (for a detailed discussion, see Wolters, *Zechariah*, 382–88); but the idea that that "thirty (shekels) of silver" would serve to refer to YHWH's own value remains awkward, and does suggest that the mention of the "lordly price" (אדר היקר) is intended ironically here. Alternatively, another interpretive option is to assume that the second part of the divine speech switches back to the prophet, who would be the referent of "I was valued by them" (as suggested by Boda, *Zechariah*, 670 note c). This is an interesting solution, but one may note that the distinction between YHWH and the prophet should not be posited too rigidly in this chapter (see already v. 10). In this case, the problem raised by the reference to YHWH being valued by the merchants persists in the line of interpretation as well. In any event, this issue is not decisive for the present argument and may be left open here.

32 For a review of earlier interpretations, see Foster, "Shepherds," 746–48. As argued above (note 27), the plural form עמים must refer here to other nations, and not to Israel. The idea that Zech 11:10 would refer here to the annulment of YHWH's covenant with Israel (e.g., Meyers and Meyers, *Zechariah*, 270–71; Redditt, *Zechariah*, 85; Wolters, *Zechariah*, 377–78) is therefore unconvincing. Admittedly, the nature of the covenant with the peoples mentioned in Zech 11:10 remains difficult to interpret because of the allusive character of this verse. However, the context of Zech 11:4–17 clearly implies that the "inhabitants of the land" will be delivered to other nations (v. 6) and that some of them will be taken into captivity (v. 9). Consequently, on the basis of the parallel with Hos 2:20, the most likely explanation remains that Zech 11:10 refers to the fact that YHWH will no longer protect his people from other nations; see already, for example, Wilhelm Rudolph, *Sacharja 1–8, Sacharja 9–14, Maleachi*, KAT 13 (Gütersloh: Mohn, 1976), 9–14, 208, and more recently Jakob Wöhrle, *Der Abschluss des Zwölfprophetenbuches: Buchübergreifende Redaktionsprozesse in den späten Sammlungen*, BZAW 389 (Berlin: de Gruyter, 2008), 91 and note 85 (with further references to earlier literature). David L. Petersen (*Zechariah 9–14 and Malachi. A Commentary*, OTL [Louisville: Westminster John Knox, 1995], 95–96) proposes that Zech 11:10 involves a reversal of the covenant with Noah in Gen 9: "In Genesis 9, Yahweh

staff, for its part, is identified with the breaking of the "kinship" (אחוה) between Judah and Israel (v. 14). The obvious parallel between the smashing (גדע) of the two staffs in vv. 10 and 14, which frames the development found in vv. 11–13, indicates that the separation between Judah and Israel mentioned in v. 14 is part of a broader scenario of general disruption of the social, economic and political order, already referenced in v. 10. We will have more to say about this below.

Zechariah 11:14 provides us with an important piece of evidence regarding early anti-Samaritan polemics. In fact, there is arguably no other passage in the Hebrew Bible that articulates so clearly the idea of a definitive separation between the two communities. Earlier scholars, such as Gustav Hölscher,[33] Wilhelm Rudolph,[34] or Mathias Delcor,[35] identified this verse as the first reference to the "schism" that would have taken place after the building of the Samaritan sanctuary on Mt. Gerizim which, based on the authority of Josephus,[36] they dated to the last third of the fourth century BCE. However, it is clear now that this interpretation of Zech 11:14, and the underlying reconstruction of the social-historical context for this passage, are problematic in several respects. To begin with, the excavations on Mt. Gerizim have shown that the building of the sanctuary on that site is in fact earlier, going back to the middle of the fifth century BCE.[37] Fur-

---

appears to promise that he will not act as an enemy agent against all humanity, whereas in Zechariah 11, Yahweh indicates that he will let earthly powers operate without control" (ibid., 96). However, as noted by Foster ("Shepherds," 747–48), the parallel with Noah's covenant is not really accurate: contrary to Gen 9, Zech 11 is not concerned with the destruction of humankind in general, but of the Israelites specifically. Foster himself argues that Zech 11:10 should be viewed as an intertextual allusion to texts, such as Isa 42 and 49 which refer to the role of the "Servant" in the liberation of Judean captives. Consequently, the breaking of the first staff would mean "that YHWH reverses the promise to [continue to] bring the Jews back to their homeland from north, south, east and west, from the ends of the earth" (Foster, "Shepherd," 749). However, this reading seems rather unconvincing. The intertextuality with Second Isaiah is weak, and passages, such as Isa 42:6 and 49:8 speak of a "covenant with the people" (ברית עם), not with the "peoples" (עמים). Furthermore, even on the topical level the connection between these texts remains rather vague. The oracles in Isa 42 and 49 are specifically concerned with the repatriation of former captives to the Judean homeland, whereas Zech 11 is more generally concerned with the extermination of the people living in the land (see, esp. Zech 11:9).

33 Gusatv Hölscher, *Palaestina in der persischen und hellenistischen Zeit* (Berlin: Weidmann, 1902), 43.
34 Rudolph, *Sacharja*, 209.
35 Mathias Delcor, "Hinweise auf das samaritanische Schism im Alten Testament," *ZAW* 74 (1962): 285–91.
36 Josephus, *Ant.* 11:321–324.
37 See Yitzhaq Magen, "The Dating of the First Phase of the Samaritan Temple on Mount Gerizim in Light of the Archaeological Evidence," in *Judah and the Judeans in the Fourth Century*

thermore, the idea that the building of the sanctuary on Mt. Gerizim would have been followed by the separation between Jews and Samaritans is contradicted by other writings from the late Persian / early Hellenistic periods, such as Chronicles. As a matter of fact, the separation between the two communities is now commonly viewed as the result of a much longer and significantly more complex process in Antiquity.[38] So the question remains: What is the origin of the concept stated in Zech 11:14, and what historical evidence does it provide for the emergence of anti-Samaritan polemics in the Second Temple period? In our view, this issue can only be properly addressed when Zech 11:14 is re-contextualized in the broader context of Zech 9–14.

To begin with, it is important to observe that the smashing of the two staffs in Zech 11:10 and 14 corresponds to the two main shifts taking place within the collection formed by Zech 9–14.[39] The bulk of this collection consists of three scenarios describing the eschatological war fought by Judah, followed by the eventual restoration of the community: Zech 9–10; 12–13, 14. The obvious differences between these three scenarios at the lexical, stylistic and topical levels strongly suggest that they were successively added, as proposed by Odil Steck and others: each new scenario takes up and revises the previous materials.[40] One major shift between these scenarios concerns the identity of the nations fighting against Judah. In Zech 9–10, the war opposes the "sons of Zion" and the "sons of Iāwān," which refers to the Greeks. But in the following scenarios, Judah's war is now against "all the nations" (כל העמים, Zech 12:2, 3, 6; 14:12), which gather around Jerusalem to capture the city. This shift toward a generalization of the conflict is made clear in Zech 11:10 through the reference to the

---

BCE, ed. Oded Lipschits, Gary N. Knoppers, and Rainer Albertz (Winona Lake, IN: Eisenbrauns, 2007), 157–211; Magen, Mitsgav, and Tsfania, *Inscriptions*.

38 Among recent studies, see Knoppers, *Jews and Samaritans*.

39 For this observation, see already Mark J. Boda, "Reading Between the Lines: Zechariah 11.4–16 in its Literary Contexts," in *Bringing out the Treasure: Inner Biblical Allusion in Zechariah 9–14*, JSOTSup 370, ed. Mark J. Boda and Michael H. Floyd (London: Sheffield Academic Press, 2003) 290–91; idem, *Zechariah*, 672. Few authors, however, have addressed in detail the implications of this observation for the construction of Judean-Samarian relations in Zech 9–14.

40 Odil H. Steck, *Der Abschluss der Prophetie im Alten Testament: Ein Versuch zur Frage der Vorgeschichte des Kanons*, Biblisch-Theologische Studien 17 (Neukirchen-Vluyn: Neukirchen Verlag, 1991), 25–60; and compare James Nogalski, *Redactional Processes in the Book of the Twelve*, BZAW 218 (Berlin: de Gruyter, 1993), 213–47; as well as Paul L. Redditt, "Israel's Shepherds: Hope and Pessimism in Zechariah 9–14," *CBQ* 51 (1989): 631–42. On the structure and composition of Zech 9–14, see also the remarks by Gonzalez, "Zechariah 9–14," 8–12. For an alternative view that identifies layers running throughout the collection comprised in Zech 9–14, see Wöhrle, *Abschluß*, 67–138.

smashing of the staff representing YHWH's covenant with "all the nations" (again with the phrase כל העמים).⁴¹ Note that if, as argued above, the smashing of the first staff refers to the notion that YHWH will no longer protect his people from other nations, this conception would also fit well with the dystopian scenario recounted at the beginning of Zech 14, which describes the capture of the city by foreign nations and the deportation of a portion of the population.⁴² Likewise, the smashing of the second staff in 11:14 highlights the other major transition taking place between Zech 9–10 and 12–14, namely, the disappearance of the northern tribes. The first scenario, in Zech 9–10, still considers a subordinated role for Ephraim (the northern tribes) in the war between the "sons of Zion" and the "sons of Iāwān." According to Zech 9:13, Judah and Ephraim will both serve as the weapons of the divine warrior, YHWH, defending his sanctuary on Mt. Zion.

כי־דרכתי לי יהודה קשת מלאתי אפרים
ועוררתי בניך ציון על־בניך יון ושמתיך כחרב גבור

For I [i.e., YHWH] have bent Judah as my bow and nock it with Ephraim [or: and nock it, Ephraim]: I will arise your [f.] sons, Zion, against your [f.] sons, Iāwān, and wield you [f.] like a warrior's sword.

The relationship between Judah and Ephraim in the first hemistich is not entirely clear. The MT's division takes קשת, "bow," with v. 13aβ rather than 13aα, and this reading has been followed by some authors.⁴³ The LXX, for its part, adopts another division of v. 13a, associating the word "bow" (τόξον) with Judah rather than with Ephraim. In our view, a more compelling solution is to consider that קשת is the object of both the verbs דרך and מלא in v. 13a.⁴⁴ This approach leaves us with two interpretive options (both of which are reflected in the translation proposed above): either "Ephraim" is taken as the indirect object of the verb מלא, or as an apposition to this verb. In the first option, the meaning of v. 13a would be that YHWH will bend Judah as his bow, and "fill" (i.e., nock)

---

41 On the relationship between the use of the phrase כל העמים in Zech 11:10 and in the rest of Zech 9–14, see above note 28.
42 See, especially, Zech 14:1–2, further 14:5.
43 In this case, the first hemistich should be rendered with: "I will bend Judah for myself (or: to me), and fill Ephraim (like) a bow." For this rendering, see, for example, Redditt, *Zechariah 9–14*, 34; but note, however, that in his later comment on this verse (ibid., 45) he apparently adopts the alternative translation presented below, which identifies Judah with YHWH's bow and Ephraim with its arrow.
44 As argued, in particular, by Shalom M. Paul, "A Technical Expression from Archery in Zechariah IX 13a," *VT* 39 (1989): 496.

it with Ephraim. In other words, Judah is identified here with YHWH's bow, while Ephraim is the arrow mounted on the bow.⁴⁵ In the second option, the meaning is different, and both Judah and Ephraim are effectively identified with YHWH's bow. In any case, what is clear is that both Judah and Ephraim, as YHWH's weapons, are apparently subsumed in the second hemistich under the "sons of Zion," at war with the "sons of Iāwān" (v. 13b). Although the context is clearly distinct, the underlying conception presents some striking affinities with the view of Chronicles discussed above: the presence of the northern tribes alongside Judah is legitimate, but only insomuch as they protect the sanctuary on Mt. Zion, and thereby acknowledge its authority. Evidently, this conception implies a subordinated role for Ephraim. This trend, introduced in Zech 9:13, is taken up and developed in Zech 10, where it becomes clear that Judah, which is identified with YHWH's "majestic horse in the battle" (סוס הודו במלחמה, Zech 10:3b), will have the leadership in the upcoming war (Zech 10:4–5), whereas Ephraim's role is described only briefly and in much more modest terms (Zech 10:7).⁴⁶

---

45 This interpretation is adopted by several commentators; see, for example, Wolters, *Zechariah*, 288. As pointed out by Paul ("Technical Expression"), the possibility that the verb מלא is used here as a technical term referring to the fitting of an arrow on a bowstring is supported by the parallel Akkadian idiom *qašta mullû*. Alternatively, Boda (*Zechariah*, 582–83), proposes to interpret v. 13 in the sense that Ephraim, here, is identified with YHWH's hand "mounted" (מלא) on the bow; this interpretation is also adopted by Suk Yee Lee, *An Intertextual Analysis of Zechariah 9–10 – The Earlier Restoration Expectations of Second Zechariah*, LHBOTS 599 (London: Bloomsbury T&T Clark, 2015), 131–32. In this case, the relationship between Judah and Ephraim would be reversed, and Judah (the bow) would be identified with a weapon placed in the hand of Ephraim. However, this reading rests heavily upon the parallel with 2 Kgs 9:24, which, however, has a distinct construction; in the case of Zech 9:13 the idea that the verb מלא should refer to the setting of the bow on the archer's hand, rather than to the setting of an arrow on the bowstring, is not obvious. Boda himself admits that the second reading is in fact equally possible (*Zechariah*, 583). Furthermore, the idea that Ephraim would represent the "hand" of the divine archer, and Judah the weapon in the service of Ephraim, is not consistent with the second half of the verse and, more generally, with the construction of the relationship between Judah and Ephraim in Zech 9–10.

46 In particular, v. 4 raises considerable philological and textual issues, which cannot be discussed in detail here. What is clear, however, is that this verse refers to Judah's leaders, which are then identified in v. 5 with "warriors" (גברים) prevailing over their enemies and putting them to shame because they have YHWH's support. By contrast, in the case of the northern tribes v. 7a merely mentions that "Ephraim will be *like* a *gibbôr* (כגבור)," whose heart is filled with a joy comparable to the intoxication induced by wine. While some authors assume that v. 7 implies that Ephraim will have a role similar to Judah's in the battle (e.g., Redditt, *Zechariah 9–14*, 66; Boda, *Zechariah*, 624), the differences in the wording of vv. 5 and 7 make this conclusion unlikely in our opinion. In any event, the sequence construed by Zech 10 implies that Eph-

In short, the northern tribes are consistently represented in Zech 9–10 as military auxiliary forces assisting Judah, either in the defense of Mt. Zion as the sanctuary of the divine warrior (Zech 9) or in the final victory against YHWH's (and Judah's) enemies (Zech 10). In the following two scenarios of Zech 12–13, and 14, however, the situation has radically changed: the northern tribes are no longer represented as fighting alongside Judah, and the action exclusively takes place in the land of Judah, especially around or in Jerusalem. Accordingly, the pair "Judah/Ephraim" in Zech 9–10 has been consistently replaced with a new pair, "Jerusalem and Judah," which recurs throughout Zech 12–14.[47] Just as Zech 11:10 introduces the shift from the war against "Iāwān" in Zech 9–10 to the war against "all the nations" in chapters 12–14, Zech 11:14 serves to introduce the disappearance of Ephraim as an auxiliary force fighting against Judah and, consequently, the exclusion of the northern tribes from the rewards of the eschatological war.

However, this reading merely accounts for the function of Zech 11:14 within the larger context of Zech 9–14. It does not yet explain the reason for this shift in the role assigned to the northern tribes between Zech 9–10 and 12–14. For this, we must make another observation. The first mention of "Ephraim" in Zech 9–14 (and, for that matter, in the entire book of Zechariah), occurs in Zech 9:10, in the context of a short oracle describing the entry in Jerusalem of a royal figure who will have dominion over a vast kingdom.

9 Rejoice greatly, Daughter of Zion!
Shout aloud, Daughter of Jerusalem!
Lo, your king is coming to you:
He is righteous and delivered (Greek: σῴζων, "savior"!),
Humble and mounted on a donkey—
On a jackass, a purebred.[48]
10 I will (G: he will) remove the chariot from Ephraim,
And the horse from Jerusalem:

---

raim's involvement in the battle will be subsequent to Judah's. More generally, the asymmetry noted here between Judah's and Ephraim's role in the upcoming war may arguably be related to the fact that in the case of the northern tribes, the focus in Zech 10:6–12 seems to lie much more in their repatriation to the homeland (already introduced in v. 6, and continued in vv. 8–12) than in their participation in battle.

[47] See Zech 12:2, 5, 6, 7; 14:14, 21; by contrast, the pair Judah/Jerusalem is never used before Zech 12. The connection between the disappearance of the northern tribes after Zech 9–11 and the introduction of the joint mention of Jerusalem and Judah has already been noted by various authors: see, for example, Redditt, *Zechariah 9–14*, 93.

[48] For this rendering of the Hebrew in the last line of v. 9, see Kenneth C. Way, "Zechariah 9:9 and Lexical Semantics," *JBL* 129 (2010): 105–14; compare also Boda, *Zechariah*, 561 note g.

> The battle-bow will be cut off,
> And he will announce peace to the nations;
> His dominion will be from sea to sea,
> From the River to the ends of the land.

Like other passages in Zech 9–14, this short oracle raises considerable interpretive difficulties, not the least because of the differences between the MT and the LXX regarding the role ascribed to this royal figure.[49] For the present essay, however, a few brief remarks will suffice. Verse 10b, which mentions the king's dominion (משל) takes up almost verbatim Ps 72:8, which describes the extent of Solomon's kingdom.[50] Additionally, as several authors have pointed out, the language used to describe the royal figure in v. 9 is reminiscent of the phraseology already used in some Davidic psalms.[51] This observation, combined with the citation of Ps 72:8 in v. 10b, suggests that Zech 9:9–10 effectively refers to a ruler, presumably of Davidic origins, who will recreate the mythical kingdom associated with the founding figures of David and Solomon.[52] This conclusion, in turn, suggests that the reason why Zech 9–10 consistently represents the northern tribes fighting alongside Judah as they battle the Greeks is because this scenario still retains the expectation of a unified kingdom under a Davidic ruler, at least

---

[49] In the MT, the king is exclusively tasked to "announce peace to the nations", whereas in LXX he is conferred a more active role in the cessation of war. See further on this the remarks in Christophe Nihan, "Utopies royales et origins du messianisme dans la Bible hébraïque," in *Encyclopédie des messianismes*, ed. David Hamidović (forthcoming).

[50] On this aspect of the description of Zech 9:9–10, see, for example, Andreas Kunz, *Ablehnung des Krieges – Untersuchungen zu Sacharja 9 und 10*, Herders Biblische Studien 17 (Freiburg: Herder, 1998), 128–29.

[51] In particular, the reference in the MT to the king being "humble" (עָנִי) and "delivered" (נוֹשָׁע) recalls the language used in various prayers associated with David: see, especially, Ps 12:6; 18:28 and 34:7. On this aspect of the oracle, see, for example, Meyers and Meyers, *Zechariah*, 172–73. Even the wording of the LXX in v. 9, according to which the king is "savior," σῴζων, and not "delivered" as in the MT, finds an echo in some royal psalms, especially Ps 72 (Ps 71 LXX), which refers to the Davidic king as the agent of the people's deliverance (see Ps 72:4, 13 / 71:4, 13 LXX).

[52] Alternatively, some authors have proposed to identify the royal agent described in the oracle as a collective figure, rather than an individual one: see, for example, Petersen, *Zechariah*, 58–9; Kunz, *Ablehnung*, 132. However, there is little textual support for this interpretation. Contrast, for example, the recent treatment by Anthony R. Petterson, *Behold your King: The Hope for the House of David in the Book of Zechariah*, LHBOTS 513 (New York: T&T Clark International, 2009), 135–42; Boda, *Zechariah*, 564–65, who does identify this figure with a Davidic ruler but assumes that it refers to Zerubbabel specifically. The latter suggestion also has little support in the text, and would only make sense with a significantly earlier dating for Zech 9–10 than the one adopted in this essay.

in the present form of these chapters.⁵³ In particular, this interpretation accounts for the fact that the first mention of "Ephraim" in Zech 9–14 occurs precisely in 9:10a, as noted above.

In the following two scenarios (i.e., Zech 12–13 and 14), however, the situation regarding Davidic rulership is markedly distinct. In Zech 14, the third and last scenario, a Davidic ruler is no longer mentioned, and the only form of kingship envisioned corresponds to YHWH's rule in Jerusalem (cf. 14:16–21).⁵⁴ In Zech 12–13, the Davidic dynasty is still mentioned, but its role has been thoroughly re-signified. First, Zech 12 (more exactly, 12:1–13:1)⁵⁵ no longer refers to an individual figure, as in Zech 9:9–10, but to the "house of David" (בית דויד) as a collective entity.⁵⁶ Presumably, in the context of Zech 12–13, this expression refers to a number of associated families that could trace their lineage to David.⁵⁷ Second, the "house of David" is no longer associated with the Davidic kingdom but exclusively with the city of Jerusalem. As a matter of fact, the description of Zech 12:7–13:1, with its repeated reference to "the house of David" and the "inhabitants of Jerusalem" (יושב/יושבי ירושלם),⁵⁸ always in the same order, suggests that the "house of David" represents the group of leading families in Jerusalem. Third, and lastly, it is striking to observe that the role conferred to the house of

---

53 The question of the place of Zech 9:9–10 in the composition of Zech 9–10 is a complex one, which cannot be addressed here. While there is some evidence suggesting that Zech 9–10 is not of one hand, there is no consensus on the reconstruction of the compositional history of these two chapters. For the present argument, it is enough to observe that Zech 9:11–17 cannot predate the oracle in 9:9–10, especially because the second feminine singular address in vv. 11–17 appears to presuppose the reference to Zion and Jerusalem in v. 9.
54 This difference has long been noted by scholars; compare the following comment by Konrad R. Schaefer ("Zechariah 14: A Study in Allusion," *CBQ* 57 [1995]: 72): "The king of 9:9–10 is eclipsed in chap. 14 where all authority is subsumed under YHWH." For a list of further authors holding a similar view, see Petterson, *Behold*, 243 and note 135. Petterson (*Behold*, 243–44) is arguably correct that the two forms of kingship (i.e., Davidic and divine) should not be too readily pitted against each other. The point remains nevertheless that their relationship remains somewhat unclear and ambiguous in the final shape of Zech 9–14, and that in Zech 14 the emphasis is on divine rather than human kingship.
55 The occurrence of the phrase והיה ביום ההוא נאם יהוה צבאות at the beginning of 13:2 signals that, within Zech 12–13, a major break takes place after 13:1.
56 Zech 12:7, 8, 10, 12; 13:1. Significantly enough, this expression does not otherwise occur in Zechariah. Elsewhere in the Hebrew Bible, it is primarily used in Samuel, Kings and Chronicles, where it consistently refers to the Davidic dynasty.
57 For the persistence of the Davidic line after the end of Judean monarchy, see, especially, 1 Chr 3:17–24. For a similar view, compare Boda, *Zechariah*, 707; *contra* Petersen, *Zechariah*, 116.
58 While Zech 12 consistently uses the singular form (יושב ירושלם), Zech 13:1 has the plural (יושבי ירושלם). However, this alternation is not necessarily significant, as the singular form can also take a collective meaning.

David is no longer military or political (at least not explicitly), but strictly *ritual*. Following Judah's and Jerusalem's victory over the nations that besieged the city (12:2–9), the house of David will lead the penitential liturgy in Jerusalem (12:10–14)[59] and will eventually be rewarded with opening a "source" (according to the MT)[60] in the city.

These remarks suggest, therefore, that the definitive separation between Judah and Israel which is announced in Zech 11:14 reflects shifting attitudes toward the tradition of the Davidic kingdom within Zech 9–14. In Zech 9–10 this tradition is still retained, albeit in a revised form, and accordingly the northern tribes (i.e., "Ephraim") are depicted as fighting alongside Judah. In Zech 12–14, however, the notion of a great Davidic kingdom has been abandoned: the Davidic dynasty is exclusively associated with Jerusalem, and the tribe of Judah is no longer allied with the northern tribes during the eschatological war. In this regard, the discourse on the northern tribes in Zech 9–14 is both strikingly similar to, and markedly distinct from, the discourse of Chronicles. In both works, the tradition, or the memory, of a united kingdom under David and Solomon is the key factor in assessing the place and status of the northern tribes vis-à-vis Judah. But in Chronicles, this memory is maintained and even reaffirmed, whereas in Zech 9–14 the expectation of the reunification of Israel with Judah within a Davidic kingdom is gradually revised, and even rejected, in the more recent scenarios that comprise the second part of that collection.

---

59 In Zech 12:10 the house of David is mentioned first as the recipient of the "spirit of favor and supplication" (רוח חן ותחנונים) sent by YHWH to enable the subsequent penitential liturgy. Later, in Zech 12:12–14, the "clan of the house of David" (משפחת בית־דויד) is also mentioned first among the families that mourn the mysterious figure of the "pierced one."

60 The textual situation in this verse (13:1) is admittedly complex. It is difficult to explain the shorter text transmitted by the LXX as the result of either a textual accident or an intentional omission; rather, we must probably assume here that the LXX preserves an alternative, and even, in part perhaps, an earlier version than that of the MT. On the other hand, the LXX reading πᾶς τόπος, "any place," instead of the MT's מקור, "source," is less likely to be original, and may arguably reflect a confusion between *mem* and *resh* (מקור / מקום). In the context of MT's version, the reference to the opening of a "source" in Jerusalem is presumably related first and foremost to the topic of purification from "sin" and "impurity" (e.g., Petersen, *Zechariah*, 123–24), although in the broader ancient Near Eastern context it may also serve to call up additional images of the city's restoration to a mythical state of prosperity and abundance. On the latter aspect, see, for example, the comments by Meyers and Meyers (*Zechariah*, 399): "The idea of a 'fountain' being opened by Yahweh [...] draws upon imagery of Jerusalem as the sacred center of the universe, where the living waters are part of the quasi-mythic character of Zion's everlasting sanctity. This imagery contributes to the eschatological thrust of the oracle and implies that the cleansing wrought by the cosmic waters will be an ongoing feature of the future age, so that Israel's leadership will never again be impure."

While this development within Zech 9–14 is clear, it is more difficult to say what historical factors underlie the rejection of the united kingdom in this collection. Returning to the pivotal account of Zech 11:4–17, the language of this passage does suggest that this development is closely related to the experience of foreign domination in the southern Levant. This point is already indicated by the formulation of v. 6, which refers to the "inhabitants of the land" being delivered "each into the hand of his neighbor *and in the hand of his king*" (ביד־רעהו וביד מלכו).[61] This topic of foreign oppression, which is introduced in v. 6, is then taken up and developed in vv. 15–17. These verses comprise a new sign-act announcing the arrival of a "foolish" shepherd who will feed on his flock instead of protecting his animals (vv. 15–16), followed by a woe oracle against the shepherd (v. 17).[62]

15 ויאמר יהוה אלי עוד קח־לך כלי רעה אולי: 16 כי הנה־אנכי מקים רעה בארץ הנכחדות לא־יפקד הנער
לא־יבקש והנשברת לא ירפא הנצבה לא יכלכל ובשר הבריאה יאכל ופרסיהן יפרק:
17 הוי רעי האליל עזבי הצאן
חרב על־זרועו ועל־עין ימינו
זרעו יבוש תיבש ועין ימינו כהה תכהה:

15 Then YHWH said to me: Take again the equipment of a foolish shepherd. 16 For take note, I am about to raise up a shepherd in the land: he will not care for the ones being wiped out, he will not seek the strays,[63] he will not heal the injured,[64] he will not take care of the bloated [?];[65] but he will eat the flesh of the fat one, and tear off their hooves. 17 Woe to the worthless shepherd[66] forsaking the flock!
A sword against his arm and against his right eye.
His arm will surely wither,
and his right eye will surely go blind.

---

61 It is unclear whether מלכו "his king" takes a singular or a distributive meaning here, and both readings are advocated in the scholarly literature. In our view, however, the obvious parallel in the construction of the phrase ביד־רעהו וביד מלכו suggests that מלכו, like רעהו, has a distributive meaning and therefore refers to a plurality of kings.
62 While some authors have argued that vv. 15–17 form a single unit, it is more satisfactory to distinguish between the sign-act itself in vv. 15–16 and the woe oracle in v. 17. For a recent and detailed assessment of this position, with references to previous scholars, see Boda, *Zechariah*, 677.
63 For this reading of נַעַר in this context, see Wolters, *Zechariah*, 392–93; Boda, *Zechariah*, 675.
64 Possibly, the verb שבר in this context refers to broken limbs specifically; see Boda, *Zechariah*, 675–76.
65 For this reading, see Wolters, *Zechariah*, 394, who proposes to repoint the MT from נִצָּבָה to נְצָבָה, the Niphal participle of נצב, "to swell up."
66 Alternatively, one can also translate "the shepherd of worthless gods," as recently argued by Boda, *Zechariah*, 679.

Based on v. 17, there have been various attempts to relate the "shepherd" mentioned in these verses with a specific historical character. As numerous commentators have observed, however, this interpretation is problematic and leads to no convincing solution.[67] It is more likely, therefore, that the "foolish" or "worthless" shepherd in vv. 15–17 implies a rather general reference to communal leaders rather than to a unique historical figure. Furthermore, various authors have also noted that the description of the shepherd in v. 16 is reminiscent of the earlier description of the "shepherds of Israel" found in Ezek 34:3–4, where it denotes the past rulers of the people:

3 את־החלב תאכלו ואת־הצמר תלבשו הבריאה תזבחו הצאן לא תרעו: 4 את־הנחלות לא חזקתם ואת־החולה לא־רפאתם ולנשברת לא חבשתם ואת־הנדחת לא השבתם ואת־האבדת לא בקשתם ובחזקה רדיתם אתם ובפרך:

3 You [pl.] eat the fat,[68] you wear the wool, you butcher the fat one; but you do not tend the flock, 4 you have not strengthened the weak, you have not healed the sick, you have not bound up the injured, you have not brought the stray back, and you have not sought the lost. With harshness and ruthlessness you have mistreated them (?).[69]

There are clear topical, structural,[70] and even phraseological[71] parallels between the two texts, which make it likely that Zech 11:16 is reusing Ezek 34:3–4. In the case of Ezek 34, however, the critique of the bad shepherds introduces the theme of YHWH's intervention for his people, which includes (among other things) the reestablishment of a Davidic ruler (see 34:23–24).[72] This topic is continued later in Ezek 37, which develops the description of a reunited kingdom governed by a

---

[67] See, for example, the comments by Meyers and Meyers, *Zechariah*, 284.
[68] Following the MT's pointing; alternatively, the consonantal החלב can also be read as "milk" (*heḥālāb*), as per the LXX (γάλα).
[69] The translation of this last clause is difficult. The reading adopted here follows Daniel I. Block, *The Book of Ezekiel – Chapters 25–48*, NICOT (Grand Rapids, MI: Eerdmans, 1998), 25–48, 278.
[70] Namely, both Ezek 34:3b–4a and Zech 11:16 use a series of negations (introduced by לא) to describe the actions of the shepherd(s).
[71] See, especially, the reference to "seeking" (בקש) the lost or the stray; "healing" (רפא) the injured or the sick; the reference to the "injured" animal (נשברת) occurs in both texts, albeit at different places. Additionally, the accusation of "eating (אכל) the flesh of the fat one (הבריאה)" in Zech 11:16b recalls the language used in Ezek 34:3a.
[72] The question of whether the critique of the shepherds in Ezek 34 refers to local (i.e., Israelite) or foreign rulers has been the subject of some dispute. It is arguably preferable to consider that both categories may be included in this designation.

Davidic ruler (37:15–28; cf. esp. 34:23–24 with 37:24–25).⁷³ The reuse of Ezek 34:3–4 in Zech 11 goes, however, in an entirely different direction. While Ezek 34 and 37 foretell the coming of a Davidic figure who will replace the bad kings of the past and reunite the northern tribes with Judah, Zech 11, by taking up the language of Ezek 34:3–4, now declares that YHWH will in fact send a shepherd/king like the bad shepherds/kings of the past. Hence earlier postexilic prophecies of restoration, such as the restoration of the united kingdom in Ezekiel, are here revised considering more recent events related to foreign domination in the southern Levant. This makes perfect sense considering the classical dating of Zech 9–14 in the context of the late Persian and early Hellenistic periods (fourth and third century BCE), that is, at a time of significant political and military transition in the Levant.

To conclude: The aim of this essay was to reexamine two passages from Chronicles and Zech 9–14 that have arguably significant implications for understanding Judean constructions of Samaria in the late Persian and early Hellenistic periods. The previous discussion highlights two broader points for future discussions, which can be briefly summarized here.

First, the comparison between these two passages indicates that we must count with a broad variety of responses, in Judean circles, to the new situation created by the building of the sanctuary on Mt. Gerizim during the middle of the fifth century BCE. Even works like Chronicles and Zech 9–14, which were composed in the same period, in the same sociological setting (the temple of Jerusalem), and perhaps even by the same circles of Levitical scribes,⁷⁴ could promote very different agendas regarding the Samarians. In Chronicles, this agenda corresponds to what we have called here the "cultic annexation" of the north to Jerusalem. In Zech 9–14 (esp. in the second part of that collection), the future of Jerusalem involves a very different scenario: namely, the separation from the north. It should be clear that this is only a sample of the Judean responses to

---

73 On the restoration of Davidic rule in Ezek 34 and 37, and the relationship between these two chapters, see Christophe Nihan, "Reconsidering Davidic Kingship in Ezekiel," in *Leadership, Social Memory and Judean Discourse in the Fifth–Second Centuries BCE*, ed. Diana Edelman and Ehud Ben Zvi, Worlds of the Ancient Near East and Mediterranean (Sheffield: Equinox, 2016), 89–110.

74 The implication of Levitical scribes in the composition of Chronicles has long been recognized, and need not be reassessed here. In the case of Zech 9–14, the evidence is more complex and rests primarily (albeit not exclusively) on the mention of the "house of Levi" in Zech 12:13 and the identification of the "clan of Shimei," which presumably represents a peripheral clan of Levites claiming to descend from Shimei, the son of Gershon and grandson of Levi (cf. Exod 6:17; Num 3:18, 21; 1 Chr 6:2; 23:6–11). For a recent reassessment of this issue, see Gonzalez, "Observations."

the growing rivalry between Judah and Samaria from the Persian period onward, which should be compared with what can be seen in other writings of that time. Moving forward, we would need a new *mapping* of the various ways in which Judean-Samarian relationships have been construed in the postexilic writings considering the archaeological and epigraphic evidence that is available to us.

Second, the comparison between 2 Chr 7:12 and Zech 11:14 also highlights the importance of *memorial traditions* in postexilic Judean constructions of the Samarians, especially regarding the tradition of the Davidic kingdom. In both works, the tradition, or the memory, of a united kingdom under David and Solomon is the key factor in assessing the place and status of the northern tribes *vis-à-vis* Judah. In Chronicles, this memory is maintained and even reaffirmed: consequently, the temple of Jerusalem built by Solomon, identified with Deuteronomy's central place (2 Chr 7:12–16), can serve as the national shrine not only for Judah but also for the northern tribes. In Zech 9–14, on the other hand, the expectation of the reunification of Israel with Judah within a Davidic kingdom is gradually revised and rejected in the more recent scenarios that comprise the second part of that collection (Zech 12–14); and this shift, in turn, is explicitly articulated in the prophetic account of Zech 11:4–17. Here also, a more comprehensive examination of the role played by memorial traditions in the representation of Samaria in Judean writings from the Persian and Hellenistic periods would merit further study.

Raik Heckl
The Composition of Ezra-Nehemiah as a Testimony for the Competition Between the Temples in Jerusalem and on Mt. Gerizim in the Early Years of the Seleucid Rule over Judah*

Ezra-Nehemiah contains a radical interpretation of the Torah from the Jerusalem perspective that enables us to recognize the situation in which it was created. It also testifies to the existence of a different Judaism during the Persian period. In this essay, I want to illuminate the program of the Ezra-Nehemiah composition for a Judaism that is focussed exclusively on Jerusalem. After some methodological remarks I will describe the main steps in the emergence of the Ezra-Nehemiah composition and its intention. Secondly, I want to emphasize especially the function of the Ezra story within Ezra-Nehemiah. In the third part of my work, I will discuss the connection of the older Nehemiah story with the Ezra-Nehemiah composition. The link between Neh 7–8 and Neh 10 shows how and why the authors of the composition made the Nehemiah story part of the larger composition. Two summarizing parts will conclude my essay. In the first part, I wish to reconstruct the discourses of which Ezra-Nehemiah was part and to date these discourses. In the second part, I would like to discuss the hermeneutics of Ezra-Nehemiah with respect to the Torah and the emergence of the canon of the Hebrew Bible.

1 Some Methodological Remarks

The texts of the Hebrew Bible are the authoritative Jewish canon (Tanak) and also the first part of the twofold Christian Bible. However, the *Vorlagen* of the biblical texts as well as the larger compositions did not come into being as canonical or even as authoritative literature.[1] For a long time during their literary

---

* The discussion of Ezra-Nehemiah in light of its historical background is based on my recent investigations. See Raik Heckl, *Neuanfang und Kontinuität in Jerusalem – Studien zu den hermeneutischen Strategien im Esra-Nehemia-Buch*, FAT 104 (Tübingen: Mohr Siebeck, 2016).
1 For such a view, see, for instance, Shemaryahu Talmon, "Heiliges Schrifttum und Kanonische Bücher aus jüdischer Sicht: Überlegungen zur Ausbildung der Größe 'Die Schrift' im Judentum,"

history, the texts were not yet commonly accepted as authoritative texts.[2] Instead, they should rather be regarded as intentional literature: literature that served the aim to impart concepts of identity and to reinforce particular forms of religion. That is the reason why it was possible to work on and with these texts over a long period of time. The literary history shows that the biblical authors used their *Vorlagen* in different ways. Transformations, substitutions, and summarizing excerpts of older literary texts are as likely as redactions and supplementations. If we accept the intentional nature of the biblical texts on different literary levels, it is possible to approach them via a discourse analytical concept. During their literary history, the biblical texts belonged to discourses about the national and religious identity of ancient Israel. Changes in the identity emerged together with – and have been enforced by – changes in the texts. Our problem, however, is mostly that we only possess the ancient texts without particular knowledge about their time of emergence. But considering these texts as fragments of the mentioned discourses enables us to understand the larger discourses to which the texts once belonged. The texts contain hermeneutical strategies that depend on these discourses and which are sometimes connected to the *Vorlagen* upon which the texts are based. That enables us to draw conclusions about these discourses and, paired with our philological observations, to comprehend the intention of the writers, who composed earlier stages of the text (the *Vorlagen*) itself. The exegesis should not work simply in either a synchronic or a diachronic way, but recognize indications for the literary history within the synchronic structure of the text.[3] Different from and in addition to the source criticism the proposed approach is based on the fact that the later authors of the composition had to presuppose that their recipients could know the reworked texts (*Vorlagen*).

---

in *Mitte der Schrift? Ein jüdisch-christliches Gespräch; Texte des Berner Symposions vom 6.–12. Januar 1985*, ed. Martin A. Klopfenstein, JudChr 11 (Bern: Peter Lang, 1987), 58; Uwe Becker, *Exegese des Alten Testaments: Ein Methoden- und Arbeitsbuch*, UTB 2664 (Tübingen: Mohr Siebeck, 2011), 86; Christoph Levin, "Source Criticism: The Miracle at the Sea," in *Method Matters: Essays on the Interpretation of the Hebrew Bible*, ed. Joel M. LeMon and Kent H. Richards, RBS 56 (Atlanta: Society of Biblical Literature, 2009), 41.
2 See Heckl, *Neuanfang und Kontinuität*, 17.
3 It was Eckart Otto who showed that the singular/plural-oscillation in Deuteronomy is a means to provide a theological structure in the service of its hermeneutics (*Deuteronomium 1–11*, HThKAT [Freiburg: Herder, 2012], 261). The literary works of Deuteronomistic authors on the oldest levels of Deuteronomy created and further developed it. See further the discussion of Deut 12 by Eckart Otto, *Deuteronomium 12,1–23,15*, HThKAT (Freiburg: Herder, 2016), 1182.

2 The Recontextualization of the Aramaic Temple Chronicle

The most important step in the emergence of the Ezra-Nehemiah composition was the use and integration of one older literary text – the Aramaic-Temple-Chronicle (Ezra 5:1–6:18).[4] A. Bertholet assumed already in 1902 that within the Aramaic temple chronicle in Ezra 6 there existed an older version of the Cyrus decree than that which is found in Ezra 1:2–4.[5] And if we take into account that the elders of the Jews report the existence and contents of the command of Cyrus to rebuild the temple in Jerusalem to the Persian official Tattenai, there is a second version of the decree besides that of Ezra 1.[6] There are, however, huge differences between these three texts in their contexts. The decree in Ezra 1, in particular, differs very much from both of the passages in the Aramaic temple chronicle. According to the critical analysis of this literary development, it is quite clear that Ezra 1 uses the content of Ezra 5:13–15 and 6:2–5, as well as other information[7] from the account of Ezra 5–6 to create a new form of the decree and its context. But the author of the Ezra-Nehemiah composition not only supplemented the older story by adding some new verses. With the Cyrus decree as an introduction he already anticipates the main contents of the Aramaic tem-

---

[4] Against Julius Wellhausen and W. H. Kosters, Eduard Meyer saw especially the Persian letters as authentic documents and decrees. Scholars followed him by seeing Ezra 5–6 as the older source underlying the Chronicler's work within the book of Ezra. See further Wilhelm Rudolph, *Esra und Nehemia: samt 3. Esra*, HAT 20 (Tübingen: Mohr Siebeck, 1949), 47; Antonius Gunneweg, *Esra*, KAT 19,1 (Gütersloh: Gütersloher Verlagshaus, 1985), 95; Reinhard G. Kratz, *Die Komposition der erzählenden Bücher des Alten Testaments: Grundwissen der Bibelkritik*, UTB 2157 (Göttingen: Vandenhoeck & Ruprecht, 2000), 67.

[5] See Alfred Bertholet, *Die Bücher Esra und Nehemia*, KHC 19 (Tübingen: Mohr Siebeck, 1902), 25.

[6] See Thomas Willi, *Juda, Jehud, Israel: Studien zum Selbstverständnis des Judentums in persischer Zeit*, FAT 12 (Tübingen: Mohr Siebeck, 1995), 51; Baruch Halpern, "A Historiographic Commentary on Ezra 1–6: A chronological Narrative and Dual Chronology in Israelite Historiography," in *The Hebrew Bible and its Interpreters*, ed. William H. Propp, Baruch Halpern, and David N. Freedman, Biblical and Judaic Studies 1 (Winona Lake, IN: Eisenbrauns, 1990), 85; and Maria Häusl, "'Eine Schriftrolle, darin ist geschrieben' (Esr 6,2): Zur Bedeutung der Schriftlichkeit im Buch Esra/Nehemia," in *'Ich werde meinen Bund mit euch niemals brechen!' (Ri 2,1): Festschrift W. Groß*, ed. Erasmus Gaß and Hermann-Josef Stipp, Herders Biblische Studien 62 (Freiburg im Breisgau: Herder, 2011), 183.

[7] See Ralf Rothenbusch, *"...abgesondert zur Tora Gottes hin": Ethnisch-religiöse Identitäten im Esra/Nehemiabuch*, Herders Biblische Studien 70 (Freiburg: Herder, 2012), 108; Heckl, *Neuanfang und Kontinuität*, 45 f.

ple chronicle, and did that in a sharply focussed way.⁸ In my opinion, the Cyrus decree in Ezra 1 serves as a hermeneutical key to Ezra 1–6 generally and to the paraphrase of the Cyrus decree by the elders of the Jews (Ezra 5:13–15) and its memorandum (Ezra 6:2–5) specifically.⁹

The most important feature is that the quotation of the Cyrus decree happens at the level of the narrative and claims thereby higher authority than the supposed later reproductions. In the introduction of the quotation, we find an additional suggestion of how the three versions should be understood by the reader: Ezra 1:1 notes that there were two different channels, an oral and a written, of spreading the royal decree in the Persian empire, which Ezra 1:2–4 supposedly quotes. Ezra 1:1 establishes a direct link to both versions of the decree within the Aramaic temple chronicle. The reader of the Ezra-Nehemiah composition who just got to know the supposedly authentic content of the decree in Ezra 1:1–4 should understand its older versions as an oral reproduction and as something like a written record. The intention of this hermeneutical instrument is to persuade the reader to accept the new contents of Ezra 1 with its theological features as authentic and more reliable than the older versions of the Aramaic temple chronicle that he could know as an independent text.¹⁰

Ezra 1 is, however, part of a larger recontextualization of the original Aramaic temple chronicle. Thus, in Ezra 3:7 and 4:3 the Cyrus decree is mentioned, and it appears to be the basis of all following events. The entire context of Ezra 1–4 seems to be created as the new context of the Aramaic temple chronicle. Thus, some details of the temple chronicle were emphasized. Others became reinterpreted and supplemented. Ezra 1 explains, for instance, who the so-called Sheshbazzar (cf. Ezra 5:14) is and calls him the נשיא ליהודה ("the leader of Judah").¹¹ The recontextualization emphasizes the introduction of the regular cult and the pilgrimage feasts with their festive celebrations. Not only does the

---

8 The author develops the idea that the Cyrus-decree caused a change in the course of salvation history (Heckl, *Neuanfang und Kontinuität*, 390 f.). Its basis is a theological universalism which instrumentalizes the Persian kings. See Heckl, *Neuanfang und Kontinuität*, 365 f, and recently Sebastian Grätz: "Den persischen Herrschern ist von JHWH bewusst und gewollt die Weltherrschaft gegeben, und mit diesem Sachstand ist nun im Positiven wie im Negativen umzugehen" ("Kyroszylinder, Kyrosedikt und Kyrosorakel: Der König als Medium göttlicher Geschichtsmächtigkeit," in *Geschichte und Gott: XV. Europäischer Kongress für Theologie. 14.–18. September 2014 in Berlin*, ed. Michael Meyer-Blanck and Laura Schmitz, Veröffentlichungen der Wissenschaftlichen Gesellschaft für Theologie 44 [Leipzig: Evangelische Verlagsanstalt, 2016], 349 f.).
9 See Heckl, *Neuanfang und Kontinuität*, 55 ff.
10 In the new composition of Ezra 1–6, the discovery of the memorandum in Ezra 6:2–5 becomes the etiology of the Cyrus-decree in Ezra 1:2–4. See Heckl, *Neuanfang und Kontinuität*, 56.
11 See Heckl, *Neuanfang und Kontinuität*, 45.

cult begin after preparing the altar right before the beginning of the building process itself, but the building of the temple is double framed by Ezra 3 and Ezra 6 through the pilgrimage feasts and festive celebrations.¹² Ezra 3 and 6:16–21 form a concentric structure¹³:

A Pilgrimage feast (Ezra 3:6)
   B Festive beginning of the temple building (Ezra 3:8–10)
   B Festive conclusion of the temple building (6:16–18)
A Pilgrimage feast (6:19–21)

In the context of the temple building story of Ezra 1–6, chapter 4 is a retarding element.¹⁴ Since the language changes in this chapter from Hebrew to Aramaic and since the whole chapter forms a contrast to the visit of Tattenai in Jerusalem and to the reactions of Darius in Ezra 6, it is a central part of the recontextualization of the older Aramaic passage of the temple building and now serves as its introduction. Indirectly, Ezra 4 shows the Persian king in a disgraceful light because he only acts in response to accusations.¹⁵

In its present form the Aramaic temple chronicle fits within its context so seamlessly that literary criticism does not seem to be able to reconstruct its original beginning, as R. G. Kratz notes with some regret.¹⁶ In my opinion, it is indeed impossible to reconstruct the beginning, because Ezra 5:1 f. was completely rewritten in order to harmonize the content of the original Aramaic temple chronicle with the information taken from the books of Haggai and Zechariah. Besides mentioning both of these postexilic prophets, the most important indi-

---

12 Ezra 3 and 6:16–21 form a concentric structure: Ezra 3:6 (pilgrimage feast) > 3:8–10 (festive beginning of the temple building) – 6:16–18 (festive conclusion of the temple building) > 6:19–21 (pilgrimage feast). See further Heckl, *Neuanfang und Kontinuität*, 194.
13 See further Heckl, *Neuanfang und Kontinuität*, 194.
14 See Heckl, *Neuanfang und Kontinuität*, 100; Grätz, "Kyroszylinder," 349.
15 See Heckl, *Neuanfang und Kontinuität*, 190. In spite of the use of some of the Persian kings as pious servants of the God of Israel, the Ezra-Nehemiah composition contains again and again a hidden critique of the Persian domination. Julius Wellhausen already saw Ezra-Nehemiah more or less dealing with a situation under the Persian rule: "Man wohnte zwar wieder im Lande der Väter, aber das persische Joch, weil es den Verheißungen so gänzlich widersprach, wurde drückender empfunden, als vordem das chaldäische. Die Krisis war eingetreten und doch war alles beim Alten geblieben, das Gefängnis war gewandt und doch mußte die eigentliche Wendung erst kommen" (*Israelitische und Jüdische Geschichte* [Berlin: de Gruyter, 1921], 155 f.). It seems to me that E. Meyer's assertion, that Ezra 1–6 contained authentic documents, was still influential more than 100 years later, so that these critical voices could not be heard.
16 See Kratz, *Komposition*, 56; Heckl, *Neuanfang und Kontinuität*, 124.

cation of the harmonization is, that Zerubbabel and Jeshua seem to determine the plot of the Aramaic temple chronicle, because they are, as in chapters Ezra 2, 3, and 4, mentioned in its introduction (Ezra 5:2). But differently from Ezra 2–4 the already mentioned tension between Zerubbabel (Ezra 5:2), Sheshbazzar (Ezra 5:14), and the nameless mentioning of the governor of the Jews (Ezra 6:7) testifies that Zerubbabel, Joshua together with Haggai and Zechariah were introduced from the content of the prophetic books.[17]

The direct frame of the Aramaic source by Ezra 4 and Ezra 6:19–21 is of utmost importance in order to understand the pragmatics of Ezra 1–6. Ezra 4:2 introduces adversaries which offer their support in the rebuilding process. Since the 19th century, scholars believe that these people refer to the Samarians.[18] In spite of their offered support, they are regarded as foreign people who have settled in the region because of Assyrian imperial policy.

After Zerubbabel rejects their help, Ezra 4 becomes a story about intrigues, bribery, and defamation aiming at the disruption of the building process. Several letters are mentioned and one is quoted as an example in Ezra 4:8–24. Scholars interpret it as a misplaced passage about the building of the city and its walls. It concludes that it is something like the prehistory of the Nehemiah story because only this third part of Ezra-Nehemiah discusses the building of the walls.[19] This view, however, does not sufficiently take the present context into account. The letter contains the accusation that inhabitants of the rebellious city had started rebuilding the city, working toward the completion of the walls and the repair of the foundations. It is possible to assume from this repeatedly presented reproach that it deals with the building of the city walls. However, this becomes nowhere explicit because the phrases in Ezra 4:12, 13, 16 do not contain a clarifying suffix which connects the walls with the city. Furthermore, the accusation is based on blaming Jerusalem's past as being the reason for its destruction. The reproach

---

[17] So earlier Kratz, *Komposition*, 59f.
[18] See Eduard Meyer, *Die Entstehung des Judentums: Eine historische Untersuchung* (Halle: Niemeyer, 1896), 40f.; Charles C. Torrey, *Ezra Studies* (Chicago: The University of Chicago Press, 1910), 326; Gustav Hölscher, "Die Bücher Esra und Nehemia," in *Die Heilige Schrift des Alten Testaments: 2. Hosea bis Chronik*, ed. Emil Kautzsch, HSAT (Tübingen: Mohr Siebeck, 1923), 491; Gunneweg, *Esra*, 79f.
[19] See Meyer, *Entstehung*, 56f., and for the recent discussion, Rothenbusch, "...abgesondert," 57f. Oded Lipschits used Ezra 4:7–24 as a testimony for "an attempt to build fortifications around Jerusalem during the reign of Artaxerxes I, before the arrival of Nehemiah" ("Achaemenid Imperial Policy, Settlement Processes in Palestine and the Status of Jerusalem in the Middle of the Fifth Century B.C.E.," in *Judah and the Judeans in the Persian period*, ed. Oded Lipschits and Manfred Oeming [Winona Lake, IN: Eisenbrauns, 2006], 39).

generally remains unclear and it is obviously based on the Deuteronomistic History, which reveals the letter as a constructed accusation.

It is striking that the accusations are connected to the decree of Cyrus in Ezra by the phrase די יהודיא די סלקו מן לותך עלינא ("that the Judeans who came up to us from you") in Ezra 4:12. Because the letter presupposes that the king already knows about Cyrus' decree, the accusation could not deal with the building of the temple. According to the decree of Cyrus, the building of the temple was not only allowed, but also expressly desired. In order to make the king act against the Jews and the temple building, the letter had to resort to other felonies of the Jews in Jerusalem. The ancient addressees, however, should recognize that the accusations are constructed as an attempt of the Samarians – successful for the time being – to prevent the Judeans from building the temple. Thus, the Samarians with their attempts to hinder the realization of the Cyrus decree became responsible for delaying the completion of the temple by an outrageous charge. With reference to the so-called adversaries in Ezra 4:2, the constructed blaming letter not only explains the delay of the temple building, but also testifies to the legitimacy and the early beginnings of the Jerusalem temple. Furthermore, it emphasizes the continuity of the famous history of Jerusalem by mentioning the great kings that ruled over the land at the other side of the Euphrates.[20]

The various self-introductions of the adversaries in Ezra 4:2 and of the originators of the letter in Ezra 4:9–10 consistently show the adversaries as strangers, but with different identities and with conflicting views of their history. However, we must see both self-introductions as perspective voices. They are explicitly not part of the narrative context, but are utterances of characters. That the adversaries introduce themselves twice in different ways in this context serves as a signal. The intended addressees should, on the one hand, notice their discrepancy and, on the other, understand the existing temple on Mt. Gerizim as an illegitimate cultic place built by non-Israelites who took it upon themselves to offer sacrifices to the God of Israel.[21] In order to understand the passage, the perspective is crucial. Utterances of characters, such as those found in the accusatory letter, cannot be seen as testimonies for a following argument about the building process of the city, even if the context was inspired by the controversies depicted in the older Nehemiah account. Neither can they be used as evidence for the assumption of S. Japhet and others, that the Ezra-Nehe-

---

20 Heckl, *Neuanfang und Kontinuität*, 98 f.
21 In *Ant.* 12.257, Josephus already interprets the context in this way: "They also said they were colonists from the Medes and Persians, and they are, in fact, colonists from these peoples" (καὶ λέγοντες αὐτοὺς Μήδων ἀποίκους καὶ Περσῶν καὶ γάρ εἰσιν τούτων ἄποικοι).

miah composition presupposes that Samaria was inhabited by foreign people since the time of the Neo-Assyrian Empire.[22]

Differently from the perspective embodied in 2Kings 17 and coherent with the idea of Chronicles,[23] Ezra 1–6 presupposes that there are Israelites among other people in the areas outside the Judean territory. These are the people who separate themselves from the uncleanliness of the gentiles and take part in the Passover celebration at the rebuilt temple (Ezra 6:21). The participation of these Israelites is connected to the Passover feast under Hezekiah and Josiah. As in 2 Chr 30:1 ff. and 35:18, the arrival of some inhabitants of Samaria indicates the legitimacy of the Jerusalem temple. So does the arrival of some of the Samarian people in Ezra 6:21. It shows that the Jerusalem temple was rebuilt by the returnees very early and is supposed to represent the elected cultic place.

Ezra 1–6 is, therefore, a comprehensive recontextualization of the Aramaic chronicle of the building of the temple, which was harmonized according to information from the books of Haggai and Zechariah. Its author did not have an historical interest, but accepted the basic relevance of these Jewish texts and tried to create innovations by their recontextualization in new literary contexts. The background of his innovations was a culmination of the conflict between Jerusalem and Samaria.

3 Ezra and the Torah

By using the Cyrus decree, the beginnings of the regular cult and the building of the temple are claimed to have happened just after the end of the exile. The text aims to prove that the temple of Jerusalem is the legitimate cult place. This is

---

22 See Sara Japhet, "The Relationship Between Chronicles and Ezra-Nehemiah," in *Congress Volume, Leuven, 1989*, ed. John A. Emerton, VTSup 43 (Leiden: Brill, 1991), 256 f.; Erhard Blum, "Volk oder Kultgemeinde? Zum Bild des nachexilischen Judentums in der alttestamentlichen Wissenschaft," *Neukirchener Theologische Zeitschrift* 10 (1995): 30.
23 Differently from the perspective evident in 2 Kgs 17, the book of Chronicles (1 Chr 5:25 f.) mentions a deportation of the Reubenites, the Gadites, and half of the tribe Manasseh by the Assyrians as a punishment from Yhwh. Possibly 2 Kgs 17 is a polemical enhancement of an earlier literary account which the writer of 1 Chr 5:25 f. knew; see Heckl, *Neuanfang und Kontinuität*, 212 f. Regarding the ideology of the empty land, see Hans M. Barstad, *The Myth of the Empty Land: A Study in the History and Archaeology of Judah During the "Exilic" Period*, SO 28 (Oslo: Scandinavian University Press, 1996), 77 ff. There is evidence to challenge the view of Japhet (*Relationship*, 306) that Chronicles used Ezra-Nehemiah as a source. See Heckl, *Neuanfang und Kontinuität*, 387–97 (summary). Instead, the Ezra-Nehemiah composition, by creating Ezra 1–4, built a bridge between the already existing Chronicles and the Aramaic temple chronicle.

done by asserting the continuity of the place (Ezra 1:3–5; 3:1), by an interpretation of the Pentateuch from a Jerusalem perspective (Ezra 3:2, 4), by emphasizing the order of the Persian kings (Ezra 1:2–4), and by the testimony of the alleged adversaries (Ezra 4:1f.). The opening of the Ezra-story has a similar function: It starts with the genealogy of Ezra (Ezra 7:1ff.) which serves to connect Jerusalem and the Torah directly through Ezra. Differently from the position of J. Pakkala,[24] I do not view it as an originally independent story.[25] Ezra is introduced by a genealogy that connects him to Aaron and follows the line of high priests from the Second Temple period. Genealogies legitimate persons, people, or institutions, Ezra 7:1ff. serves in that sense to directly connect Jerusalem and the Torah through Ezra.[26] Among all people who appear in Ezra 7:1–5, Ezra is the only one who is not a high-priest, but he is the son of the last high priest at the First Temple and therefore the potential high-priest of the exilic period. Ezra, as the person who goes up to Jerusalem with the Torah in his hands (Ezra 7:14: בדת אלהך די בידך), is also the grandson of Hilkiah the high-priest who discovered the Torah in the temple during the reign of Josiah. Ezra, being the scribe of God's law and the grandson of Hilkiah, establishes a direct continuity of the relationship between the Torah and Jerusalem.[27] Indirectly, the text suggests that Seraiah, the father of Ezra, took the Torah with himself into exile. Thus, Ezra can bring it back to Jerusalem to its rightful place where he, Ezra, reads it aloud to the public in the narrative of Nehemiah 8.

Because of form and content related indications, there is no reason to eliminate the genealogy of Ezra as the starting point of the story, as Pakkala proposes. Such a literary operation would prevent us from understanding that the character of Ezra serves the same aim as the Cyrus decree and the early return of the Judeans to Jerusalem. With the Ezra-figure, the authors built a direct connection to the preexilic period. The narrated Ezra according to Ezra 7ff., however, cannot be thought of as a figure of the fifth or even fourth century but much earlier. The position of Ezra explains the strange view of postexilic history by mentioning the

---

[24] See Juha Pakkala, *Ezra the Scribe: The Development of Ezra 7–10 and Nehemiah 8*, BZAW 347 (Berlin: de Gruyter, 2004), 179.
[25] I follow Kratz, *Komposition*, 94; Jacob L. Wright, *Rebuilding Identity: The Nehemiah-Memoir and its Earliest Readers*, BZAW 348 (Berlin: de Gruyter, 2004), 87f.
[26] Raik Heckl, "Esra als Hohepriester und die Verkündigung der Tora im Lichte einer Notiz bei Hekataios von Abdera," *Leqach* 9 (2009): 76ff.; Heckl, *Neuanfang und Kontinuität*, 223.
[27] Heckl, *Neuanfang und Kontinuität*, 232.

Persian kings in Ezra 4–7. It is not possible to connect them with our knowledge about Persian rule from Herodotus and other sources.[28]

According to Ezra 1–6 and 7–8, it seems that Ezra went up to Jerusalem shortly after the building of the temple, leading to an early introduction of the Torah. In that way the Ezra-story uses another decree that can easily be seen as the continuation of the fictional documents in Ezra 1–6. The form and language of all the so-called Artaxerxes firman in Ezra 7 point to a Hellenistic time of composition, as S. Grätz has pointed out.[29] It is also of importance because the foreign ruler makes himself a worshiper of the God of Israel and a supporter of his cult and the community of the returnees. In that way the text does not have anything to do with the so-called imperial authorization of the Torah,[30] but is a legend that explains how a pious Persian emperor ensured that the Torah came back to its rightful place and served its rightful function. It is possible in this text to detect hopes, which had been arising since the beginning of the Hellenistic era. The kings would support the cult and the worship of the only God, which we find, for instance, in the story of Alexander's visit to Jerusalem[31] and in the letter of Aristeas.

Ezra 7, however, overemphasizes these hopeful expectations unrealistically because Ezra does not only receive an autonomy in the jurisdiction, but also the free usage of the financial resources of the province.[32] With that view of the Ezra-story, the observation of R. G. Kratz is proved: There is no subject in the Ezra story independent from the Nehemiah story.[33] Most likely, Ezra is portrayed as the forerunner of the pious governor and more important than him.

---

28 One would expect the mentioning of Cambyses and also a different order. See Heckl, *Neuanfang und Kontinuität*, 376. Because of these chronological problems, Torrey (*Ezra-studies*, 38) suggested at the beginning of the 20th century that Ezra-Nehemiah mentioning Darius already focussed on the alleged Darius the Mede who preceded Cyrus. In my opinion, however, we can only be sure that this later Jewish concept is present in 1 Esdras. See Raik Heckl, "Die Gotteserkenntnis und das Bekenntnis des Darius in Dan 6,27 f. (LXX) als inhaltliches Zentrum von 1Esdras: 1Esdras als Metatext in der spätnachexilischen Literatur," in *Gotteserkenntnis in der Septuaginta*, ed. E. Dafne, WUNT 387 (Tübingen: Mohr Siebeck), 2017.
29 See Sebastian Grätz, *Das Edikt des Artaxerxes: Eine Untersuchung zum religionspolitischen und historischen Umfeld von Esra 7,12–26*, BZAW 337 (Berlin: de Gruyter, 2004), 295.
30 Against Peter Frei, "Zentralgewalt und Lokalautonomie im Achämenidenreich," in *Reichsidee und Reichsorganisation im Perserreich*, ed. Peter Frei and Klaus Koch, OBO 55 (Freiburg: Universitätsverlag, 1996), 6–131.
31 Josephus' story (*Ant.* 11, 326–329) starts with Alexander's intent to punish Jerusalem. It closes with his sacrifices to the God of Israel, with the bestowal of great honours to the priests and the permission to observe their country's laws, amongst others.
32 See Heckl, *Neuanfang und Kontinuität*, 268.
33 See Kratz, *Komposition*, 78.

At the same time, the author of the composition connected a second return to Ezra, according to the pattern of Ezra 1–6. So the Ezra-story serves not only to anticipate and go beyond the Nehemiah story, but also to connect the two main subjects of the temple and the Torah.

4 The Returnees as Builders of the Temple and the Community of the Covenant on the Basis of the Torah

The report of the return of the Judeans and Benjaminites after the Cyrus decree (Ezra 1f.) defines the group responsible for the new beginning, or better, for the continuation of the history of God with Jerusalem. The reason for placing the emphasis on Jerusalem and the returnees is the existence of the temple on Mt. Gerizim and the competing community in Samaria. It suggests that the rival temple was erected by the adversaries and most importantly later than the one in Jerusalem.

Scholars have been speculating about the original function of the list of the returnees (Ezra 2) since the end of the 19th century.[34] Up to now, it has become clear that the number of people exceeds by far the number of inhabitants of Judah in the early Persian era as far as we know from archaeological surveys. From form and content, the list, however, must have been a recontextualized passage. Its frame makes one expect a list of people responding to the call of Cyrus but its content is rather a statistical register of the regional population. Ezra 2 seems to not only focus on Yehud because it contains some place names which are situated outside the Judean territory.[35] The list must have had a connection to the temple of Jerusalem as the last verses show (Ezra 2:68f.). Its reuse as the list of the returnees made it most likely necessary to delete some names of places and persons which contradicted its new context. Accordingly, now only the returnees are claimed to be building the temple. That

---

[34] Regarding the research on Ezra 2, see Heckl, *Neuanfang und Kontinuität*, 58ff.
[35] According to Diana V. Edelman, Lod and Ono (Ezra 2:33//Neh 7:37) only became part of the Hasmonean territory during the second century BCE, and both places are near Samaria (*The Origins of the 'Second' Temple: Persian Imperial Policy and the Rebuilding of Jerusalem* [London: Equinox, 2005], 243).

could be the reason why the total number of names of the list is much higher than the sum of the mentioned groups.[36]

The literary connections between Ezra 1 and 3 and the Aramaic temple chronicle lead directly to an answer as to from where the list was taken.[37] The Aramaic temple chronicle (Ezra 5 f.) is structured by two main questions of the Persian official, Tattenai: At first, he asks by whom the permission to build the temple was given and, secondly, who the responsible people were. The first question was answered by paraphrasing the command of Cyrus, but the second question remains unanswered, although Tattenai states that he wrote down the names in order to send them to the king. However, there is no trace of such a list in the context of Ezra 5 or 6. The solution is that the list of Ezra 2//Neh 7 is taken from the Aramaic temple chronicle. Like other details of this passage it was used in a shortened form at the beginning of Ezra-Nehemiah and included in Ezra 2. It had to be shortened in order to fit into the new context and to create a new coherence. As Cyrus's decree in Ezra 1 overshadows the mention of his commands in Ezra 5 f. the list in Ezra 2 tries to persuade the readers who could still know the original list that the new form and its new compositional context are more reliable. While it was originally supposed to be written by the Persian official, Tattenai, it now becomes a part of the narrative, and as such, claims to be more trustworthy.

It is likely that the list was translated into Hebrew just like the other information of the Aramaic temple chronicle that were reused in Ezra 1.[38] In that way a list of the temple builders became the register of the returnees who immediately started building the temple after their return from the exile.

There is, however, a second reason for this recontextualization. After Ezra 2 the list was inserted yet another time in Neh 7. After the building of the city walls Nehemiah decides to carry out a census because very few people lived in Jerusalem. But then he finds a list, and so the census can be cancelled (Neh 7:5b). The subsequent quotation (Neh 7:6–72) shows that it is the list from Ezra 2. The fact,

---

36 Interestingly, the rabbinic sources explain the difference by regarding the others to have belonged to different tribes. Compare Seder Olam Rabbah 29 and see Henreich W. Guggenheimer, *Seder Olam: The Rabbinic View of Biblical Chronology* (Lanham: Rowman & Littlefield, 2005), 247.
37 Concerning the details, see Heckl, *Neuanfang und Kontinuität*, 177 ff.
38 There are, however, several Aramaic forms of the names in the list, which support the conclusion that the list was originally written in Aramaic, just as the Aramaic temple chronicle still is. According to David Marcus the entire book of Nehemiah could originally have been written in Aramaic. See David Marcus, "Is the Book of Nehemiah a Translation from Aramaic?" in *Boundaries of the Ancient Near Eastern World: A Tribute to Cyrus H. Gordon*, ed. Meir Lubetski, Claire Gottlieb, and Sharon R. Keller, JSOTSup 273 (Sheffield, England: Sheffield Academic Press, 1998), 104–10.

that it could be used instead of the census shows that it is supposed to establish a personal and a temporal connection between the time of the return and Nehemiah's time. At first a connection with the so-called synoicism seems natural. However, in Neh 11 the synoicism takes place by an election with a lottery. It logically follows that the demographic policy cannot be the reason for the quotation. One reason is rather that the character Nehemiah from the older Nehemiah story becomes a witness of the recontextualized and reformulated list (Ezra 2) and hence he witnesses the literary concept of the return and the building of the temple in Ezra 1–6.[39] In that way the older text suggests the age and the special importance of the new composition with the list. Another reason is that the list should serve as a hermeneutical key also in the Nehemiah story. It is now the starting point for the story of presenting the Torah to the public. The narrative interestingly starts with the same words as the narrative of the altar building in Ezra 3. That, however, has not been done by a careless interpolator who did not realize that he quoted the first sentence of the following story.[40] Instead, the seventh month is necessary for the Nehemiah context, too. Thus, it starts close to the festival of the booths when entire Israel gathers. This time, however, the reason is not the building of the temple but the reading of the Torah according to Moses' command in Deut 31. And as in Ezra 3 the people present in Neh 7f. are now connected to the return. For the following context Neh 7 suggests again that it is only returnees and their descendants who are present. Hence, the quotation links the different parts of the Ezra-Nehemiah composition very closely and binds all events to the returnees in order to portray them as the entire Israel.

If we agree that there is a connection between the return of the Torah through the figure of Ezra and the presentation of the Torah in Neh 8 the emphasis on the returnees also affects the covenant in Neh 10. Through the preceding scenery of the presentation of the Torah the covenant and the arrangements on the basis of the Torah become dependent on its reading. In that way, the commitment in Neh 10 becomes a quintessential acceptance of the Torah. In my opinion the procedure is similar to that in the recontextualization of the Aramaic temple chronicle. A partial acceptance of the commandments of the Torah by a clearly confined public becomes a general acceptance of the Torah.

It is significant that there are many names in Neh 10 which already appear in the list of Neh 7 (and Ezra 2). That is an indication of a partially identical com-

---

[39] This observation was made by Wright: "Nehemiah discovers 'the book of the genealogies of those who came up first' (7:5b), which he employs to enroll the residents of the newly built Jerusalem (7:6ff.), nowhere else than in Ezra 1–6, as Spinoza proposed long ago" (*Rebuilding Identity*, 303).
[40] Neh 7:72b; 8:1a is parallel to Ezra 3:1 with the exception of the location information.

munity.⁴¹ So Neh 7 f. together with the older covenant text in Neh 10 repeats what we have seen in Ezra 7 with the return of Ezra. The events of the building of the walls, the presentation of the Torah and the covenant are placed relatively close to the end of the exile. The quotation of Ezra 2 in Neh 7 and the consequent presence of the entire Jewish population make the people who accept the covenant in Neh 10 to be the community of the first returnees, who are still alive, and their descendants. And as Jerusalem appears as the elected place for the temple, the presentation of the Torah is also inseparably linked to Jerusalem. In that way no legitimate use and interpretation of the Torah in Samaria remains possible.

5 The Book of Ezra-Nehemiah as a Programmatic Text in the Conflict between Jerusalem and Samaria

The book of Ezra-Nehemiah is a late postexilic programmatic text. Its intention is to show the return from the Babylonian exile, the Jerusalem temple, and the Jerusalem interpretation of the Torah as the only foundations of postexilic Israel. Its background is the argument with and against the community which arose around the temple on Mt. Gerizim as their religious centre. The new beginning is based on an allegedly unbroken continuity of the election of Jerusalem and on a corresponding interpretation of the Torah, and is directed against the other temple and its interpretation. The various reasons given for the election of Jerusalem are quite conspicuous and show the actuality of the conflict: why are the references to the election of Jerusalem, the command of Cyrus as the will of God, the temple equipment, and the offer of the alleged adversaries used to testify to Jerusalem's claim of election? And why is the interpretation of the Torah, which is linked to Jerusalem, supposed to have started very early with the community of the returnees?

The repeated justification of Jerusalem's legitimacy can only mean that the election of Jerusalem had not been self-evident at the time when Ezra-Nehemiah was composed. My view is that in the time of the Diadochi, Jews of Jerusalem connected to its shrine intensified their efforts to show that it was the correct place of worship instead of Mt. Gerizim.⁴² The Ezra-Nehemiah composition in-

---

41 See Heckl, *Neuanfang und Kontinuität*, 340 ff. According to Gunneweg, the repeated names demonstrate the continuity, and together with the new names Neh 10 is an etiology for a new situation (*Nehemiah*, 133 f.).
42 Concerning the discussion of the time of origin, see Heckl, *Neuanfang und Kontinuität*, 403 ff.

tended to commit the Jews/Israelites in Palestine and in the diaspora to the temple in Jerusalem or rather to detach them from the temple on Mt. Gerizim. In my opinion, it is likely that the respective temples had financial interests in gaining support from the diaspora. And without doubt many argumentative efforts were needed to attract members of the competing community to be loyal to Jerusalem. That was the intention of the Ezra-Nehemiah composition for the Jews in Palestine and in the diaspora. The context from which these conflicts arose must have been a community to which the Israelites or Jews of Samaria and Judah both belonged. Because of this background one can assume that the building of the Jerusalem temple did not necessarily precede the existence of the temple on Mt. Gerizim.

The political background of these developments cannot have been the imperial policy of the Persians, but it must have been the attempts of the Jews of Jerusalem to gain some autonomy for Judah and Jerusalem with the temple as its centre. Concessions were granted several times, and possibly already since the destruction of Samaria by Alexander, the Jews of Jerusalem could enjoy positive developments. The most positive concession of a general tax reduction and other privileges was given by Antiochus III.[43] The situation is connected to the time of the Persians, although it was composed in the Hellenistic era, because it should legitimate the later possession of the Jerusalem temple.[44] In that way, it is presented as if its wealth stems from the donations of past kings and from the voluntary gifts of the Judean people. In my opinion these are strategies to legitimate the possessions of the Jerusalem temple against the withdrawal of the privileges granted earlier by the Seleucid empire. We have to remember that the Seleucids had to pay a huge tribute to the Romans after the battle of Magnesia. In my opinion there seems to be a connection to the events reported in 2 Macc 3:4ff. in the so-called Heliodorus affair.[45] The Ezra-Nehemiah composition created a projection into the past of the Persians for this development possibly because of the incalculability of the Seleucid policy and the non-binding nature of their promises.[46]

---

43 See the comparison between Ezra 7:12–26 and Josephus, *Ant.* 12.138–144 by Grätz, *Das Edikt*, 144ff.
44 See Heckl, *Neuanfang und Kontinuität*, 407f.
45 Ibid.
46 See Heckl, *Neuanfang und Kontinuität*, 408.

6 The Interpretation of the Pentateuch to which Ezra-Nehemiah Reacts

The main authority in the background of the discourse with Samaria to which the composition of Ezra-Nehemiah belonged seems to be the Pentateuch. Its acceptance is used to show that an interpretation of the Torah from the Jerusalem perspective was the only appropriate perspective to the interpretation of the Torah. The focus is of course on the holy place: Following, for instance, the reports of Chronicles on the Passover of Hezekiah and that of Josiah (2 Chr 30:11; 35:18), Ezra-Nehemiah claims that only the Jerusalem cult is in accordance with the Torah. It is, however, significant that the Pentateuch itself does not claim to be connected to one particular place. And if we take the great efforts by Ezra-Nehemiah into account, there must have been other interpretations available. Even in the Deuteronomistic historical books, the election of Jerusalem is not yet fixed in the way it is in Ezra-Nehemiah. In Joshua to 1 Kings a conceptual succession of places plays a predominant role in which the election of the place was expressed by the continuity of the cultic vessels, especially the Ark of Covenant. And the end of 2 Kings, which narrates the destruction of the temple of Jerusalem, indicates an end of the time of this holy place. In my opinion, the permanent election of Jerusalem could not be claimed without doubt after the destruction of the Jerusalem temple.[47] We have to take into account that the Deuteronomistic movement was housed in Palestine,[48] and that Haggai and Zechariah did still not know that Jerusalem and Judah were empty during the exile. In the Aramaic papyri from Elephantine the governors and officials of the provinces of Judah and Samaria worked together in religious matters. The existence of two temples in which the same Torah was introduced during the Persian era fits very well to the concept that after the exile no certainty existed about the place where God would continue his election. If we also bear in mind that Jerusalem and Yehud stood in the shadows of the more influential Samaria[49] and that the introduction of the Torah must

---

[47] In my monograph, I expressed the view that Jeremiah's attitude against Jerusalem might have been playing an important role in the emergence of this concept. See Heckl, *Neuanfang und Kontinuität*, 416.
[48] See Timo Veijola, *Verheissung in der Krise: Studien zur Literatur und Theologie der Exilszeit anhand des 89. Psalms*, Annales Academiae Scientiarum Fennicae, ser. B 220 (Helsinki: Suomalainen Tiedakatemia, 1982), 198 ff.
[49] See Wolfgang Zwickel, "Jerusalem und Samaria zur Zeit Nehemias – Ein Vergleich," *BZ* 52 (2008): 220.

have been a compromise, as C. Nihan pointed out,[50] the building of the temples at both places must have been the result of agreements or at least acceptance.

The original Nehemiah story, which predates Ezra-Nehemiah, already saw the political and religious influence by Samaria as a problem and propagated the political and religious independence of Jerusalem. This might be an important testimony for the time in which the relationship between Jerusalem/Yehud and Gerizim/Samaria started to become difficult. The Ezra-Nehemiah composition went further concerning the polemics and revoked the initial compromise of which the Pentateuch gives testimony until today. The starting partition was performed by the aim to present Jerusalem and the Jerusalemite interpretation of the Torah as the only foundation of Israel. Although we normally associate Judaism with Jerusalem, the Pentateuch previously existed as the authoritative text of a more decentralized Judaism.[51] The Judaism of the period of the Persian Empire[52] must be distinguished from the Judaism that emerged during and after the Hellenistic period that Ezra-Nehemiah demands. Due to the confrontation with Samaria and its temple on Mt. Gerizim, it becomes now strongly connected to Jerusalem, while at the same time the community of the Samaritans emerges.

It seems that after the end of the Persian rule over Palestine a great change in the identity concepts happened. On the side of Jerusalem, the older books written from a Jerusalem perspective most likely played an important role in the emergence of the Jerusalem Judaism. These books – all the prophetic books, some other late and some polemical books such as Chronicles and Ezra-Nehemiah – then became the three-part canon of the Hebrew Bible and of the Judaism of Jerusalem. That does not necessarily mean that Samaritanism is the direct continuation of the Israel from the Persian period, but our view of an unbroken continuation of the Judaism since the return from exile seems to be the result of a projection and an ideology from a much later time which was created

---

[50] See Christophe Nihan, "The Torah between Samaria and Judah: Shechem and Gerizim in Deuteronomy and Joshua," in *The Pentateuch as Torah: New Models for Understanding its Promulgation and Acceptance*, ed. Gary N. Knoppers and Bernard M. Levinson (Winona Lake, IN: Eisenbrauns, 2007), 223.

[51] The Pentateuch played an important role in this Judaism. Its intention was to legitimate the cult of the God of Israel at different places. See Raik Heckl, "Ein vollendeter Text für den Surrogat-Tempel: Struktur, Chronologie und Funktion des Pentateuchs in Anschluss an Benno Jacob," *ZABR* 22 (2016): 185–221.

[52] While older research used to see the Samaritans as a Jewish sect, modern theses assume a relatively early existence of two independent temple communities. See Reinhard Pummer, "Samaritanism – A Jewish Sect or an Independent Form of Yahwism?" in *Samaritans: Past and Present: Current studies*, ed. Menachem Mor and Friedrich V. Reiterer, SJ 53; StSam 5 (Berlin: de Gruyter, 2010), 10–16; idem, *The Samaritans: A Profile* (Grand Rapids, MI: Eerdmans, 2016), 15–25.

from the Jerusalem perspective.⁵³ Neither are the Samaritans a sectarian movement nor are Judaism and the Samaritans two different Yahwistic communities.⁵⁴ Both, Samaritans with Mt. Gerizim and Jews with Jerusalem, became two competing communities during the Hellenistic period, while they previously had been both part of a more decentralized Judaism in the Persian period.

---

53 It is also possible to say that the Samaritans defined their identity from the perspective of their own cultic centre, after the conflicts with Jerusalem had deepened. This is in accordance with Magnar Kartveit, who points out that the building of the temple is the *terminus post quem* for talking about "Samaritans" (*The Origin of the Samaritans* VTSup 128 [Leiden: Brill, 2009], 351).

54 This is a view that was originally developed by Blum ("Volk," 30). Christian Frevel has adopted this view in his description of the postexilic history (*Geschichte Israels*, Kohlhammer Studienbücher Theologie 2 [Stuttgart: Kohlhammer, 2015], 318 ff.). It is also the basic position in the recent study of Benedikt Hensel, who assumes an ethnic and cultural continuity of the Samarian population that is based in the preexilic history of Israel before 722 (*Juda und Samaria: Zum Verhältnis zweier Jahwismen in nach-exilischer Zeit*, FAT 110 [Tübingen: Mohr Siebeck, 2016] 91–102). Indeed, the existence under the imperial rule of the Assyrians, Babylonians and Persians did not completely change the cultural identity of the regions. However, because of the independent existence of Judah until the exile and because the devastation of the land by the Babylonians occurred primarily in the south we must assume that a cultural mixture emerged. Wolfgang Schütte detected and analysed Israelite traditions within written prophetic works, which were influenced by the exile of Israelites in Judah after 722 (*Israels Exil in Juda: Untersuchungen zur Entstehung der Schriftprophetie*, OBO 279 [Fribourg: Academic Press Fribourg, 2016], 226). The Pentateuch tradition is an important testimony of this development. Gary N. Knoppers has a similar view, even if he speaks of different communities (*Jews and Samaritans: The Origins and History of their Early Relations* [Oxford: Oxford University Press, 2013], 133). Apart from the Pentateuchal traditions we also have epigraphic evidence for this cultural mixture. See Johannes Renz, *Schrift und Schreibertradition: Eine paläographische Studie zum kulturgeschichtlichen Verhältnis von israelitischem Nordreich und Südreich*, ADPV 23 (Wiesbaden: Harrassowitz, 1997), 51. After the destruction of the Jerusalem temple a more decentralized self-conception emerged, which is suggested in the extrabiblical texts of the Elephantine community. The thesis of independent communities from the preexilic time cannot explain the affinities between Judaism and Samaritans. See the description of the problem by Pummer: "Thus, despite its association with the North, Samaritanism is at the same time a Jewish sect" ("Samaritanism," 17). Pummer refers to the study of James R. Linville, who mainly sees a terminological problem (*Israel in the Book of Kings: The Past as a Project of Social Identity*, JSOTSup 272 [Sheffield: Sheffield Academic Press, 1998], 28). Most of the biblical texts speak of Israel. Because of that it seems necessary to redefine the position of the Samaritans, which is what Pummer recently did with the statement that the Samaritans might be "a branch of Yahwistic Israel in the same sense as the Jews" (*Samaritans*, 25). In my opinion, it is possible to combine the observations in the following way: nearly all the books of the *Nevi'im* and *Ketuvim* speak of Israel from the Jerusalem perspective. That the Pentateuch does not go in this direction yet is not the result of the acceptance of the Pentateuch by the Samarians, but an indication that it was composed during the Persian period within a broader Jewish context.

Benedikt Hensel

Ethnic Fiction and Identity-Formation: A New Explanation for the Background of the Question of Intermarriage in Ezra-Nehemiah[1]

1 Introduction

The separation "from everything foreign" (Neh 13:30: מִכָּל־נֵכָר) is one of the leading themes of the Ezra-story in Ezra 7–10/Neh 8–10, and finds pointed expression especially in the restrictive regulations regarding intermarriage and their implementation within the early restoration community (Esr 9–10/Neh 8–10). One gets the impression that the fear of foreign infiltration expressed in this theme must have become a defining problem for the Jerusalem YHWH-community relatively soon after the return from exile. Terminologically, the category of "foreigner" is marked in Hebrew with the expressions נֵכָר and נָכְרִי (or בְּנֵי נֵכָר, "son of the stranger"). Thus, on the surface of the text the boundaries were directed against peoples and individuals who possessed neither cultural nor ethnic-genealogical commonalities with "Israel" – or in any case with "Israel," according to the specifically exclusivistic manner in which it was defined in the Ezra-tradition. On this, more will be said momentarily. In the foreground, the community's fear that its own identity could be endangered by a mixture with cultural, and therefore also religious, foreign elements seems to stand out.

At this point, a question should be asked about the historical background of the Ezra tradition. Because of an enormous growth of non-biblical archaeological, epigraphic and iconographic finds in recent years, it is now possible to establish a quite reliable picture of the population of Yehud (and this applies also to the neighboring province of Samaria) – as a kind of critical litmus-test for the biblical texts. The great significance that the Ezra story attributes to the question of intermarriage and the processes of foreign infiltration within the Jerusalem community has, oddly enough, no equivalent in the non-biblical evidence. If

---

[1] This article is an expanded version of a paper given at the 22nd Congress of International Organization for the Study of the Old Testament (IOSOT), Stellenbosch, 4.–9.9.2016. The article is part of a project financed by the German Research Foundation (DFG) on "Judean-Samarian Relations in the Post-Exilic Period" at the Johannes Gutenberg-University Mainz/Germany.

one looks at the archaeology of the Persian and Hellenistic periods, there seems to have been no foreign infiltration of this extent in the Levant heartland.

A look at the external evidence will be carried out in detail in the following. At the same time, the understanding of the "foreigner" in the relevant texts of Ezra-Nehemiah should/will be investigated in view of the material culture. This is because the category of "foreigner"/"stranger" is not tied to an objectively measurable demarcation line that is consistently defined by all text-producing groups or parts thereof. What genealogically or ethnically is "still allowed" for "Israel," and what qualifies as endogamy or exogamy, are not universally agreed upon.[2] In view of the entire biblical corpus and its various genres, such as genealogies, legal regulations, and narratives, the ethnic boundaries of "Israel" will be in each case refined and developed. Here, one need only recall the Moabite woman, and therefore "foreign woman," Ruth, who according to Ruth 4:1–12, 17 (and against other traditions such as the so-called Moabite paragraph in Deut 23:4–7; cf. Neh 13:1–3), is prominently and provocatively integrated into the Davidic-Israelite line.

In the same way, attention should be given to the correlation between the term "foreigner" and the term "Israel," because in the Persian and Hellenistic Periods "Israel" hardly presented a clearly definable collective term. Instead, its external boundaries and internal differentiating structures were – as I have shown in a new monograph[3] – highly controversial, both theologically and ideologically, among the various groups of early Judaism.[4] The coextensive identification of Jewish Yahwism or of Judaism with the term "Israel, which is often explicitly or implicitly presupposed in the scholarship, is therefore especially problematic, and distorts the view of the religio-sociological and -political developments of the post-exilic period.[5] In any case, other groups also asserted the claim to be

---

[2] On this, Thomas Hieke, *Die Genealogien der Genesis*, Herders Biblische Studien 39 (Freiburg: Herder, 2003), is fundamental.

[3] On this, see my *Juda und Samaria: Zum Verhältnis zweier Jahwismen in nach-exilischer Zeit*, FAT 110 (Tübingen: Mohr Siebeck, 2016).

[4] See the two contrasting conceptions of Israel in Ezra-Nehemiah (exclusivist) and Chronicles (inclusive: twelve-tribe system). On this issue, see recently Kristin Weingart, *Stämmevolk – Staatsvolk – Gottesvolk? Studien zur Verwendung des Israel-Namens im Alten Testament*, FAT II/68 (Tübingen: Mohr Siebeck, 2014), 67–82, 99–153.

[5] This image is admittedly influenced by the Deuteronomistic and Chronistic traditions, as Konrad Schmid some time ago once again reminded; see Konrad Schmid, "Die Samaritaner und die Judäer: Die biblische Diskussion um ihr Verhältnis in Josua 24," in *Die Samaritaner und die Bibel. Historische und literarische Wechselwirkungen zwischen biblischen und samaritanischen Traditionen*, ed. Jörg Frey, Ursula Schattner-Rieser, and Konrad Schmid, SJ 70; StSam 7 (Berlin: de Gruyter, 2012), 31–37. In the framework of the historical fiction of DtrG it is merely the group of Judean

"Israel," which is now if nothing else clearly attested by the sources for the Samaritan Yʜᴡʜ-worshippers.⁶

2 The Problem of Intermarriages in Ezra 9–10/Neh 8–10

Ezra 9–10 recounts the dissolution of mixed marriages (Esr 9:2, ערב√), which are said to have existed in a significant number among the returning families. These "people of Israel" are already in Ezra 9:1 (הָעָם יִשְׂרָאֵל) positioned in contrast to the other peoples, particularly the eight "peoples of the lands" (עַמֵּי הָאֲרָצוֹת). Individuals from the Jerusalem community are said to have married women from these peoples, who are qualified as "foreign women" (נָשִׁים נָכְרִיּוֹת; Greek: γυναῖκας ἀλλοτρίας) in Ezra 10:2, 10, 11, 14, 17, 18, 44. According to the perspective of the scribe Ezra, these marriages should be ended, and the women sent away, which was immediately carried out in Ezra 10:1–17. The drama of the situation is interpreted and reviewed through Ezra's public penitential prayer and plea, which qualifies the problem theologically (Ezra 9:5–15).⁷ The men who married foreign women were thereby made responsible for the poor situation in Yehud.

In relation to the use of the term "Israel," it is important to note that Ezra 9–10 sees the Galuth-community in Jerusalem as the *exclusive representatives* of Israel. Neither the twelve-tribe system, as it is established for instance in the similarly post-exilic book of Chronicles, nor other possible cultural and ethnic-genealogical markers that could imply a broader understanding of the term "Israel," occurs in the textual world of the Ezra story, as Weingart once again recently demonstrated.⁸

---

emigrants who succeeded in overcoming the catastrophe of exile, and continued the tradition of "Israel" in the post-exilic period. Weippert therefore once described this research-history-shaped reading of the "history of Israel" as "sub-Deuteronomistic"; see Manfred Weippert, "Geschichte Israels am Scheideweg," *ThR* 58 (1993): 73. This observation also applies *cum grano salis* for New Testament scholarship, on which see Martina Böhm, "Wer gehörte in hellenistisch-römischer Zeit zu 'Israel'?," in *Die Samaritaner und die Bibel. Historische und literarische Wechselwirkungen zwischen biblischen und samaritanischen Traditionen*, ed. Jörg Frey, Ursula Schattner-Rieser, and Konrad Schmid, SJ 70; StSam 7 (Berlin: De Gruyter, 2012), 181–202.
6 On this issue, see immediately below.
7 On the prayer, see Thomas Hieke, *Die Bücher Esra und Nehemia* (Stuttgart: Katholisches Bibelwerk, 2005), 146–149.
8 On conceptions of Israel in the Ezra-story, see Weingart, *Stämmevolk*, 78–81.

Nehemiah 8–10 continues this ideological line, but no longer refers to marriage with "foreign women," but rather in general to foreign partners; the people should separate themselves from the "sons of the stranger" (בְּנֵי נֵכָר; Neh 9:2), who are later identified with the "peoples of the land" (עַמֵּי הָאֲרָצוֹת; Neh 10:29). In parallel to Ezra 9–10, the term "sons of Israel" (בְּנֵי יִשְׂרָאֵל; Neh 7:72 with 8:1) is applied exclusively to the community gathered to listen to the Torah (Neh 8:2,14). This "Torah-community" is described in Neh 8:17a as כָּל־הַקָּהָל הַשָּׁבִים מֵהַשְּׁבִי, that is, as the "returned community," and is subsequently addressed as בְּנֵי יִשְׂרָאֵל (Neh 8:17b). As already in Ezra 9–10, this results in an *exclusive identification* of the Torah-observant Jerusalem community with "Israel," with whose number it is coextensive.[9] Thus, the texts build up a clear contrast between this "Israel" and "everything else": the "foreigners".

The negative judgement of intermarriage and the "foreigner" is based on the fear of syncretism and falling away from YHWH. The Jerusalem "Torah-community" is described as the "holy seed" (Ezra 9:2: זֶרַע הַקֹּדֶשׁ; cf. also Isa 6:12 as well as the "Godly seed" in Mal 2:15). This alludes to comparable formulations in Leviticus, Numbers, and Deuteronomy, where "Israel" or its representatives, namely the Priests and Levites, are labeled "holy people" (Deut 28:9; but also Lev 19:2; 11:44; 20:7,26; Num 15:40).[10] The special place of the people of God is captured in the image of the "seed of Abraham" (e.g. Deut 1:8).[11] Through the application and modification of this idea in the Ezra-tradition, a *radical*[12] and elevated consciousness of the election of the Ezra-group is expressed. Whereas in the Torah holiness is especially and exclusively reserved for certain special

---

[9] On the usage of "Israel" as a collective (vv. 1, 3) or as a description for the people (vv. 5, 25), see in detail Weingart, *Stämmevolk*, 78–79.

[10] For a detailed analysis of the conception of election, see especially Horst Dietrich Preuß, *Theologie des Alten Testaments*, vol. 1, *Theologie des Alten Testaments* (Stuttgart: Kohlhammer, 1991), 27–30; vol. 2, *Theologie des Alten Testaments* (Stuttgart: Kohlhammer, 1992), 305–27; for a good summary of the various traditions of election in the Old Testament, see Rolf Rendtorff, "Die 'Erwählung' Israels in der Hebräischen Bibel," in *Kontexte der Schrift, 1: Text. Ethik. Judentum und Christentum. Gesellschaft. E. W. Stegemann zum 60. Geburtstag*, ed. Gabriella Gelardini (Stuttgart: Kohlhammer, 2015), 319–27; Klaus Seybold, "Erwählung. I Altes Testament," *RGG* 2 (1999): 1478–81; and Horst Seebass, "בחר III: Gebrauch im AT," *ThWAT* I (1973): 608–594. On the various concepts of election in Genesis and Deuteronomy, see Benedikt Hensel, *Die Vertauschung des Erstgeburtssegens in der Genesis: Eine Analyse der narrativ-theologischen Grundstruktur des ersten Buches der Tora* (Berlin: de Gruyter, 2011), 316–18.

[11] Likewise, Bob Becking, "On the Identity of the Foreign Women in Ezra 9–10," in *Ezra, Nehemiah, and the Construction of Early Jewish Identity*, ed. Bob Becking (Tübingen: Mohr Siebeck, 2011), 59.

[12] Similarly, Becking, "On the Identity", 59.

figures or representatives of the people, such as priests and Levites, in Ezra the concept is extended to the entire community, that is, to "all Israel."[13]

This category serves as a clear *boundary marker* of the *in-Group* "Israel," and sets it apart from all other peoples, who therefore – expressed according to cult-terminology – are regarded as "impure" (Ezra 9:11: נִדָּה), and their practices could be described as "abominations" (תּוֹעֵבָה; Ezra 9:1,11,14; cf. Mal 2:11; Lev 18:22,26,27,29,30). With Becking, it can be affirmed that for Ezra, "The idea of divine election is thus reformulated in biological categories."[14] Intermarriage with those peoples is accordingly seen as a breach of duty (מַעַל) against YHWH (Ezra 9:2,4; 10:10), and concretely, against the duties received in the Torah (Ezra 10:3). Already the term מַעַל makes a bridge between the cultic practices of the "foreign peoples" and their sexual transgressions, as they are prohibited in Leviticus 18. There the "manner of the land of Canaan" (Lev 18:3), especially particular sexual practices, was harshly condemned and described as an "abomination" (Lev 18:26,27,29), which has polluted the land. "Israel" as holy, that is, a pure people (Lev 19:2–3) should not fall for the same practices.[15] This cultic dimension is also decisive for Neh 9–10. The people gathered in Jerusalem fast and separate themselves from all that is not "Israel" (Neh 9:2): וַיִּבָּדְלוּ זֶרַע יִשְׂרָאֵל מִכֹּל בְּנֵי נֵכָר, "And those of the seed of Israel separated themselves from all the sons of the stranger."

The Ezra-tradition thereby combines in its conception of "Israel" the concepts of cultic purity, restricted sexual practices, and endogamy, as well as a religious identity as the chosen people of God, with the claim of separation from other peoples. Only where all these factors come together is "Israel" to be spoken of. Conversely, this means that the "foreigner" stands primarily for everything ethnic-genealogically – but also religiously – *non-Israelite*.

3 Internal "Israelite" Differentiation Processes

It may be asked whether and to what extent text-external grounds could have precipitated the thematic concentration on the question of intermarriage in the Ezra-tradition. In the historical fiction of the Ezra-tradition, intermarriage by one's own people seems to severely threaten one's own group identity. However, only in Ezra 9–10 is the actual implementation of the intermarriage prohibition

---

13 Similarly, Tamara Cohn Eskenazi, *In an Age of Prose: A Literary Approach to Ezra-Nehemiah* (Atlanta: Scholars Press, 1988), 68.
14 Becking, "On the Identity", 58.
15 On this, see also Hieke, *Die Bücher Esra und Nehemia*, 140–143.

reported, and therefore the enforced divorces of the mixed marriages addressed. As scholars often presume, a historical kernel could lie in this.[16]

One assumes that the authorities within the restoration community saw themselves confronted with a Jerusalem group that was in practice multi-ethnic and multi-religious. The politics of intermarriage reflects "Israel's" search for and reassurance of their own identity after the turbulent time in exile and the uncertainty of the new beginning in the period shortly after the exile. It is often presumed that after the loss of its nationhood "Israel" was anxious to preserve its religious identity, for which reason the protection of its ethnic population was of decisive significance, and the fear of the tendency to assimilate was very great within their own group.[17] Thus, for instance, as Hieke formulates it:

> After the loss of territorial sovereignty with the exile, the danger of mixing with the other peoples at the cost of their own identity and religion was a constant, virulent problem, which many of the more particularistic-oriented texts of the Old Testament address, and which strikingly finds its concrete expression directly in the question of endogamy or exogamy.[18]

---

16 Armin Lange, "'Eure Töchter gebt nicht ihren Söhnen und ihre Töchter nehmt nicht für eure Söhne' (Esra 9,12): Die Frage der Mischehen im Buch Esra/Nehemia im Licht der Textfunde von Qumran," in *Was ist der Mensch, dass du seiner gedenkst? (Psalm 8,5): Aspekte einer theologischen Anthropologie – Festschrift für Bernd Janowski zum 65. Geburtstag*, ed. Michaela Bauks (Neukirchen-Vluyn: Neukirchener Verlag, 2008), 295–311. Fundamentally, scholarship has held the text of Ezra 9–10 to be at heart historical. The question, then, is whether these repudiations were actually carried out (e.g. Antonius Gunneweg, *Esra: Mit einer Zeittafel von Alfred Jepsen* (Gütersloh: Gütersloher Verlagshaus Mohn, 1985), 162; David Janzen, *Witch-hunts, Purity and Social Boundaries: The Expulsion of the Foreign Women in Ezra 9–10* (London: Sheffield Academic Press, 2002), 53) or merely demanded by Ezra, but then not carried out, or whether Ezra 9–10 presents a midrashic interpretation of Ezra 7 (W.T. In der Smitten, *Nehemia: Quellen, Überlieferung und Geschichte* (Assen: Van Gorcum, 1973), 66). On this entire issue, see also the discussion of the literature offered by Weingart, *Stämmevolk*, 103.

17 So e.g. concisely formulated by Thomas Willi, *Juda – Jehud – Israel: Studien zum Selbstverständnis des Judentums in persischer Zeit* (Tübingen: Mohr, 1995), 80–81.

18 The original quote in German: *"Nach dem Verlust der territorialen Eigenstaatlichkeit mit dem Exil ist die Gefahr der Vermischung mit den anderen Völkern unter Preisgabe der eigenen Identität und Religion ein ständig virulentes Problem, das sich durch viele eher partikularistisch orientierte Texte des Alten Testaments zieht und auffälligerweise gerade in der Frage von Endogamie oder Exogamie seinen konkreten Ausdruck findet"*; Hieke, *Die Bücher Esra und Nehemia*, 139–140. Donald Moffat, *Ezra's Social Drama: Identity Formation, Marriage and Social Conflict in Ezra 9 and 10* (New York: Bloomsbury, 2013), esp. 1–2, 134–95, offers an up to date discussion of the scholarly debate. On the socio-political and economic background of the intermarriage problematic, see Willa Johnson, *The Holy Seed Has Been Defiled: The Interethnic Marriage Dilemma in Ezra 9–10* (Sheffield: Phoenix Press, 2011), 15–26.27–55.

Likewise, socio-economic, historical backgrounds are presumed. The small size of Persian-period Yehud as well as the settlement politics of the Persian authorities made mixed marriages and the preservation of the heritage of "Israel" into a central problem of post-exilic Judaism.[19] Precisely over-against the Persian cultural pressure and in clarification of the role of "Israel" within the enormous, multi-ethnic Persian Empire, the debate over intermarriage is said to have been decisive.[20]

However, the historical horizons envisaged here are quite vague. For the Jerusalem group in the post-exilic period, the question of identity may have actually been a question of their own, to be addressed from many sides. But it was certainly not first in this period that the question was so decisive; it also played a role in the pre-exilic period. Viewed historically, a "mixing" of diverse ethnicities is in any case a common occurrence. With the community of Judeo-Aramaeans in Elephantine, for example, "intermarriage" was entirely normal.[21] What certainly changes with the Ezra-tradition is the *evaluation* of this ethnic diversity.

The historical debate can also be approached from another vantage point. Becking recently investigated the epigraphic and onomastic sources of Israelite provenance for indications regarding to what extent one can speak of a multi-ethnic and multi-religious community in the Persian period, in the sense of Ezra's interpretation of a "foreign-infiltration" of Jewish-Judean identity.[22] BECKING discusses the lists of names in Ezra 2/Neh 7, the Ammonite list of names that was preserved on Tell el-Mazār Ostrakon VII (4th century BCE),[23] the Ostracon 283[24] from Makkeda/Idumea (most likely to be identified with Ḫir-

---

19 So e.g. Michael Satlow, *Jewish Marriage in Antiquity* (Princeton: Princeton University Press, 2001), 133–140; Hieke, *Die Bücher Esra und Nehemia*, 143–46; and D.L. Smith-Christopher, "The Mixed Marriage Crisis in Ezra 9–10 and Nehemiah 13: A Study of the Sociology of the Post-Exilic Judean Community," in *Temple and Community in the Persian Period*, vol. 2 of *Second Temple Studies*, ed. Tamara Cohn Eskenazi (Sheffield: JSOT Press,1994), 242–65.
20 See Bob Becking, "The Idea of Torah in Ezra 7–10: A Functional Analysis", *ZABR* 7 (2001): 273–286.
21 At Elephantine mixed marriages were apparently common, as the corresponding marriage contracts show. For the marriage contracts at Elephantine see Jan Dušek, "Aramaic in the Persian Period," *HBAI* (2013): 249. The marriage contracts in Elephantine seem to suggest that no distinction was made between exogamous and endogamous marriages; see Hélène Nutkowicz, "Les mariages mixtes à Éléphantine à l'époque perse," *Transeu* 36 (2008): 125–139.
22 Becking, "On the Identity", 62–70.
23 *Editio Princeps:* Khair Yassine / Javier Teixidor, "Ammonite and Aramaic Inscriptions from Tell el-Mazār," *BASOR* 264 (1986): 48–49, n. 7, fig. 9.
24 The ostracon was first published in 2002 by André Lemaire, *Nouvelles Inscriptions araméennes d'Idumée Tome II* (Paris: Gabalda, 2002), 149–156 [the text is also in Dirk Schwiderski,

bet el-Qōm[25]; 4th century BCE) and the personal names in the papyrus finds at Wadi ed-Daliyeh. Becking's results show that though a little evidence for a mingling of diverse ethnicities is certainly to be found, on the basis of their low number this could not have been any serious threat to Jewish identity.[26] Becking's findings for Tell el-Mazār are therefore especially significant, since Hübner still came to the conclusion in 1992 that a broad spectrum of multi-ethnic, multi-religious peoples lived on Tell el-Mazār in the Persian period.[27] Becking discerned neither at Tell el-Mazār, nor in the other sources he investigated, signs of a high degree of multi-ethnic or multi-religious character for the people of Yehud, as seems to be imagined in the Ezra-tradition.

Against the background of the not yet conclusive debate regarding the time of origin of the Ezra-tradition, the analysis of the epigraphic material should be extended up to the Hellenistic period. Here a comparable picture is apparent, as I have recently shown.[28] The Samaria Papyri, discovered at Wadi ed-Daliyeh in the 1960s, are to be dated to the transition from the Persian to the Hellenistic periods and include 117 personal names, as Dušek has shown[29] (and not just the 37 names that Becking describes[30] with references to the now outdated edition (2001) from Gropp[31]). The onomasticon largely contains personal names with the theophoric element referring to El or Yhwh, or other West-Semitic linguistic markers, and those attested also in other Jewish literature and inscriptions. In total, "Israelite" personal names dominate the onomasticon of Wadi ed-Daliyeh with 63 percent. No more than 12 percent of the personal names

---

Die alt- und reichsaramäischen Inschriften / The Old and Imperial Aramaic Inscriptions, vol. 2, *Texte und Bibliographie* (Berlin: De Gruyter. 2004), 275].

25 On localization, see the overview of the various suggestions by D. A. Dorsey, "The Location of Biblical Makkedah," *TA* 7 (1980): 185. On the widely accepted identification of Makkeda with Ḥirbet el-Qōm, see Manfred Weippert, *Historisches Textbuch zum Alten Testament: Mit Beiträgen von Joachim Friedrich Quack, Bernd Ulrich Schipper und Stefan Jakob Wimmer* (Göttingen: Vandehoeck & Ruprecht, 2010), 502–3; Dorsey, "The Location," 185–202; and Diether Kellermann, "Überlieferungsprobleme alttestamentlicher Ortsnamen," *VT* 28 (1978): 428, n. 24.

26 See Becking, "On the Identity", 70.

27 See Ulrich Hübner, *Die Ammoniter: Untersuchungen zur Kultur und Religion eines Transjordanischen Volkes des 1. Jahrtausend v.Chr.* (Wiesbaden: Harrassowitz, 1992), 33–35. It may be assumed, as Hübner states, "dass der Tell el-Mazār in der achämenidischen Zeit von einer religiös (und ethnisch) gemischten Bevölkerung besiedelt gewesen ist." (Hübner, *Die Ammoniter*, 33).

28 See Hensel, *Juda und Samaria*, 138–48.

29 The essential edition is Jan Dušek, *Les manuscrits araméens du Wadi Daliyeh et la Samarie vers 450–332 av. J.-C.* (Leiden: Brill, 2009)

30 Becking, "On the Identity", 66.

31 Cf. D.M. Gropp, *Wadi Daliyeh II: The Samaria Papyri from Wadi ed-Daliyeh* (Oxford: Oxford University Press, 2001).

have theophoric elements of foreign deities (e. g. Qôs, Šamaš, Šin; so also only at Wadi ed-Daliyeh, not on Gerizim, where the names containing El and Yhwh predominate), so foreign elements appear to be very rare, and even then it is to be asked whether those who bore those foreign names actually lived in Samaria, or – much more likely, corresponding to the character of the papyri (exclusively contract documents) – involve foreign traders.

The onomasticon of the votive inscriptions from Gerizim, which largely stem from the 3rd and 2nd centuries BCE, points in the same direction:[32] In total, 55 different names are attested there, of which 35 are Hebrew, 13 are Greek, four Arabic, one Persian, one Palmyrene, and two names whose categorization remains unclear. Therefore, also in the Hellenistic period foreign influences are certainly present, but marginal.

In this context it seems probable that the intermarriage problematic in Ezra-Nehemiah involves a different historical situation. I take it to be very likely that the category of "foreigner" is a cipher for other forms of Yahwism of the post-exilic period, and by this literary means secures ideologically the identity and the uniqueness of the Judean "Israel"-denomination. Essentially, the term נָכְרִי already functions in the biblical literature as a cipher: Most of the people mentioned in the list of eight "foreign peoples" in Ezra 9:1–2 is stereotypical within the biblical literature, and Deut 7:1–6 (mentioning the Hittites, the Amorites, the Canaanites, the Perizzites, and the Jebusites, as Ezra 9:1 does) in combination with Dtn 23,2–9 (adding from there Moab and Ammon to the list in Ezra 9,2) may be the closest reference texts.[33] The list of peoples in Neh 9:8a builds analogously upon those lists, in reusing the standard lists of the Pentateuch: "Canaanites, Hittites, Amorites, Perizzites, Jebusites and Girgashites." The peoples named here serve within the Pentateuch as a common cipher, which can be

---

[32] *Editio Princeps:* Yitzhak Magen, Haggai Misgav and Levana Tsfania, *The Aramaic, Hebrew and Samaritan Inscriptions*, vol. 1 of *Mount Gerizim Excavations*, Judea and Samaria Publications 2 (Jerusalem: Israel Antiquities Authority, 2004). For a reevaluation and thorough comparative-palaeological classification of the inscriptions, see Jan Dušek, *Aramaic and Hebrew Inscriptions from Mt. Gerizim and Samaria between Antiochus III and Antiochus IV Epiphanes* (Leiden: Brill, 2012).
[33] Over Dtn 7:1–6 as reference text in Ezra 9 is a broad consensus, see Sebastian Grätz, "Zuwanderung als Herausforderung: Das Rutbuch als Modell einer sozialen und religiösen Integration von Fremden im nachexilischen Judäa," *EvT* 65 (2005): 304–5; Hieke, *Die Bücher Esra und Nehemia*, 140–142; H. G. M. Williamson, *Ezra, Nehemiah* (Dallas: Word Books, 1985), 131; Joseph Blenkinsopp, *Ezra-Nehemiah: A Commentary* (Philadelphia: Westminster, 1988), 175–76; and Lester Grabbe, *Ezra-Nehemiah*, OTR (New York: Routledge, 1998), 32–33. On the reuse of this list and the inclusion of peoples from Deut 23, see the nuanced discussion of Michael Fishbane, *Biblical Interpretation in Ancient Israel* (Oxford: Clarendon, 1985), 115–121.123–128.

used in every period as a paraphrase for the "enemies of Israel," as for example in Gen 15:19–21; Exod 3:8,17; 13:5; 23:23, 28; 33:2; Deut 7:1; 23:4–9; Neh 13:1–3,13 ff.[34] In the Ezra-story they are now used in the same sense. The foreign peoples become symbolic opponents to "Israel," as it is defined in the Ezra-story: that is, opponents of the Galuth-community.

We know today that in the post-exilic period significantly different regional forms of Yahwism existed. Examples known from the sources include the Yahu-community in Elephantine, in Makkeda (Idumea), Leontopolis, *al-Yahudu* and perhaps also in the Ammanitis in the post-exilic period.[35] About their religious profile, however, too little is known to be able to further stress the argument here. The most prominent and, as far as the sources are concerned, best-attested representative of a non-Judean Yahwism is certainly Samaria. The Samaritan YHWH-worshippers described themselves as "Israelites" (Delos-Inscriptions[36]), and they were also seen as such from the outside. This view is confirmed by those literary sources that stem from the *pre*-Hasmonean period and are *non-Samaritan* origin. In 2 Macc 5:22–23; 6:1–2, as well as Sir 50:25–26 (Hebrew version) the Samaritan YHWH-worshippers are seen as part of the same γένος as are the Jews. The Samaritan YHWH-worshippers had their central sanctuary on Gerizim from the Persian period on.[37] The material culture of the neighboring

---

34 On the biblical allusions, see esp. Gary N. Knoppers, "Intermarriage, Social Complexity, and Ethnic diversity in the Genealogy of Judah," *JBL* 120 (2001): 29–30; Dalit Rom-Shiloni, *Exclusive Inclusivity: Identity Conflicts Between Exiles and the Peoples Who Remained (6th-5th Centuries BCE)*, LHBOTS 543 (London: T&T Clark, 2013), 45.

35 On these Yahwisms, see, among others, Christian Frevel, "Der Eine oder die Vielen? Monotheismus und materielle Kultur in der Perserzeit," in *Gott – Götter – Götzen. XIV. Europäischer Kongress für Theologie (11.–15. September 2001, Zürich)*, ed. Christoph Schwöbel, Veröffentlichungen der Wissenschaftlichen Gesellschaft für Theologie 38 (Leipzig: Evangelische Verlagsanstalt, 2013), 238–65.

36 On the two Greek inscriptions found on Delos (2nd/3rd century BCE), which mention "Israelites" who "bring their taxes/tributes/offerings to Gerizim," see Magnar Kartveit, *The Origin of the Samaritans* (Leiden: Brill, 2009), 216–35.

37 On the archaeological finds on Gerizim, see Yitzhak Magen, *A Temple City*, vol. 2 of *Mount Gerizim Excavations*, Judea and Samaria Publications 2 (Jerusalem: Israel Antiquities Authority, 2008). A current critical examination of the findings appears in: Jürgen Zangenberg, "Berg des Segens – Berg des Streits. Heiden, Juden, Christen und Samaritaner auf dem Garizim," *TZ* 63 (2007): 289–309; idem, "The Sanctuary on Mount Gerizim. Observations on the Results of 20 Years of Excavation," in *Temple Building and Temple Cult. Architecture and Cultic Paraphernalia of Temples in the Levant (2.–1. Mill. B.C.E.). Proceedings of a Conference on the Occasion of the 50th Anniversary of the Institute of Biblical Archaeology at the University of Tübingen (28–30 May 2010)*, ed. Jens Kamlah (Wiesbaden: Harrasowitz, 2012), 399–420; and Benedikt Hensel, "Das

provinces of Samaria and Judah show very clearly that the two people-groups also in the post-exilic period (still) shared the same cultural context.³⁸ The texts relevant to the intermarriage problematic may be aimed especially at the disqualification of the Gerizim community.³⁹ The application of the "foreigner-category" to the Samaritan Yhwh-worshippers allows this "Israel" community to appear *de facto* as "gentiles." To them neither the privileges nor the obligations of the giving of the Torah applied, nor was it possible for them to properly participate in "Israel's" divine service.⁴⁰ They therefore do not belong directly to "Israel" – according to the expression of the Ezra-Nehemiah group – and are in principle not eligible for the cult.

In this polemic of Judean provenance, which one may call "Ethnic-fiction" (German *terminus technicus: Ethnofiktion*), the "Samaritans" rise to the position of "foreign colonists" and become the prototype of the "non-Israelites." This historical fiction is fundamentally comparable with the similar ideological *topoi* in

---

JHWH-Heiligtum am Garizim: ein archäologischer Befund und seine literar- und theologiegeschichtliche Einordnung," *VT* 68 (2018): 73–93.

38 On this, see esp. Gary Knoppers, "Aspects of Samaria's Religious Culture During the Early Hellenistic Period," in *The Historian and the Bible: Essays in Honour of Lester L. Grabbe*, ed. Philip Davies (New York: T&T Clark International, 2010): 159–174; idem, *Jews and Samaritans: The Origins and History of Their Early Relations* (New York: Oxford University Press, 2013, 103–134; Yigal Levin, "Judea, Samaria and Idumea: Three Models of Ethnicity and Administration in the Persian Period," in *From Judah to Judaea. Socio-Economic Structures and Processes in the Persian Period*, ed. J. U. Ro (Sheffield: Sheffield Phoenix Press, 2012): 4–53; and Benedikt Hensel, "Samaritanische Identität in persisch-hellenistischer Zeit im Spiegel der biblischen Überlieferung und der epigraphischen Befunde," in *Nationale Identität im Alten Testament*, ed. Wolfgang Zwickel, Kleine Arbeiten zum Alten und Neuen Testament 12 (Kamen: Hartmut Spenner, 2015), 67–115.

39 Raik Heckl in his article "The Composition of Ezra-Nehemiah as a Testimony for the Competition Between the Temples in Jerusalem and on Mt. Gerizim in the Early Years of the Seleucid Rule over Judah" in this volume thinks that the book of Ezra-Nehemiah as a whole is to be seen as a programmatic text in the conflict between Jerusalem and Samaria.

40 On the aspect of Torah see Reinhard Pummer, "The Samaritans and Their Pentateuch," in *The Pentateuch as Torah: New Models for Understanding Its Promulgation and Acceptance*, ed. Gary N. Knoppers and Bernard M. Levinson (Winona Lake, IN: Eisenbrauns, 2007), 237–269; Gary N. Knoppers, "Parallel Torahs and Inner-Scriptural Interpretation: The Jewish and Samaritan Pentateuchs in Historical Perspective," in *The Pentateuch: International Perspectives on Current Research*, ed. Thomas B. Dozeman, Konrad Schmid, and Baruch J. Schwartz, FAT 78 (Tübingen: Mohr Siebeck, 2011), 507–531; idem, *Jews and Samaritans*, and Benedikt Hensel, "Von ‚Israeliten' zu ‚Ausländern': Zur Entwicklung anti-samaritanischer Polemik ab der hasmonäischen Zeit," *ZAW* 126 (2014): 488–490.

the Egyptian cultural context,[41] or in the ethnic history of Greece[42] in the Hellenistic period. In social anthropology this process of elevating one's self and social image, while classifying people or groups with other characteristics as "different," is described as *othering*.[43] This process creates over time an image of the enemy, the content of which certainly need not itself be historical grounded. Precisely this process could stand in the background of the "foreigner" polemic. Seen historically, the differences between these two groups are marginal; in the literary interpretation and imagination they are all the more clearly emphasized.

4 Nehemiah 13: The Disambiguation of a Cipher

The coded identification of the Gerizim community with "foreigners" in the Ezra-tradition is unambiguously spelled out in Nehemiah 13. The concluding chapter of the book of Ezra-Nehemiah may in many ways count as the thematic "summary" of the whole book,[44] and therefore to be attributed to a redactor

---

[41] On this, see Jan Assmann, "Zum Konzept der Fremdheit im alten Ägypten," in *Die Begegnung mit dem Fremden: Wertungen und Wirkungen in Hochkulturen vom Altertum bis zur Gegenwart*, ed. Meinhard Schuster, Colloquium Rauricum 4 (Stuttgart: Teubner, 1996), 77–99.

[42] The earliest attestation is in the Greek epics, e.g., Homer's Iliad, but then also in the beginning *Dekadenztheorien* of the late antique poetry (Xenophon, later Aeschylus) and in Herodotus. On these and other sources, see Reinhold Bichler, "Wahrnehmung und Vorstellung fremder Kultur: Griechen und Orient in archaischer und frühklassischer Zeit," in *Die Begegnung mit dem Fremden: Wertungen und Wirkungen in Hochkulturen vom Altertum bis zur Gegenwart*, ed. Meinhard Schuster, Colloquium Rauricum 4 (Stuttgart: Teubner, 1996), 51–74. In Herodotus, the leading thoughts regarding ethnic and cultural identity are concentrated into a proper *Geschichtsphilosophie* (philosophy of history), as on the long evolutionary line of civilization (as Herodotus describes it) from the *barbaroi* to the Hellenes (which were seen as the highest state of civilization) each people has its own obligations, privileges and limitations in cultural history (depending on which part of the evolutionary line they've already reached); on this see Walter Nicolai, *Versuch über Herodots Geschichtsphilosophie* (Heidelberg: Winter, 1986).

[43] The term "othering" describes there the use of, and the distancing or differentiating from, other groups, in order to assert one's own "normality." The term was first coined in 1985 by Gayatri Spivak, "The Rani of Sirmur," in *Europe and its Others*, vol. 1, *Proceedings of the Essex Conference on the Sociology of Literature*, ed. Francis Barker (Colchester: University of Essex, 1985), 128–51. A generally usable German translation does not exist; see also Julia Reuter, *Ordnungen des Anderen: Zum Problem des Eigenen in der Soziologie des Fremden* (Bielefeld: Transcript, 2002).

[44] Nehemiah 13:1–31 concludes the Nehemiah-story, and simultaneously the book of Ezra-Nehemiah, with a theological summary of the most important themes. After the construction of the Temple (Ezra 1–6), the construction of the wall and city are brought to an end in Neh 11:1–12:47,

who already had the Temple-construction narrative (Ezra 1–6), the Nehemiah story, and even the Ezra-tradition in view, and who chose once again and finally to demand the segregation of the "foreign elements" within "Israel" (Neh 13:1–3). As one of two examples, which should illustrate that with the urgency of the separation of the mixed marriages, the daughter of Sanballat, the Samaritan governor, is specified (v. 28). She is expelled from the "Israel" community as one of the "foreign women" (vv. 26–27: MT: נָשִׁים נָכְרִיּוֹת; Greek: γυναῖκας ἀλλοτρίας; cf. v. 30: מִכָּל־נֵכָר). From the context it is clear that also here the ethnic-genealogical dimension of the "foreign"-markers are transcended and aimed at the cultic de-classification of the "foreign" group. The reference to the mixed marriages of Solomon in v. 26b ("foreign women also led him [= Solomon] to sin;" גַּם־אוֹתוֹ הֶחֱטִיאוּ הַנָּשִׁים הַנָּכְרִיּוֹת) serve to bring the theme of "sin" against Yhwh into connection with the mixed marriages and ethnic categories,[45] and to lend to the discussion a particular theological edge. Marriage with foreign women constitutes nothing less than betrayal of Yhwh (Neh 13:27, לִמְעֹל בֵּאלֹהֵינוּ).

Sanballat is hereby declassified to a "foreigner," and with him also the people-group he signifies:[46] the Samaritan people and therefore also the Sa-

---

and the preconditions for a renewed commitment to the Torah are present. Nehemiah 12 and 13 report on the realization of these provisions, first reporting the reorganization of the Jerusalem community and its cultic personal at the Jerusalem Temple (Neh 12:1–47), then in Neh 13 describing the outer boundaries of the "Israel community" (conceived ethnically as well as cultically), in distinction from "foreign elements." This "Israel" is none other than that which the profiling of the comprehensive approach of the book of Ezra-Nehemiah and all its literary precursors are striving after, namely the returnee community. Thus, it is hardly surprising that at the end once again the theme of "identity" stands at the center. Content-wise, the concluding chapter corresponds to the dissolution of the mixed marriages under Ezra (Ezra 7–10 and Neh 8–10), as well as the commitment to the Torah, including the public reading of the Torah and the covenant documents (Neh 7:5–10:40), which for its part again includes the prohibition against intermarriage as a characteristic feature of the Torah community (Neh 10:31); similarly, Böhler views Neh 13:4–31 as a *"wichtiges Schlusswort"* [Dieter Böhler, *Die heilige Stadt in Esdras a und Esra-Nehemia: Zwei Konzeptionen der Wiederherstellung Israels* (Freiburg, Schweiz: Univ.-Verl., 1989), 369]. Differently, Grabbe, *Ezra-Nehemiah*, 68, sees Neh 13 merely as a kind of "epilogue", as the climax of Ezra-Nehemiah – in his eyes – was already reached with the end of chapter 12.

45 Williamson sees the reference to Solomon as "his trump rhetorical card" [H. G. M. Williamson, "The Belief System of the Book of Nehemiah," in *The Crisis of Israelite Religion: Transformation of Religious Tradition in Exilic and Post-Exilic Times*, ed. Bob Becking (Leiden: Brill, 1999), 279].

46 The description of Sanballat and the other two opponents of Nehemiah (Geshem and Tobiah) is thoroughly topical, but not interested in the historical constellation of people or facts [see esp. Sebastian Grätz, "The Adversaries in Ezra/Nehemiah – Fictitious or Real?" in *Between*

maritan Yhwh-worshippers. Sanballat's disqualification as "foreigner" is thereby ideological-religious, and not ethnically motivated. Dušek sees this differently, following the majority view.[47] He points out that the "foreigner"-status is to be grounded in the actually *foreign* – that is Babylonian – origins of Sanballat. Indeed, the personal name of the Samaritan governor is to be derived from Sîn-uballiṭ and is therefore of Babylonian origin. Dušek's observation regarding the etymology of the name is certainly to be accepted, but not his conclusion from it. Again and again the names of well-known Judean leaders of the restoration period are of "Mesopotamian origins." Zerubbabel is very likely[48] a Hebraizing of the well-attested Akkadian name *zēr-bābili*, "scion of Babel," and precisely the same onomastic source is also to be assumed for Sheshbazar (שֵׁשְׁבַּצַּר).[49] As far as I know, no foreign cultural or religious roots are speculated concerning these individuals. On the other hand, it is known from the Elephantine correspondence particularly that Sanballat had two sons who exhibit theophoric Yhwh-elements in their names: Delaiah (דליה) und Shelemiah (שלמיה).[50] If one assumes that the Sanballat from Nehemiah is a literary resonance of the historically attested Sanballat, then it is to be inferred that either he or his children were not basically distant from Yhwh-belief.

Cooperation and Hostility: Multiple Identities in Ancient Judaism and the Interaction with Foreign Powers, ed. Rainer Albertz and Jakob Wöhrle, Journal of Ancient Judaism, Supplements 11 (Göttingen: Vandenhoeck & Ruprecht, 2013), 73–88; and Reinhard Kratz, *Das Judentum im Zeitalter des Zweiten Tempels* (Tübingen: Mohr Siebeck, 2004), 102–4]. The opponents of Nehemiah represent (Grätz) or symbolize (Kratz) in this way the threat and danger that the restoration community saw itself exposed to, or which the text-producing elites wished to be seen as problems.
47 Dušek, *Aramaic and Hebrew Inscriptions*, 99.
48 See Benedikt Hensel, Art. "Serubbabel", *WiBiLex*. URL: http://www.bibelwissenschaft.de/stichwort/28453.
49 On this, see Benedikt Hensel, Art. "Serubbabel", *WiBiLex*. URL: http://www.bibelwissenschaft.de/stichwort/28453. See also Reinhard Pummer, "Samaritanism – A Jewish Sect or an Independent Form of Yahwism?" in *Samaritans: Past and Present: Current Studies*, ed. Menahem Mor (Berlin: de Gruyter, 2010), 14–15, with n. 70 (bibliography).
50 Attested 407 BCE in TAD A4.7,29; 4.8,28; 4.9,1. The same Delaiah is also mentioned in WDSP 11r and WD 22 (see on this Dušek, *Les manuscrits araméens*, 321–331). Whether the abbreviations דל and של are truly related to the two sons of Sanballat [Ya'akov Meshorer, *Samarian Coinage*, Numismatic Studies and Researches 9 (Jerusalem: Israel Numismatic Society: 1999)], is doubtful.

5 Conclusions

The conclusions may be summarized as follows: First, it is shown that in reference to "separation from all foreigners" the Ezra-tradition presupposes a very specific, exclusivistic use of the term "Israel," which essentially sees only the returnee-community as representatives of the *Qahal Yiśrael*. The decisive marker of the "foreigner" for the intermarriage question is preeminently and for the purposes of the narrative logic *ethnic-genealogically* determined, but it is aimed at the *cultic-religious* demarcation of the Galuth-community from "the other." The designation of the "foreigner" functions in the text as a cipher for a particular conflict, by which the "Israelite" authors of Ezra demarcate themselves from other groups, who are defined as "not Israel." It has been suggested in this essay that behind the usage of the term "foreigner" may lie other post-exilic Yahwisms, which likewise applied the "Israel" title to themselves positively and, when these other post-exilic Yahwisms are viewed historically, were equivalent to the Judean form of Yahwism. In particular, this Judean boundary-marking polemic may refer to the Samarian Yhwh-worshipers, because these worshipers were certainly no marginal religio-historical phenomenon in the post-exilic period (a "Jewish sect"), but instead were the most theological-historically significant form of Yahwism in the Levant heartland, outside of Judah.[51] Within the *ethnic fiction* of the Ezra-tradition (and essentially of the entire book of Ezra-Nehemiah[52]), which developed concerning the question of intermarriage, the Samaritan YHWH-community is declassified as a group that is impure, ineligible for the cult, and multi-ethnic, and consequently delegitimized as representatives of "Israel"; the Ezra-tradition stands in line with a tradition of "foreigner" polemic against the Samaritans that continues up to the modern period.[53]

---

[51] On this issue, see now Hensel, *Juda und Samaria*, 409–13. As a matter of fact, the very categorization of the Samaritans as a "Jewish sect", as even modern scholarship still tends to qualify them, is highly problematic. It sees the Samaritans as a *deviation* of Judaism, with its roots *within* Judaism. All the available evidences from the Samaritans themselves suggest that they did not view themselves as Jews, but rather as Israelites. On this see esp. Knoppers, *Jews and Samaritans*, 103–134. In an older article, he rightfully states: "Viewing the Samaritans as a breakaway Jewish sect is too simplistic. The Yahwistic Samarian community must be granted its own historical integrity", Gary N. Knoppers, "Mt. Gerizim and Mt. Zion. A Study in the Early History of the Samaritans and the Jews," *SR* 34 (2005): 313. On the problem of seeing Samaritans as a Jewish sect see the nuanced discussion given by Reinhard Pummer, *The Samaritans. A Profile* (Grand Rapids, MI/Cambridge: Wm. B. Eerdmans Publishing Co., 2016), 9–25.

[52] In detail, see Hensel, *Juda und Samaria*, 391–400.

[53] An overview of this phenomenon is in Hensel, "Von ‚Israeliten' zu ‚Ausländern'", 475–93.

The concrete cause for the sharp polemic of the Ezra-story is the situation that the (Judean) authors stand against a denomination of "Israel" that was in every way comparable to the post-exilic Yahwism of Jerusalem. The Samaritan YHWH-worshippers likewise understood themselves as "Israel," were perceived as such from outside, shared a "common Pentateuch" with Judah and operated their own central Yahwistic sanctuary. Literarily and ideologically, a clear, restrictive boundary between the two denominations of "Israel" was drawn over the polemic. Only through the discrediting of the Samaritan YHWH-cult could the exclusive legitimacy and therefore the justifiable uniqueness of the Judean YHWH-faith (particularly that of the Jerusalem Temple) be ensured.

In the idealistic reconstruction of the restoration of this "Israel," which within the Ezra-story ultimately experiences its normative founding in the recapitulation and promulgation of the Torah (Ezra 7),[54] the grounds may be sought for the fact that the Gerizim community is never explicitly mentioned, and a cipher is used. The claim is developed in the texts that the Torah – as essential spiritual center[55] of the Jerusalem community – unrestrictedly serves to decipher all political religious and social questions, and as an authoritative medium possesses an undisputed significance. Because the Torah does not (explicitly) mention the Samaritans or the Gerizim community as an individual group or "people,"[56] these terms are also not available to the Ezra-community. One is reliant on the application of pertinent categories of foreign peoples and enemies, in order to criticize the "Samaritans."

The results do not mean that the cipher in the comparison "foreigner" = "other post-exilic Yahwisms" is the only way the term "foreigners" should be understood, as the literary achievement of the cipher is just to enable a certain interpretive openness. As such it could be used as allusion to several problems of religious, ethnic or political nature which were contemporary to the authors of the texts or to later generations. For the authors of the Ezra-story, however, the differentiation process of their own group identity among the mélange of various "Israelite" identities would have certainly been the most pressing problem.

---

[54] On this see the article of Raik Heckl, "The Composition of Ezra-Nehemia as a Testimony for the Competition Between the Temples in Jerusalem and on Mt. Gerizim in the Early Years of the Seleucid Rule over Judah" in this volume.

[55] Sebastian Grätz, "Esra 7 im Kontext hellenistischer Politik: Der königliche Euergetismus in hellenistischer Zeit als ideeller Hintergrund von Esr 7," in *Die Griechen und das antike Israel: Interdisziplinäre Studien zur Religions- und Kulturgeschichte des Heiligen Landes*, ed. Stefan Alkier (Fribourg: Acad. Press, 2004), 153.

[56] In any case, not in a negative sense, because in the post-exilic period the Torah is still understood as a "compromise document" of both Israel-groups in Judah and Samaria.

Reinhard Pummer
An Update of Moses Gaster's "Chain of Samaritan High Priests"

The head of the Samaritan community is the high priest. According to Samaritan tradition the present representative is the 132nd in the line that began with Aaron, the brother of Moses. The importance of tracing the descent of the community's high priests from the earliest time of the existence of Israel to the present manifests itself in the careful recording of the names and times of all the high priests throughout history. The extant Samaritan chronicles and treatises of Samaritan chronology all contain lists of Samaritan high priests. Some such lists are also available in modern travelers' reports. To cite only one example from a traveler's report of the nineteenth century, John Mills in his book, *Three Months' Residence at Nablus*,[1] published a chronology which the priest Jacob b. Aaron[2] drew up for him, the same priest who copied for Moses Gaster the "Chain of Samaritan High Priests."[3] Mills' list begins with the creation of the world and Adam and ends in 6295 *anno mundi* which is equated with 1857 CE.[4] Thus, according to this Samaritan calculation, the world was created in 4439 BCE. Besides the names of the Patriarchs and the high priests, the lists contain more or less detailed notes of important events, secular as well as religious, that occurred during a given priest's term of office. An example of a modern list of high priests was drawn up by John Macdonald on the basis of his edition and translation of parts of *Chronicle II*, reaching from Aaron's son Eleazar to Nethanel in the time of Nebuchadnezzar.[5] The most detailed and extensive discussion and presentation of Samaritan chronology and priestly lists is contained in

---

1 John Mills, *Three Months' Residence at Nablus and an Account of the Modern Samaritans* (London: John Murray, 1864).
2 *Three Months' Residence*, 330–335; his dates are approximately the same as in Gaster's "Chain." Jacob b. Aaron b. Salama lived from AH 1255/1841 CE to AH 1336/1916 CE, and was high priest from AH 1291/1870 CE to his death.
3 Moses Gaster, "The Chain of Samaritan High Priests: A Synchronistic Synopsis," *JRAS* (1909): 483. The article was reprinted in Moses Gaster, *Studies and Texts in Folklore, Magic, Medieval Romance, Hebrew Apocrypha and Samaritan Archaeology*, Vol. 1 (London: Maggs Bros., 1971), 483–502 (Introduction and English translation) and Moses Gaster, *Studies and Texts in Folklore, Magic, Medieval Romance, Hebrew Apocrypha and Samaritan Archaeology*, Vol. 3 (London: Maggs Bros., 1971), 131–38 (Hebrew text).
4 From 70 CE on, Mills lists the Christian dates.
5 John Macdonald, *The Samaritan Chronicle No. II (or: Sepher Ha-Yamim) From Joshua to Nebuchadnezzar*, BZAW 107 (Berlin: de Gruyter, 1969), 216–17.

https://doi.org/10.1515/9783110581416-009

Maurice Baillet's entry "Samaritains" in the *Dictionnaire de la Bible*.[6] For his computation, Baillet took into account the figures given in the Samaritan Pentateuch, the *Kitāb al-Tarīkh* of Abū 'l-Fatḥ, the *Tulida* (*Chronicle Neubauer*), the *Chain of Samaritan High Priests*, the *New Chronicle* (*Chronicle Adler*), and *Chronicle II*. Baillet's tables extend from Adam to Jacob II who died in March 1985. Nathan Schur in his book *History of the Samaritans* presents a list of high priests from the beginning of the Ottoman period to 1987.[7] The Samaritans, on their web site www.israelite-samaritans.com/religion, list the high priests of the Ihtamar family from 1624 CE until 2013. According to the Samaritans, the present high priest, Abdel b. Asher, is the 132nd high priest since Aaron, the son of Amram and brother of Moses, as previously mentioned.[8]

In the course of their history, the Samaritans used a variety of eras, taking significant events as points of reference: the creation of the world or of Adam, the Flood, the Exodus from Egypt, the Entrance of the Israelites into Canaan, the beginning of the *Fanūta* (*pnwth*) or time of Divine Disfavour (God's turning away with the disappearance of the Tabernacle during the high priesthood of Uzzi), Sabbatical years, the reigns of high priests, the Hijra, and various others.[9] Samaritan lists of high priests are intimately connected with Samaritan chronology in general and with the Samaritan calendar. This is not the place to enter into a discussion of either of these issues. Suffice it to point out that a thorough study of Samaritan chronologies was undertaken by Paul Stenhouse in his article "Samaritan Chronology"[10] which includes a table that graphically shows the major variants of the totals of the Samaritan eras from Adam to Baba Rabbah. A possible reason for these discrepancies, Stenhouse conjectures, could be that "some authors (scribes) drew for the Era totals on one source, and for the

---

6 Maurice Baillet, "Samaritains," in *DBSup* 11 (1991), 926–60.

7 Nathan Schur, *History of The Samaritans: 2nd Revised and Enlarged Edition*, BEATAJ 18 (Frankfurt am Main; Bern; New York; Paris: Peter Lang, 1992), 231. The list extends from Pinḥas b. Eleazar (1509–1549) to Joseph b. Ab Ḥisda b. Yaʻaqov (1987–1998).

8 See also the lists in the new work by Benyamim Tsedaka, *The History of the Israelite Samaritans Based on Their Own Sources, From the Entrance of the People of Israel to the Land of Canaan Till 2015 CE [3654 Years]* (Holon – Mount Gerizim: A.B. Institute of Samaritan Studies Press, 2016), א–יד (Hebrew).

9 Cf. Leib Khaimovich Vilsker, *Manuel d'araméen samaritain*, Études et Répertoires publiés par l'Institut de Recherche et d'Histoire des Textes. Traduit du russe par Jean Margain (Paris: Centre National de la Recherche Scientifique, 1981), 95–96. Paul Stenhouse, "Samaritan Chronology," in *Proceedings of the First International Congress of the Société d'Études Samaritains*, ed. Abraham Tal and Moshe Florentin (Tel-Aviv: Chaim Rosenberg School of Jewish Studies, Tel-Aviv University, 1988), 175.

10 See above note 9.

consecutive listing, on another."¹¹ Moreover, priests from communities other than the Nablus community – such as Damascus, Egypt, Gaza, and others – may have been included.¹² In addition, "different calendars were in use over the long period covered by our chronologists."¹³

The list under discussion was published by Gaster in 1909 in Hebrew and in English in the *Journal of the Royal Asiatic Society* under the title "The Chain of Samaritan High Priests: A Synchronistic Synopsis." The name of the work stems from Gaster. In Hebrew it is called שלשת הכהנים הגדולים. The list is based on Gaster's manuscript 862 (identified by him as Codex A in the article; now BL Or. 10141), written at Gaster's request by the aforementioned high priest Jacob b. Aaron b. Salama, and dated AH 1325 = 1907 CE.¹⁴ In addition, Gaster used his MS 877 (identified by him as Codex B in the article [now JR 286]) to complement MS 862.¹⁵ He also compared the text with that of *Chronicle Neubauer*,¹⁶ *Chronicle Adler*,¹⁷ and *Kitāb al-Tarīkh* of Abū 'l-Fatḥ.¹⁸ The "Chain" spans the time from Adam to Jacob b. Aaron b. Salama and contains these data: the age at the birth of the first son (for the Patriarchs) or the number of years a high priest was

---

11 Stenhouse, "Samaritan Chronology," 186.
12 Stenhouse, "Samaritan Chronology," 187.
13 Stenhouse, "Samaritan Chronology," 186. For a thorough treatment of the questions connected with the Samaritan calendar, including an edition and translation of the *Kitāb Ḥisāb as-Sinīn*, a complete calendar for the year 6403 *anno mundi* (= 1964/65 CE), see Sylvia Powels, *Der Kalender der Samaritaner anhand des Kitāb ḥisāb as-sinīn und anderer Handschriften*, StSam 3 (Berlin and New York: de Gruyter, 1977); eadem, "The Samaritan Calendar and the Roots of Samaritan Chronology," in *The Samaritans*, ed. A.D. Crown (Tübingen: J.C.B. Mohr [Paul Siebeck], 1989), 691–742.
14 On the manuscript see Alan David Crown, *A Catalogue of the Samaritan Manuscripts in the British Library* (London: British Library, 1998), 32–33 (according to Crown, the date is May 1906); on the spine, the manuscript is called שלשלה; Gaster, in his Handlist, describes it as ספר התולדות after the opening words (see Moses Gaster, *Handlist of Gaster Manuscripts, held mostly in the British Library [formerly British Museum], London, and in the John Rylands Library, Manchester*. Preface by Brad Sabin Hill. [London: Hebrew Section, Oriental and India Office Collections, The British Library, 1995], 66.)
15 Both manuscripts are described by Gaster in his "Chain" 490 (the page numbers given here are those of the reprint in *Studies and Texts*); MS 877 is also described in Robertson, *Catalogue* 2, 209–211.
16 Adolf Neubauer, "Chronique samaritaine, suivie d'un appendice contenant de courtes notices sur quelques autres ouvrages samaritains," *JA* 14 (1869): 385–470.
17 Elkan Nathan Adler and Max Séligsohn, "Une nouvelle chronique samaritaine," *REJ* 44 (1902): 188–222; 45 (1902): 70–98; 223–254; 46 (1903): 123–146.
18 Gaster used Eduardus Vilmar, ed. *Abulfathi Annales Samaritani quos ad fidem codicum manu scriptorum Berolinensium Bodlejani Parisini edidit et prolegomenis instruxit Eduardus Vilmar* (Gothae: Sumtibus Frederici Andreae Perthes, 1865).

in office; the date of the Era of Creation; the date of the Era of the Entry into Canaan; and the date according to the Muslim calendar.

The updating of Gaster's list in this paper includes the following elements: (1) the addition of the high priests who officiated after AH 1325/1907 CE, the year in which Gaster's list ends; (2) the addition of references to the individual passages in the Samaritan chronicles in which the respective high priests are spoken about or mentioned on the basis of the new editions and translations that appeared since the time of Gaster, i.e. the *Tulida* in the edition of Moshe Florentin[19], Abū 'l-Fatḥ's *Kitāb al-Tarīkh* in the edition and translation by Paul Stenhouse,[20] and *The* Continuatio *of the Samaritan Chronicle of Abū l-Fatḥ al-Sāmirī al-Danafī*, edited and translated by Milka Levy-Rubin;[21] (3) additional references from the following sources: (a) an addition to the *Tulida* as edited by Moshe Florentin; (b) the reference work *Personalities in Eretz-Israel 1799 – 1948*, ed. Yaacov Shavit, Yaacov Goldstein, Haim Be'er;[22] (c) Reinhard Pummer, *Samaritan Marriage Contracts and Deeds of Divorce*;[23] (d) A.B. – *The Samaritan*

---

19 Moshe Florentin, *The Tulida: A Samaritan Chronicle: Text, Translation, Commentary* (Jerusalem: Yad Yitzchak Ben Zvi; The Rabbi David Moshe and Amalia Rosen Foundation, 1999 [Hebrew]).

20 Paul Stenhouse, "The Kitāb al-Tarīkh of Abu 'l-Fatḥ: A New Edition with Notes" (PhD diss., Sydney: University of Sydney, 1980), and Paul Stenhouse, *The Kitāb al-Tarīkh of Abū 'l-Fatḥ: Translated into English with Notes*, Studies in Judaica, 1 (Sydney: Mandelbaum Trust, University of Sydney, 1985). The *Kitāb al-Tarīkh* contains a chronology from Adam to the disappearance of the Tabernacle in Chapter I (pp. 4–7 in the translation by Stenhouse), and a list of Patriarchs and high priests from Adam to the time of Muhammad in Chapter LV (pp. 187–90 in Stenhouse). According to Abū 'l-Fatḥ, Muhammed came at the end of the life of Eleazar VIII (see Stenhouse, *Kitāb*, 184 and 190). High priests are also mentioned throughout the text of the chronicle. For the differences between the high priests in the *Tulida* and the *Kitāb al-Tarīkh* see Moritz Heidenheim, "Die samaritan. Chronik des Hohenpriesters Elasar aus dem 11. Jahrhundert, übersetzt und erklärt," *Vierteljahrsschrift für deutsch- und englisch-theologische Forschung und Kritik* 4 (1870): 347–89.

21 Milka Levy-Rubin, *The* Continuatio *of the Samaritan Chronicle of Abū l-Fatḥ al-Sāmirī al-Danafī*, Studies in Late Antiquity and Early Islam, 10 (Princeton, NJ: Darwin Press, 2002). There is so far no new edition of the *Chronicle Adler*; the references are given here in the following way: The first page number in the annotations below refers to the publication in *REJ* (1 = *REJ* 44 [1902] 188–222; 2 = 45 [1902] 70–98; 3 = 45 [1902] 223–254; 4 = 46 [1903] 123–146), the second to the separate publication (Paris: Durlacher, 1903).

22 Yaacov Shavit, Yaacov Goldstein, and Haim Be'er, eds., *Personalities in Eretz-Israel 1799 – 1948: A Biographical Dictionary* (Tel-Aviv: Am Oved Publishers, 1983), (Hebrew). The entries on Samaritans were written by Benjamim Tsedaka (oral information from the author of the entries).

23 Reinhard Pummer, *Samaritan Marriage Contracts and Deeds of Divorce*, 2 vols. (Wiesbaden: Otto Harrassowitz, 1993 and 1997).

News, the bi-monthly Samaritan periodical published by Benyamim and Yefet Tsedaka in Ḥolon, Israel; (4) the listing of names of the high priests side by side in English and in Hebrew whereby I have substituted Gaster's English spellings of biblical names with those of the New Revised Standard Version; and finally, (5) the addition of the Gregorian dates, beginning with the first mention of an *anno Hegirae* date to the present.[24]

Concerning the Gregorian dates, the following points are to be noted: to obtain the year in which Eleazar IX became high priest, the eighteen years of his term of office (column I) were subtracted from AH 38, the Muslim year in which his term of office ended according to the "Chain" (column IV), whereby AH 38 corresponds to 658/9 CE.[25] For the next high priest, Aqbon VII, his 30 years of office are to be added to AH 38; the result, in terms of the Gregorian calendar, would be 688/9 CE. However, AH 68, the date when Aqbon's office ended according to column IV in the "Chain," corresponds to 687/8 CE. In the updated list, the CE dates are those that correspond to the AH date in Gaster's source.[26] A comparison of the dates of the most recent high priests included in the "Chain" with dates available in modern sources, shows that some dates are only approximate.

Similar to the Jews, the Samaritans base themselves on the figures of the Bible, in particular on the ages of the Patriarchs. Because the Samaritan Pentateuch differs in certain figures from the Masoretic text, and because the Jews rely on additional sources apart from the Pentateuch, Jewish and Samaritan dates of the Creation differ – the Jewish Year 1 of Creation corresponds to 3760 BCE, while the most common Samaritan Year 1 corresponds to 4439 BCE. The difference between the Samaritan and the Jewish Era of Creation is, therefore, 679 years. But even in Samaritan writings the date of Creation is not uniform (although the dis-

---

[24] Gaster's notes with the short texts of the events that took place in the time of some of the high priests can be consulted in the original publication. In particular, no attempts are made to reconcile dates in different sources. Photographs of some of the recent high priests are contained in *Personalities* and in various issues of *A.B. – The Samaritan News*.

[25] The Hijra dates were converted with the help of the Wüstenfeld-Mahler'sche *Vergleichungstabellen* (Bertold Spuler and Joachim Mayr, eds., *Wüstenfeld-Mahler'sche Vergleichungs-Tabellen zur muslimischen und iranischen Zeitrechnung mit Tafeln zur Umrechnung orient-christlicher Ären. Dritte, verbesserte und erweiterte Auflage der "Vergleichungs-Tabellen der mohammedanischen und christlichen Zeitrechnung"* [Wiesbaden: Franz Steiner, 1961]).

[26] It should be noted that Macdonald arrived at different results. His point of departure is a "fix" from which he worked backwards and forwards. He chose as "fix" the Northern Exile (722/1 B.C.E.); moreover, he understood the Hijra-dates in Gaster's "Chain" to indicate the *beginning* of a high priest's office, rather than the end (Macdonald, *The Samaritan Chronicle No. II*, 222–23).

crepancies are smaller than the one between the Samaritan and the Jewish dates). Chronological inconsistencies for later periods, too, are found in Samaritan writings due to additions or omissions in high priestly lists. Year 1 of the Era of Entry in the "Chain" is 2794 of the Era of Creation, as is the case in all chronicles;[27] AH 1 (622 CE) corresponds to 2107 of the Era of Entry and to 4901 of the Era of Creation.

As in Gaster's publication, the columns in the following tables indicate: I = age at the birth of the first son (Patriarchs) or years of office (high priests); II = Era of Creation; III = Era of Entry into Canaan; IV = year in the Muslim calendar in which the respective high priest's term of office ended; V = term of office in the Gregorian calendar; VI = name of the high priest in Hebrew and English.

The list published by Gaster contains probably an ancient classical tradition, and for this reason it is useful and interesting in spite of certain shortcomings.[28]

Originally, this update was undertaken at the suggestion of Professor Sergio Noja Noseda. It was to be published in his *Festschrift* to celebrate his 65th birthday. Unfortunately, the project of the *Festschrift* as an independent monograph did not come to fruition; only offprints were produced.[29] The present version is a revision and update of the earlier offprint of my contribution. I dedicate the paper to Prof. Noja's memory in appreciation for his contributions to Samaritan studies and for his friendship.

	I	II	III	IV	V	VI
I. Date of Birth and Priesthood.						
II. The Order of the Perfect Book (the Law) (i.e. Date of Creation).						
[1] *Tulida* 6א1 *Chronicle Adler* 1, 191/3		130	130			אדם Adam

---

27 Except for the *Asaṭir*. See the table in Ayala Loewenstamm, "Samaritans. Samaritan Chronology," in *Encyclopaedia Judaica* 17 (732–738, 2007), 734; this table does not include Gaster's "Chain." See now also Christophe Bonnard, "Asfår Asāṭīr, le 'Livre des Légendes,' une réécriture araméenne du Pentateuque samaritain: présentation, édition critique, traduction et commentaire philologique, commentaire comparatif" (PhD diss., Strasbourg: University of Strasbourg, 2015), 365.

28 As pointed out by Baillet, "Samaritains," 920, it contains some errors and Gaster disregarded the differences in the calendars.

29 The title of the book was to be *I primi sessanta anni di scuola: Studie dedicati dagli amici a Sergio Noja Noseda nel suo 65° compleanno, 7 Luglio 1996* (Lesa: Fondazione Ferni Noja Noseda, n.d.).

Continued

	I	II	III	IV	V	VI	
Abū 'l-Fatḥ 4 [5],[30] 187 [247]							
[2] *Tulida* 6א2 *Chronicle Adler* 1, 192/4 Abū 'l-Fatḥ 4 [5]; 187 [247]	105	235				שת	Seth
[3] *Tulida* 6א3 *Chronicle Adler* 1, 192/4 Abū 'l-Fatḥ 4 [5]; 187 [247]	90	325				אנוש	Enosh
[4] *Tulida* 6א4 *Chronicle Adler* 1, 192/4 Abū 'l-Fatḥ 4 [5]; 187 [247]	70	390				קינן	Kenan
[5] *Tulida* 6א5 *Chronicle Adler* 1, 192/4 Abū 'l-Fatḥ 4 [5]; 187 [247]	65	460				מהללאל	Mahalel
[6] *Tulida* 6א6 *Chronicle Adler* 1, 192/4 Abū 'l-Fatḥ 4 [5]; 187 [247]	62	522				ירד	Jared
[7] *Tulida* 6א7 *Chronicle Adler* 1, 193/5 Abū 'l-Fatḥ 4 [5]; 187 [247]	65	58				חנוך	Enoch
[8] *Tulida* 6א8 *Chronicle Adler* 1, 193/5 Abū 'l-Fatḥ 4 [5]; 187 [247]	67	654				מתושלח	Metuselah
[9] *Tulida* 6א9 *Chronicle Adler* 1, 193/5 Abū 'l-Fatḥ 4 [5]; 187 [247]	53	707				למך	Lamech
[10] *Tulida* 6א10 *Chronicle Adler* 1, 193–196/ 5–8 Abū 'l-Fatḥ 4 [5]; 187 [247]	502	1209				נח	Noah
[11] *Tulida* 6א11 *Chronicle Adler* 1, 196/8	100	1309				שם	Shem

---

30 The first figure refers to the page in the Arabic manuscript edited in Stenhouse, "Kitāb" (1980), the second, in brackets, to the page in Stenhouse's translation, "Kitāb" (1985). Reference is always to the first mention of a name.

Continued

	I	II	III	IV	V	VI	
Abū 'l-Fatḥ 5 [6]							
[12] *Tulida* 6א12 *Chronicle Adler* 1, 197/9 Abū 'l-Fatḥ 5 [6]; 187 [247]	135	1444				ארפכשד	Arpachshad
[13] *Tulida* 6א13 *Chronicle Adler* 1, 197/9 Abū 'l-Fatḥ 5 [6]; 187 [247]	130	1574				שלח	Shelah
[14] *Tulida* 6א14 *Chronicle Adler* 1, 197/9 Abū 'l-Fatḥ 5 [6]; 187 [247]	135	1708				עבר	Eber
[15] *Tulida* 6א15 *Chronicle Adler* 1, 197/9 Abū 'l-Fatḥ 5 [6]; 188 [247]	130	1838				פלג	Peleg
[16] *Tulida* 6א16 *Chronicle Adler* 1, 197/9 Abū 'l-Fatḥ 5 [6]; 188 [247]	132	1970				רעו	Reu
[17] *Tulida* 6א17 *Chronicle Adler* 1, 197/9 Abū 'l-Fatḥ 5 [6]; 188 [247]	130	2100				שרוג	Serug
[18] *Tulida* 6א18 *Chronicle Adler* 1, 197/9 Abū 'l-Fatḥ 5 [6]; 188 [247]	79	2179				נחור	Nahor
[19] *Tulida* 6א19 *Chronicle Adler* 1, 197/9 Abū 'l-Fatḥ 5 [6]; 188 [247]	70	2249				תרח	Terah
[20] *Tulida* 6א21 *Chronicle Adler* 1, 198/10 Abū 'l-Fatḥ 5 [6]; 188 [247]	100	2349				אברהם	Abraham
[21] *Tulida* 6א22 *Chronicle Adler* 1, 198–199/ 10–11 Abū 'l-Fatḥ 6 [7]; 188 [247]	60	2409				יצחק	Isaac
[22] *Tulida* 6א23 *Chronicle Adler* 1, 199–200/ 11–12	87	2496				יעקב	Jacob

Continued

	I	II	III	IV	V	VI	
Abū 'l-Fatḥ 6 [7]; 188 [247]							
[23] *Tulida* 6א24 *Chronicle Adler* 1, 200/12 Abū 'l-Fatḥ 7 [7]; 188 [247]	52	2547				לוי	Levi
[24] *Tulida* 6א25 *Chronicle Adler* 1, 200–210/ 12–13 Abū 'l-Fatḥ 7 [7]; 188 [247]	71	2619				קהת	Kohath
[25] *Tulida* 6א26 *Chronicle Adler* 1, 201/13 Abū 'l-Fatḥ 7 [7]; 187 [247]	52	2671				עמרם	Amram
[26] [*Tulida* 6א27 [*Chronicle Adler* 1, 201/13 [*Tulida* 6א28 [*Chronicle Adler* 1, 201/13 Abū 'l-Fatḥ 7 [7]; 187 [247]	83 40	2754 2794				אהרן משה	Aaron I[31] Moses
III. The Entry of the Children of Israel into the Land of Canaan.							
[27] *Tulida* 6ב31 *Chronicle Adler* 1, 201–202/ 13–14 Abū 'l-Fatḥ 28 [33]; 188 [247]	50	2844	50			אלעזר	Eleazar I
[28] *Tulida* 6ב32 *Chronicle Adler* 1, 202–203/ 14–15 Abū 'l-Fatḥ 38 [43]; 188 [247]	60	2904	110			פינחס	Phinehas I
[29] *Tulida* 6ב33 *Chronicle Adler* 1, 203–204/ 15 Abū 'l-Fatḥ 39 [45]; 188 [247]	40	2944	150			אבישע	Abisha I
[30] *Tulida* 6ב34 *Chronicle Adler* 1, 204/16 Abū 'l-Fatḥ 39 [45]; 188 [247]	50	2994	200			ששי	Sheshai I
[31] *Tulida* 6ב35	35	3029	235			בחקי	Baḥqi I

---

[31] I have added ordinal numbers where necessary, even if they are absent from Gaster's text.

Continued

I	II	III	IV	V	VI	
Chronicle Adler 1, 204–205/ 16–17 Abū 'l-Fatḥ 39 [45]; 188 [247]						
[32] Tulida 6ב36 Chronicle Adler 1, 205–206/ 17–18 Abū 'l-Fatḥ 39 [45]; 188 [247][32]	25	3053	260		עזי	Uzzi I
[33] Tulida 6ב40 Chronicle Adler 1, 206–207/ 18–19 Abū 'l-Fatḥ 54 [64]; 188 [247]	39	3093	299		שישי	Sheshai II
[34] Tulida 7א55 Chronicle Adler 1, 207/19 Abū 'l-Fatḥ 55 [65]; 188 [247]	23	3116	322		בחקי	Baḥqi II
[35] Tulida 7א56 Chronicle Adler 1, 207/19 Abū 'l-Fatḥ 55 [65]; 188 [247]	28	3144	350		שבט	Shebeṭ
[36] Tulida 7א57 Chronicle Adler 1, 208/20 Abū 'l-Fatḥ 55 [65]; 188 [247]	55	3169	375		שלום	Shalom I
[37] Tulida 7א58 Chronicle Adler 1, 208/20 Abū 'l-Fatḥ 55 [65]; 188 [247]	20	3189	395		חזקיה	Hezekiah I
[38] Tulida 7א 59 (יהונן) Chronicle Adler 1, 208/20 Abū 'l-Fatḥ 55 [65]; 188 [247]	28	3217	423		יהונתן	Jonathan I
[39] Chronicle Adler 1, 208/20 Abū 'l-Fatḥ 55 [65]; 188 [247][33]	22	3239	445		יאיר	Jair I
[40] Tulida 7א60 Chronicle Adler 1, 208/20 Abū 'l-Fatḥ 59 [70]; 188 [247]	25	3264	470		דליה	Daliah I

---

[32] Abū 'l-Fatḥ adds: "The end of the Raḍwān and the disappearance of the Tabernacle ... From Ozzi to the appearance of Muḥammad was 1993 years."

[33] Abū 'l-Fatḥ inserts: "Ṣadaqīa, 28 years; Aḥiyūd, 20 years; Mājar, 21 years; Yūṣadaq, 25 years" (59 [70]; 188 [247]).

Continued

	I	II	III	IV	V	VI	
[41] Tulida 7א61 Chronicle Adler 1, 208/20 Abū 'l-Fatḥ 59 [70]; 188 [248]	19	3224?	489			יאיר	Jair II
[42] Tulida 7א 62 (יהונן) Chronicle Adler 1, 209–210/ 21–22 Abū 'l-Fatḥ 59 [70]; 188 [248]	28	3311	517			יהונתן	Jonathan II
[43] Tulida 7א63 Chronicle Adler 1, 210/22 Abū 'l-Fatḥ 59 [70]; 188 [248]	26	3337	543			ישמעאל	Ishmael
[44] Tulida 7א64 Chronicle Adler 1, 211/23 Abū 'l-Fatḥ 59 [70]; 188 [248]	28	3365	571			טוביה	Tobiah I
[45] Tulida 7ב65 Chronicle Adler 1, 211–212/ 23–24 Abū 'l-Fatḥ 59 [70]; 189 [248]	20	3385	591			צדוק	Zadok
[46] Tulida 8א84 Chronicle Adler 1, 212/24 Abū 'l-Fatḥ 60 [71]; 189 [248]	28	3413	619			עמרם	Amram I
[47] Tulida 8א85 Chronicle Adler 1, 212/24 Abū 'l-Fatḥ 60 [71]; 189 [248]	24	3437	643			חלקיה	Hilkiah
[48] Tulida 8א86 Chronicle Adler 1, 213/25 Abū 'l-Fatḥ 60 [71]; 189 [248]	28	3475	681			עמרם	Amram II
[49] Tulida 8א87 Chronicle Adler 1, 213/25 Abū 'l-Fatḥ 60 [71]; 189 [248]	36	3511	717			עקוב	Aqob I
[50] Tulida 8א88 Chronicle Adler 1, 213–215/ 25–27 Abū 'l-Fatḥ 60 [71];[34] 189 [248]	39	3550	756			עקביה	Aqbiah

---

34 Abū 'l-Fatḥ adds: "it was in his day that Nebuchadnezzar came."

Continued

	I	II	III	IV	V	VI	
[51] *Tulida* 8א89 *Chronicle Adler* 1, 215/27 Abū 'l-Fatḥ 65 [78]; 189 [248]	45	3595	501			חלאל	Hilal (Hillel?)
[52] *Tulida* 8א90 *Chronicle Adler* 1, 215/27 Abū 'l-Fatḥ 65 [78]; 189 [248]	40	3635	841			שריה	Seraiah
[53] *Tulida* 8א216 *Chronicle Adler* 1, 216/28 Abū 'l-Fatḥ 66 [79]; 189 [248]	50	3685	891			לוי	Levi I
[54] *Tulida* 8א92 *Chronicle Adler* 1, 216–217/ 28–29 Abū 'l-Fatḥ 66 [79]; 189 [248]	51	3737	943			נתנאל	Nethanel I
[55] *Tulida* 8א93 *Chronicle Adler* 1, 217–218/ 29–30 Abū 'l-Fatḥ 66 [79]; 189 [248]	35	3772	978			עזריה	Azariah
[56] *Tulida* 8א94 *Chronicle Adler* 1, 218–220/ 30–32 Abū 'l-Fatḥ 66 [79]; 189 [248]	40	3812	1018			עבדאל	Abdael I
[57] *Tulida* 8א95 *Chronicle Adler* 1, 220–222/ 32–34 Abū 'l-Fatḥ 80 [96]; 85 [103]; 189 [248]	30	3842	1084			חזקיה	Hezekiah II
[58] *Tulida* 8א96 *Chronicle Adler* 1, 222/34 Abū 'l-Fatḥ 85 [103]; 189 [248]	24	3866	1072			חניה	Hananiah
[59] *Tulida* 8א97 *Chronicle Adler* 2, 70–72/ 34–36 Abū 'l-Fatḥ 85 [103]; 189 [248]	32	3898	1104			עמרם	Amram III
[60] *Tulida* 8א98 *Chronicle Adler* 2, 72/37 Abū 'l-Fatḥ 91 [112]; 189 [248]	25	3924	1029			חנן	Hanan

Continued

	I	II	III	IV	V	VI	
[61] *Tulida* 8ב99 *Chronicle Adler* 2, 73/37 Abū 'l-Fatḥ 91 [112];[35] 102 [126]; 189 [248]	21	3944	1150			חזקיה	Hezekiah III
[62] *Tulida* 8ב100 *Chronicle Adler* 2, 73–75/38–39 Abū 'l-Fatḥ 102 [126]; 189 [248]	42	3986	1192			דליה	Daliah II
[63] *Tulida* 8ב101 *Chronicle Adler* 2, 75/39 Abū 'l-Fatḥ 189 [248]	40	4026	1222			עקוב	Aqob II
[64] *Tulida* 8ב102 *Chronicle Adler* 2, 75/39 Abū 'l-Fatḥ 189 [248]	35	4061	1157			עקביה	Aqabiah II
[65] *Tulida* 8ב103 *Chronicle Adler* 2, 75/39–40 Abū 'l-Fatḥ 189 [248]	41	4102	1298			לוי	Levi II
[66] *Tulida* 8ב104 *Chronicle Adler* 2, 75/40 Abū 'l-Fatḥ 189 [248]	44	4146	lacuna			אלעזר	Eleazar II
[67] *Tulida* 8ב105 *Chronicle Adler* 2, 75/40 Abū 'l-Fatḥ 189 [248]	36	4182	1388			מנשה	Manasseh
[68] *Tulida* 8ב106 *Chronicle Adler* 2, 75/40 Abū 'l-Fatḥ 189 [248]	39	4221	1427			יאיר	Jair III
[69] *Tulida* 8ב107 *Chronicle Adler* 2, 75/40 Abū 'l-Fatḥ 113 [143]; 189 [248]	41	4262	1468			[נתנאל]	[Nethanel] II

---

[35] Abū 'l-Fatḥ notes: "In the days of this Ḥezeqīa the High Priest, Alexander came from Macedon to fight Darius king of Persia."

Continued

	I	II	III	IV	V	VI	
[70] *Tulida* 108ב8 *Chronicle Adler* 2, 76–77/40 Abū 'l-Fatḥ 116 [147]; 189 [248]	[32	4294	1500]			יהיקם	Jojaqim[36]
[71] *Tulida* 109ב8 *Chronicle Adler* 2, 77/41–42 Abū 'l-Fatḥ 117 [147]; 189 [248]	27	4321	1527			יהונתן	Jonathan III
[72] *Tulida* 110ב8 *Chronicle Adler* 2, 78/42 Abū 'l-Fatḥ 117 [148]; 189 [248]	33	4354	1550			אלישמע	Elishama
[73] *Tulida* 111ב8 *Chronicle Adler* 2, 78/42 Abū 'l-Fatḥ 117 [149]; 189 [248]	10	4364	1560			שמעיה	Shemaiah
[74] *Tulida* 112ב8 *Chronicle Adler* 2, 78/42 Abū 'l-Fatḥ 117 [149]; 189 [248]	8	4372	1568			טוביה	Tobiah II[37]
[77] *Tulida* 113ב8 *Chronicle Adler* 2, 78–80/42–44 Abū 'l-Fatḥ 117 [149]; 189 [248]	9	4381	1277			עמרם	Amram IV
[78] *Tulida* 114ב8 *Chronicle Adler* 2, 80–84/44–48 Abū 'l-Fatḥ 118 [149];[38] 189 [248]	30	4411	1607			עקבון	Aqbon I

---

36 The "Chain" adds to the name of the high priest the note: "In his days Jesus appeared in Bethlehem." See also Abū 'l-Fatḥ *ad locum:* "In his days the Messiah was born, son of Mary, son of the Rabbi – peace be upon him – Joseph the Carpenter" (see footnote no. 600 in Stenhouse's translation). The *Tulida* reads יהקים; *Chronicle Adler* reads יהוקים.

37 Gaster notes that Abū 'l-Fatḥ inserts here two more names – [75] 'Amram, 11 years; [76] 'Aḳob, 9 years.

38 According to Abū 'l-Fatḥ 118 [149], 'Aḳbon ('Aqūb) was succeded by 'Amram, who was succeded by 'Aqbūn (122 [155]).

Continued

	I	II	III	IV	V	VI	
[79] *Tulida* 8ב115 *Chronicle Adler* 2, 84/48 Abū 'l-Fatḥ 128 [162]; 189 [248]	40	4451	1647			פינחס	Phinehas II
[80] *Tulida* 8ב116 *Chronicle Adler* 2, 84–85/ 48–49 Abū 'l-Fatḥ 128 [162]; 189 [248]	25	4476	1682			לוי	Levi III
[81] *Tulida* 8ב117 *Chronicle Adler* 2, 85/49 Abū 'l-Fatḥ 128 [162]; 189 [248]	32	4507	1714			אלעזר	Eleazar III
[82] *Tulida* 8ב118 *Chronicle Adler* 2, 85/49 (טביה) Abū 'l-Fatḥ 128 [162]; 189 [248][39]	28	4536	1742			בבא	Baba I
[83] *Tulida* 8ב119 *Chronicle Adler* 2, 85/49 Abū 'l-Fatḥ 128 [162]; 189 [248]	41	4577	1783			אלעזר	Eleazar IV
[84] *Tulida* 9א120 *Chronicle Adler* 2, 85–86/50 Abū 'l-Fatḥ 128 [163]; 189 [248]	23	4600	1806			עקבון	Aqbon II
[—] *Tulida* 9א121 *Chronicle Adler* 2, 86–87/ 50–51 Abū 'l-Fatḥ 135 [172]; 189 [248]	32	4632	1838			נתנאל	Nethanel III
[85] *Tulida* 10א139 *Chronicle Adler* 3, 223–227/ 63–67 Abū 'l-Fatḥ 161 [206]; 189 [248]	26	4658	1864			עקבון	Aqbon III

---

39 Abū 'l-Fatḥ reads Ṭobīa, as does *Chronicle Adler*. The *Tulida* reads בבא.

Continued

	I	II	III	IV	V	VI	
[86] *Tulida* 10א140 *Chronicle Adler* 3, 228–230/ 76–70 Abū 'l-Fatḥ 170 [219]; 190 [248]	31	4689	1895			נתנאל	Nethanel IV
[87] *Tulida* 10א141 *Chronicle Adler* 3, 231/71 Abū 'l-Fatḥ 176 [230]; 190 [248]	20	4709	1915			עקבון	Aqbon IV
[88] *Tulida* 10א142 *Chronicle Adler* 3, 231–232/ 71–72 Abū 'l-Fatḥ 176 [230]; 190 [248]	25	4734	1940			אלעזר	Eleazar V
[89] *Tulida* 10א143 *Chronicle Adler* 3, 232–234/ 72–74 Abū 'l-Fatḥ 177 [232]; 190 [248]	24	4758	1964			עקבון	Aqbon V
[90] *Tulida* 10א144 *Chronicle Adler* 3, 234/74 Abū 'l-Fatḥ 180 [236]; 190 [248]	17	4775	1981			אלעזר	Eleazar VI
[91] *Tulida* 10א145 *Chronicle Adler* 3, 234/74 Abū 'l-Fatḥ 180 [236]; 190 [248]	30	4805	2011			עקבון	Aqbon VI
[92] *Tulida* 10א146 *Chronicle Adler* 3, 234–235/ 74 Abū 'l-Fatḥ 180 [237]; 190 [248]	40	4845	2051			אלעזר	Eleazar VII
[93] *Tulida* 10א147 *Chronicle Adler* 3, 235–237/ 75–76 Abū 'l-Fatḥ 182 [239]; 190 [248]	31	4876	2084			נתנאל	Nethanel V

Continued

	I	II	III	IV	V	VI	
[94] *Tulida* 10א148 *Chronicle Adler* 3, 237–240/ 76–81 Abū ʾl-Fatḥ 184 [242];[40] 190 [248]	25	4901	2107			אלעזר	Eleazar VIII
[95] *Tulida* 11א163 *Chronicle Adler* 3, 241/81 Abū ʾl-Fatḥ 190 [248]	20	4921	2127			נתנאל	Nethanel VI
IV. The Era of the Muhammedans.							
[96] *Tulida* 11א164 *Chronicle Adler* 3, 242/81–82 Abū ʾl-Fatḥ 190 [248]	18	4939	2145	38	640/1– 658/9	אלעזר	Eleazar IX
[97] *Tulida* 11א165 *Chronicle Adler* 3, 242–243/ 82–83 *Continuatio* 51	30	4969	2175	68	658/9– 687/8	עקבון	Aqbon VII
[98] *Tulida* 11א166 *Chronicle Adler* 3, 244/83 *Continuatio* 51	16	4985	2191	84	687/8– 703	אלעזר	Eleazar X
[99] *Tulida* 11א167 *Chronicle Adler* 3, 244/83	20	5005	2211	104	703– 722/3	עקבון	Aqbon VIII
[100] *Tulida* 11א168 *Chronicle Adler* 3, 244/84	22	5027	2233	126	722/3– 743/4	אלעזר	Eleazar XI
[101] *Tulida* 11א169 *Chronicle Adler* 3, 244–245/ 84–85	21	5048	2254	147	743/4– 764/5	עקבון	Aqbon IX

---

40 Abū ʾl-Fatḥ adds: "At the end of the High Priesthood of this Eleazar [viz. Eleazar VIII in Gaster's list] Muḥammad came."

Continued

	I	II	III	IV	V	VI	
[102] *Tulida* 11א170 *Chronicle Adler* 3, 245/85	26	5074	2280	173	764/5– 789/90	אלעזר	Eleazar XII
[103] *Tulida* 11א171 *Chronicle Adler* 3, 246/85–86	7	5081	2287	180	789/90– 796/7	שמעון	Simeon
[104] *Tulida* 11א172 *Chronicle Adler* 3, 246/86	31	5012	2318	211	796/7– 826/7	לוי	Levi IV
[105] *Tulida* 11א173 *Chronicle Adler* 3, 246–50/ 86–90	12	5124	2330	223	826/7– 837/8	פינחס	Phinehas III
[106] *Tulida* 11א174 *Chronicle Adler* 3, 250/90	2	5126	2332	225	837/8– 839/40	נתנאל	Nethanel VII
[107] *Tulida* 11א175 *Chronicle Adler* 3, 250–251/ 90	11	5137	2343	236	839/40– 850/1	בבא	Baba II
[108] *Tulida* 11א176 *Chronicle Adler* 3, 251/90	9	5146	2352	245	850/1– 859/60	אלעזר	Eleazar XIII
[109] *Tulida* 11א177 *Chronicle Adler* 3, 251/90–91	20	5166	2372	265	859/60– 878/9	נתנאל	Nethanel VIII
[110] *Tulida* 11א178 *Chronicle Adler* 3, 251/91 Continuatio 105	7	5173	2379	272	878/9– 885/6	אלעזר	Eleazar XIV
[111] *Tulida* 11א179 *Chronicle Adler* 3, 251/91	8	5181	2387	280	885/6– 893/4	פינחס	Phinehas IV
[112] *Tulida* 11א180 *Chronicle Adler* 3, 251–2/91	55	5236	2442	335	893/4– 946/7	נתנאל	Nethanel IX

Continued

	I	II	III	IV	V	VI	
[113] Tulida 11א181 Chronicle Adler 3, 252/91	[16	5252	2458	351]	946/7–962	עבדאל	Abdael II
[114] Tulida 11א182 Chronicle Adler 3, 252–3/91–2	35	5287	2493	386	962–996	אלעזר	Eleazar XV
[115] Tulida 11א183 Chronicle Adler 3, 253/92–93	20	5307	2513	406	996–1015/6	עבדאל	Abdael III
[116] Tulida 12א200 Chronicle Adler 3, 254/93	38	5345	2551	444	1015/6–1052/3	אלעזר	Eleazar XVI
[117] Tulida 12א201 Chronicle Adler 3, 254/93–94	14	5359	2565	458	1052/3–1065	אהרן	Aaron II
[118] Tulida 12א202 Chronicle Adler 4, 123–4/94–5	12	5371	2577	470	1065–1087/8	צדקה	Ṣadaqa I
[119] Tulida 12א203 Chronicle Adler 4, 124/95	39	5410	2616	509	1087/8–1115/6	עמרם	Amram V
[120] Tulida 12א204 Chronicle Adler 4, 124–126/95–97	[22	5432	2638	531]	1115/6–1136/7	אהרן	Aaron III
[121] Tulida 13ב1 Chronicle Adler 4, 126/97	28	5460	2666	559	1136/7–1163/4	עמרם	Amram VI
[122] Tulida 13ב2 Chronicle Adler 4, 127/97–98	26	5486	2692	585	1163/4–1189/90	אהרן	Aaron IV
[123] Tulida 13ב3 Chronicle Adler 4, 127/98	19	5505	2711	604	1189/90–1207/8	נתנאל	Nethanel X

Continued

	I	II	III	IV	V	VI	
[124]		48	5553	2759	652	1207/8– 1254/5	איתמר Ithamar
Tulida 13ב16 *Chronicle Adler* 4, 127/98							
[125]		15	5568	2774	667	1254/5– 1268/9	עמרם Amram VII
Tulida 13ב17 *Chronicle Adler* 4, 127–128/ 98–99							
[126]		22	5590	2766	689	1268/9– 1290	עזי Uzzi II
Tulida 13ב18 *Chronicle Adler* 4, 128–129/ 99–100							
[127]		19	5609	2815	708	1290– 1308/9	יוסף Joseph I
Tulida 13ב21 *Chronicle Adler* 4, 129–130/ 100–101							
[128]		56	5665	2871	764	1308/9– 1362/3	פינחס Phinehas V[41]
Tulida 14א22 *Chronicle Adler* 4, 130/101							
[129]		25	5690	2896	789	1362/3– 1387	אלעזר Eleazar XVII[42]
Tulida 14א24 *Chronicle Adler* 4, 131/101							
[130]		56	5746	2952	845	1387– 1441/2	פינחס Phinehas VI[43]
Tulida 14א25 *Chronicle Adler* 4, 131/102							
[131]		34	5780	2986	879	1441/2– 1474/5	אבישע Abisha II[44]
Tulida 14א28 *Chronicle Adler* 4, 131/102							
[132]		36	5816	5022!	915	1474/5– 1509/10	אלעזר Eleazar XVIII[45]
Tulida 14א29 *Chronicle Adler* 4, 131–132/ 102–103							

---

41 פינחס בן יוסף
42 אלעזר בן פינחס בן יוסף
43 פינחס בן אבישע בן פינחס בן יוסף
44 פינחס בן אבישע בן פינחס בן יוסף – son of אבישע בן פינחס בן אבישע.
45 אבישע בן פינחס בן יוסף – son of אלעזר בן אבישע בן פינחס.

Continued

	I	II	III	IV	V	VI	
[133] *Tulida* 14ב37 *Chronicle Adler* 4, 132–133/ 103–104	41	5857	3063	956	1509/10– 1549	פינחס	Phinehas VII[46]
[134] *Tulida* 14ב38 *Chronicle Adler* 4, 133/104	48	5905	3111	1004	1549– 1595/6	אלעזר	Eleazar XIX[47]
[135] *Tulida* 14א39 *Chronicle Adler* 4, 134/104	19	5924	3130	1023	1595/6– 1614/5	פינחס	Phinehas VIII[48]
[136] *Tulida* 14ב40 *Chronicle Adler* 4, 134–135/ 104–105	10	5935	3140	1033	1614/5– 1623/4	שלמיה	Shelemiah[49]
[137] *Tulida* 18ב3 *Chronicle Adler* 4, 135/105– 106	27	5961	3167	1060	1623/4– 1650	צדקה	Ṣadaqa II[50]
[138] *Tulida* 18ב4 *Chronicle Adler* 4, 135–6/106	45	6006	3212	1105	1650–1694	יצחק	Isaac I[51]
[139] *Tulida* 18ב5 *Chronicle Adler* 4, 136/106– 107	40	6046	3252	1145	1694–1732	אברהם	Abraham[52]
[140] *Tulida* 18ב6 *Chronicle Adler* 4, 136–137/ 107	20	6066	3272	1165	1733–1752	לוי	Levi V[53]

---

46 פינחס בן אלעזר
47 אלעזר בן פינחס
48 פינחס בן אלעזר
49 שלמיה בן פינחס. End of original line.
50 צדקה בן טביה הלוי
51 יצחק בן צדקה
52 אברהם בן יצחק בן צדקה
53 לוי בן אברהם; cf. Pummer, *Samaritan Marriage Contracts* I, 151.

Continued

	I	II	III	IV	V	VI	
[141] *Tulida* 18ב7 *Chronicle Adler* 4, 137–138/ 107–109	36	6102	3308	1201	1752–1787	טביה	Ṭabia IV[54]
[142] *Tulida* 18ב8 *Chronicle Adler* 4, 138–140/ 109–111	42	6144	3350	1243	1798–1828	שלמה	Salama[55]
[143] *Tulida* 18ב9[56] *Chronicle Adler* 4, 140–144/ 111–114	33	6177	3383	1276	1828–1859/60	עמרם	Amram VIII
[144] *Tulida* 18ב (addition) *Chronicle Adler* 4, 144–146/ 115–116	49	6226	3432	1335[57]	1859/60–1916	יעקב	Jacob I[58]
(145) *Tulida* 18ב (addition)				1336–1351	1917/8–1932	יצחק	Isaac II[59]
(146) *Tulida* 18ב (addition)				1351–1362	1933–1943	מצליח	Maṣliaḥ[60]

---

54 טביה בן יצחק; cf. Pummer, *Samaritan Marriage Contracts* I, 153.
55 שלמה בן טביה בן יצחק – lived 1784–1855, was high priest 1788–1828; he was only four years old when his father died and was the only member left of the priestly family; the community filled in for him until he was installed as high priest at the age of 15 *(Personalities*, 494); cf. Pummer, *Samaritan Marriage Contracts* I, 152–153.
56 1272–1291 (1855/6–1874/5 CE) according to the addition on 18ב (p. 125 in the ed. by Florentin).
57 1325 in Gaster's text is the date of the compilation of the list.
58 יעקב בן אהארן בן שלמה – lived 1840–1916; was high priest 1870–1916 *(Personalities* 256). 1291–1336 (= 1874–1917/18) according to the addition to 18ב (p. 125 in the edition by Florentin); Pummer, *Samaritan Marriage Contracts* I, 149–150. According to Robert T. Anderson and Terry Giles, *The Keepers: An Introduction to the History and Culture of the Samaritans* (Peabody, MA: Hendrickson, 2002), 138, he was born in 1841 and was high priest from 1861 to his death in 1916.
59 יצחק בן עמרם בן שלמה – lived 1855–1932, was high priest 1916–1932 *(Personalities*, 259); Pummer, *Samaritan Marriage Contracts* I, 147.
60 מצליח בן פינחס בן יצחק בן שלמה – lived 1868–1943, was high priest 1932–1943 *(Personalities*, 323); Pummer, *Samaritan Marriage Contracts* I, 151.

Continued

	I	II	III	IV	V	VI	
(147) *Tulida* ב18 (addition)				1362–1380	1943–1960	אבישע	Abisha III[61]
(148) *Tulida* ב18 (addition)				1380–1400	1960–1980	עמרם	Amram IX[62]
(149) *Tulida* ב18 (addition)				1400–1402	1980–1982	אשר	Asher[63]
(150) *Tulida* ב18 (addition)				1402–1404	1982–1984	פינחס	Phinehas IX[64]
(151) *Tulida* ב18 (addition)				1404–1407	1984–1987	יעקב	Jacob II[65]
(152) *Tulida* ב18 (addition)				1407–1419	1987–1998	יוסף	Joseph II[66]
(153)				1419–1422	1998–2001	לוי	Levi VI[67]
(154)				1422–1424	2001–2004	שלום	Shalom II[68]

---

[61] אבישע בן פינחס בן יצחק בן שלמה – lived 1880–1960, was high priest 1943–1960 (*Personalities*, 17); Pummer, *Samaritan Marriage Contracts* I, 141–142. Brother of מצליח בן פינחס בן יצחק בן שלמה.

[62] עמרם בן יצחק בן עמרם בן שלמה – lived 1889–1980, was high priest 1960–1980 (*Personalities*, 383–384). A.B. – *The Samaritan News* 256 (16.3.1980) 1–14 (Hebrew), 20; 257 (1.4.1980) 3–7 (Hebrew); Pummer, *Samaritan Marriage Contracts* I, 144.

[63] אשר בן מצליח בן פינחס – lived 1895–1982, was high priest 1980–1982 (cf. *Personalities*, 64). A.B. – *The Samaritan News* 304 (15.2.1982) 3–7 (Hebrew).

[64] פינחס בן מצליח – lived 1899–1984, was high priest 1982–1984 (cf. *Personalities*, 396). A.B. – *The Samaritan News* 272 (1.11.1984): 5–22 (Hebrew). Brother of אשר בן מצליח בן פינחס.

[65] יעקב בן עזי בן אהרון – lived 1900–1987 (cf. *Personalities*, 256), was high priest 1984–1987. Cf. A.B. – *The Samaritan News* 208–209 (21.4.1978): 15–29; 428–429 (1.2.1987): 8–11 (Hebrew), 51–52.

[66] יוסף בן אב חסדא בן יעקב – lived 1919–1998, was high priest 1987–1998. Cf. A.B. – *The Samaritan News* 705–706 (1.3.1998): 1, 11–39, 44–46 (Hebrew), 76–78.

[67] לוי בן אבישע – lived 1920–2001, was high priest 1998–2001. A.B. – *The Samaritan News* 705–706 (1.3.1998): 6–7; 791–794 (1.6.2001): 157–158 (Hebrew).

[68] שלום בן עמרם – lived 1922–2004, was high priest 2001–2004. See A.B. – *The Samaritan News* 851 (14.5.2004): unpaginated insert.

Continued

	I	II	III	IV	V	VI	
(155)				1425–1431	2004–2010	אלעזר	Eleazar[69] XX
(156)				1431–1434	2010–2013	אהרון	Aaron V[70]
(157)				1434-	2013-	עבדאל	Abdel[71] IV

---

69 אלעזר בן צדקה בן יצחק; born 1927, died 2010; high priest 2004–2010. See also *A.B. – The Samaritan News* 1055–1056 (26.2.2010): 8–10. Cousin of שלום.

70 אהרון בן אב־חיסדה בן יעקב בן אהרון; born 1 Feb. 1927, died 19 April 2013. See *A.B. – The Samaritan News* 1055–1056 (26.2.2010): 1–2, 5–7; *A.B. – The Samaritan News* 1059–1060 (28.4.2010): 2, and *A.B. – The Samaritan News* 1140–1141 (10.5.2013): 84–88.

71 עבד־אל בן אשר בן מצליח Abdel b. Asher b. Maṣliaḥ; born 1935; high priest 2013-. Cf. *A.B. – The Samaritan News* 1140–1141 (10.5.2013): 1, and *A.B. – The Samaritan News* 1142–1143 (14.6.2013): 97–99.

Bibliography

Abel, Félix-Marie. "Notre exploration à Naplouse." RB 31 (1922): 89–99.
Adler, Elkan Nathan and Max Séligsohn. "Une nouvelle chronique Samaritaine." *REJ* 44 (1902): 188–222; 45 (1902): 70–98; 45 (1902): 223–254; 46 (1903): 123–146. Also published separately: Paris: Durlacher, 1903.
Aejmelaeus, Anneli. "Septuagintal Translation Techniques: A Solution to the Problem of the Tabernacle Account." Pages 116–30 in *On the Trail of the Septuagint Translators: Collected Essays*. Edited by Anneli Aejmelaeus. Kampen: Kok Pharos, 1993.
Ahlström, Gösta. *The History of Ancient Palestine*. Sheffield: Sheffield Academic Press, 1993.
Albertz, Rainer. *From the Exile to the Maccabees*. Vol. 2 of *A History of Israelite Religion in the Old Testament Period*. London: SCM Press, 1992. English translation of *Religionsgeschichte Israels in alttestamentlicher Zeit*, Teil 2: *Vom Exil bis zu den Makkabäern*. Göttingen: Vandenhoeck & Ruprecht, 1992.
Albertz, Rainer. *Vom Exil bis zu den Makkabäern*. Vol. 2 of *Religionsgeschichte Israels in alttestamentlicher Zeit*. GAT 8.2. Göttingen: Vandenhoeck & Ruprecht, 1992.
Albertz, Rainer. "Purity Strategies and Political Interest in the Policy of Nehemiah." Pages 199–206 in *Confronting the Past: Archaeological and Historical Essays on Ancient Israel in Honor of William G. Dever*. Edited by S. Gitin, J. E. Wright, and J. P. Dessel. Winona Lake, IN: Eisenbrauns, 2006.
Albright, William Foxwell. "A Biblical Fragment from the Maccabaean Age: The Nash Papyrus." *JBL* 56 (1937): 145–76.
Allen, Leslie C. *The Greek Chronicles: The Relationship of the Septuagint of I and II Chronicles to the Masoretic Text – Part II Textual Criticism*. VTSup 27. Leiden: Brill, 1974.
Alon, Gedaliah. *The Jews in Their Land in the Talmudic Age (70–640 C.E.)*. Vol. 2. Edited and translated by Gershon Levi. Jerusalem: Magnes Press, Hebrew University, 1984.
Alt, Albrecht. "Die Rolle Samarias bei der Entstehung des Judentums (1934)." Pages 316–37 in *Kleine Schriften zur Geschichte des Volkes Israels II*. 2nd ed. Munich: Kaiser, 1959.
Alt, Albrecht. "Judas Nachbarn zur Zeit Nehemias." Pages 338–45 in *Kleine Schriften zur Geschichte des Volkes Israels II*. 2nd ed. Munich: Kaiser, 1959.
Anbar, Moshe. *Josué et l'Alliance de Sichem (Josué 24:1–28)*. BBET 25. Frankfurt am Main: Peter Lang, 1992.
Anderson, Robert T. and Terry Giles. *The Keepers: An Introduction to the History and Culture of the Samaritans*. Peabody, MA: Hendrickson, 2002.
Assmann, Jan. "Zum Konzept der Fremdheit im alten Ägypten." Pages 77–99 in *Die Begegnung mit dem Fremden: Wertungen und Wirkungen in Hochkulturen vom Altertum bis zur Gegenwart*. Edited by Meinhard Schuster. Colloquium Rauricum 4. Stuttgart: Teubner, 1996.
Baillet, Maurice. "Phylactère." Pages 149–57 in *Les 'petites grottes' de Qumrân: exploration de la falaise, les grottes 2Q, 3Q, 5Q, 7Q à 10Q, le rouleau de cuivre*. Edited by Maurice Baillet, Józef Tadeusz Milik, and Roland de Vaux. DJD 3. 2 vols. Oxford: Clarendon, 1962.
Baillet, Maurice. "Samaritains." In *DBSup* 11 (1991): 773–1047.
Barkai, Rachel. "Samaritan Sarcophagi of the Roman Period from the Land of Israel." M.A. thesis. Jerusalem: Hebrew University, 1984 (Hebrew).

Barkai, Rachel. "Four Samaritan Sarcophagi of the Roman Period." *ErIsr* 19 (1987): 6–18 (Hebrew).
Barkai, Rachel. "Samaritan Sarcophagi." Pages 310–38 in *The Samaritans*. Edited by Ephraim Stern and Hanan Eshel. Jerusalem: Yad Ben-Zvi Press; Israel Antiquities Authority, 2002 (Hebrew).
Barstad, Hans M. *The Myth of the Empty Land: A Study in the History and Archaeology of Judah During the "Exilic" Period.* SO 28. Oslo: Scandinavian University Press, 1996.
Becker, Uwe. "Jakob in Bet-El und Sichem." Pages 159–85 in *Die Erzväter in der biblischen Tradition: Festschrift Matthias Köckert.* Edited by Anselm C. Hagedorn and Henrik Pfeiffer. BZAW 400. Berlin: de Gruyter, 2009.
Becker, Uwe. *Exegese des Alten Testaments: Ein Methoden- und Arbeitsbuch.* 3rd ed. UTB 2664. Tübingen: Mohr Siebeck, 2011.
Becking, Bob. *The Fall of Samaria: An Historical and Archaeological Study.* SHANE 2. Leiden: Brill, 1992.
Becking, Bob. "The Idea of Torah in Ezra 7–10: A Functional Analysis." *ZABR* 7 (2001): 273–86.
Becking, Bob. "Do the Earliest Samaritan Inscriptions Already Indicate a Parting of the Ways?" Pages 213–22 in *Judah and the Judeans in the Fourth Century B.C.E.* Edited by Oded Lipschits, Gary N. Knoppers, and Rainer Albertz. Winona Lake, IN: Eisenbrauns, 2007.
Becking, Bob. "On the Identity of the Foreign Women in Ezra 9–10." Pages 58–73 in *Ezra, Nehemiah, and the Construction of Early Jewish Identity.* Edited by Bob Becking. Tübingen: Mohr Siebeck, 2011.
Becking, Bob. "Is There a Samaritan Identity in the Earliest Documents?" Pages 51–65 in *Die Samaritaner und die Bibel: Historische und literarische Wechselwirkungen zwischen biblischen und samaritanischen Traditionen / The Samaritans and the Bible: Historical and Literary Interactions between Biblical and Samaritan Traditions.* Edited by Jörg Frey, Ursula Schattner-Rieser, and Konrad Schmid. SJ 70; StSam 7. Berlin: de Gruyter, 2012.
Bertholet, Alfred. *Die Bücher Esra und Nehemia.* KHC 19. Tübingen, Leipzig: Mohr Siebeck, 1902.
Bichler, Reinhold. "Wahrnehmung und Vorstellung fremder Kultur: Griechen und Orient in archaischer und frühklassischer Zeit." Pages 51–74 in *Die Begegnung mit dem Fremden: Wertungen und Wirkungen in Hochkulturen vom Altertum bis zur Gegenwart.* Edited by Meinhard Schuster. Colloquium Rauricum 4. Stuttgart: Teubner, 1996.
Bieberstein, Klaus. *Josua—Jordan—Jericho: Archäologie, Geschichte und Theologie der Landnahmeerzählungen Jos 1–6.* OBO 143. Fribourg: Universitätsverlag; Göttingen: Vandenhoeck & Ruprecht, 1995.
Blenkinsopp, Joseph. *Ezra-Nehemiah: A Commentary.* OTL. Philadelphia: Westminster, 1988.
Blenkinsopp, Joseph. "Was the Pentateuch the Civic and Religious Constitution of the Jewish Ethnos in the Persian Period?" Pages 41–62 in *Persia and Torah: The Theory of the Imperial Authorization of the Pentateuch.* Edited by James W. Watts. SBL Symposium Series 17. Atlanta, GA: Society of Biblical Literature, 2001.
Block, Daniel I. *The Book of Ezekiel – Chapters 25–48.* NICOT. Grand Rapids, MI: Eerdmans, 1998.
Blum, Erhard. *Die Komposition der Vätergeschichte.* WMANT 57. Neukirchen-Vluyn: Neukirchener Verlag, 1984.

Blum, Erhard. "Volk oder Kultgemeinde? Zum Bild des nachexilischen Judentums in der alttestamentlichen Wissenschaft." *Neukirchener Theologische Zeitschrift* 10 (1995): 24–42.

Blum, Erhard. "Der kompositionelle Knoten am Übergang von Josua zu Richter: Ein Entflechtungsvorschlag." Pages 181–212 in *Deuteronomy and Deuteronomic Literature: Festschrift C.H.W. Brekelmans*. Edited by M. Vervenne and J. Lust. BETL 133. Leuven: Peeters, 1997.

Boda, Mark J. "Reading Between the Lines: Zechariah 11.4–16 in Its Literary Contexts." Pages 277–91 in *Bringing out the Treasure: Inner Biblical Allusion in Zechariah 9–14*. Edited by Mark J. Boda and Michael H. Floyd. JSOTSup 370. London: Sheffield Academic Press, 2003.

Boda, Mark J. *The Book of Zechariah*. NICOT. Grand Rapids, MI: Eerdmans, 2016.

Böhler, Dieter. *Die heilige Stadt in Esdras α und Esra-Nehemia: Zwei Konzeptionen der Wiederherstellung Israels*. OBO 158. Freiburg, Schweiz: Universitätsverlag, 1997.

Böhm, Martina. "Wer gehörte in hellenistisch-römischer Zeit zu 'Israel'?" Pages 181–202 in *Die Samaritaner und die Bibel. Historische und literarische Wechselwirkungen zwischen biblischen und samaritanischen Traditionen / The Samaritans and the Bible: Historical and Literary Interactions between Biblical and Samaritan Traditions*. Edited by Jörg Frey, Ursula Schattner-Rieser, and Konrad Schmid. SJ 70; StSam 7. Berlin: de Gruyter, 2012.

Bonnard, Christophe. "Asfår Asāṭīr, le 'Livre des Légendes,' une réécriture araméenne du Pentateuque samaritain: présentation, édition critique, traduction et commentaire philologique, commentaire comparatif." PhD diss., Strasbourg: University of Strasbourg, 2015.

Bourgel, Jonathan. "The Destruction of the Samaritan Temple by John Hyrcanus: A Reconsideration." *JBL* 135 (2016): 505–23.

Bowman, John. *Transcript of the Original Text of the Samaritan Chronicle Tolidah*. University of Leeds, 1954 (mimeographed).

Campbell, Edward F. "Shechem." *NEAEHL* 4:1345–54 (New York: Simon & Schuster, 1993).

Carr, David McLain. *The Formation of the Hebrew Bible: A New Reconstruction*. Oxford: Oxford University Press, 2011.

Catastini, Alessandro. *Storia di Guiseppe (Genesi 37–50)*. Venezia: Marsilio, 1994.

Chalcraft, David J., ed. *Sectarianism in Early Judaism: Sociological Advances*. London: Equinox, 2007.

Collins, Billie Jean, Bob Buller, and John F. Kutsko, eds. *The SBL Handbook of Style for Biblical Studies and Related Disciplines*. 2nd ed. Atlanta: Society of Biblical Literature, 2014.

Collins, John J. *Beyond the Qumran Community: The Sectarian Movement of the Dead Sea Scrolls*. Grand Rapids, MI: Eerdmans, 2009.

Collins, John J. *The Invention of Judaism: Torah and Jewish Identity from Deuteronomy to Paul*. Oakland, CA: University of California Press, 2017.

Cook, Stanley Arthur. "A Pre-Massoretic Biblical Papyrus." *Proceedings of the Society of Biblical Archaeology* 25 (1903): 34–56.

Crown, Alan David. *A Catalogue of the Samaritan Manuscripts in the British Library*. London: British Library, 1998.

Crüsemann, Frank. *Die Tora: Theologie und Sozialgeschichte des alttestamentlichen Gesetzes*. München: Chr. Kaiser, 1992.

Delcor, Mathias. "Hinweise auf das samaritanische Schisma im Alten Testament." *ZAW* 74 (1962): 281–91.
Delcor, Mathias. "Le trésor de la maison de Yahweh des origines à l'exil." *VT* 12 (1962): 353–77.
Dion, Paul-Eugène. "La religion des papyrus d'Éléphantine: un reflet du Juda d'avant l'exil." Pages 243–54 in *Kein Land für sich allein: Studien zum Kulturkontakt in Kanaan, Israel/Palästina und Ebirnâri für Manfred Weippert zum 65. Geburtstag*. Edited by Ulrich Hübner and Ernst Axel Knauf. OBO 186. Freiburg, Schweiz: Universitätsverlag; Göttingen: Vandenhoeck & Ruprecht, 2002.
Donner, Herbert. *Geschichte des Volkes Israel und seiner Nachbarn in Grundzügen*. 2nd ed. GAT 4/2. Göttingen: Vandenhoeck & Ruprecht, 1995.
Dorival, Gilles. *La Bible d'Alexandrie, 4: Les Nombres*. Paris: Cerf, 1994.
Dorsey, D. A. "The Location of Biblical Makkedah." *TA* 7 (1980): 185–202.
Dozeman, Thomas and Konrad Schmid, eds. *A Farewell to the Yahwist? The Composition of the Pentateuch in Recent European Interpretation*. SBLSS 34. Atlanta: Society of Biblical Literature, 2006.
Dušek, Jan. *Les manuscrits araméens du Wadi Daliyeh et la Samarie vers 450–332 av. J.-C.* CHANE 30. Leiden: Brill, 2007.
Dušek, Jan. *Aramaic and Hebrew Inscriptions from Mt. Gerizim and Samaria between Antiochus III and Antiochus IV Epiphanes*. CHANE 54. Leiden: Brill, 2012.
Dušek, Jan. "Aramaic in the Persian Period." *HBAI* 2 (2013): 243–64.
Edelman, Diana V. *The Origins of the 'Second' Temple: Persian Imperial Policy and the Rebuilding of Jerusalem*. London: Equinox, 2005.
Edenburg, Cynthia and Reinhard Müller. "A Northern Provenance for Deuteronomy? A Critical Review." *HBAI* 4 (2015): 148–61.
Eshel, Esther. "4QDeut^n: A Text That Has Undergone Harmonistic Editing." *HUCA* 62 (1991): 117–154.
Eskenazi, Tamara Cohn. *In an Age of Prose: A Literary Approach to Ezra-Nehemiah*. Atlanta: Scholars Press, 1988.
Falk, Daniel K., Andrew B. Perrin, and Kyung S. Baek, eds. *Reading the Bible in Ancient Traditions and Modern Editions: Studies in Textual and Reception History in Honour of Peter W. Flint*. SBL Early Judaism and Its Literature Series. Atlanta: Society of Biblical Literature, forthcoming.
Finkelstein, Israel. "Seilun, Khirbet." *ABD* 5:1069–72.
Finkelstein, Israel. "The Territorial Extent and Demography of Yehud/Judea in the Persian and Early Hellenistic Periods." *RB* 117 (2010): 39–54.
Finkelstein, Israel. *The Forgotten Kingdom: The Archaeology and History of Northern Israel*. SBL Ancient Near East Monographs 5. Atlanta: Society of Biblical Literature, 2013.
Fishbane, Michael. *Biblical Interpretation in Ancient Israel*. Oxford: Clarendon, 1985.
Fleming, Daniel. *The Legacy of Israel in Judah's Bible: History, Politics, and the Reinscribing of Tradition*. Cambridge: Cambridge University Press, 2012.
Flint, Peter, *The Dead Sea Psalms Scrolls and the Book of Psalms*. STDJ 17. Leiden: Brill, 1997.
Flint, Peter W. and Tae Hun Kim, eds. *The Bible at Qumran: Text, Shape, and Interpretation*. Studies in the Dead Sea Scrolls and Related Literature. Grand Rapids, MI: Eerdmans, 2001.

Flint, Peter W. and Patrick D. Miller, Jr., eds. *The Book of Psalms: Composition and Reception.* VTSup 99. Leiden: Brill, 2005.
Flint, Peter W. and Eugene C. Ulrich. *Qumran Cave 1. II: The Isaiah Scrolls.* 2 vols. DJD 32. Oxford: Clarendon, 2010.
Flint, Peter W. *The Dead Sea Scrolls.* Nashville, TN: Abingdon, 2013.
Florentin, Moshe, ed. and transl. *The Tulida: A Samaritan Chronicle.* Jerusalem: Yad Izhak Ben-Zvi, 1999 (Hebrew).
Frankel, Zacharias. *Über den Einfluss der palästinischen Exegese auf die alexandrinische Hermeneutik.* Leipzig: J. A. Barth, 1851.
Frankel, Zacharias. *Vorstudien zu der Septuaginta.* Leipzig: Fr. Chr. Wilh. Vogel, 1941.
Frei, Peter. "Zentralgewalt und Lokalautonomie im Achämenidenreich." Pages 6–131 in *Reichsidee und Reichsorganisation im Perserreich.* Edited by Peter Frei and Klaus Koch. 2nd ed. OBO 55. Göttingen: Vandenhoeck & Ruprecht, 1996. Freiburg: Universitätsverlag, 1996.
Frevel, Christian. "Der Eine oder die Vielen? Monotheismus und materielle Kultur in der Perserzeit." Pages 238–65 in *Gott – Götter – Götzen. XIV. Europäischer Kongress für Theologie (11.–15. September 2001, Zürich).* Edited by Christoph Schwöbel. Veröffentlichungen der Wissenschaftlichen Gesellschaft für Theologie 38. Leipzig: Evangelische Verlagsanstalt, 2013.
Frevel, Christian. *Geschichte Israels.* Kohlhammer Studienbücher Theologie 2. Stuttgart: Kohlhammer, 2016.
Fritz, Volkmar. *Das Buch Josua.* HAT I/7. Tübingen: Mohr Siebeck, 1994.
Gaster, Moses. "The Chain of Samaritan High Priests: A Synchronistic Synopsis." *JRAS* (1909): 393–420. Reprinted in Moses Gaster. *Studies and Texts in Folklore, Magic, Mediaeval Romance, Hebrew Apocrypha and Samaritan Archaeology.* Vol 1, 483–502 (English translation) and vol. 3, 131–38 (Hebrew). New York: Ktav, 1971.
Gaster, Moses. *Handlist of Gaster Manuscripts: held mostly in the British Library (formerly British Museum), London, and in the John Rylands Library, Manchester.* Preface by Brad Sabin Hill. London: Hebrew Section, Oriental and India Office Collections, The British Library, 1995.
Geiger, Abraham. המקרא ותרגומיו. Jerusalem: Mosad Bialik, 1972.
Gerleman, Gillis. *Synoptic Studies in the Old Testament.* Lund: Gleerup, 1948.
Gertz, Jan C. et al. *T&T Clark Handbook of the Old Testament: An Introduction to the Literature, Religion and History of the Old Testament.* London: T&T Clark, 2012.
Gertz, Jan C., Konrad Schmid and Markus Witte, eds. *Abschied vom Jahwisten: Die Komposition des Hexateuch in der jüngsten Diskussion.* BZAW 215. Berlin: de Gruyter, 2002.
Gesenius, Wilhelm. *De Pentateuchi Samaritani origine, indole et auctoritate commentatio philologico-critica.* Halle: Bibliotheca Rengeriana, 1815.
Gonzalez, Hervé. "Zechariah 9–14 and the Continuation of Zechariah during the Ptolemaic Period." *JHebS* 13 (2013): 1–43.
Gonzalez, Hervé and Jan Rückl. "*Lectio difficilior potior?* Zacharie 11,7a.11b dans le texte massorétique et la Septante." *Sem* 56 (2014): 333–57.
Gonzalez, Hervé. "Zacharie 9–14 et le temple de Jérusalem: Observations sur le milieu de production d'un texte prophétique tardif." *Judaïsme Ancien – Ancient Judaism* 5 (2017): 23–77.

Gooding, David Willoughby. "On the Use of the LXX for Dating Midrashic Elements in the Targums." *JTS* 25 (1974): 1–11.
Grabbe, Lester L. *The Roman Period.* Vol. 2 of *Judaism from Cyrus to Hadrian.* Minneapolis: Fortress, 1992.
Grabbe, Lester L. *Ezra-Nehemiah.* OTR. New York: Routledge, 1998.
Granerød, Gard. *Dimensions of Yahwism in the Persian Period: Studies in the Religion and Society of the Judaean Community at Elephantine.* BZAW 488. Berlin: de Gruyter, 2016.
Grätz, Sebastian. "Esra 7 im Kontext hellenistischer Politik: Der königliche Euergetismus in hellenistischer Zeit als ideeller Hintergrund von Esr 7." Pages 131–154 in *Die Griechen und das antike Israel: Interdisziplinäre Studien zur Religions- und Kulturgeschichte des Heiligen Landes.* Edited by Stefan Alkier. OBO 201. Fribourg: Academic Press, 2004.
Grätz, Sebastian. "Zuwanderung als Herausforderung: Das Rutbuch als Modell einer sozialen und religiösen Integration von Fremden im nachexilischen Judäa." *EvT* 65 (2005): 294–309.
Grätz, Sebastian. "Zu einem Essay von Albrecht Alt: Die Rolle Samarias bei der Entstehung des Judentums." Pages 171–84 in *Kontexte: Biografische und forschungsgeschichtliche Schnittpunkte der alttestamentlichen Wissenschaft: Festschrift Hans Jochen Boecker.* Edited by Thomas Wagner et al. Neukirchen-Vluyn: Neukirchener Verlag, 2008.
Grätz, Sebastian. "The Adversaries in Ezra/Nehemiah – Fictitious or Real?" Pages 73–88 in *Between Cooperation and Hostility: Multiple Identities in Ancient Judaism and the Interaction with Foreign Powers.* Edited by Rainer Albertz and Jakob Wöhrle. Journal of Ancient Judaism. Supplements 11. Göttingen: Vandenhoeck & Ruprecht, 2013.
Grätz, Sebastian. *Das Edikt des Artaxerxes. Eine Untersuchung zum religionspolitischen und historischen Umfeld von Esra 7,12–26.* BZAW 337. Berlin; New York: de Gruyter, 2004.
Grätz, Sebastian. "Kyroszylinder, Kyrosedikt und Kyrosorakel: Der König als Medium göttlicher Geschichtsmächtigkeit." Pages 339–53 in *Geschichte und Gott: XV. Europäischer Kongress für Theologie (14.–18. September 2014 in Berlin).* Edited by Michael Meyer-Blanck and Laura Schmitz. Veröffentlichungen der Wissenschaftlichen Gesellschaft für Theologie 44. Leipzig: Evangelische Verlagsanstalt, 2016.
Greenberg, Moshe. "The Stabilization of the Text of the Hebrew Bible Reviewed in the Light of the Biblical Materials from the Judean Desert." *JAOS* 76 (1956): 157–67.
Greenspoon, Leonard J. "Between Alexandria and Antioch: Jews and Judaism in the Hellenistic Period." Pages 346–49 in *The Oxford History of the Biblical World.* Edited by Michael D. Coogan. Oxford: Oxford University Press, 1998.
Gropp, D.M. *Wadi Daliyeh II: The Samaria Papyri from Wadi ed-Daliyeh.* DJD 28. Oxford: Oxford University Press, 2001.
Gudme, Anne Katrine de Hemmer. *Before the God in This Place for Good Remembrance: A Comparative Analysis of the Aramaic Votive Inscriptions from Mount Gerizim.* BZAW 441. Berlin: de Gruyter, 2013.
Guggenheimer, Heinrich W. *Seder Olam: The Rabbinic View of Biblical Chronology.* Lanham, MD: Rowman & Littlefield, 2005.
Guillaume, Philippe. *Waiting for Josiah: The Judges.* JSOTSup 385. London: T&T Clark, 2004.
Gunneweg, Antonius H. J. *Esra. Mit einer Zeittafel von Alfred Jepsen.* KAT 19/1. Gütersloh: Gütersloher Verlagshaus Mohn, 1985.
Gunneweg, Antonius H. J. *Nehemia.* KAT 19/2. Gutersloh: Gütersloher Verlagshaus Mohn, 1987.

Halpern, Baruch. "A Historiographic Commentary on Ezra 1–6: A Chronological Narrative and Dual Chronology in Israelite Historiography." Pages 81–142 in *The Hebrew Bible and its Interpreters*. Edited by William H. Propp, Baruch Halpern and David N. Freedman. Biblical and Judaic Studies 1. Winona Lake, IN: Eisenbrauns, 1990,

Hardmeier, Christof. "Zur Quellenevidenz biblischer Texte und archäologischer Befunde: Falsche Fronten und ein neues Gespräch zwischen alttestamentlicher Literaturwissenschaft und Archäologie." Pages 11–24 in *Steine—Bilder—Texte: Historische Evidenz außerbiblischer und biblischer Quellen*. Edited by Christof Hardmeier. Arbeiten zur Bibel und ihrer Geschichte 5. Leipzig: Evangelische Verlagsanstalt, 2001.

Häusl, Maria. "'Eine Schriftrolle, darin ist geschrieben' (Esr 6,2): Zur Bedeutung der Schriftlichkeit im Buch Esra/Nehemia." Pages 175–94 in *'Ich werde meinen Bund mit euch niemals brechen!' (Ri 2,1): Festschrift W. Groß*. Edited by Erasmus Gaß and Hermann-Josef Stipp. Herders Biblische Studien 62. Freiburg im Breisgau: Herder, 2011.

Heckl, Raik. "Esra als Hohepriester und die Verkündigung der Tora im Lichte einer Notiz bei Hekataios von Abdera." *Leqach* 9 (2009): 71–78.

Heckl, Raik. "Ein vollendeter Text für den Surrogat-Tempel: Struktur, Chronologie und Funktion des Pentateuchs in Anschluss an Benno Jacob." *ZABR* 22 (2016): 185–221.

Heckl, Raik. *Neuanfang und Kontinuität in Jerusalem: Studien zu den hermeneutischen Strategien im Esra-Nehemia-Buch*. FAT 104. Tübingen: Mohr Siebeck, 2016.

Heckl, Raik. "Die Gotteserkenntnis und das Bekenntnis des Darius in Dan 6,27 f. (LXX) als inhaltliches Zentrum von 1 Esdras: 1 Esdras als Metatext in der spätnachexilischen Literatur." In *Gotteserkenntnis in der Septuaginta*. Edited by E. Dafne. Tübingen: Mohr Siebeck, (forthcoming).

Heidenheim, Moritz. "Die samaritan. Chronik des Hohenpriesters Elasar aus dem 11. Jahrhundert, übersetzt und erklärt." *Vierteljahrsschrift für deutsch- und englisch-theologische Forschung und Kritik* 4 (1870): 347–89.

Heller, Chaim. *Untersuchungen über die Peschitta zur gesamten hebräischen Bibel, I*. Berlin: Poppelauer, 1911.

Hendel, Ronald S. *The Text of Genesis 1–11: Textual Studies and Critical Edition*. New York: Oxford University Press, 1998.

Hensel, Benedikt. *Die Vertauschung des Erstgeburtssegens in der Genesis: Eine Analyse der narrativ-theologischen Grundstruktur des ersten Buches der Tora*. BZAW 423. Berlin: de Gruyter, 2011.

Hensel, Benedikt. "Von 'Israeliten' zu 'Ausländern': Zur Entwicklung anti-samaritanischer Polemik ab der hasmonäischen Zeit." *ZAW* 126 (2014): 475–93.

Hensel, Benedikt. "Samaritanische Identität in persisch-hellenistischer Zeit im Spiegel der biblischen Überlieferung und der epigraphischen Befunde." Pages 67–115 in *Nationale Identität im Alten Testament*. Edited by Wolfgang Zwickel. Kleine Arbeiten zum Alten und Neuen Testament 12. Kamen: Hartmut Spenner, 2015.

Hensel, Benedikt. "Serubbabel." *WiBiLex*. URL: http://www.bibelwissenschaft.de/stichwort/28453.

Hensel, Benedikt. *Juda und Samaria. Zum Verhältnis zweier Jahwismen in nach-exilischer Zeit*. FAT 110. Tübingen: Mohr Siebeck, 2016.

Hensel, Benedikt. "Das JHWH-Heiligtum am Garizim: ein archäologischer Befund und seine literar- und theologiegeschichtliche Einordnung." *VT* 68 (2018): 73–93.

Hermann, Siegfried. *Geschichte Israels*. Stuttgart: Kohlhammer, 1973.
Hieke, Thomas. *Die Genealogien der Genesis*. Herders Biblische Studien 39. Freiburg: Herder, 2003.
Hieke, Thomas. *Die Bücher Esra und Nehemia*. NSKAT 9/2. Stuttgart: Katholisches Bibelwerk, 2005.
Himbaza, Innocent. "'Le lieu que Yhwh aura choisi': Une perspective narrative, historique et philologique." *Sem* 58 (2016): 115–34.
Hjelm, Ingrid. *The Samaritans and Early Judaism: A Literary Analysis*. JSOTSup 303. Sheffield: Sheffield Academic Press, 2000.
Hjelm, Ingrid. "What do Samaritans and Jews Have in Common? Recent Trends in Samaritan Studies." *Currents in Biblical Research* 3 (2004): 9–59.
Hjelm, Ingrid. *Jerusalem's Rise to Sovereignty: Zion and Gerizim in Competition*. JSOTSup 404. London: T&T Clark, 2004.
Hjelm, Ingrid. "Northern Perspectives in Deuteronomy and its Relation to the Samaritan Pentateuch." *HBAI* 4 (2015): 184–204.
Hölscher, Gustav. *Palaestina in der persischen und hellenistischen Zeit*. Berlin: Weidmann, 1902.
Hölscher, Gustav. "Die Bücher Esra und Nehemia." Pages 491–562 in *Die Heilige Schrift des Alten Testaments: 2. Hosea bis Chronik*. Edited by Emil Kautzsch. HSAT. Tübingen: Mohr Siebeck, 1923.
Houston, Walter. "Between Salem and Mount Gerizim: The Context of the Formation of the Torah Reconsidered." *Journal of Ancient Judaism* 5 (2014): 311–34.
Hübner, Ulrich. *Die Ammoniter: Untersuchungen zur Kultur und Religion eines transjordanischen Volkes des 1. Jahrtausend v. Chr*. Wiesbaden: Harrassowitz, 1992.
Hurvitz, Avi. "Terms and Epithets Relating to the Jerusalem Temple Compound in the Book of Chronicles: The Linguistic Aspect." Pages 165–83 in *Pomegranates and Golden Bells: Studies in Biblical, Jewish, and Near Eastern Ritual, Law, and Literature in Honor of Jacob Milgrom*. Edited by David P. Wright, David N. Freedman, and Avi Hurvitz. Winona Lake, IN: Eisenbrauns, 1995.
Husser, Jean-Marie. "L'histoire de Joseph." Pages 12–22 in *La Bible et sa culture: Ancien Testament*. Edited by Michel Quesnel and Philippe Gruson. Paris: Desclée de Brouwer, 2000.
Jamieson-Drake, David. *Scribes and Schools in Monarchic Judah: A Socio-archaeological Approach*. JSOTSup 109. Sheffield: Sheffield Academic Press, 1991 [repr. Winona Lake, IN: Eisenbrauns, 2010].
Janzen, David. *Witch-hunts, Purity and Social Boundaries: The Expulsion of the Foreign Women in Ezra 9–10*. JSOTSup 350. London: Sheffield Academic Press, 2002.
Japhet, Sara. "The Relationship Between Chronicles and Ezra-Nehemiah." Pages 298–313 in *Congress Volume, Leuven, 1989*. Edited by John A. Emerton. VTSup 43. Leiden: Brill, 1991.
Japhet, Sara. *I & II Chronicles: A Commentary*. OTL. Louisville: Westminster John Knox, 1993.
Japhet, Sara. *The Ideology of the Book of Chronicles and Its Place in Biblical Thought*. BEATAJ 9. Frankfurt: Peter Lang, 1997. 3rd ed. Winona Lake, IN: Eisenbrauns, 2009.
Jaroš, Karl. *Sichem: Eine archäologische und religionsgeschichtliche Studie mit besonderer Berücksichtigung von Jos 24*. OBO 11. Fribourg: Universitätsverlag, 1976.
Jericke, Detlef. "Der Berg Garizim im Deuteronomium." *ZAW* 124 (2012): 213–28.

Johnson, Willa. *The Holy Seed Has Been Defiled: The Interethnic Marriage Dilemma in Ezra 9–10*. Sheffield: Phoenix Press, 2011.
Johnstone, William. *1 and 2 Chronicles. Volume 1: 1 Chronicles 1–2 Chronicles 9. Israel's Place among the Nations*. JSOTSup 253. Sheffield: Sheffield Academic Press, 1997.
Kahle, Paul. "Untersuchungen zur Geschichte des Pentateuchtextes." *TSK* 88 (1915): 399–439; repr. pages 3–37 in id., *Opera Minora*. Leiden: Brill, 1956.
Kartveit, Magnar. *The Origin of the Samaritans*. VTSup 128. Leiden; Boston: Brill, 2009.
Kartveit, Magnar. "Josephus on the Samaritans – His *Tendenz* and Purpose." Pages 109–20 in *Samaria, Samarians, Samaritans: Studies on Bible, History, and Linguistic*. Edited by József Zsengellér. SJ 88; StSam 6. Berlin: de Gruyter, 2011.
Kartveit, Magnar. "Samaritan Self-Consciousness in the First Half of the Second Century B.C.E. in Light of the Inscriptions from Mount Gerizim and Delos." *JSJ* 45 (2014): 449–70.
Kartveit, Magnar. "The Place That the Lord Your God Will Choose." *HBAI* 4 (2015): 205–18.
Kautzsch, Emil, ed. *Die Heilige Schrift des Alten Testaments: 2. Hosea bis Chronik*. HSAT. Tübingen: Mohr Siebeck, 1923.
Kellermann, Diether. "Überlieferungsprobleme alttestamentlicher Ortsnamen." *VT* 28 (1978): 423–432.
Kippenberg, Hans G. *Garizim und Synagoge: Traditionsgeschichtliche Untersuchungen zur samaritanischen Religion der aramäischen Periode*. RVV 30. Berlin: de Gruyter, 1971.
Knauf, Ernst Axel. "Audiatur et altera pars. Zur Logik der Pentateuchredaktion." *BK* 53 (1998): 118–126.
Knauf, Ernst Axel. "Bethel: The Israelite Impact on Judean Language and Literature." Pages 291–349 in *Judah and the Judeans in the Persian Period*. Edited by Oded Lipschits and Manfred Oeming. Winona Lake, IN: Eisenbrauns, 2006.
Knauf, Ernst Axel. *Josua*. ZBKAT 6. Zürich: Theologischer Verlag, 2008.
Knierim, Rolf P. "The Composition of the Pentateuch." Pages 393–415 in *SBL Seminar Papers 24*. Atlanta, GA: Scholars Press, 1985.
Knoppers, Gary N. "An Achaemenid Imperial Authorization of Torah in Yehud?" Pages 115–34 in *Persia and Torah: The Theory of the Imperial Authorization of the Pentateuch*. Edited by James W. Watts. SBL Symposium Series 17. Atlanta, GA: Society of Biblical Literature, 2001.
Knoppers, Gary N. "Intermarriage, Social Complexity, and Ethnic Diversity in the Genealogy of Judah." *JBL* 120 (2001): 15–30.
Knoppers, Gary N. "In Search of Post-Exilic Israel: Samaria after the Fall of the Northern Kingdom." Pages 150–180 in *In Search of Pre-Exilic Israel: Proceedings of the Oxford Old Testament Seminar*. Edited by John Day. JSOTSup 406. London: T&T Clark, 2004.
Knoppers, Gary N. *I Chronicles 1–9: A New Translation with Introduction and Commentary*. AB 12. New York: Doubleday, 2004.
Knoppers, Gary N. "Mt. Gerizim and Mt. Zion: A Study in the Early History of the Samaritans and Jews." *SR* 34 (2005): 309–38.
Knoppers, Gary N. "Revisiting the Samarian Question in the Persian Period." Pages 265–89 in *Judah and the Judeans in the Persian Period*. Edited by Oded Lipschits and Manfred Oemin,. Winona Lake, IN: Eisenbrauns, 2006.
Knoppers, Gary N., and Bernard M. Levinson, eds. *The Pentateuch as Torah: New Models for Understanding Its Promulgation and Acceptance*. Winona Lake, IN: Eisenbrauns, 2007.

Knoppers, Gary N. "Aspects of Samaria's Religious Culture During the Early Hellenistic Period." Pages 159–174 in *The Historian and the Bible: Essays in Honour of Lester L. Grabbe*. Edited by Philip Davies and Diana V. Edelman. LHBOTS 530. New York: T&T Clark International, 2010.

Knoppers, Gary N. "Parallel Torahs and Inner-Scriptural Interpretation: The Jewish and Samaritan Pentateuchs in Historical Perspective." Pages 507–31 in *The Pentateuch: International Perspectives on Current Research*. Edited by Thomas B. Dozeman, Konrad Schmid, and Baruch J. Schwartz. FAT 78. Tübingen: Mohr Siebeck, 2011.

Knoppers, Gary N. "Samaritan Conceptions of Jewish Origins and Jewish Conceptions of Samaritan Origins: Any Common Ground?" Pages 81–118 in *Die Samaritaner und die Bibel: historische und literarische Wechselwirkungen zwischen biblischen und samaritanischen Traditionen*. Edited by Jörg Frey, Ursula Schattner-Rieser, and Konrad Schmid. SJ 70; StSam 7. Berlin: de Gruyter, 2012.

Knoppers, Gary N. "The Samaritan Schism or the Judaization of Samaria? Reassessing Josephus's Account of the Mt. Gerizim Temple." Pages 163–78 in *Making a Difference: Essays on the Bible and Judaism in Honour of Tamara Cohn Eskenazi*. Edited by David J. A. Clines, Kent Richards, and Jacob L. Wright. Hebrew Bible Monographs 49. Sheffield: Sheffield Phoenix, 2012.

Knoppers, Gary N. *Jews and Samaritans: The Origins and History of Their Early Relations*. Oxford; New York: Oxford University Press, 2013.

Knoppers, Gary N. "The Northern Context of the Law-Code in Deuteronomy." *HBAI* 4 (2015): 162–83.

Knoppers, Gary N. "Toward a Critical Edition of the Samaritan Pentateuch: Reflections on Issues and Methods." In *Reading the Bible in Ancient Traditions and Modern Editions: Studies in Textual and Reception History in Honour of Peter W. Flint*. Edited by Daniel K. Falk, Andrew B. Perrin, and Kyung S. Baek. SBL Early Judaism and Its Literature Series. Atlanta: Society of Biblical Literature, forthcoming.

Kohn, Samuel. *De Pentateucho Samaritano ejusque cum versionibus antiquis nexu*. Leipzig: Kreysing, 1865.

Koopmans, William T. *Joshua 24 as Poetic Narrative*. JSOTSup 93. Sheffield: Sheffield Academic Press, 1990.

Kratz, Reinhard G. *Die Komposition der erzählenden Bücher des Alten Testaments: Grundwissen der Bibelkritik*. UTB 2157. Göttingen: Vandenhoeck & Ruprecht, 2000.

Kratz, Reinhard G. "Der vor- und der nachpriesterschriftliche Hextateuch." Pages 295–323 in *Abschied vom Jahwisten: Die Komposition des Hexateuch in der jüngsten Diskussion*. Edited by Jan C. Gertz, Konrad Schmid and Markus Witte. BZAW 215. Berlin: de Gruyter, 2002.

Kratz, Reinhard G. *Das Judentum im Zeitalter des Zweiten Tempels*. FAT 42. Tübingen: Mohr Siebeck, 2004.

Kratz, Reinhard G. *The Composition of the Narrative Books of the Old Testament*. Translated by John Bowden. London: T&T Clark, 2005. Translation of *Die Komposition der erzählenden Bücher des Alten Testaments: Grundwissen der Bibelkritik*, 2000.

Kratz, Reinhard G. *Historical and Biblical Israel*. Translated by Paul Michael Kurtz. Oxford: Oxford University Press, 2015. Translation of *Historisches und biblisches Israel: drei Überblicke zum Alten Testament*. Tübingen: Mohr Siebeck, 3rd ed. 2017.

Kunz, Andreas. *Ablehnung des Krieges – Untersuchungen zu Sacharja 9 und 10*. Herders Biblische Studien 17. Freiburg: Herder, 1998.
Kutscher, Edward Yechezkel. *The Language and Linguistic Background of the Isaiah Scroll (1 Q Is^a)*. STDJ 6. Leiden: Brill, 1974.
L'Hour, Jean. "L'alliance de Sichem." *RB* 69 (1962): 5–36, 161–84, 350–68.
Lange, Armin. "'Eure Töchter gebt nicht ihren Söhnen und ihre Töchter nehmt nicht für eure Söhne' (Esra 9,12): Die Frage der Mischehen im Buch Esra/Nehemia im Licht der Textfunde von Qumran." Pages 295–311 in *Was ist der Mensch, dass du seiner gedenkst? (Psalm 8,5): Aspekte einer theologischen Anthropologie: Festschrift für Bernd Janowski zum 65. Geburtstag*. Edited by Michaela Bauks. Neukirchen-Vluyn: Neukirchener Verlag, 2008.
Lapp, Nancy L. "The Stratum V Pottery from Balâṭah (Shechem)." *BASOR* 257 (1985): 19–43.
Lapp, Nancy L. *Shechem IV: The Persian-Hellenistic Pottery of Shechem/Tell Balâṭah*. ASOR Archaeological Reports 11. Boston: American Schools of Oriental Research, 2008.
Lee, Kyong-Jin. *The Authority and Authorization of the Torah in the Persian Period*. CBET 64. Leuven: Peeters, 2011.
Lee, Suk Yee. *An Intertextual Analysis of Zechariah 9–10: The Earlier Restoration Expectations of Second Zechariah*. LHBOTS 599. London: Bloomsbury T&T Clark, 2015.
Lemaire, André. *Nouvelles Inscriptions araméennes d'Idumée Tome II*. Transeu Supplèment 9. Paris: Gabalda, 2002.
Lemmelijn, Bénédicte. *A Plague of Texts? A Text-Critical Study of the So-Called 'Plagues Narratives' in Exodus 7:14–11:10*. OTS 56. Leiden: Brill, 2009.
Levin, Christoph. *The Old Testament: A Brief Introduction*. Translated by Margaret Kohl. Princeton: Princeton University Press, 2005.
Levin, Christoph. "Source Criticism: The Miracle at the Sea." Pages 39–61 in *Method Matters: Essays on the Interpretation of the Hebrew Bible*. Edited by Joel M. LeMon and Kent H. Richards. RBS 56. Atlanta: Society of Biblical Literature, 2009.
Levin, Yigal. "Judea, Samaria and Idumea: Three Models of Ethnicity and Administration in the Persian Period." Pages 4–53 in *From Judah to Judaea: Socio-Economic Structures and Processes in the Persian Period*. Edited by J. U. Ro. Sheffield: Sheffield Phoenix Press, 2012.
Levinson, Bernard M. *Deuteronomy and the Hermeneutics of Legal Innovation*. Oxford: Oxford University Press, 1997.
Levinson, Bernard M. and Jeffrey Stackert. "Between Covenant Code and Esarhaddon's Succession Treaty: Deuteronomy 13 and the Composition of Deuteronomy." *Journal of Ancient Judaism* 3 (2012): 123–40.
Levy-Rubin, Milka. *The Continuatio of the Samaritan Chronicle of Abū l-Fatḥ al-Sāmirī al-Danafī*. Studies in Late Antiquity and Early Islam, 10. Princeton, NJ: Darwin Press, 2002.
Lieberman, Saul. *Hellenism in Jewish Palestine*. 2nd ed. New York: Jewish Theological Seminary, 1962.
Linville, James Richard. *Israel in the Book of Kings: The Past as a Project of Social Identity*. JSOTSup 272. Sheffield: Sheffield Academic Press, 1998.
Lipschits, Oded. "Demographic Changes in Judah between the Seventh and the Fifth Centuries B.C.E." Pages 323–76 in *Judah and the Judeans in the Neo-Babylonian Period*. Edited by Oded Lipschits and Joseph Blenkinsopp. Winona Lake, IN: Eisenbrauns, 2003.

Lipschits, Oded. "Achaemenid Imperial Policy, Settlement Processes in Palestine, and the Status of Jerusalem in the Middle of the Fifth Century B.C.E ." Pages 19–52 in *Judah and the Judeans in the Persian period*. Edited by Oded Lipschits and Manfred Oeming. Winona Lake, IN: Eisenbrauns, 2006.

Loewenstamm, Ayala. "Samaritans. Samaritan Chronology." *EncJud*, 2nd ed., 2007:732–38.

Lohfink, Norbert. "Fortschreibung? Zur Technik von Rechtsrevisionen im deuteronomischen Bereich, erörtert an Deuteronomium 12, Ex 21,2–11 und Dtn 15,12–18." Pages 127–71 in *Das Deuteronomium und seine Deutungen*. Edited by Timo Veijola. Schriften der Finnischen Exegetischen Gesellschaft 62. Göttingen: Vandenhoeck & Ruprecht, 1996.

Maas, Paul. *Textual Criticism*. Translated by Barbara Flower. Oxford: Clarendon, 1958 = "Textkritik." In *Einleitung in die Altertumswissenschaft*, I, VII. Edited by Alfred Gercke and Eduard Norden. 3rd ed. Leipzig: Teubner, 1957.

Macdonald, John. *The Samaritan Chronicle No. II (or: Sepher Ha-Yamim): From Joshua to Nebuchadnezzar*. BZAW 107. Berlin: de Gruyter, 1969.

Magen, Yitzhak. "Qedumim." *NEAHL* 4:1225–27.

Magen, Yitzhak. "The 'Samaritan' Sarcophagi." Pages 149–66 in *Early Christianity in Context: Monuments and Documents*. Edited by Frédéric Manns and Eugenio Alliata. SBFCMa 38. Jerusalem: Franciscan Printing Press, 1993.

Magen, Yitzhak. "Mount Gerizim – Temple City." *Qad* 120 (2000): 74–118.

Magen, Yitzhaq. "The Dating of the First Phase of the Samaritan Temple on Mount Gerizim in Light of the Archaeological Evidence." Pages 157–211 in *Judah and the Judeans in the Fourth Century B.C.E*. Edited by Oded Lipschits, Gary N. Knoppers, and Rainer Albertz. Winona Lake, IN: Eisenbrauns, 2007.

Magen, Yitzhak. *A Temple City*. Vol. 2 of *Mount Gerizim Excavations*. Judea and Samaria Publications 8. Jerusalem: Israel Antiquities Authority, 2008.

Magen, Yitzhak. *The Samaritans and the Good Samaritan*. Judea and Samaria Publications 7. Jerusalem: Israel Antiquities Authority, 2008.

Magen, Yitzhak. *Flavia Neapolis: Shechem in the Roman Period*. Vol. 1. Judea and Samaria Publications 11. Jerusalem: Israel Antiquities Authority, 2009.

Magen, Yitzhak, Haggai Misgav, and Levana Tsfania. *The Aramaic, Hebrew and Samaritan Inscriptions*. Vol. 1 of *Mount Gerizim Excavations*. Judea and Samaria Publications 2. Jerusalem: Israel Antiquities Authority, 2004.

Magness, Jodi. "Ossuaries and the Burials of Jesus and James." *JBL* 124 (2005): 121–54.

Marcus, David. "Is the Book of Nehemiah a Translation from Aramaic?" Pages 103–10 in *Boundaries of the Ancient Near Eastern World: A Tribute to Cyrus H. Gordon*. Edited by Meir Lubetski, Claire Gottlieb and Sharon R. Keller. JSOTSup 273. Sheffield: Sheffield Academic Press, 1998.

Martone, Corrado. "From Chaos to Coherence and Back: Some Thoughts on the Phenomenon of Harmonization in the Bible and the Dead Sea Scrolls." Pages 29–38 in *"Let the Wise Listen and Add to Their Learning" (Prov 1:5): Festschrift for Günter Stemberger on the Occasion of his 75th Birthday*. Edited by Constanza Cordoni and Gerhard Langer. SJ 90. Berlin: de Gruyter, 2016.

Mayes, Andrew D. H. *The Story of Israel between Settlement and Exile: A Redactional Study of the Deuteronomistic History*. London: SCM Press, 1983.

Meshorer, Ya'akov. *Samarian Coinage*. Numismatic Studies and Researches 9. Jerusalem: Israel Numismatic Society, 1999.

Metzger, Manfred. *Grundriss der Geschichte Israels*. Neukirchen-Vluyn: Neukirchener Verlag, 1963.
Meyer, Eduard. *Die Entstehung des Judentums: Eine historische Untersuchung*. Halle: Niemeyer, 1896.
Meyers, Carol L. and Eric M. Meyers. *Zechariah 9–14: A New Translation with Introduction and Commentary*. AB 25C. New York: Doubleday, 1993.
Milik, Józef Tadeusz. "Tefillin, Mezuzot et Targums (4Q128–4Q157)." Pages 33–79 in *Qumrân grotte 4.II: I. Archéologie, II. Tefillin, Mezuzot et Targums (4Q128–4Q157)*. Edited by Roland de Vaux and Józef Tadeusz Milik. 2 vols. DJD 6. Oxford: Clarendon, 1977.
Miller, J. Maxwell and John H. Hayes. *A History of Ancient Israel and Judah*. Philadelphia: Westminster, 1986.
Mills, John. *Three Months' Residence at Nablus, and an Account of the Modern Samaritans*. London: John Murray, 1864.
Moffat, Donald. *Ezra's Social Drama: Identity Formation, Marriage and Social Conflict in Ezra 9 and 10*. LHBOTS 579. New York: Bloomsbury, 2013.
Mölle, Herbert. *Der sogenannte Landtag zu Sichem*. Forschung zur Bibel 42. Würzburg: Echter, 1980.
Mommer, Peter. *Samuel: Geschichte und Überlieferung*. WMANT 65. Neukirchen-Vluyn: Neukirchener Verlag, 1991.
Montgomery, James A. *Samaritans: The Earliest Jewish Sect: Their History, Theology, and Literature*. Philadelphia: John C. Winston, 1907 [repr. New York: Ktav, 1968].
Na'aman, Nadav. "The 'Conquest of Canaan' in the Book of Joshua and in History." Pages 218–81 in *From Nomadism to Monarchy: Archaeological and Historical Aspects of Early Israel*. Edited by Nadav Na'aman and Israel Finkelstein. Jerusalem: Israel Exploration Society, 1994.
Na'aman, Nadav. "The Law of the Altar in Deuteronomy and the Cultic Site Near Shechem." Pages 141–61 in *Rethinking the Foundations. Historiography in the Ancient World and in the Bible. Essays in Honour of John Van Seters*. Edited by Steven L. McKenzie and Thomas Römer. BZAW 294. Berlin: de Gruyter, 2000.
Na'aman, Nadav. "Saul, Benjamin and the Emergence of Biblical Israel." *ZAW* 121 (2009): 216–224, 335–349.
Na'aman, Nadav. "The Israelite-Judahite Struggle for the Patrimony of Ancient Israel." *Bib* 91 (2010): 1–23.
Na'aman, Nadav and Israel Finkelstein, eds. *From Nomadism to Monarchy: Archaeological and Historical Aspects of Early Israel*. Jerusalem: Israel Exploration Society, 1994.
Naveh, Joseph and Yitzhak Magen. "Aramaic and Hebrew Inscriptions of the Second-Century BCE at Mount Gerizim." *'Atiqot* 32 (1997): 9*–17*.
Neubauer, Adolf. "Chronique Samaritaine." *JA* 14 (1869): 385–470.
Nicolai, Walter. *Versuch über Herodots Geschichtsphilosophie*. Heidelberg: Winter, 1986.
Niemann, Hermann Michael. *Herrschaft, Königtum und Staat: Skizzen zur soziokulturellen Entwicklung im monarchischen Israel*. FAT 6. Tübingen: Mohr Siebeck, 1993.
Nihan, Christophe. "The Torah between Samaria and Judah: Shechem and Gerizim in Deuteronomy and Joshua." Pages 187–223 in *The Pentateuch as Torah: New Models for Understanding Its Promulgation and Acceptance*. Edited by Gary N. Knoppers and Bernard M. Levinson. Winona Lake, IN: Eisenbrauns, 2007.

Nihan, Christophe. "Garizim et Ébal dans le Pentateuque: Quelques remarques en marge de la publication d'un nouveau fragment du Deutéronome." *Sem* 54 (2011): 185–210.

Nihan, Christophe. "Cult Centralization and the Torah Traditions in Chronicles." Pages 253–88 in *The Fall of Jerusalem and the Rise of the Torah*. Edited by Peter Dubovský, , Dominik Markl, and Jean-Pierre Sonnet. FAT 107. Tübingen: Mohr Siebeck, 2016.

Nihan, Christophe. "Reconsidering Davidic Kingship in Ezekiel." Pages 89–110 in *Leadership, Social Memory and Judean Discourse in the Fifth–Second Centuries BCE*. Edited by Diana Edelman and Ehud Ben Zvi. Worlds of the Ancient Near East and Mediterranean. Sheffield: Equinox, 2016.

Nihan, Christophe. "Utopies royales et origines du messianisme dans la Bible hébraïque." In *Encyclopédie des messianismes*. Edited by David Hamidović. Forthcoming.

Nodet, Étienne. "Israelites, Samaritans, Temples, Jews." Pages 121–71 in *Samaria, Samarians, Samaritans: Studies on Bible, History and Linguistics*. Edited by József Zsengellér. SJ 66; StSam 6. Berlin: de Gruyter, 2011.

Nocquet, Dany R. *La Samarie, la Diaspora et l'achèvement de la Torah: territorialités et internationalités dans l'Hexateuque*. OBO 284. Fribourg: Academic Press; Göttingen: Vandenhoeck & Ruprecht, 2017.

Nogalski, James. *Redactional Processes in the Book of the Twelve*. BZAW 218. Berlin: de Gruyter, 1993.

Nutkowicz, Hélène. "Les mariages mixtes à Éléphantine à l'époque perse." *Transeu* 36 (2008): 125–139.

Nutt, John W. *Fragments of a Samaritan Targum: Edited from a Bodleian Manuscript, with an Introduction, Containing a Sketch of Samaritan History, Dogma and Literature*. London: Trübner, 1874.

Nyberg, Henrik Samuel. "Das textkritische Problem des Alten Testaments am Hoseabuche demonstriert." *ZAW* 52 (1934): 241–54.

Olyan, Saul. "Purity Ideology in Ezra-Nehemiah as a Tool to Reconstitute the Community." *JSJ* 35 (2004): 4–10.

Oswald, Wolfgang. *Israel am Gottesberg: Eine Untersuchung zur Literaturgeschichte der vorderen Sinaiperikope Ex 19–24 und deren historischem Hintergrund*. OBO 159. Göttingen: Vandenhoeck & Ruprecht, 1998.

Otto, Eckart. *Das Deuteronomium: Politische Theologie und Rechtsreform in Juda und Assyrien*. BZAW 284. Berlin: de Gruyter, 1999.

Otto, Eckart. "Die Rechtshermeneutik des Pentateuch und die achämenidische Rechtsideologie in ihren altorientalischen Kontexten." Pages 71–116 in *Kodifizierung und Legitimierung des Rechts in der Antike und im Alten Orient*. Edited by Markus Witte and Marie Theres Fögen. BZABR 5. Wiesbaden: Harrassowitz, 2005.

Otto, Eckart. *Deuteronomium 1–11*. HThKAT. Freiburg, Basel, Wien: Herder, 2012.

Otto, Eckart. *Deuteronomium 12,1–23,15*. HThKAT. Freiburg, Basel, Wien: Herder, 2016.

Pakkala, Juha. *Ezra the Scribe: The Development of Ezra 7–10 and Nehemiah 8*. BZAW 347. Berlin, New York: de Gruyter, 2004.

Paul, Shalom M. "A Technical Expression from Archery in Zechariah IX 13a." *VT* 39 (1989): 495–97.

Petersen, David L. *Zechariah 9–14 and Malachi: A Commentary*. OTL. Louisville: Westminster John Knox, 1995.

Petterson, Anthony R. *Behold your King: The Hope for the House of David in the Book of Zechariah*. LHBOTS 513. New York: T&T Clark International, 2009.

Powels, Sylvia. *Der Kalender der Samaritaner anhand des Kitāb ḥisāb as-sinīn und anderer Handschriften*. StSam 3. Berlin – New York: de Gruyter, 1977.

Powels, Sylvia. "The Samaritan Calendar and the Roots of Samaritan Chronology." Pages 691–742 in *The Samaritans*. Edited by Alan D. Crown. Tübingen: J.C.B. Mohr (Paul Siebeck), 1989.

Preuß, Horst Dietrich. *Theologie des Alten Testaments*. Vol. 1, *Theologie des Alten Testaments*. Stuttgart: Kohlhammer, 1991.

Preuß, Horst Dietrich. *Theologie des Alten Testaments*. Vol. 2, *Theologie des Alten Testaments*. Stuttgart: Kohlhammer, 1992.

Prijs, Leo. *Jüdische Tradition in der Septuaginta*. Leiden: Brill, 1948.

Pummer, Reinhard. *The Samaritans*. Iconography of Religions 23.5. Leiden: Brill, 1987.

Pummer, Reinhard. "Samaritan Material Remains and Archaeology." Pages 135–77 in *The Samaritans*. Edited by Alan D. Crown. Tübingen: J.C.B. Mohr (Paul Siebeck), 1989.

Pummer, Reinhard. *Samaritan Marriage Contracts and Deeds of Divorce*. Vol. I. Wiesbaden: Harrassowitz, 1993.

Pummer, Reinhard. "The Samaritans and Their Pentateuch." Pages 237–69 in *The Pentateuch as Torah: New Models for Understanding Its Promulgation and Acceptance*. Edited by Gary N. Knoppers and Bernard M. Levinson. Winona Lake, IN: Eisenbrauns, 2007.

Pummer, Reinhard. *The Samaritans in Flavius Josephus*. TSAJ 129. Tübingen: Mohr Siebeck, 2009.

Pummer, Reinhard. "Samaritanism – A Jewish Sect or an Independent Form of Yahwism?" Pages 1–24 in *Samaritans: Past and Present. Current Studies*. Edited by Menahem Mor and Friedrich V. Reiterer. SJ 53; StSam 5. Berlin; New York: de Gruyter, 2010.

Pummer, Reinhard, *The Samaritans. A Profile*. Grand Rapids, MI: Eerdmans, 2016.

Pummer, Reinhard. "Was There an Altar or a Temple in the Sacred Precinct on Mt. Gerizim?" *JSJ* 47 (2016): 1–21.

Pummer, Reinhard. "Synagogues – Samaritan and Jewish: A New Look at Their Differentiating Characteristics." In *Proceedings of the Ninth Congress of Samaritan Studies*, edited by Jan Dušek. SJ; StSam. Berlin: de Gruyter, forthcoming.

Pury, Albert de. "P^g as the Absolute Beginning." Pages 99–128 in *Les dernières rédactions du Pentateuque, de l'Hexateuque et de l'Ennéateuque*. Edited by Konrad Schmid and Thomas Römer. BETL 203. Leuven: Peeters, 2007.

Rapp, Hans A. *Jakob in Bet-El: Gen 35,1–15 und die jüdische Literatur des 3. und 2. Jahrhunderts*. Herders Biblische Studien 29. Freiburg/New York: Herder, 2001.

Redditt, Paul L. "Israel's Shepherds: Hope and Pessimism in Zechariah 9–14." *CBQ* 51 (1989): 631–42.

Redditt, Paul L. *Zechariah 9–14*. IECOT. Stuttgart: Kohlhammer, 2012.

Rendtorff, Rolf. "Die 'Erwählung' Israels in der Hebräischen Bibel." Pages 319–27 in *Kontexte der Schrift, Bd. 1: Text. Ethik. Judentum und Christentum. Gesellschaft. E. W. Stegemann zum 60. Geburtstag*. Edited by Gabriella Gelardini. Stuttgart: Kohlhammer, 2015.

Renz, Johannes. *Schrift und Schreibertradition: Eine paläographische Studie zum kulturgeschichtlichen Verhältnis von israelitischem Nordreich und Südreich*. ADPV 23. Wiesbaden: Harrassowitz, 1997.

Reuter, Julia. *Ordnungen des Anderen: Zum Problem des Eigenen in der Soziologie des Fremden*. Bielefeld: Transcript, 2002.

Ro, Johannes Unsok. "The Portrayal of Judean Communities in Persian Era Palestine Through the Lens of the Covenant Code." *Sem* 56 (2014): 249–89.

Robertson, Edward. *Catalogue of the Samaritan Manuscripts in the John Rylands Library of Manchester*. Vol. 2. Manchester: John Rylands Library, 1962.

Rofé, Alexander. "Historico-Literary Aspects of the Qumran Biblical Scrolls." Pages 30–39 in *The Dead Sea Scrolls: Fifty Years After Their Discovery: Proceedings of the Jerusalem Congress, July 20–25, 1997*. Edited by Lawrence H. Schiffman, Emanuel Tov, and James C. VanderKam. Jerusalem: Israel Exploration Society and the Shrine of the Book, Israel Museum, 2000.

Römer, Thomas. *Israels Väter: Untersuchungen zur Väterthematik im Deuteronomium und in der deuteronomistischen Tradition*. OBO 99. Fribourg: Universitätsverlag and Göttingen: Vandenhoeck & Ruprecht, 1990.

Römer, Thomas. "Joseph approché: Source du cycle, corpus, unité." Pages 73–85 in *Le livre de traverse: De l'exégèse biblique à l'anthropologie*. Edited by Oliver Abel and Françoise Smyth. Patrimoines. Paris: Cerf, 1992.

Römer, Thomas. *The So-Called Deuteronomistic History: A Sociological, Historical and Literary Introduction*. London: T & T Clark, 2005.

Römer, Thomas. "Das doppelte Ende des Josuabuches: einige Anmerkungen zur aktuellen Diskussion um 'deuteronomistisches Geschichtswerk' und 'Hexateuch.'" *ZAW* 118 (2006): 523–48.

Römer, Thomas. "Der Pentateuch." Pages 52–166 in Walter Dietrich et al., *Die Entstehung des Alten Testaments*. Theologische Wissenschaft 1. Stuttgart: Kohlhammer, 2014.

Römer, Thomas and Marc Z. Brettler. "Deuteronomy 34 and the Case for a Persian Hexateuch." *JBL* 119 (2000): 401–19.

Rom-Shiloni, Dalit. *Exclusive Inclusivity: Identity Conflicts Between Exiles and the Peoples Who Remained (6th–5th Centuries BCE)*. LHBOTS 543. London: T&T Clark, 2013.

Rösel, Martin. "Die Septuaginta und der Kult: Interpretationen und Aktualisierungen im Buch Numeri." Pages 25–40 in *La double transmission du texte biblique: Études d'histoire du texte offertes en hommage à A. Schenker*. Edited by Yohanan Goldman and Christoph Uehlinge,. OBO 179. Fribourg/Göttingen: Éditions Universitaires/Vandenhoeck & Ruprecht, 2001.

Rothenbusch, Ralf. *"...abgesondert zur Tora Gottes hin": Ethnisch-religiöse Identitäten im Esra/Nehemiabuch*. Herders Biblische Studien 70. Freiburg, Basel, Wien: Herder, 2012.

Rothstein, J. W. *Juden und Samaritaner: Die grundlegende Scheidung von Judentum und Heidentum: Eine kritische Studie zum Buch Haggai und zur jüdischen Geschichte im ersten nachexilischen Jahrhundert*. BZAW 3. Leipzig: Hinrichs, 1908.

Rudolph, Wilhelm. *Esra und Nehemia: samt 3. Esra*. HAT 20. Tübingen: Mohr Siebeck, 1949.

Rudolph, Wilhelm. *Haggai, Sacharja 1–8, Sacharja 9–14, Maleachi*. KAT 134. Gütersloh: Mohn, 1976.

Rütersworden, Udo. "Die persische Reichsautorisation der Thora: Fact or Fiction." *ZABR* 1 (1995): 47–61.

Sacchi, Paolo. *The History of the Second Temple Period*. JSOTSup 285. Sheffield: Sheffield Academic Press, 2000.

Safrai, Shmuel. *Das jüdische Volk im Zeitalter des Zweiten Tempels*. Neukirchen-Vluyn: Neukirchener Verlag, 1978.
Satlow, Michael. *Jewish Marriage in Antiquity*. Princeton: Princeton University Press, 2001.
Schaefer, Konrad R. "Zechariah 14: A Study in Allusion." *CBQ* 57 (1995): 66–91.
Schaper, Joachim. "The Jerusalem Temple as an Instrument of the Achaemenid Fiscal Administration." *VT* 45 (1995): 528–39.
Schaper, Joachim. "Auf der Suche nach dem alten Israel? Text, Artefakt und 'Geschichte Israels' in der alttestamentlichen Wissenschaft vor dem Hintergrund der Methodendiskussion in den historischen Kulturwissenschaften." *ZAW* 118 (2006): 1–21, 181–96.
Schenker, Adrian. "Le Seigneur choisira-t-il le lieu de son nom ou l'a-t-il choisi? L'apport de la Bible grecque ancienne à l'histoire du texte samaritain et massorétique." Pages 339–51 in *Scripture in Transition: Essays on Septuagint, Hebrew Bible, and Dead Sea Scrolls in Honour of Raija Sollamo*. Edited by Jutta Jokiranta, and Anssi Voitila. Leiden: Brill, 2008.
Schmid, Konrad. *Genesis and the Moses Story: Israel's Dual Origins in the Hebrew Bible*. Translated by James D. Nogalski. Siphrut 3. Winona Lake, IN: Eisenbrauns, 2010.
Schmid, Konrad. "Die Samaritaner und die Judäer: Die biblische Diskussion um ihr Verhältnis in Josua 24." Pages 31–49 in *Die Samaritaner und die Bibel: Historische und literarische Wechselwirkungen zwischen biblischen und samaritanischen Traditionen/The Samaritans and the Bible: Historical and Literary Interactions between Biblical and Samaritan Traditions*. Edited by Jörg Frey, Ursula Schattner-Rieser, and Konrad Schmid. SJ 70; StSam 7. Berlin: de Gruyter, 2012.
Schmid, Konrad. *The Old Testament: A Literary History*. Translated by Linda M. Maloney. Minneapolis: Fortress, 2012.
Schmitt, Götz. *Der Landtag von Sichem*. AzTh I/15. Stuttgart: Calwer, 1964.
Schorch, Stefan. "La formation de la communauté samaritaine au 2e siècle avant J.–Chr. et la culture de lecture du Judaïsme." Pages 5–20 in *Un carrefour dans l'histoire de la Bible*. Edited by Innocent Himbaza and Adrian Schenker. OBO 233. Göttingen: Vandenhoeck & Ruprecht, 2007.
Schorch, Stefan. "The Samaritan Version of Deuteronomy and the Origin of Deuteronomy." Pages 23–37 in *Samaria, Samarians, Samaritans: Studies on Bible, History and Linguistics*. Edited by József Zsengellér. SJ 66; StSam 6. Berlin: de Gruyter, 2011.
Schorch, Stefan. "Der Pentateuch der Samaritaner: Seine Erforschung und seine Bedeutung für das Verständnis des alttestamentlichen Bibeltextes." Pages 5–29 in *Die Samaritaner und die Bibel: Historische und literarische Wechselwirkungen zwischen biblischen und samaritanischen Traditionen*. Edited by Jörg Frey, Ursula Schattner-Rieser, and Konrad Schmid. SJ 70; StSam 7. Berlin: de Gruyter, 2012.
Schorch, Stefan. "A Critical *editio maior* of the Samaritan Pentateuch: State of Research, Principles, and Problems." *HBAI* 2 (2013): 100–20.
Schorch, Stefan. "Der Samaritanische Pentateuch in der Geschichte des hebräischen Bibeltextes." *VF* 60 (2015): 18–29.
Schur, Nathan, *History of the Samaritans: 2nd Revised and Enlarged Edition*, BEATAJ 18. Frankfurt am Main; Bern; New York; Paris: Peter Lang, 1992.
Schütte, Wolfgang. *Israels Exil in Juda: Untersuchungen zur Entstehung der Schriftprophetie*. OBO 279. Fribourg: Academic Press Fribourg, 2016.

Schweitzer, Steven James. *Reading Utopia in Chronicles*. LHBOTS 442. New York: T&T Clark International, 2007.

Schwiderski, Dirk. *Die alt- und reichsaramäischen Inschriften / The Old and Imperial Aramaic Inscriptions*. Vol. 2: *Texte und Bibliographie*. Berlin: de Gruyter. 2004.

Seebass, Horst. "בחר III: Gebrauch im AT." *ThWAT* 1:594–608.

Seger, Joe D. "Shechem." *OEANE:* 19–23.

Seybold, Klaus. "Erwählung. I Altes Testament." *RGG* 2:1478–81.

Shavit, Yaacov, Yaacov Goldstein, and Haim Be'er, eds. *Personalities in Eretz-Israel 1799–1948: A Biographical Dictionary*. Tel-Aviv: Am Oved Publishers, 1983 (Hebrew).

Ska, Jean-Louis. "'Persian Imperial Authorization': Some Question Marks." Pages 161–82 in *Persia and Torah: The Theory of the Imperial Authorization of the Pentateuch*. Edited by James W. Watts. SBL Symposium Series 17. Atlanta, GA: Society of Biblical Literature, 2001.

Skehan, Patrick W. "Exodus in the Samaritan Recension from Qumran." *JBL* 74 (1955): 182–87.

Smith-Christopher, D.L. "The Mixed Marriage Crisis in Ezra 9–10 and Nehemiah 13: A Study of the Sociology of the Post-Exilic Judean Community." Pages 242–65 in *Temple and Community in the Persian Period*. Vol. 2 of *Second Temple Studies*. Edited by Tamara Cohn Eskenazi. JSOTSup 175. Sheffield: JSOT Press, 1994.

Smitten, Wilhelm T. in der. *Esra: Quellen, Überlieferung und Geschichte*. Assen: Van Gorcum, 1973.

Soggin, J. Alberto. *Einführung in die Geschichte Israels und Judas: Von den Ursprüngen bis zum Aufstand Bar Kochbas*. Darmstadt: Wissenschaftliche Buchgesellschaft, 1991.

Sperber, Alexander. *The Bible in Aramaic*. Vol. 4a. Leiden: Brill, 1968.

Spilsbury, Paul and Chris Seeman. *Judean Antiquities 11. Flavius Josephus: Translation and Commentary*. Vol. 6 A. Leiden: Brill, 2017.

Spivak, Gayatri. "The Rani of Sirmur." Pages 128–151 in *Europe and its Others*. Vol. 1 of *Proceedings of the Essex Conference on the Sociology of Literature*. Edited by Francis Barker. Colchester: University of Essex, 1985.

Spuler, Bertold and Joachim Mayr, eds. *Wüstenfeld-Mahler'sche Vergleichungs-Tabellen zur muslimischen und iranischen Zeitrechnung mit Tafeln zur Umrechnung orient-christlicher Ären*. Dritte, verbesserte und erweiterte Auflage der "Vergleichungs-Tabellen der mohammedanischen und christlichen Zeitrechnung". Wiesbaden: Franz Steiner, 1961.

Steck, Odil Hannes. *Der Abschluss der Prophetie im Alten Testament: Ein Versuch zur Frage der Vorgeschichte des Kanons*. Biblisch-theologische Studien 17. Neukirchen-Vluyn: Neukirchen Verlag, 1991.

Stenhouse, Paul, ed. *The Kitāb al-Tarīkh of Abū 'l-Fatḥ: A New Edition with Notes*. 3 vols. Microfiches of Ph.D. thesis. Sydney, 1980.

Stenhouse, Paul, transl. *The Kitāb al-Tarīkh of Abū 'l-Fatḥ*. Studies in Judaica, 1. Sydney: Mandelbaum Trust, University of Sydney, 1985.

Stenhouse, Paul. "Samaritan Chronology." Pages 173–187 in *Proceedings of the First International Congress of the Société d'Études Samaritaines, Tel-Aviv, April 11–13, 1988*. Edited by Abraham Tal and Moshe Florentin. Tel-Aviv: Chaim Rosenberg School for Jewish Studies, Tel Aviv University, 1991.

Stern, Ephraim. *The Assyrian, Babylonian, and Persian Periods (732–332 B.C.E.)*. Vol. 2 of *Archaeology of the Land of the Bible*. ABRL. New York: Doubleday, 2001.

Stern, Ephraim and Yitzhak Magen. "Archaeological Evidence for the First Stage of the Samaritan Temple on Mount Gerizim." *IEJ* 52 (2002): 49–57.
Stern, Menahem. *Greek and Latin Authors on Jews and Judaism, I.* Jerusalem: The Israel Academy of Sciences and Humanities, 1974.
Steymans, Hans Ulrich. *Deuteronomium 28 und die adê zur Thronfolgeregelung Asarhaddons. Segen und Fluch im Alten Orient und in Israel.* OBO 145. Göttingen: Vandenhoeck & Ruprecht, 1995.
Steymans, Hans Ulrich. "Deuteronomy 28 and Tell Tayinat." *Verbum et Ecclesia* 34 (2013): 1–13.
Tal, Abraham. *Tibåt Mårqe: The Ark of Marqe: Edition, Translation, Commentary.* StSam. Berlin: de Gruyter, in preparation.
Tal, Oren, and Itamar Taxel. "Samaritan Burial Customs Outside Samaria: Evidence from Late Roman and Byzantine Cemeteries in the Southern Sharon Plain." *ZDPV* 130 (2014): 155–80.
Tal, Oren, and Itamar Taxel. *Samaritan Cemeteries and Tombs in the Southern Coastal Plain: The Archaeology and History of the Samaritan Settlement Outside Samaria (Ca. 300–700 CE).* ÄAT 82. Münster: Ugarit-Verlag, 2015.
Talmon, Shemaryahu. "Heiliges Schrifttum und kanonische Bücher aus jüdischer Sicht: Überlegungen zur Ausbildung der Größe 'Die Schrift' im Judentum." Pages 45–79 in *Mitte der Schrift? Ein jüdisch-christliches Gespräch.* Texte des Berner Symposions vom 6. – 12. Januar 1985. Edited by Martin A. Klopfenstein. JudChr 11. Bern, Frankfurt am Main, New York, Paris: Lang, 1987.
Teeter, David Andrew. *Scribal Laws: Exegetical Variation in the Textual Transmission of Biblical Law in the Late Second Temple Period.* FAT 92. Tübingen: Mohr Siebeck, 2014.
Teitelbaum, Dina. "The Jewish Ossuary Phenomenon: Cultural Receptivity in Roman Palestine." PhD thesis. Ottawa: University of Ottawa, 2005.
Toepler, Theophilus Eduardus. *De Pentateuchi interpretationis alexandrinae indole critica et hermeneutica.* Halle: C. Schwetschke, 1830.
Toorn, Karel van der. "Anat-Yahu, Some Other Deities, and the Jews of Elephantine." *Numen* 39 (1992): 80–101.
Torrey, Charles C. *Ezra Studies.* Chicago: The University of Chicago Press, 1910.
Tov, Emanuel. "The Nature and Background of Harmonizations in Biblical Manuscripts." *JSOT* 31 (1985): 3–29.
Tov, Emanuel. "Approaches towards Scripture Embraced by the Ancient Greek Translators." pages 213–28 in *Der Mensch vor Gott: Forschungen zum Menschenbild in Bibel, antikem Judentum und Koran: Festschrift für Herrmann Lichtenberger zum 60. Geburtstag.* Edited by Ulrike Mittmann-Richert et al. Neukirchen-Vluyn: Neukirchener Verlag, 2003.
Tov, Emanuel. "Textual Harmonizations in the Ancient Texts of Deuteronomy." Pages 271–82 in *Hebrew Bible, Greek Bible, and Qumran: Collected Essays.* TSAJ 121. Tübingen: Mohr Siebeck, 2008.
Tov, Emanuel. *Textual Criticism of the Hebrew Bible.* 3rd ed., revised and expanded. Minneapolis: Fortress Press, 2012.
Tov, Emanuel. "The Samaritan Pentateuch and the Dead Sea Scrolls: The Proximity of the Pre-Samaritan Qumran Scrolls to the SP." Pages 59–88 in *Keter Shem Tov: Essays on the Dead Sea Scrolls in Memory of Alan Crown.* Edited by S. Tzoref and I. Young.

Perspectives on Hebrew Scriptures and Its Contexts 20. Piscataway, NJ: Gorgias Press, 2013. Revised version pages 387–410 in vol. 3 of *Textual Criticism of the Hebrew Bible, Qumran, Septuagint: Collected Writings.* Edited by Emanuel Tov. VTSup 167. Leiden: Brill, 2015.

Tov, Emanuel. "Textual Harmonization in the Stories of the Patriarchs." Pages 166–88 in vol. 3 of *Textual Criticism of the Hebrew Bible, Qumran, Septuagint: Collected Writings.* Edited by Emanuel Tov. VTSup 167. Leiden: Brill, 2015.

Tov, Emanuel. "The Harmonizing Character of the Septuagint of Genesis 1–11." Pages 470–89 in vol. 3 of *Textual Criticism of the Hebrew Bible, Qumran, Septuagint: Collected Writings.* Edited by Emanuel Tov. VTSup 167. Leiden: Brill, 2015.

Tov, Emanuel. "The Source of Source Criticism: The Relevance of Non-Masoretic Textual Witnesses." Pages 283–301 in *Text – Textgeschichte – Textwirkung: Festschrift zum 65. Geburtstag von Siegfried Kreuzer.* Edited by Thomas Wagner et al. AOAT 419. Münster: Ugarit-Verlag, 2015.

Tov, Emanuel. "The Development of the Text of the Torah in Two Major Text Blocks." *Text* 26 (2016): 1–27. http://www.hum.huji.ac.il/units.php?cat=5020&incat=4972

Tov, Emanuel. "The Septuagint Translation of the Torah as a Source and Resource for the Post-Pentateuchal Translators." Pages 316–28 in vol. 3 of *Die Sprache der Septuaginta, The Language of the Septuagint, Handbuch zur Septuaginta, Handbook of the Septuagint,* LXX.H. Edited by Eberhard Bons and Jan Joosten. Gütersloh: Gütersloher Verlag, 2016.

Tov, Emanuel. "The Shared Tradition of the Septuagint and the Samaritan Pentateuch." Pages 277–93 in *Die Septuaginta: Orte und Intentionen.* Edited by Siegfried Kreuzer et al. WUNT 361. Tübingen: Mohr Siebeck, 2016.

Tov, Emanuel. "The *Tefillin* from the Judean Desert and the Textual Criticism of the Hebrew Bible." Pages 277–92 in *Is There a Text in This Cave? Studies in the Textuality of the Dead Sea Scrolls in Honour of George J. Brooke.* STDJ 119. Leiden: Brill, 2017.

Tov, Emanuel. "The Textual Base of the Biblical Quotations in Second Temple Compositions." Pages 280–302 in *Hā-'îsh Mōshe: Studies in Scriptural Interpretation in the Dead Sea Scrolls and Related Literature in Honor of Moshe J. Bernstein.* Edited by Binyamin Y. Goldstein, Michael Segal, and George Brooke, STDJ 122. Leiden: Brill, 2017.

Tov, Emanuel. "Textual Harmonization in Exodus 1–24." *TC: A Journal of Biblical Textual Criticism* 22 (2017). http://rosetta.reltech.org/TC/v22/TC-2017-Tov.pdf

Tov, Emanuel. "Textual Harmonization in Leviticus." forthcoming;

Tov, Emanuel. "The Septuagint of Numbers as a Harmonizing Text." forthcoming;

Tsedaka, Benyamim. *The History of the Israelite Samaritans Based On Their Own Sources, From the Entrance of the People of Israel to the Land of Canaan Till 2015 CE [3654 Years].* Holon – Mount Gerizim: A.B. Institute of Samaritan Studies Press, 2016 (Hebrew).

Uehlinger, Christoph. "Bildquellen und 'Geschichte Israels': Grundsätzliche Überlegungen und Fallbeispiele." Pages 25–77 in *Steine—Bilder—Texte: Historische Evidenz außerbiblischer und biblischer Quellen.* Edited by Christof Hardmeier. Arbeiten zur Bibel und ihrer Geschichte 5. Leipzig: Evangelische Verlagsanstalt, 2001.

Uehlinger, Christoph. "Fratrie, filiations et paternités dans l'histoire de Joseph (Genèse 37–50*)." Pages 303–28 in *Jacob: Commentaire à plusieurs voix de Gen. 25–36:*

Mélanges offerts à Albert de Pury. Edited by Jean-Daniel Macchi, and Thomas Römer. MdB 44. Genève: Labor et Fides, 2001.

Ulrich, Eugene C. *Dead Sea Scrolls and the Developmental Composition of the Bible.* VTSup 169. Leiden: Brill, 2015.

Valentin, Heinrich. *Aaron: Eine Studie zur vor-priesterschriftlichen Aaron-Überlieferung.* OBO 18. Fribourg: Universitätsverlag and Göttingen: Vandenhoeck & Ruprecht, 1978.

Van Seters, John. "The Altar Law of Ex 20,24–26 in Critical Debate." Pages 157–74 in *Auf dem Weg zur Endgestalt von Genesis bis II Regum: Festschrift für Hans-Christoph Schmitt zu seinem 65. Geburtstag.* Edited by Martin Beck and Ulrike Schorn. BZAW 370. Berlin: de Gruyter, 2006.

Veijola, Timo. *Verheissung in der Krise: Studien zur Literatur und Theologie der Exilszeit anhand des 89. Psalms.* Annales Scientiarum Fennicae, ser. B 220. Helsinki: Suomalainen Tiedakatemia, 1982.

Vilmar, Eduard, ed. *Abulfathi Annales Samaritani.* Gotha: Friedrich Andreas Perthes, 1865.

Vilsker, Leib Kheimovitch. *Manuel d'araméen samaritain.* Traduit du russe par Jean Margain. Paris: Editions de Centre National de la Recherche Scientifique, 1981.

Vincent, L.-H. "Un hypogée antique à Naplouse." *RB* 29 (1920): 126–35.

Wächter, Ludwig. "Zur Lokalisierung des sichemitischen Baumheiligtums." *ZDPV* 103 (1987): 1–12.

Way, Kenneth C. "Donkey Domain: Zechariah 9:9 and Lexical Semantics." *JBL* 129 (2010): 105–14.

Weingart, Kristin. *Stämmevolk – Staatsvolk – Gottesvolk? Studien zur Verwendung des Israel-Namens im Alten Testament.* FAT II/68. Tübingen: Mohr Siebeck, 2014.

Weippert, Manfred. "Geschichte Israels am Scheideweg." *TRu* 58 (1993): 71–103.

Weippert, Manfred. *Historisches Textbuch zum Alten Testament: Mit Beiträgen von Joachim Friedrich Quack, Bernd Ulrich Schipper und Stefan Jakob Wimmer.* Göttingen: Vandehoeck & Ruprecht, 2010.

Wellhausen, Julius. *Israelitische und Jüdische Geschichte.* 8th ed. Berlin, Leipzig: de Gruyter, 1921.

Wenzel, Heiko. *Reading Zechariah with Zechariah 1:1–6 as the Introduction to the Entire Book.* CBET 59. Leuven: Peeters, 2011.

Wevers, John William. *Notes on the Greek Text of Numbers.* SBLSCSS 46. Atlanta: Scholars Press, 1998.

Widengren, Geo. "The Persian Period." Pages 489–538 in *Israelite and Judean History.* Edited by John H. Hayes and J. Maxwell Miller. London: SCM Press, 1977.

Willi, Thomas. *Juda – Jehud – Israel. Studien zum Selbstverständnis des Judentums in persischer Zeit.* FAT 12. Tübingen: Mohr Siebeck, 1995.

Williamson, H. G. M. *Ezra. Nehemiah.* WBC 16. Dallas: Word Books, 1985.

Williamson, H. G. M. "The Belief System of the Book of Nehemiah." Pages 276–87 in *The Crisis of Israelite Religion: Transformation of Religious Tradition in Exilic and Post-Exilic Times.* Edited by Bob Becking. Leiden: Brill, 1999.

Williamson, H. G. M., ed. *Understanding the History of Ancient Israel.* Oxford: Oxford University Press, 2007.

Witte, Markus. "Die Gebeine Josefs." Pages 139–56 in *Auf dem Weg zur Endgestalt von Genesis bis II Regum: Festschrift Hans-Christoph Schmitt zum 65. Geburtstag.* Edited by Martin Beck and Ulrike Schorn. BZAW 370. Berlin: de Gruyter, 2006.

Wöhrle, Jakob. *Der Abschluss des Zwölfprophetenbuches: Buchübergreifende Redaktionsprozesse in den späten Sammlungen*. BZAW 389. Berlin: de Gruyter, 2008.
Wolters, Al. *Zechariah*. HCOT. Leuven: Peeters, 2014.
Wright, Jacob L. *Rebuilding Identity: The Nehemiah-Memoir and its Earliest Readers*. BZAW 348. Berlin, New York: de Gruyter, 2004.
Yassine, Khair and Javier Teixidor. "Ammonite and Aramaic Inscriptions from Tell el-Mazār." *BASOR* 264 (1986): 45–50.
Zakovitch, Yair. "The Object of the Narrative of the Burial of Foreign Gods at Shechem (Gen 35:2, 4)." *Bet Mikra* 25 (1979–1980): 30–37 (Hebrew).
Zangenberg, Jürgen. *ΣΑΜΑΡΕΙΑ: Antike Quellen zur Geschichte und Kultur der Samaritaner in deutscher Übersetzung*. Texte und Arbeiten zum neutestamentlichen Zeitalter 15. Tübingen: Francke, 1994.
Zangenberg, Jürgen. "Between Jerusalem and the Galilee: Samaria in the Time of Jesus." Pages 393–432 in *Jesus and Archaeology*. Edited by James H. Charlesworth. Grand Rapids, MI: William B. Eerdmans, 2006.
Zangenberg, Jürgen. "Berg des Segens – Berg des Streits: Heiden, Juden, Christen und Samaritaner auf dem Garizim." *TZ* 63 (2007): 289–309.
Zangenberg, Jürgen. "The Sanctuary on Mount Gerizim. Observations on the Results of 20 Years of Excavation." Pages 399–420 in *Temple Building and Temple Cult: Architecture and Cultic Paraphernalia of Temples in the Levant (2.–1. Mill. B.C.E.). Proceedings of a Conference on the Occasion of the 50th Anniversary of the Institute of Biblical Archaeology at the University of Tübingen (28–30 May 2010)*. Edited by Jens Kamlah. Wiesbaden: Harrasowitz, 2012.
Zsengellér, József. *Gerizim as Israel: Northern Tradition of the Old Testament and the Early Traditions of the Samaritans*. Utrechtse Theologische Reeks 38. Utrecht: University of Utrecht, 1998.
Zwickel, Wolfgang. "Jerusalem und Samaria zur Zeit Nehemias – Ein Vergleich." *BZ* 52 (2008): 204–18.

List of Contributors

Hervé Gonzalez, Attaché temporaire d'enseignement et de recherche à la chaire Milieux bibliques, Collège de France, Paris, and PhD Candidate (*doctorant*), Université de Lausanne, Switzerland.

Raik Heckl, Außerplanmäßiger Professor, Institut für alttestamentliche Wissenschaft, Universität Leipzig, Germany.

Benedikt Hensel, Privatdozent; Wissenschaftlicher Mitarbeiter am Lehrstuhl für Alttestamentliche Wissenschaft und frühjüdische Religionsgeschichte (Konrad Schmid), Theologische Fakultät, Universität Zürich, Switzerland.

Magnar Kartveit, Emeritus Professor of Old Testament, VID Specialized University / School of Mission and Theology, Stavanger, Norway.

Gary N. Knoppers, John A. O'Brien Professor of Theology, University of Notre Dame, USA.

Christophe Nihan, Professeur associé en Bible hébraïque et Histoire de l'Israël ancien, Université de Lausanne, Switzerland.

Reinhard Pummer, Emeritus Professor of Religious Studies, University of Ottawa, Canada.

Thomas Römer, Professor of Hebrew Bible, Collège de France, Paris, France, University of Lausanne, Switzerland, and University of Pretoria, South Africa.

Konrad Schmid, Professor für alttestamentliche Wissenschaft und frühjüdische Religionsgeschichte, Universität Zürich, Switzerland.

Emanuel Tov, J. L. Magnes Professor of Bible Emeritus, Hebrew University, Jerusalem, Israel.

Index of Modern Authors

Abel, F.-M. 74
Adler, E. 151
Aejmelaeus, A. 52
Ahlström, G. 19, 28
Albertz, R. 2, 22, 26, 62, 79, 93, 96, 104, 146
Albright, W. F. 36
Allen, L. 94
Alon, G. 76
Alt, A. 21
Anbar, M. 23, 25
Anderson, R. T. 170
Assmann, J. 144

Baek, K. 4
Baillet, M. 36, 150, 154
Barkai, R. 75–76
Barstad, H. 122
Be'er, H. 152
Becker, U. 26, 116
Becking, B. 23, 71, 96–97, 136–137, 139–140
Bertholet, A. 117
Bichler, R. 144
Bieberstein, K. 25
Blenkinsopp, J. 79–80, 141
Block, D. 112
Blum, E. 25, 27, 29, 122, 132
Boda, M. 101–102, 104, 106–109, 111
Böhler, D. 145
Böhm, M. 135
Bonnard, C. 154
Bourgel, J. 60
Brettler, M. 90
Buller, B. 1

Campbell, E. 28
Carr, D. 6, 15, 31
Catastini, A. 91
Chalcraft, D. 21
Collins, B. J. 11
Collins, J. J. 15, 21
Cook, S. 36

Crown, A. 151
Crüsemann, F. 79

Delcor, M. 101, 103
Dion, P. 63,
Dessel, J. 26
Donner, H. 19
Dorival, G. 37
Dorsey, D. 140
Dozeman, T. 24
Dušek, J. 60, 62–63, 65–69, 97, 139–141, 146

Edelman, D. 125
Edenburg, C. 81–82
Eshel, E. 35–36, 56, 75
Eskenazi, T. 137

Falk, D. 4
Finkelstein, I. 22, 80, 85
Fishbane, M. 141
Fleming, D. 18
Flint, P. 4–5, 8
Florentin, M. 152, 170
Foster, R. 101
Frankel, Z. 33, 37, 43
Frei, P. 79, 124
Frevel, C. 15, 19–21, 132, 142
Fritz, V. 25

Gaster, M. 149, 151, 153–154, 157, 162, 165, 170
Geiger, A. 46
Gerleman, G. 55
Gertz, J. 24
Gesenius, W. 50–51
Giles, T. 170
Gitin, S. 26
Goldstein, Y. 152
Gooding, D. 41
Gonzalez, H. 93, 101, 104, 113
Grabbe, L. 20–21, 141, 145
Granerød, G. 81

Grätz, S. 21, 80, 118–119, 124, 129, 141, 145–146, 148
Greenberg, M. 55
Greenspoon, L. 20
Gropp, D. 140
Gudme, A. 61–62, 65, 68
Guggenheimer, H. 126
Guillaume, P. 18
Gunneweg, A. 117, 120, 128, 138

Halpern, B. 117
Hardmeier, C. 18
Hayes, J. 19
Häusl, M. 117
Heckl, R. 11, 115–119, 121–126, 128–131, 143, 148
Heidenheim, M. 152
Heller, C. 54
Hendel, R. 32, 37, 48, 53
Hensel, B. 11, 15, 29, 57, 60, 64–65, 132, 136, 140, 142–143, 146–147
Herrmann, S. 19
Hieke, T. 134–135, 137–139, 141
Himbaza, I. 83
Hjelm, I 6–7, 20, 23, 27, 88, 90, 98
Hölscher, G. 103, 120
Houston, W. 88
Hübner, U. 140
Hurvitz, A. 96
Husser, J.M. 91

In der Smitten, W. T. 138

Jamieson-Drake, D. 21
Janzen, D. 138
Japhet, S. 95, 97, 100, 121–122
Jaroš, K. 28
Jericke, D. 88
Johnson, W. 138
Johnstone, W. 95

Kahle, P. 55
Kartveit, M. 7, 9, 15, 17, 23, 65, 84, 98, 132, 142
Kellermann, D. 140
Kippenberg, H. 21
Knauf, E. 18, 79, 90

Knierim, R. 80
Knoppers, G. 7–8, 14–15, 17, 19, 22–23, 61, 69–71, 79–80, 88, 93, 96–98, 104, 132, 142–143, 147
Koch, K. 79
Kohn, S. 50
Koopmans, W. 23
Kratz, R. 17, 24, 117, 119, 120, 123–124, 146
Kunz, A. 108
Kutscher, E. 55

L'Hour, J. 31
Lange, A. 138
Lapp, N. 64
Lee, K. 79
Lee, S. 106
Lemaire, A. 139
Lemmelijn, B. 32
Levin, C. 17, 116
Levin, Y. 143
Levinson, B. 80, 82, 87
Levy-Rubin, M. 152
Lieberman, S. 55
Linville, J. 132
Lipschits, O. 80, 120
Loewenstamm, A. 154
Lohfink, N. 84

Maas, P. 51
Macdonald, J. 149, 153
Magen, Y 2–3, 22–23, 58, 60–72, 74–76, 80, 97, 103–104, 141–142
Magness, J. 74
Marcus, D. 126
Martone, C. 32
Mayes, A. 23, 27
Mayr, J. 153
Meshorer, Y. 146
Meyer, E. 117, 120
Meyers, C. 101–102, 108, 110, 112
Meyers, E. 101–102, 108, 110, 112
Miller, M. 19
Metzger, M. 19
Milik, J. T. 36
Miller, P. 4
Mills, J. 149
Misgav, H. 3, 60–61, 64–71, 97, 104, 141

Moffat, D.   138
Mölle, H.   23 – 24
Mommer, P.   25
Montgomery, J.   7 – 8, 20
Müller, R.   82

Na'aman, N.   18, 21, 26, 82, 88
Naveh, J.   68
Neubauer, A.   151
Nicolai, W.   144
Niemann, H.   21
Nihan, C.   27, 82, 88, 96, 98, 100, 108, 113, 131
Nodet, É.   15
Nocquet, D.   7
Nogalski, J.   104
Noseda, S. N   154
Nutkowicz, H.   139
Nutt, J.   50
Nyberg, S.   55

Olyan, S.   25
Oswald, W.   87
Otto, E.   87, 116

Pakkala, J.   123
Paul, S.   105 – 106
Perrin, A.   4
Petersen, D.   102, 108 – 110
Petterson, A.   108 – 109
Powels, S.   151
Preuß, H.   136
Prijs, L.   33
Pummer, R.   7, 15, 57 – 62, 71, 74, 96, 131 – 132, 143, 146 – 147, 152, 169 – 171
Pury, A. de   25

Rapp, H.   26
Redditt, P.   101 – 102, 104 – 107
Rendtorff, R.   136
Renz, J.   132
Reuter, J.   144
Ro, J.   87
Robertson, E.   151
Rofé, A.   55
Römer, T.   23, 26 – 28, 80, 83, 90 – 91
Rom-Shiloni, D.   142

Rösel, M.   37
Rothenbusch, R.   117, 120
Rothstein, J.   20
Rückl, J.   101
Rudolph, W.   102 – 103, 117
Rüterswörden, U.   79

Sacchi, P.   19
Safrai, S.   19
Satlow, M.   139
Schaefer, K.   109
Schaper, J.   18, 101
Schenker, A.   83
Schmid, K.   4, 17 – 18, 24, 134
Schmitt, G.   23
Schneider, A. M.   2
Schorch, S.   7, 17, 82
Schur, N.   150
Schütte, W.   132
Schweitzer, S.   100
Schwiderski, D.   139 – 140
Seebass, H.   136
Seeman, C.   14, 59, 63
Seger, J.   58
Séligsohn, M   151
Seybold, K.   136
Shavit, Y.   152
Ska, J.   79
Skehan, P.   1 – 2
Smith-Christopher, D.   139
Soggin, J.   19
Sperber, A.   54
Spilsbury, P.   14, 59, 63
Spivak, G.   144
Spuler, B.   153
Stackert, J.   82
Steck, O. H.   104
Stenhouse, P.   150 – 152, 155, 162
Stern, E.   22, 28, 80
Stern, M.   63
Steymans, H.   82

Tal, A.   9
Tal, O.   73, 75 – 76
Talmon, S.   115 – 116
Taxel, I.   73, 75 – 76
Teeter, A.   33, 44 – 45, 52, 55

Teitelbaum, D.   74
Teixidore, J.   139
Toepler, T.   37
Toorn, K. van der   91
Torrey, C.   120, 124
Tov, E.   2, 6, 8, 31–56
Tsedaka, B.   150, 152
Tsfania, L.   3, 60–61, 64, 71, 97, 104, 141

Uehlinger, C.   18, 91
Ulrich, E.   98

Valentin, H.   25
Van Seters, J.   87
Veijola, T.   130
Vilmar, E.   151
Vilsker, L.   150
Vincent, L.   74–75

Wächter, L.   28
Way, K.   107

Weingart, K.   18, 134–136, 138
Weippert, M.   18, 135, 140
Wellhausen, J.   117, 119
Wenzel, H.   94
Wevers, J.   37, 42
Widengren, G.   19
Willi, T.   117, 138
Williamson, H. G. M.   18, 141, 145
Witte, M.   24
Wöhrle, J.   102, 104, 146
Wolters, A.   101–102, 106, 111
Wright, D.   96
Wright, J. E.   26
Wright, J. L.   15, 123, 127

Yassine, K.   139

Zakovitch, Y.   26
Zangenberg, J.   22, 74, 142
Zsengellér, J.   6
Zwickel, W.   130, 143

Index of Ancient Texts

Old Testament

Genesis
1	80
1:9 LXX	42
4:10–11 LXX	35
9	102f
11–12	27
11:31	43
12	10, 27
12:1–9	89
12:6	27, 90
12:6–7	89
12:6, 8	24
12:7	89
15:19–21	142
17:8	25
17:14	42
20:14	43
20:16	43
22	10, 90
22:2	90
24:2b, 4	24
24:10–14	33
24:15–27	33
24:33–49	33
32:18	43
32:19	43
32:20	43
35	26
35:1–5	24
35:2b	24, 26
35:4	26
36:8–9	24
37–50	10
39:7–13	33
39:14–15	33
39:17–19	33
40:9–12	33
40:12–15, 18–19	33
40:16–17	33
41:1–7	33
41:25–36	33
41:47–57	33
41:51–52	91
49	50
50:25	24, 42
50:26	90

Exodus
2:11	39
2:23	41
3:8, 17	142
4:18	41
4:25–26	35
6:17	113
6:20	41
7–11	42, 46, 51
7:10	50
7:15	39
9:29	50
10:24	50
12	44
12–13	35
12:9	44
12:50	36
13:3, 5, 9	36
13:3–10	44
13:5	142
13:19	24, 42, 90
14	25
14:4, 8–9, 23	25
14:9, 17–18, 23, 26	25
14:28	25
15:27	39
16:10	42, 52
17:9	41, 42
17:10	42
18:25	41
19:10	41
19:13	41
19:16	41
20	8, 36f,
20:8–11	36

20:22–26	87	17:4	34–35
20:24	87	17:15	33
20:24–26	87–89, 92	18:3	137
21–22	86	18:22, 26–27, 29–30	137
21:1	87	18:26–27, 29	137
21:2	45	19:2	136
21:11	44	19:2–3	137
21:12	41	19:33	42, 52
21:28	45	20:7, 26	136
21:33	45	20:18	35
21:35	45	22:18	38
22:3	45	23:5–14	44
22:9	45f	23:12	45
22:13	46	23:13	45
23:4	46	23:41	35
23:15	35	25:25	39
23:15, 18	44	25:46	39
23:23, 28	142	25:50	38
25–31	86f, 88	26:20	38
28:41	43	26:21	39
30:20	42	26:24	39
31:16	45	26:41	34
33:2	142	27:30–33	44
34:6	50		
34:6–7 LXX	40	**Numbers**	
34:15	52	1:18	35
34:18, 25	44	2:2b	43
35–40	52, 86f, 88	3:10	41
		3:18, 21	113
Leviticus		4:14	34
1–6	71	7:88	43
1:10	45	9:1–14	44
5:5, 21	34	9:14	42, 52
6:8	38	14:10	42, 52
7:25	45	14:18	50
10:9	42	14:18 LXX	40
10:15	38	14:23 LXX	42
11:25, 28, 40	33–34	14:31	55
11:40b LXX	34	15:14	42
11:44	136	15:36	43
12:3	42	15:40	136
12:5, 7	35	17:12	34
13:39b	38	18:7	41
13:43	38	18:21–32	44
15:3	34–35	21–24	46
15:5	34	21:2	52
15:5–10, 21–22, 27	33	21:21	50

22:11	39	12:13–18	83–84, 86
22:18	39	12:14	86–87
23:3b	42	13:16	35
23:7	39	13:17	34
24:2	39	14:22–29	44
25:16	39	14:23–24	96
26:1 LXX	38	14:23–25	95
26:33	39	15:12–18	44
26:59	41	15:20	95
27:12	39, 41, 52	15:22	45
28:16–25	44	16:1–8	44
29:11	38	16:2, 6–7, 11, 15–16	95
30:6	50	16:2, 6, 11	96
31:6	38	16:7	44
32:11	41	16:17	83
33:9	39	17:8, 10	95
35:21	39, 44	18:6	95
		21:12	34
Deuteronomy		22:2	34
1–3	46, 52	23:4–7	134
1:8	136	23:4–9	142
1:39	41, 55	23:12	34
2:26	50	23:17	95
5	8, 36	26:2	95–96
5; 8; 10; 11; 32	35	27	82, 88
5; 11; 32	35	27:2–8	8
5:1	35	27:4	62, 96, 98
5:3, 32	36	27:12	39
5:15	36	28:9	136
7:1	142	28:15	33
7:1–6	141	28:20	83
10:13, 18, 22	36	30:10 LXX	33
10:13, 21	36	31:11	95
11:1	33	32	40
11:2, 4, 6–8, 10–11, 13	36	32:49	39, 41, 52
11:10, 12, 16	36	34	80
11:29–30	8	34:2–3	89
11:29–32	82	34:4	89
12	82–87, 92, 96–97, 99	**Joshua**	
12–26	86	4:20	62
12:2–7	86	6:5	41
12:4	87	9:27	95
12:5	86	24	23–29, 89–90, 92
12:5, 11, 14, 18, 21, 26	95	24:1	26
12:5, 11, 21	96	24:2	27
12:8–12	86, 99	24:2–4	24

24:5	25	**Jeremiah**	
24:6–7	25	3:18	29
24:7, 11	25	7	92
24:13–28	24	7:12–14	85
24:14–14	28	30:3, 8–9	29
24:26	89	31:27–28, 31–34	29
24:32	24, 90		
		Ezekiel	
1 Samuel		34:3–4	112–113
9:3	42	34:23–24	112
		34:23–31	29
2 Samuel		37:15–28	29, 113
7:1	99		
		Hosea	
1 Kings		2:20	102
5:17–18	99		
8	97	**Obadiah**	
8:16	96	18–21	29
8:30, 33, 35, 42, 44, 48	97		
9:3	94–95	**Zechariah**	
9:4–9	94	9–10	104
12	85	9–14	93–94, 101, 104, 107–111, 113–114
12:1	27	9:9–10	108–109
18:36	42	9:9–13	29
		9:10	107
2 Kings		9:11–17	109
9:24	106	9:13	105–106
17	27, 122	10:3	106
17:21–40	19	10:4–5	106
17:24–31	27	10:6–12	29, 107
17:24–41	27, 59	10:7	106
17:24–40	20	10:9	101
17:29–34	28	11:4–14	100
17:33	28	11:4–17	101–102, 111, 114
17:34, 41	28	11:9	103
18:13–20:11	54	11:10	102–105, 107
24:18–25:30	54	11:14	10–11, 93, 100, 103–105, 107, 110, 114
Isaiah		11:16	112
6:12	136	12:2–4, 6	101, 104
11:11–16	29	12:2, 5–7	107
36:1–38:8	54	12:7–8, 10, 12	109
42:6	103	12:7–13:1	109
49:8	103	12:10	110
56:7	97	12:12–14	110
66:1	99		

12:13	113	5:1	119
13:2	109	5:2	120
13:7–9	101	5:13–15	12, 117–118
14:1–2	105	5:14	118, 120
14:4	105, 107	6:2–5	12, 117–118
14:12	101, 104	6:7	120
14:16–21	109	6:16–21	119
14:21	107	6:19–21	120
		6:21	122
Malachi		7:1	123
2:11	137	7:12–26	129
		7:14	123
Psalms		9:1	135
12:6	108	9:1, 11, 14	137
18:28	108	9:1–2	141
34:7	108	9:2	136
72:4, 13	108	9:2, 4	137
72:8	108	9:5–15	135
78:64	84	9:11	137
132:13–14	99	10:1–17	135
		10:2, 10–11, 14, 17–18	135
Ruth		10:3	137
4:1–12, 17	134	10:10	137
		10:44	135
Daniel			
6:27	124	**Nehemiah**	
		1:9	83, 95
Ezra		2:1–10	3
1:1	118	7	115, 126–128, 139
1:2–4	117–118, 123	7:5	126
1:3–5	123	7:5–10:40	145
2:33	125	7:6–72	126
2:68	125	7:37	125
3:1	123, 127	7:72	136
3:2, 4	123	8	123, 127
3:6	119	8–10	133, 135–136, 145
3:7	118	8:1	136
3:8–10	119	8:2, 14	136
4:1	123	8:17	136
4:1–5	20	9–10	137
4:2	120–121	9:2	136–137
4:3	118	9:8	141
4:8–24	120	10:29	136
4:9–10	121	10:31	145
4:12	121	11	127
4:12–13, 16	120	11:1–12:47	144
5:1–6:18	117	12:1–47	145

13	139, 144–145	6:25, 27	94
13:1–3	134, 145	6:26	94
13:1–3, 13	142	6:28	94
13:1–31	144	6:34, 38	95
13:4–31	145	7:11–22	94
13:27	145	7:12	10–11, 71, 93–100, 114
13:28	13, 88		
13:28–30	20, 25	7:12–16	95, 97, 114
13:30	12, 133	7:13	95
		7:15	97
1 Chronicles		7:16	95, 96
3:17–24	109	13:8	100
5:25	122	13:8–12	98, 100
6:2	113	30–31	100
17:1	99	30:1	122
22:9–10	99	30:1–18	20
23:6–11	113	30:11	130
28:2	99	35:18	122, 130
2 Chronicles		**2 Maccabees**	
3:1	90	3:4	129
5:2–7:10	94	5:22–23	142
6:5–6	96	6:1–2	142
6:12	95		
6:21	94	**Sirach**	
6:21,24, 26, 32, 34, 38	97	50:25–26	142
6:22–29	95		

Dead Sea Scrolls

1QIs^a	55	4QpaleoExod^m	1–2, 4, 8, 53
4QComm Gen A	51	4QPhyl G	36
4QDeut^h	55	4QRP^a	53
4QDeut^j	35	4QRP^b	53
4QDeut^{k1}	35	4QTestimonia	51
4QDeut^n	36, 56	8QPhyl III	36
4QExod-Lev^f	53	11QT^a	50–51
4QMez	36	11QT^a XIII, 20	50
4QNum^b	4, 52, 53		

Josephus

Jewish Antiquities		11.30	64
9.288–291	59	11.297–347	59

11.302	3,	12.138–144	129
11.302–312	88	12.257	121
11.303	59	13.74–79	91
11.306–312	14, 60	13.254	61
11.309–312	88	13.254–256	60
11.310–311	60	13.256	60
11.316–320	60	18.86	70
11.321–322	91	22.323	61
11.321–324	103		
11.321–325	3	**Jewish War**	
11.322–324	60	1.62	61
11.323	59	1.62–63	60
11.326–369	124	1.63	60
11.346	59, 88	4.449	70
12.7–10	91		

Index of Subjects

Aaron   13–14, 25, 123, 149–150
Abdael   160, 167
Abdel b. Asher   150
Abijah   98, 100
Abisha   157, 168, 171
Abraham   24, 27, 43, 89–90, 92, 136, 156, 169
Abrahamic Descendants   25, 136
Abram   10, 43
Abū 'l-Fatḥ   150–152, 155–165
Ai   89
'Aḳbon   162
Alexander the Great   3, 59–60, 63–64, 70, 124, 129, 161
Altar(s)   14, 42–43, 62, 87–88, 98, 119, 127
Altar, Abraham's   24, 27, 89–90
Altar, Mt. Gerizim   8–9, 58–59, 71, 82, 88
Ammanitis   142
Ammon   141
Ammonite   139–140
Amorite(s)   28, 141
Amram   8, 69, 150, 157, 159–160, 162, 167–171
Amulets   73
Andromachus   63
Animal Bones   2, 62, 71
Anti-Samaritan   13, 26–27
Anti-Samaritan Polemic   103–104
Antiochus III   67, 129
Aqbiah   159
Aqob   159, 161
'Ar'ara   75
Arabian(s)   25
Aramaic Temple Chronicle   12, 117–120, 122, 126
Archaeology   21, 26, 60–61, 72, 134
Aristeas, Letter of   124
Arpachshad   156
Art traditions   85, 130
Artaxerxes I   120, 124
'Askar   75
Assyrian   82, 132
Assyrian Policy   120

'Avarta   70
Azariah   160

Baba Rabbah   153
Babylonian Diaspora   80, 89
Babylonian Exile   128, 132
Bagavahyah   81
Bagohi   63, 69, 96
Baḥqi   157–158
Bar-Kokhba   76
Benjamin, Tribe   70, 125
Beth-El   8
Beth She'an   76
Beth She'arim   76
Bethel   18, 85, 89
„Book of the Law of God"   89
Byzantine Period   9, 13, 58, 66, 72–73, 76

Caesarea   75
Calendar(s)   150–152
Canaan   23, 41, 89, 137, 150, 152, 154
Canaanite(s)   101, 141
Carmel   76–77
Centralization   10, 79–92, 95–100
Chronicle Adler   150–152, 154–171
Chronicle Neubauer   See Tulida
Chronicler   94, 97, 100, 117
Circumcision   63
Coin(s)   61–64, 67, 73, 146
Covenant Code   82, 85–87, 92
Curtius Rufus   63
Cuthean(s)   59
Cyrus Edict   12, 117–118, 121–122, 125–126, 128

Damascus   60, 151
Dan   85
Daphna   69
Darius I   79
Darius II   60, 62
Darius III   60
David   85–86, 99, 108–109
David, House of   108–110
David and Solomon   100, 108, 110, 114

Davidic Dynasty   93, 100, 108–110, 113, 134
Davidic Kingdom   109–110, 114
Decalogue   24, 36
Delos   9, 13, 142
Deuteronomistic History   10, 19, 23, 84–86, 92, 121, 130, 134
Diadochi   128
Diaspora Communities   88, 91, 129
Delaiah   63, 69, 81, 96, 146
Divine law   8, 89, 123

Ebal, Mount   74, 98
Eber   156
Edomite(s)   25
Egypt   22, 28, 36, 42, 89–92, 144, 150–151
Egypt, Population   9
Egyptian Diaspora   80, 89, 91–92
Elder(s)   14, 26, 59, 92, 117–118
Elders, Seventy   70
Eleazar   38, 69–70, 149
Eleazar, High Priest(s)   157, 161, 163–169
Elephantine   63, 81, 91, 132, 139, 142, 146
Elephantine, Letter   62–63, 71
Elephantine, Temple   96–97
Elephantine Papyri   71, 130
Eli   14
Elishama   162
Eliashib   25, 88
Elnatan   69
Endogamous Marriage   137, 139
Enoch   155
Enosh   155
Ephraim   69, 91, 105–106
Ephraim, Tribe   10, 84, 105–107, 109–110
Epigraphy   57, 65, 99, 114, 132–133, 139–140, 143
Era of the Judges   18
Esarhaddon, Loyalty Oath   82
Euphrates   27, 89, 121
Exogamous Marriage   139
Ezra-Nehemiah   11–15, 25, 115–132, 133–148

Falsifications   7
Fanūta   150
Foreign(er)   13–14, 54, 59, 69, 105, 120, 122, 124, 133–148

Foreign Domination   111, 113
Foreign Infiltration   133–134, 139
Foreign Policy   11
Foreignness   12, 15
Fortress, Egyptian   63
Fortress, Persian   64

Galuth-Community   135, 142, 147
Gaster, Moses   149–172
Gaza   151
Genealogy   14, 123, 133–135, 137, 145
Genesis Apocryphon   51
Gerizim   13, 22, 82, 88, 131, 141, 143–144, 148
Gerizim, Mount   75, 77, 88, 93–94, 96–98, 103, 113, 115, 131–132
Gerizim, Excavations   1–2, 5–6, 57
Gerizim, Inscriptions   66–71, 77
Gerizim, Josephus   63–65
Gerizim, Sanctuary   58–61, 81, 90–91
Gerizim, Temple   3, 10, 22, 62–63, 77, 80–81, 88, 90–92, 104, 113, 115, 121, 125, 128–129, 142
Gershon   113
Gesenius, Wilhelm   50–51
Geshem   145
Gilgal   98
Girgashite(s)   141
Gods, Foreign   24–26, 140–141
Göttingen   2

Ḥajja   70
Hanan   160
Hananiah   160
Harmonization   6, 31–49, 52–54, 120
Hasmonean(s)   61, 72, 125
Hasmonean Period   93, 142
Hasmonean State   60
Heliodorus Affair   129
Hellenistic Period   9, 13, 22, 28, 91, 93, 98–99, 104
Hellenistic Period, Ezra   124, 129, 131–132, 140–141, 144
Hellenistic Period, Inscriptions   66
Hellenistic Period, Josephus   91
Hellenistic Period, Mt. Gerizim   57, 61, 69, 71, 77

Hellenistic Period, Gerizim Temple 3
Hellenistic Period, Zechariah 113–114
Hellenization 70
Hexateuch 7, 23–25, 89–90
Hezekiah 122, 130, 158, 160
Ḥezeqīa, High Priest 161
High Priesthood 13–15, 25, 29, 59–60, 63–64, 67, 71, 88, 123, 149–172
Hijra 150, 153
Ḥilal 160
Hilkiah 123, 159
Ḥirbet el-Qōm 139–140
Hittites 141
Holy of Holies 62
„Holy Seed" 136
House of Sacrifice 70–71, 94–99

Idol Worship 27
Idumea 139, 142
Iliad 144
Inscription(s) 1–2, 9, 13, 57, 79, 146
Inscriptions, Delos 9
Inscriptions, Mount Gerizim 65–77, 96–97, 141–142
Intermarriage 133–148
International Organization for the Study of the Old Testament (IOSOT) 3–5
Isaac 156, 169–170
Isaac, Sacrifice of 90
Ishmael 159
Issus 60
Ithamar 168

Jacob 26, 69, 89, 156
Jacob I 170
Jacob II 150, 171
Jacob b. Aaron b. Salama 149, 151
Jaddus 14, 59
Jair 158–159, 161
Jared 155
Jebel eṭ-Ṭur 2, 9
Jebusite(s) 141
Jehohanan 63
Jehoiada 13–14, 25
Jerusalem 20, 22, 26, 135–139, 143, 145, 148

Jerusalem, Centralization 79–81, 83–86, 88, 90–92
Jerusalem, Elders 59
Jerusalem, Ezra-Nehemiah 115, 119–126, 128–133
Jerusalem, Priesthood 14–15, 63
Jerusalem, Pro- 13
Jerusalem, Sanctuary 5, 11, 60
Jerusalem Temple 14, 60, 81–82, 113–115, 117, 121–122, 124–125, 148
Jerusalem Temple, Centralization 92–93, 96–101
Jerusalem Temple, Chronicles 11
Jerusalem Temple, Destruction 76
Jerusalem Temple, Hellenistic Era 128, 129, 132
Jerusalem, Yahwists 10, 12, 77
Jerusalem, Zechariah 104, 107, 109–110, 113–114
Jewelry 61, 73
Johanan 59
John Hyrcanus 29, 60–61, 72, 74
Jojaqim 162
Jonathan 158–159, 162
Joseph 10, 24, 69, 89–92
Joseph's Bones 24, 90
Joseph the Carpenter 162
Josephus 70, 77, 88, 91
Josephus, Mt. Gerizim 57, 103
Josephus, Samaritan Temple 59–64
Josephus, Sources 14–15
Josiah 122–123, 130
Joshua 24, 89
Joshua, Book of 23–24, 27, 89–90
Joshua's Farewell Address 23, 26–28
Jubilees, Ethiopic 51
Judah 22–23, 81, 91, 143, 147–148
Judah, Ezra-Nehemiah 115, 118, 125, 129–132
Judah, Governor 63
Judah, Name 69–70
Judah, Sanctuary 84
Judah, Yahwists 10, 13, 15
Judah, Zechariah 104–108, 110, 113–114
Judah and Israel 19–20, 102–103
Judah and Samaria 5, 29, 93
Judaism, Post-Exilic 139

Judean-Samarian Relations 98, 104, 114, 133
Judeo-Arameans 139

Kafr Samir 75
Kenan 155
Kfar Ḥaggai 70
Khirbet ʿAmurieh 75
Khirbet al-ʿAura 73, 76
Khirbet al-Ḥadra 73, 76
Khirbet Samara 72
Kohath 157

Lamech 155
Language, Deuteronomistic 33
Lapidary 65, 96
Law(s) 8, 14, 26–27, 33, 44–46, 49, 52, 79–92, 96–98
Law, Deuteronomic 83, 86–88
Leontopolis 142
Levant 11, 25, 93, 111, 113, 134, 147
Levi 69, 157
Levi I-VI 160–161, 163, 166, 169, 171
Levi, House of 113
Levite(s) 13–14, 82, 113, 136–137
Literary Criticism 31, 119

Mabartha 70
Macedon 3, 161
Macedonians 64
Magnesia 129
Mahalel 155
Manasseh, High Priest 14
Manasseh, tribe 10
Manasses 14, 59
Maqom 83–84
Maṣliaḥ 170, 172
Masoretic Text (MT) 2, 6–7, 57, 83–84, 89–90, 98, 108, 145, 153
Mausoleum(s) 75
Medes 121
Memar Marqah 8
Mesopotamia 22, 27, 80, 89
Methuselah 155
Mezuzah 36, 56
Miriam 69
Moab 141

Moabite 134
More, Oak of 89
Moriah 10, 90
Moses 38–39, 41, 80–84, 87–91, 127, 157
Moses, Books of 6, 8
Mughar el-Sharaf 75
Muslim Period 75, 153–154

Nablus 72, 74, 149, 151
Nahor 27, 43, 156
Nash Papyrus 36
Neapolis 70, 75
Near East 22, 66, 110
Nebuchadnezzar 149, 159
Nethanel 149, 160–161, 163–167
Neo-Assyrian 122
Nikaso 14, 59–60
Noah 102, 155
Northern Kingdom 17, 19, 21, 27

Old Latin (OL) 83, 98
Onomastics 69, 139–141, 146
Ossuary 71, 74–75

Paleo-Hebrew 65–67
Paleography 66
Passover 100, 122, 130
Patriarch(s) 24, 32, 149, 151–154
Patriarchal era 18
Peleg 156
Pentateuch 54, 98, 123, 130–132, 141, 148
Pentateuch, Centralization 86–90, 92
Pentateuch, Development 10–13, 79–81
Pentateuchal Scholarship 1–3, 24
„Peoples of the land" 135–136
Perizzite(s) 141
Persian Ruler(s) 11, 81, 117–119, 123–126, 131–132, 139
Persian Period 9, 12–13, 80, 113–115, 125, 130–134
Persian Period, Early 20–22, 26
Persian Period, Gerizim 61–66
Persian Period, Late 91, 93, 98–99, 104
Persian Period, Yehud 139–143
Phinehas 69, 157, 163, 166, 168–169, 171
Pinḥas 67, 70, 150
Post-Exilic Period 65, 134–135, 148

Index of Subjects

Pre-Samaritan Sources   1–8, 15, 40, 48–56
Pro-Samaritan   24, 26, 89
Pseudo-Philo   51
Ptolemaic Period   60, 64, 70, 93, 139–143, 147
Ptolemies   70
Ptolemy VI   91

Qahal Yiśrael   147
Qatal   83–85
Qedumim   72
Qôs   141
Qumran   15, 21, 35–37, 39, 50–57

Rabbi(s)   36, 77
Rabbinic Sources   76, 126
Raqit   75
Religious Identity   116, 137
Recension, Samaritan   1–2, 55
Resurrection   74
Reu   156
Rewritten Bible   41, 51, 119
Roman(s)   129
Roman Period   9, 13, 58, 66, 72–73, 75–76
Roman sarcophagi   75
Roman Temple   58

Sabbathai   75
Sacerdocy   13
Sacrifice(s)   2, 11, 58, 62, 70–71, 90, 94–99, 121, 124
Ṣadaqa   167, 169
Salama   170
Samaria   3, 5, 10–13, 15, 28–29, 57, 59, 69–70, 72, 75–77, 79–82, 88, 93, 113–114, 122, 125, 128–134, 140–143, 147
Samaria, City of   63–64
Samaria Papyri   140
Samaritan Cemetery   9, 57, 71–76
Samaritan Diaspora   9, 91–92
Samaritan Pentateuch (SP)   1–8, 31–55, 62, 84, 88–90, 98, 146, 150, 153
Samaritan Sarcophagi   75–76
Samaritan Studies   1, 3, 5, 23, 57–77
Šamaš   141
Sanballat   3, 13, 25, 59–63, 81, 88, 145–146

Sarcophagi   72, 74–75
Saul   85
Scribe(s)   8, 31, 33–34, 42, 45, 80, 94, 113, 123, 135, 150
Second Temple   59
Second Temple Period   4, 57, 77, 99, 104, 123, 125
Second Zechariah   93–114
Seleucid(s)   115
Seleucid Period   3, 60, 67, 143, 148
Seleucid Policy   129
Seraiah   123, 160
Serug   156
Seth   155
Sexual Transgression(s)   137
Shalom   158, 171
Shebeṭ   158
Shechem   5, 10, 24–29, 58, 60, 64, 70–76, 80–82, 89–92, 98, 131
Shechem, Oak of   90
Shelemiah   63, 146, 169
Shelah   156
Shem   155
Shemaiah   69, 162
Shephelah   75
Sheshai   157–158
Shiloh   14, 26, 85, 90, 92
Shimei   113
Sidon   60, 63
Sin   85, 94, 110, 145
Sîn-uballiṭ   146
Šin   141
Solomon   94–100, 108, 110, 114, 145
Solomon's Prayer   94, 95, 97
Southern Kingdom   18, 22
Sub-Chronicism   5, 17–19, 21
Sub-Deuteronomism   5, 17–19, 21, 135
Succession   13, 82, 130
Synagogue   57, 73, 77

Tabernacle   46, 150, 152, 158
Tattenai   117, 119, 126
Tautology   43–44
Tefillin   6, 35–37, 40, 44, 54, 56
Tell Balatah   64, 70, 75
Tell el-Mazār   139–140
Tell er-Rās   9, 58

Tenth Commandment 8, 52
Terah 27, 43, 156
Textual Criticism 31
Theology 24–26, 32, 118, 134–135, 145, 147
Theophoric 140–141, 146
Ṭira HaCarmel 75
Tobiah 145, 159, 162
Torah 2, 8–12, 31–56, 79–92, 115, 122–131, 136–139, 143–148
Tribes of Israel 23, 26–28, 89
Tulida 150, 152, 154–171
Ṭura Ṭaba 70
Twelve Stones 62
Tyre 60, 62

Uzzi 150, 158, 168

Vessels, cultic 61, 73, 130

Wadi ed-Daliyeh 140–141

Yahu-Temple 81, 142
Yahwism 9–13, 57, 64, 132–134, 141–148
Yahwism, Post-Exilic 13, 147–148
Yahwist(s) 25, 69–70
Yehud 10–11, 21, 28–29, 69–70, 79–80, 88, 125, 130–135, 139–140
Yehudah 69–70
Yiqtol 83, 85, 102
Yoqme'am 70

Zadok 159
Zerubbabel 108, 120, 146
Zion, Mount 10, 77, 93, 105–107, 147

www.ingramcontent.com/pod-product-compliance
Lightning Source LLC
Chambersburg PA
CBHW030651230426
43665CB00011B/1042